BUSINESS FRENCH

Key words
in
CONTEXT

BUSINESS FRENCH

Key words

in

CONTEXT

A.A. Lyne

Hodder & Stoughton
LONDON SYDNEY AUCKLAND

British Library Cataloguing in Publication Data

Lyne, Anthony A.
  Business French: Key words in context.
  I. Title 443

  ISBN 0-340-54083-4

First published 1992

Typeset by Columns Design and Production Services Ltd, Reading
Printed in Great Britain for the educational publishing division of
Hodder & Stoughton Ltd, Mill Road, Dunton Green, Sevenoaks,
Kent by Biddles Ltd., Guildford.

CONTENTS

INTRODUCTION

Business French Key Words in Context will be useful to you if you speak English, not necessarily as a native speaker, and if you are either following a course in business French or are finding that you need to write letters in French at work. It assumes that you already have a grasp of the main grammatical features of French, namely the ability to choose the appropriate forms of inflected words – nouns, adjectives and verbs – and to assemble them into syntactically well-formed sentences.

   Not everybody can write an acceptable business letter in their native language, much less in a foreign one. Even a modern languages graduate who can compose, say, a fluent piece of literary criticism or a newspaper article will find that those skills do not transfer automatically to this task. Nor is it merely a matter of picking a number of stereotyped sentences from a published collection and stringing them together in the right order. This may work at a pinch with the simplest, most routine letters but it will prove a blind alley on the road to becoming a competent correspondent.

   It is not enough for a business letter to convey the desired factual information unambiguously, though this is obviously the first essential; we also need to be able to strike the right tone. On one occasion we may wish to be deliberately peremptory, on another especially deferential, and more usually somewhere between these extremes, that is, polite in the slightly stiff way which is characteristic of this register of the language. Furthermore, our individual sentences must not be simply placed end to end like a row of bricks without mortar; they need to be shaped in such a way as to complement each other and to be connected by suitable conjunctions ('car', 'de façon que', 'depuis que') and adverbial expressions ('par conséquent', 'éventuellement', 'en effet'). These interpersonal and textual features of letter writing are given the careful attention they deserve here.

   As the title implies, *Business French Key Words in Context* is concerned with the **essential** vocabulary of French business correspondence. The 1500 or so entries have been selected with great care and this selection was informed by a word-frequency count of many hundreds of authentic letters.[1] It does not set out to be in any sense a comprehensive dictionary of commercial French. The emphasis is on words which are

---

[1] For details see the author's *The Vocabulary of French Business Correspondence: word frequencies, collocations and problems of lexicometric method.* Slatkine-Champion: Geneva-Paris, 1985

characteristically frequent in business letters, especially ones concerned with export-import transactions. Other words, which are frequently used in all registers of French and which you will know how to use already, e.g. 'mais', 'tout', 'peut-être', 'parler', 'enfant', 'idée', are omitted unless business French gives them some special twist. In a specific work situation you will still need the appropriate technical glossary for the particular branch of industry you happen to be in. *Key Words in Context* should however largely enable you to dispense with a general dictionary with the attendant frustrations of searching for information which may well be there but which will be concealed amongst a mass of irrelevant material.

THE FRENCH-ENGLISH SECTION

This is the main part of the book. The entries are arranged alphabetically and each entry contains some or all of the following information.

Word Class

The abbreviations used are: *adj* adjective; *adv* adverb; *conj* conjunction; *inter* interjection; *nf* noun feminine; *nm* noun masculine; *prep* preposition; *pro* pronoun; *vimpers* verb impersonal; *vi* verb intransitive; *vpro* verb pronominal; *vt* verb transitive; *vt indir* verb transitive indirect.

A single entry often includes more than one word class, e.g. 'correspondant, -e' *nmf & adj*, but there are separate entries for particularly complex items, e.g. 'penser' *vt*, 'penser à' *vt indir*, and 'penser de' *vt indir*.

English Translation Equivalents

These are listed in alphabetical order separated by commas unless one of the following factors applies:

(1) If one translation equivalent is appropriate much more frequently than the others, it will be listed first, e.g.
commande *nf* order, indent
(2) If the French word has two or more clearly distinct senses, a semi-colon is used to separate their translation equivalents, e.g.
charger *vt* load, embark; charge, entrust
(3) If the entry includes two or more word classes, a colon is used to separate their translation equivalents, e.g.
correspondant, -e *nmf & adj* correspondent: corresponding
(4) If there is not a straightforward match between the word class of the French word and that of one of its translation equivalents, the latter is placed in square brackets, e.g.
défaut *nm* defect, fault, flaw, [alternatively, failing that, for want of].
The bracketed terms here correspond to the phrases 'à défaut', 'à défaut de' rather than to the noun 'défaut' alone. There will be a contextualized example later in the entry to illustrate this.

Tenses

It is assumed that you know the inflected forms of regular first and second conjugation verbs, e.g. 'aimer' and 'finir'. For all other verbs key forms are given as in this specimen entry for 'avoir':

Pres 1 *ai* 3 *a* 4 *avons* 6 *ont* Imp *avais* Fut *aurai* PP *eu, eue* Pres Part *ayant* Subj 1 *aie* 3 *ait* 4 *ayons* 6 *aient*

The abbreviations used are: Pres Present Indicative; Imp Imperfect Indicative; Fut Future; PP Past Participle; Pres Part Present Participle; Subj Present Subjunctive.

Using the normal productive rules of French all other required forms can be deduced from the small number of key forms actually listed, e.g. Pres 4 (nous) avons yields Pres 5 (vous) avez, while Fut (j')aurai yields not only all the other forms of the Future – 3 (il) aura, 4 (nous) aurons, 5 (vous) aurez, 6 (ils) auront – but those of the Conditional too: 1 (j')aurais, 3 (il) aurait, etc . The Past Historic – eus, eut, etc – and the Imperfect Subjunctive – eusse, eût, etc – are virtually never found in business letters and the second person singular (tu) is rare. No account is taken of them here.

Collocates

By this is meant words which co-occur regularly with the key word under consideration. Here is a specimen entry for
commande *nf* order:

COLLOCATES *adresser, ajouter à, annuler, confirmer, enregistrer, expédier, livrer, maintenir, noter, obtenir, passer, perdre, recevoir, satisfaire, transmettre; annulation, confirmation, copie, double, duplicata, exécution, expédition, réception, reliquat, solde, suspension; en cours, éventuelle, export, ferme, grosse, importante, précédente, précitée, régulière, sous rubrique, supplément-aire; en cas de, (faire) l'objet de, relative à, (faire) suite à*

The collocates are listed in alphabetical order but, in long entries such as this one, they may be separated out on the basis of their grammatical relations with the key word, hence 'adresser une commande' etc ; 'l'annulation d'une commande' etc ; 'la commande en cours' etc ; 'en cas de commande' etc .

Collocation is not an all-or-nothing matter; some co-occurrences are simply more likely than others. These lists are therefore not meant to be in any sense exhaustive. They supplement the contextualized examples later in the entry and give you an idea of the sort of company the key word keeps.

Usage Notes

Usage Notes give a variety of information depending on the requirements of the particular key word. Here are some typical examples:

'possible': 'Il est possible que' + Subjunctive.
'aujourd'hui': 'Aujourd'hui' sometimes refers to the current 24-hour period as opposed to yesterday or tomorrow, as in the first example. It

may also refer to the present time more generally, as in the second example. However, in business letters, 'aujourd'hui' is used much more rarely than 'today' is in English. (*See* jour, actuellement.)

'aussi': In the sense 'in consequence, so, therefore', 'aussi' is always found in sentence-initial position (unlike its more frequent synonym, 'donc'). This gives it a certain prominence, as in the first example. In the sense 'also' (second example), it is much more rarely used than its synonym, 'également'.

'avis': NB 'Avis' does not translate English 'advice' in the general sense of 'recommendation, helpful advice'. (*See* conseil.)

As these specimen entries illustrate, perhaps the most valuable feature of the Usage Notes is to draw your attention to similarities and differences between French words which are inevitably kept apart by being listed alphabetically, but which are nevertheless related to each other in a variety of important ways. Intelligent use of the Usage Notes in conjunction with the Collocates (see above) and the English-French index will enable you in particular to compare and contrast sets of quasi-synonyms such as 'actuellement' and 'maintenant'; 'adresser', 'envoyer', 'expédier' and 'remettre'; 'fort', 'grand', 'gros' and 'important'.

Contexts

With very few exceptions every entry contains one, sometimes several, examples of the key French word in context. These examples are all drawn from a corpus of many hundreds of authentic letters. They have been edited only where removal from a larger, very complex, context made this essential in order to maintain comprehensibility. Also, to preserve the anonymity of the firms which kindly donated the letters, names have been replaced by conventional signs – X, CIE (compagnie), MF (marque de fabrique 'trade-mark') and a few others which should be self-explanatory. Unless the French example is particularly straightforward a full or partial English translation follows it. In both the French and English parts of the example the key word, or sometimes a whole phrase, is highlighted and alternatives are often included. An example may be useful:

• Nous avons naturellement redit que CIE **n'avait pas l'habitude d'accepter** ce genre de formule. - ... *that CIE **did not usually accept / was not in the habit of accepting** this sort of arrangement.*

Since the author had a full concordance of the corpus of letters mentioned earlier it was possible for him to obtain objective evidence of the relative importance of the various collocations and grammatical environments within which the individual French key words function in business correspondence. These were the major factors taken into account in selecting and then ordering the examples within an entry. In addition, examples were chosen so as to show where a key word has more than one sense or, very importantly, where it corresponds to different English translation equivalents in different contexts, e.g. *Fr* 'important, -e': *Eng* 'important'; 'big'.

The number of examples in an entry does not necessarily reflect the importance of the key word concerned. A very frequent word may be quite straightforward to use and rate only a single example, e.g. 'adresser' *vt*, whereas a much less frequent word may occur in more varied environments and consequently deserve several, e.g. 'autant'. Many words which commercial French dictionaries tend to omit or give only cursory treatment turned out to deserve extensive exemplification. So, for instance, 'accord' *nm* is given six examples centred on the expressions 'un accord ferme', 'des accords pour. . .', 'mon accord', 'en parfait accord', 'vous vous êtes mis d'accord' and 'nous sommes d'accord pour. . . '.

THE ENGLISH-FRENCH SECTION

This section is much shorter than the French-English section and serves purely as an index to it. Each entry consists of an English word together with one or more French translation equivalents and an indication of their word class where necessary (see Word Class above for the abbreviations used). As in the main section distinct senses are separated by a semi-colon and different word classes by a colon (see English Translation Equivalents above). Here is a specimen entry:

concern concerner *vt*; (s')inquiéter *vt & pro*: entreprise *nf*

Several translation equivalents sharing roughly the same sense are separated by commas and are listed in alphabetical order unless one is much more frequently appropriate than the others, in which case it is placed first, for example:

have avoir *vt & aux*, posséder *vt*, entretenir *vt*

When a French translation equivalent consists of a multi-word expression, one or more of the component words may be highlighted to assist in locating it in the French-English section, for example:

appeal to faire **appel** à

This section includes many multi-word English expressions such as:

for the **form** pour la bonne **règle**

No attempt has been made to be exhaustive in listing these, the emphasis being on instances like this one where the head words of the expressions in the two languages are not normally translation equivalents of each other.

Finally, again as in the French-English section, where the English word and its French translation equivalent do not match straightforwardly as regards word class, the French word or expression is placed in square brackets, for example:

foregoing [précéder *vi*]

This gives access to the following example in the French-English section:

• Dans l'attente de vous lire par retour au sujet de **ce qui précède**, ... - *Looking forward to hearing from you by return regarding **the foregoing**, ...*

NB A word of warning. This section, while undoubtedly a necessary complement to the main French-English section, can be a trap for the unwary since it provides very limited information to help you choose among alternative translation equivalents. You may often only need this memory jogger to enable you to make the correct choice, but, if in doubt, you will need to check each of the alternatives in the French-English section with its wealth of contextual information.

GENERAL REMARKS

Historically, English and French are fairly closely related languages and they have grown closer over the centuries. Translation between the two therefore presents far fewer problems than between, say, English and Russian or English and Chinese. A message expressed in both English and French will normally have a very similar pattern in both languages, with a noun corresponding to a noun, a verb to a verb, and so on:

• C'est seulement maintenent que nous sommes en mesure de vous faire une offre ferme. - *It is only now that we are in a position to make you a firm offer.*

This closeness of match is however only a tendency , not a hard and fast rule. 'Word for word' translation is rarely entirely satisfactory. Whereas in English we are likely to find 'when I **visited** you', the French are more likely to write 'lors de ma **visite**'. Similarly with 'as soon as our factory **reopens**' versus 'dès la **réouverture** de notre usine'.

This French tendency to use a noun where English prefers a verb is the commonest form that this mismatch between word classes takes. There are other possibilities however: 'We **should appreciate** knowing the result' and 'Il nous **serait agréable** d'en connaître le résultat' (English verb versus French 'être' plus adjective). Or we may even find 'the **foregoing**' versus 'ce qui **précède**', where the tendency for English to prefer a verbal construction and French a nominal one is reversed. As mentioned earlier, square brackets enclose certain translation equivalents in both the sections of this book to draw your attention to expressions in the two languages which are not strictly equivalent at all, but which serve rather as clues to finding equivalence between **phrases** in the contextualized examples, e.g. 'appreciate' [agréable]. We cannot however hope to have captured more than a proportion of the possibilities in this way.

The preferred options of the two languages differ in many other ways. For example, French business letters abound in sentences with openings like the following:

'**Nous vous demandons de** limiter le poids total de vos caisses . . .'
'**Nous vous signalons que** notre client a un besoin extrèmement urgent
. . .'
'**Nous vous exprimons** notre étonnement concernant le contenu de . . .'

It is most unlikely that the corresponding sentences in an English letter would begin 'We ask you to . . .', 'We point out to you that . . .' or 'We express our astonishment to you concerning . . .'. More natural would be openings such as 'We must ask you to . . .', 'May we point out that . . .' and, in the last example, simply 'We are astonished by . . .'. In these circumstances French correspondents, as it were, say in so many words what they are doing (asking, pointing out, expressing, etc) in a way that would seem very unnatural in English. (Incidentally, they do **not** write 'Nous vous **disons** que . . .'.)

An awareness of such stylistic differences between the letter-writing registers of the two languages only comes with time and application. Simply translating into French letters which were originally written in English, with constant reference to an English-French glossary will probably do little to hasten this process. On the other hand study of complete, authentic letters in French and the French-English section of this book, providing you as it does with a distillation of many such letters, can enable you to write letters which could have been written by a French person.

Language is changing constantly. Your suggestions for alterations to possible future editions of *Business French Key Words in Context* will be gratefully received. In the meantime, sincere thanks to the many individuals and organizations who contributed letters to my corpus and thereby made this book possible.

Sheffield, 1991

A

d'abord *adv* at first, initially, from the outset, for a start, in the first instance
• Nous signalerions **d'abord** les infractions par lettre recommandée. - *We would report the offences initially by registered letter.*

abordable *adj* reasonable
• Le prix de cette machine, fabriquée en Allemagne, est très **abordable**. - *The price . . . is very reasonable.*

absence *nf* absence
• Dictée par M. X et signée **en son absence**. - *. . . signed in his absence.*

absolument *adv* absolutely, definitely
• . . . et nous vous informons ici que les résultats obtenus sont **absolument** catastrophiques. - *. . . the results obtained are absolutely catastrophic.*
• . . . il n'est **absolument** pas question pour nous de vous payer la différence. - *. . . there is absolutely/ definitely no question of our paying you the difference.*

accélérer *vt* accelerate, expedite, speed up
TENSES See *céder*
• Nous vous prions de nous fixer définitivement à ce sujet de façon à **accélérer** la décision que doit prendre l'Administration de la Marine. - *. . . so as to expedite/speed up the decision which is to be taken by the Naval Administration.*

acceptation *nf* acceptance
• Nous vous prions de trouver ci-inclus une traite de F.123 à échéance du 30 courant que nous vous demandons de bien vouloir nous retourner avec votre **acceptation**. - *. . . a draft for 123 francs falling due on 30th inst., which we ask you kindly to return to us with your acceptance.*

accepter (de) *vt* accept, agree to
• . . . il ne nous est plus possible d'**accepter** la modification demandée par votre client. - *. . . it is no longer possible for us to accept the modification . . .*
• Nous vous remercions à l'avance de nous faire retour de cette traite dûment **acceptée** et domiciliée . . . - *. . . this draft duly accepted and domiciled . . .*
• D'autre part, nous vous conseillons fortement d'**accepter de** livrer les anneaux au même prix. - *Moreover, we strongly advise you to agree to deliver the rings at the same price.*

accompagner (de) *vt* accompany, [together with]
• Nous avons prévu de faire présenter à votre banque une traite à vue, **accompagnée du** jeu de connaissements et de six factures certifiées . . . - *. . . a sight draft, accompanied by/together with the set of bills of lading and six certified invoices . . .*

accord *nm* agreement, approval, assent, consent, [agree, concur]

• ... et notre client nous a donné un **accord** ferme mais verbal pour l'achat dans les conditions prévues ci-dessus. - *... and our customer has given us a firm but verbal **agreement** to buy on the terms set out above.*

• Nous avons déjà des **accords** pour la fourniture des magasins hors taxes dans cette région. - *... **agreements** to supply the duty-free shops ...*

• Je vous confirme mon **accord** pour vous recevoir le 28 février ...

• Nous nous déclarons en parfait **accord** avec les termes de votre lettre.

• Nous savons que **vous vous êtes mis d'accord** avec vos représentants: néanmoins ... - *We know **you have agreed/reached an agreement** with your representatives: nevertheless ...*

• **Nous sommes d'accord** pour que cette opération exceptionnelle soit réalisée selon le processus que vous avez exposé. - *We **agree/assent** to this exceptional operation being carried out ...*

accorder *vt* accord, allow, confer, grant, pay
COLLOCATES *attention, crédit, escompte, facilités, permission, priorité, prix, réduction, remboursement, temps*

• ... nous vous **accordons** un escompte de 2% pour règlement comptant. - *... we are **allowing/granting** you a discount of 2% ...*

• Le client estime que la plus grande attention doit être **accordée** à ceci. - *... the closest attention should be **paid** to this.*

accréditif *nm* credit, letter of credit
• Livraison: 15 jours environ après la commande et l'ouverture de l'**accréditif**. - *... the opening of the **letter of credit**.*

• Nos règlements s'effectuent par **accréditif bancaire** sur facture pro-forma. - *Payments to us are made by*

letter of credit against pro-forma invoice.

• Paiement: **accréditif** confirmé, irrévocable, divisible et transmissible, payable contre les documents habituels. - *Payment: confirmed, irrevocable, divisible and transferable **letter of credit** payable against the usual documents.*

accueil *nm* reception, welcome
• J'ai le plaisir de vous remercier très sincèrement de l'excellent **accueil** que vous avez bien voulu me réserver lors de ma récente visite. - *... the excellent **welcome** that you were kind enough to give me ...*

accueillir *vt* receive, welcome
TENSES Pres *1,3* accueille *4* accueillons *6* accueillent Imp *accueillais* Fut *accueillerai* PP *accueilli, -ie* Pres Part *accueillant* Subj *1,3* accueille *4* accueillions *6* accueillent

• C'est avec plaisir que nous vous **accueillerons** en France avec le Dr. X au cours du mois prochain. - *... we will **receive** you in France ...*

accusé *nm* acknowledgement
• Nous sommes étonnés cependant de n'avoir pas encore reçu votre **accusé de réception** ... - *... your acknowledgement of receipt ...*

accuser *vt* acknowledge
• Nous **accusons réception** de votre lettre du 11 octobre 19... - *We acknowledge receipt ...*

achat *nm* purchase, purchasing
• Nous avons bien reçu votre contrat No 612 relatif à votre **achat** de 40 tonnes de MF et vous en remercions. - *... relative to your purchase ...*

acheminer *vt* send, route
• Ce paquet, **acheminé** par fer et mer est certainement parvenu à

destination postérieurement à la facture pro-forma ... - *This parcel, sent/routed by rail and sea ...*

acheter *vt* buy, purchase
TENSES Pres 1,3 *achète* 4 *achetons* 6 *achètent* Imp *achetais* Fut *achèterai* PP *acheté, -ée* Pres Part *achetant* Subj 1,3 *achète* 4 *achetions* 6 *achètent*
• Nous sommes déjà en relations avec cette maison, qui nous **a acheté** 200 MF. - *We already deal with this firm, which **has purchased** 200 MFs from us.*

acheteur, -euse *nmf* buyer, purchaser
• 2.5% d'escompte en faveur de l'**acheteur** par tonne.

achèvement *nm* completion, finishing
• Nous reviendrons sur cette affaire après **achèvement** du câble. - *... after completion of the cable.*

activité *nf* activity, business
• Notre **activité** se borne aux exportations de matières premières ... - *Our **business** is confined to exporting raw materials ...*
• Cette société a été formée pour reprendre à son compte et continuer les **activités** de CIE. - *... to take over and continue the **activities** of CIE.*

actuel, -elle *adj* present, current
• Néanmoins, notre situation financière **actuelle** est fort instable. - *Nevertheless, our **present/current** financial situation is very unstable.*
• Malheureusement il ne m'est pas possible de faire ce déplacement **à l'heure actuelle**. - *... to make this trip **at the present time**.*

actuellement *adv* now, at present, at the moment, currently
USAGE *This word, and not 'maintenant', is the normal translation equivalent of*

'now', 'at present'.
• Notre ingénieur principal, Monsieur X, est **actuellement** absent.
• Nous aimerions connaître vos prix **actuellement** pratiqués au distributeur de votre région. - *... the prices you are giving **now/at present** to the distributor in your region.*

admettre *vt* accept, allow, countenance, enter into
TENSES See *mettre*
• ... aucune contestation sur le matériel enlevé ne **sera admise** par CIE. - *... no dispute about the material taken away **will be countenanced/ entered into** by CIE.*

administration *nf* administration; government department, ministry
• Ce réseau est assisté d'une **administration** moderne, équipée d'ordinateurs ... - *This sales-force is backed up by a modern **administration**, equipped with computers ...*
• Je pense principalement aux **administrations** où les devis ne sont pas immédiatement suivis de commandes. - *... **government departments** where quotations are not followed immediately by orders.*

adopter *vt* adopt
• ... la cadence de livraisons que nous aimerions **adopter** pour les 2000 appareils restant ... - *... the rate of delivery which we should like to **adopt** for the 2000 appliances remaining ...*

adresse *nf* address
• Nous sommes redevables de votre **adresse** à notre Chambre Syndicale Nationale du Cycle. - *We are indebted for your **address** to our National Cycle Manufacturers' Association.*

adresser *vt* send, mail

S'ADRESSER À

USAGE *Used of letters and other documents, and small parcels.*

• Nous vous confirmons la lettre que vous **a adressée** notre bureau d'achats … - … *the letter which our purchasing department **sent** you* …

s'adresser à *vpro* apply to
• Pour tous renseignements complémentaires, veuillez **vous adresser à** Monsieur X. - … *please **apply to** Mr X.*

affaire *nf* matter; deal, transaction; business
• Pour cette **affaire**: demander M. X. - *On this **matter**: ask for Mr X.*
• Les dernières **affaires** traitées avec CIE ont été faites sur la base du tarif en livres ci-joint … - *The last **transactions/deals** we have had with CIE* …
• … une **affaire** située en Allemagne, exerçant une activité similaire à la vôtre, est actuellement à reprendre. - … *a **business** … is currently available for take-over.*

affecter *vt* affect; allocate
• Le délai contractuel du navire **ne sera pas affecté** à condition qu'une décision soit prise d'ici fin août. - *The contractual deadline **will not be affected** provided that* …
• A propos de cette affaire, nous constatons que nous lui **avons affecté** par erreur deux numéros de référence. - … *we **have allocated** to it by mistake two reference numbers.*

affirmatif, -ive *adj & nf* affirmative, [if so]
• Dans le cas d'une réponse **affirmative** il serait alors possible de … - *In the event of an **affirmative** reply* …
• Je ne sais pas si vous disposez du temps néccésaire pour nous rendre

S'AGIR DE

ce service mais, **dans l'affirmative**, soyez certain que M. X vous en serait vivement reconnaissant. - *I don't know if you have the time to do us this favour but, **if so**, you may be certain that Mr X will be extremely grateful.*

afin de/que in order to, so that
USAGE *'Afin de'* + Infinitive; *'afin que'* + Subjunctive.
• Nous vous écrivons en français **afin de** mieux exprimer notre pensée. - … *in order to express our thoughts better.*
• Par un prochain courrier nous vous indiquerons leurs nom et adresse **afin que** vous puissiez prendre contact avec eux. - … *so that you can contact them.*

agence *nf* agency, branch
• Toutes ces maisons seraient naturellement désireuses d'obtenir cette **agence**, mais nous avons pour le moment réservé notre réponse et étudions leurs propositions. - *All these firms would naturally be keen to secure this **agency**, but* …

agent *nm* agent
• Nous pensons être en mesure d'augmenter notre champ d'action en devenant l'**agent** et le diffuseur de firmes de votre pays désireuses de s'implanter sur le marché français et européen. - *We think we are in a position to extend our sphere of activity by becoming the **agent** and distributor of firms from your country* …

s'agir de *vpro impers* involve, concern, be a question of
• Il **ne s'agit pas d**'un cas unique, mais de plusieurs réclamations … - *It is **not a question of** an isolated case, but of several claims* …
• Cette plateforme a été affectée à la Société CIE, et il **s'agit d**'une installation spéciale sur un de nos

4

tracteurs. - ... *and it involves a special installation on one of our tractors.*

agréable *adj* pleasant, [appreciate, be gratified, be pleased]
• Nous espérons pouvoir continuer les **agréables** relations que nous avons entretenues dans le passé.
• Souhaitant vivement que votre démarche aboutisse, **il nous serait agréable d'en connaître** le résultat. - *Hoping very much that your approach bears fruit, we should appreciate knowing/we should be gratified to know the result.*

agréer *vt* accept, approve; suit
• Ce prix est net à nous payer et s'entend pour marchandise prise et **agréée** en nos usines, sans emballage. - ... *goods collected and accepted in our works, excluding packing.*
• Les briques seraient expédiées sur palettes de 1m. par 1m. d'un modèle **agréé** par la SNCF. - ... *of a type approved by the SNCF.*
• En espérant que ces date et heure vous **agréent**, ... - *Hoping that this date and time will suit you,* ...

aide *nf* assistance, help
COLLOCATES *apporter; précieuse*
• Nous vous remercions de l'**aide** que vous voudrez bien nous apporter ... - ... *the help which you will be kind enough to give us* ...

aider (à) *vt* assist, help
• Nous sommes à votre entière disposition pour vous **aider** dans n'importe quel problème qui se poserait. - ... *to assist you with any problem which might arise.*
• Notre cabinet est également à votre disposition pour vous **aider à** résoudre les problèmes qui vous seraient posés par vos ressortissants. - ... *to help you to resolve the problems*

put to you by your nationals.*

d'ailleurs/par ailleurs *adv* besides, furthermore, moreover
USAGE *'D'ailleurs' and 'par ailleurs' are synonymous, the former expression being the more usual. 'Par ailleurs' does however seem to be preferred when it is given special weight by being placed in sentence-initial position and followed by a comma, as in the second example.*
• Il s'agit **d'ailleurs** de la première réclamation de l'espèce sur des centaines de carabines expédiées. - *This is moreover/furthermore the first such complaint in hundreds of rifles dispatched.*
• Vous recevrez incessamment notre note de crédit pour un montant de F.123. **Par ailleurs**, si vous aviez à supporter une perte personnelle, nous serions heureux de vous assister ... - *You will shortly be receiving our credit note for 123 francs. Furthermore/moreover, if you had to bear a loss personally,* ...

aimable *adj* kind
• Nous avons bien reçu votre **aimable** lettre du 8 courant.
• **Vous seriez bien aimables de** nous documenter au sujet des desiderata de cette firme. - *It would be kind of you to fill us in as to this firm's requirements.*

aimer *vt* like
USAGE *'Aimer que' + Subjunctive.*
• Nous **aimerions** avoir livraison de cette ordre le mercredi 25 novembre courant, ... - *We should like to take delivery of this order* ...
• Nous **aimerions que** vous nous fassiez parvenir rapidement votre réponse à ces deux lettres. - *We should like you to send us your reply quickly* ...

ainsi *adv* in this way, thus

• Je crois **ainsi** avoir satisfait à votre demande et . . . - *I think I have in this way satisfied your request and . . .*

ainsi que as well as; as
• Nous avons bien reçu votre lettre du 2 juillet dernier, **ainsi que** les documents qui étaient joints. - *. . . as well as the documents which were enclosed.*
• Il nous serait agréable de recevoir les notices, **ainsi que** vous nous le proposez, sans inscription en anglais. - *We should appreciate receiving the leaflets, as you propose, without an inscription in English.*
• En effet, nous avons accepté la facture pour le prix offert de £123, **ainsi que** notre client, mais celui-ci a refusé de régler le prix facturé. - *We accepted the invoice for the quoted price of £123, as did our customer, but the latter has refused to pay the invoiced price.*

ajouter *vt* add
• Nous vous serions reconnaissants de bien vouloir **ajouter** à notre commande 721 du 3 octobre 19--: 10 MF réf. 600.
• Nous **ajoutons qu'**une facture pro-forma a été adressée au destinataire le 12 octobre 19-- . . . - *We should add that a pro-forma invoice was sent to the consignee . . .*

aller *vi & aux* go; range between
TENSES Pres 1 *vais* 3 *va* 4 *allons* 6 *vont* Imp *allais* Fut *irai* PP *allé, -ée* Subj 1,3 *aille* 4 *allions* 6 *aillent*
• . . . nous vous remettrions des spécifications plus précises pour des tonnages **allant de** 100 à 2.000 tonnes dans chacun des produits considérés. - *. . . for tonnages ranging between 100 and 2000 tons. . .*

alors *adv* then, in that case
• Si cela devait se confirmer, il

faudrait **alors** attendre quelques semaines. - *If that proved to be the case, it would then/in that case be necessary to wait a few weeks.*

alors que whereas
• Le montant de cette facture était de F1.100, **alors que** votre versement s'est élevé à F2.700. - *. . .whereas your payment amounted to 2700 francs.*

amabilité *nf* kindness, [so kind, good enough, so good]
• Je vous remercie infiniment de l'**amabilité** avec laquelle vous m'avez reçu à Londres. - *Thank you so much for the kindness with which you received me in London.*
• Voudriez-vous **avoir l'amabilité de** nous faire parvenir cette copie aussitôt que cela vous sera possible. - *Would you be so kind as/so good as to send us this copy . . .*

amélioration *nf* improvement
• Si, après trois infractions, aucune **amélioration** n'est constatée, nous résilierons le contrat. - *If, after three infractions, no improvement is noted, we shall terminate the contract.*

(s')améliorer *vt & pro* improve
• Nous envisageons d'**améliorer** encore nos ventes en engageant des représentants pour prospecter toute la Belgique. - *We anticipate further improving our sales . . .*

amende *nf* fine, penalty
• Nous désirons que le contrat **prévoie une amende** en cas de retard de livraison. - *We wish the contract to make provision for a penalty/to contain a penalty clause for late delivery . . .*

amener (à) *vt* cause, lead, give rise to; [have occasion to]
TENSES See *acheter*
• Votre lettre peut **amener** certaines

confusions. - *Your letter may cause/ give rise to certain confusions.*
• L'impossibilité d'obtenir une garantie du résultat **a amené** notre client à ne pas donner suite à cette affaire. - ... *has led our customer to drop the matter.*
• Nous recevons des communications téléphoniques de députés qui **sont amenés** à utiliser cette appareil. - ... *from MPs who have occasion to use this appliance.*

amical, -e *adj* friendly
• Faisant appel à nos anciennes relations **amicales**, je me permets aujourd'hui de vous demander un service. - *Appealing to our former friendly relations,* ...

amitié *nf* friendship
• Cependant, je suis obligé, étant donné nos rapports commerciaux et notre **amitié**, de vous tenir au courant de certaines difficultés que j'ai éprouvées. - *However, I am obliged, given our commercial ties and our friendship, to keep you informed of certain difficulties that I have had.*

an *nm* year
USAGE *Especially in 'depuis un an', 'il y a un an', 'pendant un an' and 'par an' - 'per year'. Compare 'année'.*

ancien, -ienne *adj* old, former
• CIE, une des **plus anciennes** maisons françaises de parfums et eaux de toilette, est déjà représentée en Allemagne. - *CIE, one of the oldest perfume and toilet water firms in France,* ...
• Les articles de cette commande vous seront facturés aux **anciens** prix. - ...*will be invoiced to you at the old/former prices.*

année *nf* year
USAGE *Especially in 'cette/chaque*

année', 'l'année dernière/prochaine', 'l'année précédente/suivante', 'le début/ la fin de l'année, 'les fêtes/ventes de fin d'année. Compare 'an'.*

annexe *nf* enclosure, annex, appendix, [enclosed, herewith]
• Nous accusons réception de votre lettre du 7 courant et de ses **annexes**.
• Vous trouverez, **en annexe**, notre facture commerciale en triple exemplaire, ... - *You will find, enclosed,* ...
• **Annexes**: contrat en 4 exemplaires. - *Enc.: contract in 4 copies.*

annexer (à) *vt* enclose, annex, append, attach
• Le libellé du bon de commande **annexé** à ce message diffère du précédent ... - *The wording of the order form enclosed with/attached to this message differs from the previous one* ...
• A ce sujet veuillez vous référer à notre bordereau modifié **ci-annexé**. - ... *our modified note enclosed herewith.*

annonce *nf* advertisement
• La société française qui a fait paraître l'**annonce** du 9 février dans ce journal... - *The French company which placed the advertisement of 9 February in this newspaper* ...

annoncer *vt* advise of, announce
• Monsieur X vient de m'**annoncer** votre prochaine visite à Paris. - *Mr X has just advised me of your forthcoming visit to Paris.*

annuel, -elle *adj* annual, yearly
• Nous serons fermés pour congés **annuels** du 11 au 29 août. - *We shall be closed for annual holidays* ...

annulation *nf* cancellation
• Le client maintiendra

l'**annulation** de la commande jusqu'à ce que vous ayez pris position. - *The customer will stand by the **cancellation** of the order until you have come to a decision.*

annuler *vt* cancel, revoke
• Veuillez noter que le client **annule** provisoirement sa commande.
• En nous excusant de cette erreur, nous vous adressons sous ce pli une facture rectificative **annulant** celle en votre possession. - *... a corrected invoice **cancelling** the one in your possession.*

anormal, -e *adj* abnormal, unusual
• Il est **anormal** que la marchandise mette autant de temps à arriver à Paris. - *It is **abnormal/unusual** for the goods to take so long to reach Paris.*

antérieur, -e (à) *adj* earlier, previous, prior
• Nous vous référons à notre correspondance **antérieure** au sujet des olives farcies. - *... our **previous** correspondence ...*
• De plus, lors des discussions **antérieures** à l'élaboration du bon de commande 123 du 24 mars 19--, CIE a exigé l'acceptation ... - *Furthermore, at the time of the discussions **prior to** the drawing up of the order form ...*

antérieurement *adv* earlier, previously
• Des engagements pris **antérieurement** font que, malheureusement, ni M. X ni moi-même ne serons disponibles à ce moment. - *Commitments undertaken **earlier** mean that, unfortunately, neither Mr X nor I will be free then.*

anticiper *vt* anticipate, [in advance/anticipation]
• Dans l'attente d'une réponse

favorable de votre part, et **avec nos remerciements anticipés**, ... - ... *and **thanking you in anticipation**, ...*

août *nm* August

aperçu *nm* (general) idea
• Nous vous avons adressé notre dernier catalogue français pour vous donner un **aperçu** de notre fabrication. - *... to give you a **general idea** of what we make.*

apparaître *vi* appear; [reveal, show]
TENSES See *connaître*
• Il **apparaît** clairement que l'installation actuelle dépasse largement les obligations contractuelles. - *It **appears** clearly that the present installation far exceeds the contractual obligations.*
• Cette étude **fait apparaître** que le marché anglais est actuellement très calme. - *This market research **reveals/shows** that the British market is at present very slack.*

appareil *nm* appliance, device, etc.
• A l'heure actuelle les réfrigérateurs se trouvent concurrencés par les **appareils** français qui sont mieux placés. - *At the moment refrigerators are up against competition from French **appliances** which are better placed.*

appartenir à (de) *vt indir & impers* belong to; be up to someone to, be the responsibility of someone to, rest with someone to
TENSES See *venir*
• Cet article **appartient** à notre client, M. X. - *This article **belongs to** our customer, Mr X.*
• Il vous **appartiendra de** les enlever pour transport jusqu'à Malines. - *It **will be up to you to/It will be your responsibility to** remove*

them for transport to Malines.

appel *nm* call, invitation, [appeal to, call upon]

• Nous accusons réception de votre **appel** d'offres No 123 du 18 mai, ... - *We acknowledge your **call/invitation** for tenders ...*

• Elle vous a peut-être fait part de mon **appel téléphonique**. - *She has perhaps told you about my **phone call.***

• Nous espérons que, si l'occasion s'en présente, vous voudrez bien envisager de **faire appel** à notre concours. - *... you will think of **calling upon** our assistance.*

appeler *vt* call

TENSES Pres 1,3 *appelle* 4 *appelons* 6 *appellent* Imp *appelais* Fut *appellerai* PP *appelé, -ée* Pres Part *appelant* Subj 1,3 *appelle* 4 *appelions* 6 *appellent*

• Nous vous informons que le cédrat est un agrume que nos acheteurs anglais **appellent** 'citron'. - *The 'cédrat' is a citrus fruit which our English buyers **call** 'citron'.*

application *nf* application, [apply]

• L'expérience du chantier déterminera **la nécessité de l'application de cette clause**. - *Experience on site will determine **whether this clause need apply**.*

• Il serait également souhaitable que vous nous indiquiez dans quelles **applications** pratiques cette brique a déjà été un succès. - *... in what practical **applications** this brick has been a success.*

(s')appliquer (à) *vt & pro* apply, enforce, [relevant]

• La surtaxe douanière de 15% **ne sera plus appliquée** à partir du 1er décembre prochain. - *The customs surcharge of 15% **will no longer be applied** from 1 December next.*

• Nous vous donnons ci-dessous

nouveaux prix **s'appliquant à** chacune des séries ... - ... *the new prices **applying to/relevant to** each of the series ...*

apporter *vt* bring, exercise, give, make; affect

COLLOCATES *aide, attention, démonstration, garantie, modification, perturbations, prudence, retard, soin, solution, variante*

• Nous tenons à vous remercier du soin que vous **avez apporté** dans la recherche des causes ... - *We are anxious to thank you for the care you **have taken/exercised** in seeking the causes ...*

• Vous remerciant de l'aide que vous nous **apporterez** ... - *Thanking you for the assistance you **will give** us ...*

• En cours de construction certaines modifications **ont été apportées** au cahier des charges initial. - *... certain modifications **were made** to the initial building specification.*

• Nous souffrons en effet beaucoup des quelques retards **apportés** à la dernière commande. - *... delays **which affected** the last order.*

apprécier *vt* appreciate, [popular, prized, welcome]

• Une réponse rapide et précise **serait appréciée**. - *... would be appreciated/welcome.*

• Pour cette raison même, ces miels **sont fort appréciés** par le consommateur belge. - *... these honeys **are very popular** with the Belgian consumer.*

apprendre *vt* hear (of), learn (of)

TENSES See *prendre*

• Nous **avons appris** que vous n'avez pas de représentant pour la Suisse.

• Je suis enchanté d'**apprendre** la

réaction favorable de vos amis
américains.

approfondi, -ie *adj* in depth,
thorough
• J'ai fait une enquête **approfondie**
sur la qualité des sections MF. - *I have
conducted a **thorough** inquiry into ...*

(s')approvisionner (en) *vt &*
pro furnish with, supply with;
obtain supplies, stock up
USAGE *NB The construction is
'approvisionner quelqu'un en quelque
chose'. Compare 'fournir'.*
• Nous vous remercions à l'avance
de nous fixer les dates auxquelles
vous désirez recevoir les roues afin
que nous puissions **nous
approvisionner** suffisamment tôt **en**
jantes auprès de CIE. - *... so that we
may **obtain supplies of/stock up with**
rims soon enough from CIE.*

approximatif -ive *adj* approximate,
rough
• Il est bien entendu que ces chiffres
sont **approximatifs** et considérés
comme des minima. - *... these figures
are **approximate** ...*

approximativement *adv*
approximately, roughly
• Pour votre gouverne, le délai de
livraison serait **approximativement**
de six semaines loco nos usines ... -
*... delivery would be **approximately**
six weeks ...*

après (que) *adv, prep, conj* after

d'après *prep* according to
• **D'après** les calculs qui ont été
faits, il aurait besoin de 1.500 briques
... - *According to the calculations
which have been made ...*

après-midi *nm* afternoon
USAGE *'Après-midi' can be used in the
same ways as are shown for 'matin',*

*except that 'dans l'après-midi'
corresponds to 'au matin'.*
• Le dernier numéro de cette
publication est arrivé le 14 dans
l'**après-midi**.

arriéré *nm & adj* arrears, overdue,
in arrears
• Nous vous serions très obligés de
bien vouloir nous faire parvenir cet
arriéré par un proche courrier. - *...
to forward us these **arrears** promptly.*

arrivée *nf* arrival, [arrive]
• Je vous passerai, **dès mon arrivée**,
un coup de fil pour convenir d'un
rendez-vous. - *As soon as I arrive, I
will give you a ring to arrange a
meeting.*

arriver (à) *vi* arrive, reach; come
about, happen, occur
• Il est anormal que la marchandise
mette autant de temps à **arriver à**
Paris. - *It is unusual for the goods to
take so long to **reach** Paris.*
• Dans l'espoir qu'il nous sera
possible d'**arriver à** une solution
heureuse, ... - ... *to **arrive at/reach** a
satisfactory solution.*
• C'est bien dommage que cet
accident **soit arrivé**. - *It is a great pity
that this accident **came about**.*

article *nm* article, commodity, item,
line
• ... et nous vous demandons si
vous êtes disposés à nous donner
l'exclusivité de vente de ces **articles**
pour notre pays. - *... if you are
prepared to grant us exclusive sales
rights for these **articles**...*

assez *adv* fairly
• ... et cet effort a d'ailleurs donné
d'**assez** bons résultats. - *... and this
effort has moreover yielded **fairly** good
results.*

assister *vt* assist, help

ASSISTER À

USAGE USAGE *'Aider' is the more usual word in this sense.*

• Nous serions heureux de vous **assister** en vous cédant le bénéfice que nous avons réalisé ... - ... *to assist/help you by handing over to you the profit we have made* ...

assister à *vt indir* attend, be present at, witness

• Nous **avons assisté au** montage de la dernière voûte. - *We were present at the erection of the last vault.*

assurance *nf* insurance

• Cependant, si vous décidez de couvrir l'**assurance** vous-mêmes, nous déduirons de notre prix 0,25%. - *However, if you decide to cover the insurance yourselves,* ...

• Pour gouverne, les prix que nous avons faits comprennent l'**assurance** contre tous risques, sauf rouille. - ... *the prices we have given include insurance against all risks, except rust.*

assurer *vt* assure; insure; provide

• **Soyez assurés** que nous mettrons tout en oeuvre afin de vous satisfaire. - *Rest assured that we will do everything possible to satisfy you.*

• Voulez-vous avoir l'obligeance de nous faire savoir s'il y a lieu d'**assurer** ou non la marchandise. - *Please let us know whether or not it is appropriate for us to insure the goods.*

• Mais si nous devons **assurer** un emballage maritime, celui-ci vous sera facturé. - *But if we are to provide marine packing,* ...

atteindre *vt* achieve, reach
TENSES See *joindre*

• La condition pour bénéficier d'une expédition FOB est que la commande **atteigne** la somme globale de 1.000 livres. - ... *the order should reach the total amount of £1000.*

• Notre programme de lancement

ATTENTION

des six représentants doit nous permettre d'**atteindre** notre premier but. - *Our programme for launching the six representatives should enable us to achieve our initial objective.*

attendre *vt & i* await, expect, look forward to, wait (for), [meanwhile, in the meantime]
TENSES See *rendre*

• Vous aurez à **attendre** la réception de la facture correspondante ... - *You will need to wait until you receive the corresponding invoice* ...

• Votre chambre est retenue et nous vous **attendons** le 8 octobre. - ... *and we are expecting you on 8 October.*

• **En attendant** le plaisir de vous lire à ce sujet, ... - *Looking forward to the pleasure of hearing from you* ...

• **En attendant**, nous vous avons adressé par un courrier séparé notre dernier catalogue français. - *Meanwhile, we have sent* ...

attente *nf* expectation, [looking forward to]

• **Dans l'attente du** plaisir de vous lire, ... - *Looking forward to the pleasure of hearing from you,* ...

• Nous aimerions vous lire à ce sujet dans un proche avenir et, **dans cette attente**, ... - *We should like to hear from you about this in the near future and, in this expectation,* ...

• La seule petite chance qui puisse nous rester est que, **contre toute attente**, notre voûte 2 atteigne un nombre raisonnable de coulées. - *The only faint chance that can remain for us is that, contrary to all expectation, our vault 2 may achieve a reasonable number of castings.*

attention *nf* attention, interest
COLLOCATES *avoir, retenir; accorder, appeler, attirer. réserver*

• **A l'attention de** M. X. - *For the*

attention of Mr X.
• Nous attirons tout particulièrement votre **attention** sur nos conditions générales d'achat ... - *We draw/call your **attention** particularly to our general conditions of purchase ...*
• Quelques points en particulier ont retenu notre **attention**: ... - *A few points in particular have engaged our **attention**: ...*
• Nous serions heureux si nos productions **retenaient votre attention**. - *... if our products **interested you**.*

attestation *nf* certificate
• ... notre lettre vous priant de bien vouloir nous adresser **attestation** d'assurance pour 12 ballots MF ... - *... to send us the insurance **certificate** for 12 bales of MF ...*

attirer (sur) *vt* attract, draw
• A plusieurs reprises nous **avons attiré** votre attention **sur** l'utilité qu'il y aurait à nous consulter avant de faire des réexpéditions. - *On several occasions we **have drawn** your attention **to** the fact that it would be useful to consult us ...*

aucun, -e *adj* no
• Bien entendu, nous ne pouvons **en aucun cas** accepter votre facture sur la base annoncé. - *Of course, we can **on no account** accept your invoice ...*
• Nous vous prions de **ne** faire **aucune** expédition pour cette commande avant les vacances. - *... to make **no** shipment against this order ...*

augmentation *nf* growth, increase
• Pourriez-vous nous confirmer le dernier prix, qui laisse apparaître une **augmentation** de 75 livres pour le prix CIF Dunkerque. - *... which*

*shows a **growth/increase** of £75 for the price CIF Dunkirk.*

augmenter *vi & t* grow, increase; enlarge
• Nos ventes ayant encore sensiblement **augmenté** ... - *Our sales having again **grown/increased** appreciably ...*
• Nous avons l'intention d'**augmenter** d'une unité notre flotte de navires du type ABC. - *We intend to **enlarge** by one unit our fleet ...*

aujourd'hui *adv* today, now
USAGE *'Aujourd'hui' sometimes refers to the current 24-hour period as opposed to yesterday or tomorrow, as in the first example. It may also refer to the present time more generally, as in the second example. However, in business letters, 'aujourd'hui' is used much more rarely than 'today' is in English. (See jour, actuellement.)*
• Un problème particulier me fait vous écrire **aujourd'hui**.
• Il semble **aujourd'hui** que les effets de notre prospection se fassent sentir. - *It seems **now** that the effects of our sales effort are making themselves felt.*

auprès de with, etc
• Je compte faire un dèplacement en Allemagne **auprès de** certains de nos correspondants. - *I intend making a trip to Germany **to visit** some of our correspondents.*
• Je suis disposé à **intervenir auprès de** CIE si Monsieur X le souhaite. - *I am prepared to **approach** CIE ...*

aussi in consequence, so, therefore; also; as (...as); both ... and
USAGE *In the sense 'in consequence', 'so', 'therefore', 'aussi' is always found in sentence-initial position (unlike its more frequent synonym, 'donc'). This*

gives it a certain prominence, as in the first example. In the sense 'also' (second example) it is much more rarely used than its synonym 'également'.
• Ce mode de transport paraît avoir un certain intérêt pour CIE. **Aussi** nous vous serions obligés de nous indiquer si vous pourriez ... - *This means of transport seems to hold some interest for CIE. In consequence, we should be obliged ...*
• Nous exportons **aussi** dans de nombreux pays étrangers, ... - *We **also** export to numerous foreign countries, ...*
• Nous essaierons alors de mettre au point des conditions **aussi** bonnes **que** possible pour nos amis. - *... terms which are **as** good **as** possible for our friends.*
• Cette société exploite plusieurs centrales électriques **aussi bien** en Belgique **qu**'à l'étranger. - *This company runs several power stations **both** in Belgium **and** abroad.*

autant (que/de) as many/much as, so many/much; proportionately; all the more ... because
• Il est anormal que la marchandise mette **autant de** temps à arriver à Paris. - *It is unusual for the goods to take **so much** time to reach Paris.*
• La surtaxe douanière ne sera plus appliquée. ... la marge d'exploitation sera certainement **d'autant** augmentée. - *The customs surcharge will no longer be applied. ... the trading margin will certainly be increased **proportionately**.*
• Nous serons **d'autant plus** heureux de vous rencontrer **que**, malheureusement, nous sommes sans nouvelles de votre part. - *We shall be **all the more** happy to meet you **because** we have had no news of you.*

autorisation *nf* authority,

authorization, permission
• Vos ouvriers ont déchargé sur notre chantier les fers à béton sans **autorisation** préalable. - *Your workmen unloaded the concrete reinforcing rods on our site without prior **authority/authorization**.*

autoriser *vt* authorize, empower, license
• Expéditions partielles **autorisées**. - *Part shipments **authorized**.*

autre *nmf & adj* alternative, other; [furthermore, moreover]
• Nous vous prions de bien vouloir nous en envoyer **un autre**. - *Would you kindly send us **another** of them.*
• Devons-nous vous les retourner, ou quelle **autre** solution nous proposez-vous? - *Are we to return them to you, or what **alternative** solution do you suggest?*
• **D'autre part**, nous profitons de cette occasion pour vous demander si vous n'avez pas une édition plus récente de votre brochure. - ***Furthermore/Moreover**, we take this opportunity to ask you ...*

avance *nf* advance, [anticipation]
USAGE *The three expressions, 'à l'avance', 'd'avance' and 'par avance', are used interchangeably, meaning 'in advance' or 'in anticipation'. In sentence-initial position, 'd'avance' may be preferred, as in the first example.*
• **D'avance** merci et à bientôt. - *Thanks **in anticipation** and see you soon.*
• Nous vous en remercions **par avance** et vous prions d'agréer, Messieurs, ...

avant (de/que) before, prior to; [further]
• Nous avons dû conclure que ces appareils n'avaient pas été essayés

avant leur expédition. - ... *that these devices had not been tested before/prior to dispatch.*

• Je compte aller faire une tournée en Allemagne **avant** la fin de ce mois.

• De plus, il est opportun de visiter les lots **avant de** remettre des offres, ... - *Moreover, it is as well to inspect the batches before making any offers, ...*

• ... et vous aviez manifesté un certain intérêt de principe à aller **plus avant** dans l'étude de cette question. - ... *and you had shown some interest in principle in proceeding further with the investigation of this matter.*

avantage *nm* advantage, benefit; [have pleasure in, be pleased to]

• ... ce qui réduit la part des **avantages** du MF. - ... *which reduces the advantages/benefits of the MF.*

• Nous **avons l'avantage de vous adresser** notre documentation sur le matériel ... - *We are pleased to send you/have pleasure in sending you our literature on the material ...*

avantageux, -euse *adj* advantageous, attractive, bargain, cheap, modest

COLLOCATES *affaire, conditions, prix, tarif*

• L'importance de nos achats nous permet de vous faire des prix fort **avantageux**. - *The scale of our purchases enables us to offer you very attractive/bargain prices.*

avarie *nf* damage

• Les **avaries** ne surviennent pas sur le transport Londres-Paris, mais par la suite ... - *The damage does not occur during transport from London to Paris, but subsequently ...*

avenir *nm* future

• Nous vous serions obligés de bien vouloir **à l'avenir** nous envoyer tous documents techniques pouvant servir à notre documentation. - *We should be obliged if you would kindly send us in future all technical documents ...*

s'avérer *vpro* prove, turn out

TENSES See *céder*

• Mais si un troisième voyage **s'avérait** utile, celui-ci serait à la charge de l'usine. - *But if a third trip proved/turned out to be useful, ...*

• Il **s'est avéré** qu'une de ces pièces a été mise hors d'usage par un serrage excessif ... - *It has turned out to be the case that one of these components was put out of action by overtightening ...*

avion *nm* air, aircraft

• Une facture pro-forma de cette commande a été adressée **par avion** à l'agence de Bamako. - ... *was sent by air to the Bamako agency.*

• Le mécanisme destiné à M. X sera expédié dans quelques jours **par colis postal avion**, à l'adresse ... - ... *will be dispatched by air parcel post, to the address ...*

avis *nm* advice, notice; mind, opinion, view

USAGE NB 'Avis' does not translate English 'advice' in the general sense of 'recommendation, helpful advice'. See 'conseil'.

• Comme demandé, nous vous enverrons la facture en même temps que l'**avis** d'expédition. - ... *at the same time as the advice/notice of dispatch.*

• **Sauf avis contraire de votre part**, nous adresserons donc à chacun des destinataires notre facture correspondante. - *Unless we hear from you to the contrary, ...*

• Veuillez nous faire connaître votre **avis** à ce sujet. - *Please let us know your **opinion** about this.*
• **A notre avis**, la hauteur de la partie inférieure serait . . . - *To our mind/In our opinion/view, the height of the lower part would be . . .*

aviser (de) *vt* advise (of), notify (of)
• Comme d'habitude, nous vous laissons le soin d'**aviser** votre client **de** cet envoi . . . - *As usual, we leave you to **advise/notify** your customer **of** this dispatch . . .*
• . . . nous **avons été avisés** par le service des postes **de** cet envoi. - *. . . we **have been advised/notified** by the postal authorities **of** this dispatch.*
• . . . et par télex du 14 ct. vous nous **avisiez que** vous disposiez de 100 tonnes environ. - *. . . you **advised/notified** us **that** you had about 100 tons available.*

• Nous vous demandons de nous **aviser** si nous devons maintenir votre commande pour 19--. - *. . . to **advise/notify** us whether we should maintain your order for 19--.*

avoir *nm* credit note
• . . . nous vous ferons adresser un **avoir** de F.20.8 par kilo représentant la différence entre CIF et FOB. - *. . . we will arrange for a **credit note** to be sent to you . . .*

avoir *vt & aux* have; have to, need to
TENSES Pres *1 ai 3 a 4 avons 6 ont* Imp *avais* Fut *aurai* PP *eu, eue* Pres Part *ayant* Subj *1 aie 3 ait 4 ayons 6 aient*
• . . . factures pro-forma que vous **aurez à** adresser directement à CIE. - *. . . pro-forma invoices which you **will need to** send direct to CIE.*

avril *nm April*

B

baisse *nf* decline, drop, fall, lowering
• Nous pensons qu'ainsi il pourrait être envisagé une **baisse** du prix de revient. - *We think that in this way a **lowering** of the cost price might be anticipated.*

bancaire *adj* bank, banker's
• Nous vous rappelons que nos expéditions se font contre accréditif **bancaire** ou documents **bancaires**. - *May we remind you that our shipments are made against **(banker's)** letter of credit or **banker's** documents.*

banque *nf* bank

banquier *nm* banker

• . . . nous vous indiquions que les connaissements vous parviendraient par notre **banquier**. - *. . . the bills of lading would reach you via our **banker**.*

barème *nm* scale of charges
• Ce dernier tarif vient s'ajouter à la série de tarifs et **barèmes** déjà existante. - *The latter price list is an addition to the set of price lists and **scales of charges** already in existence.*

bas *nm* bottom, foot
• Nous attirons votre attention sur les quelques pièces non livrables indiquées **au bas de** notre confirmation. - *. . . the non-deliverable items shown **at the bottom/foot of** our confirmation.*

bas, basse *adj* low
• Pourriez-vous nous indiquer si les frais de Goole à Boulogne ne seraient pas **plus bas que** les frais de Goole à Dunquerque. - ... *whether the charges from Goole to Boulogne might not be **lower than** the charges ...*

base *nf* basis, [basic]
• Nous avons vendu à Messieurs CIE sur la **base** d'un prix net. - ... *on the **basis** of a net price.*
• Nous procéderons également à la facturation des 2.200 MF à CIE France sur le prix **de base** de 123 livres, moins 35% FOB Londres. - ... *at the **basic** price of £123, less 35% FOB London.*

bateau *nm* boat, ship

bâtiment *nm* building

beaucoup *adv* a great deal, a lot, greatly, much
• Je crains de perdre **beaucoup** dans cette affaire. - *I am afraid of losing **a great deal** over this business.*
• J'ai **beaucoup** apprécié la bonne finition du tube perforé. - *I **greatly** appreciated the good finish of the perforated tube.*
• C'est avec **beaucoup de** plaisir que j'ai lu votre lettre du 7 septembre dernier. - *It was with **much** pleasure that ...*
• Nous vous avons adressé par un courrier séparé notre dernier catalogue français, qui est **beaucoup plus** complet. - ..., *which is **much more/a lot more** complete.*

bénéfice *nm* profit
• Nous avons réalisé un **bénéfice** sur ce transfert, plus élevé que normalement, ... - *We have made a **profit** on this transfer, bigger than normally, ...*

bénéficiaire *nmf & adj* beneficiary; [profit]
• Nous vous demandons de bien vouloir nous préciser si, en tenant compte de votre **marge bénéficiaire**, vous pouvez coter 225F. rendu le Creusot. - ..., *taking into account your **profit margin**, you can quote ...*

bénéficier de *vt indir* benefit from, enjoy, get, qualify for
COLLOCATES *conditions, tarif, ristourne*
• Il est entendu que pour les réparations de carrosserie de voiture nos membres **bénéficieront** d'une ristourne de 10%. - ... *our members **will enjoy** a discount of 10%.*
• M. X nous a retourné cette note de crédit et nous serions heureux de vous en faire **bénéficier**. - ..., *and we should be glad to have you **benefit** from it.*

besoin *nm* need, requirement, [require]
• Restant à votre disposition pour tous renseignements complémentaires **dont vous auriez besoin**, ... - ... *any further information **which you might need/require**, ...*
• Nous avons, en effet, un **besoin** urgent de cette matière première. - *We do, in fact, have an urgent **need** for this raw material.*
• Nous vous laissons le soin d'adresser à Bulawayo une facture **pour les besoins de la douane**. - ... *an invoice **for the requirements of the customs/for customs purposes**.*

bien *adv* well; quite, fully, properly, [good; certainly, really, indeed; safely; very]
USAGE *In business letters 'bien' is rarely equivalent to English. 'well'. As*

BIEN

*an adverb, it is used to modify verbs ('nous **voulons bien**'), adjectives ('**bien aimable**') and other adverbs ('il y a **bien longtemps**'). Being a very frequent word, it has many nuances of meaning and also enters into a number of more or less idiomatic expressions (e.g. '**bien entendu**'). The following set of examples has been chosen to illustrate the wide range of uses of 'bien' and the variety of its context-dependent English translation equivalents.*

- Toutefois, le jeudi 13 avril ne me convient pas **bien**. - *... does not suit me **well**.*
- Vous **feriez bien** de lui rembourser les 132 briques. - *You **would do well** to reimburse him for the 132 bricks.*
- Nous n'avons pas **bien** compris comment vous avez établi le compte des machines qu'il vous reste à nous livrer. - *We have not **quite/fully/ properly** understood how you have established the number of machines ...*
- Nous **voulons bien** faire cet essai. - *We are **quite prepared** to carry out this trial.*
- Nous **avons bien noté** que c'est à vous que nous nous adresserons éventuellement. - *We have **taken good note** that it is to you that we will apply in that event.*
- J'ai **bien l'impression** que notre problème n'aurait pas été pris avec la même considération. - *I **certainly/ indeed/really do have the impression** that ...*
- Nous vous confirmons qu'**il s'agit bien** d'une deuxième commande. - *... it is **indeed**/it really is a second order.*
- J'avais **bien** envisagé de me rendre à Zurich. - *I had **indeed** contemplated going to Zurich.*

BIENVEILLANCE

- Nous **avons bien reçu** votre lettre du 22 courant. - *We have **received (safely)** your letter ...*
- Nous espérons que ces échantillons vous sont maintenant **bien** parvenus. - *... these samples have by now reached you **safely**.*
- Il est **bien évident** que cette affaire dure depuis fort longtemps. - *It is **quite clear** that this business has been going on for a long time.*
- Vous seriez **bien aimables** de nous documenter au sujet des desiderata de cette firme. - *It would be **very kind** of you to fill us in regarding the requirements of this firm.*

bien entendu of course, naturally
- Vous serez, **bien entendu**, tenus au courant de l'issue de nos pourparlers avec Messieurs CIE. - *You will, **of course/naturally**, be kept informed ...*
- Il est **bien entendu que** ces chiffres sont approximatifs. - *These figures are **of course** approximate.*

bien-fondé nm justice, soundness
- Nous avons assisté à cet essai et avons dû constater le **bien-fondé** de la réclamation. - *We were present at the test and had to recognize the **justice/soundness** of the complaint.*

bien que although, (even) though
USAGE *Bien que* + Subjunctive.
- Nous tenons à vous remercier ..., **bien qu**'il ne vous ait pas été possible de donner suite à notre demande. - *We should like to thank you ..., **although/even though** it has not been possible for you to comply with our request.*

bienveillance nf sympathy, [sympathetically]
- Nous osons espérer que vous voudrez bien examiner le présent problème **avec bienveillance**. - *...*

examine the present problem **sympathetically**.

bienvenu, -e *nmf* welcome
• Dans ce programme d'offres, tous nos confrères étrangers qui voudront y coopérer seront les **bienvenus**. - ... *all our foreign colleagues who wish to cooperate will be welcome.*

bilan *nm* balance sheet
• ... ledit rapport doit accompagner le **bilan** qu'ils ont établi. - ... *the said report must accompany the balance sheet which they have drawn up.*

boîte *nf* box

bon, -ne *adj* good, careful, safe; kind
USAGE '*Bon*' *is often used simply to add a note of politeness, as in the third and fourth examples.*
• Nous vous remercions de votre lettre du 10 octobre et vous assurons que nous **avons pris bonne note de** son contenu. - ... *we have taken good/careful note of its contents.*
• Nous accusons **bonne réception** de votre lettre du 7 courant. - *We acknowledge safe receipt of your letter* ...
• Nous nous permettons de rappeler à **votre bonne attention** notre demande de prix rappelée sous rubrique. - *May we bring to your kind attention* ...
• Nous **comptons sur vos bons soins** pour l'exécution rapide de ces travaux. - *We are counting/relying on you for the rapid completion of these works.*

bon *nm* form, slip
COLLOCATES *de commande, de livraison*

• Le libellé du **bon** de commande annexé à ce message diffère du précédent sur les deux points suivants: ... - *The wording of the order form attached to this message* ...

bon à tirer *nm* final corrected proof, [pass for press]
• Notre copie vous a été remise le 15 septembre, le **bon à tirer vous a été donné** le 27 octobre, et nous recevons le premier rouleau le 5 décembre. - *Our copy was given to you on 15 September, the final corrected proof was given to you/we passed it for press on 27 October* ...

bordereau *nm* note, slip; [list]
COLLOCATES *d'achat, de chargement, d'envoi, de livraison*
• Nous vous retournons ci-jointe cette pièce, accompagnée d'une photocopie du **bordereau** de chargement correspondant, émargé par vos services. - *We are returning to you herewith this document, together with a photocopy of the corresponding cargo list, initialled by your staff.*

brièvement *adv* briefly
• Ci-joint vous trouverez une note qui expose **brièvement** les buts et les activités de notre organisation européenne. - *Enclosed you will find a note setting out briefly the aims* ...

brochure *nf* brochure, booklet, pamphlet
• Nous vous adressons par pli séparé des **brochures** que nous avons éditées récemment en anglais. - ... *brochures which we have published recently in English.*

brut, -e *adj & adv* gross
• Prix: £123 par 1015kg, **brut pour net**, pour marchandise rendue FOB

Anvers. - *Price: £123 per 1015 kilos, gross weight for net, for goods delivered FOB Antwerp.*

brutal, -e (*mpl* -aux) *adj* rough
• Après avoir réexaminé l'emballage, nous nous sommes rendu compte que l'incident pouvait à la rigueur se produire à la suite de manipulations extrèmement **brutales**. - . . . *the incident could conceivably occur following extremely rough handling.*

bureau *nm* office, department
• Nous possédons des **bureaux** en plein Paris. - . . . *offices in the heart of Paris.*

• Nous vous confirmons la lettre que vous a adressée notre **bureau** d'achats à Lyon. - *We confirm the letter which our purchasing department in Lyon sent you.*

but *nm* aim, goal, objective, purpose, target, view
• Pour atteindre ce même **but**, nous sommes à votre entière disposition pour vous aider . . . - *To attain this same goal,. . .*
• . . . et **dans le but de** vous documenter, nous vous adressons notre catalogue . . . - . . . *and with the aim/purpose of/with a view to providing you with the information you need, . . .*

C

câble *nm* cable, telegram, wire
• Nous vous confirmons les termes de notre **câble** de ce jour rédigé comme suit: . . . - . . . *the terms of our cable of today's date worded as follows: . . .*

cacher *vt* conceal, hide, [make it clear]
• Il **ne m'a pas caché** qu'il souhaite que l'étude se fasse le plus tôt possible. - *He did not conceal/hide/ He made it clear that he wished the study to be done as soon as possible.*

cadence *nf* rate
USAGE Compare *taux*.
• Nous vous prions de vouloir bien trouver ci-après la **cadence** de livraison que nous aimerions adopter pour les 2.000 appareils restant, soit: courant juillet 250, courant septembre 250, . . . - . . . *the*

rate of delivery which we should like to adopt . . .

cadre *nm* framework, scope
• Comme d'habitude, et dans le **cadre** de nos accords commerciaux, nous vous laissons le soin de . . . - . . . *and within the framework of our commercial agreements, . . .*
• Ces inconvénients, dont l'exposé détaillé dépasserait le **cadre** d'une lettre, ont été étudiés attentivement. - *These difficuties, of which a detailed account would exceed the scope of a letter, . . .*

cahier des charges *nm* schedule of conditions
• Votre offre doit être conforme aux exigences des extraits du **cahier des charges** et des plans joints à la présente et répondra en outre aux normes suivantes: . . . - *Your tender*

should comply with the requirements of the extracts from the schedule of conditions and of the plans enclosed with this letter. . .

caisse *nf* case, crate
• Nous avons eu énormément de difficultés avec vos livraisons récentes, en raison du poids considérable de vos **caisses**. - *. . . due to the considerable weight of your cases/crates.*

calcul *nm* calculation
• D'après les **calculs** qui ont été faits, il aurait besoin de 1.500 briques. - *According to the calculations which have been made, . . .*

calculer *vt* calculate, work out
• Les chiffres demandés n'étaient pas immédiatement disponibles et j'ai laissé à M. X le soin de les **calculer**. - *. . . and I have left it to Mr X to work them (the figures) out.*

camion *nm* lorry, truck
• Nous souhaiterions recevoir un prix marchandise rendue Gand par charge de **camion** complet. - *. . . a price for goods delivered to Ghent in complete lorry loads.*

campagne *nf* campaign
• Nous pouvons vous confirmer que les prix indiqués dans notre dernière liste de prix pour la **campagne** 19--/-- sont toujours valables. - *. . . the prices shown in our last price list for the 19--/-- campaign. . . .*
• Pour l'organisation de notre **campagne** publicitaire à l'occasion du Rallye de Monte Carlo, . . . - *For organizing our advertising campaign . . .*

canal *nm* channel; [through, via]

• Vous recevrez, **par le canal de** M. X, un échantillon de MF. - *You will receive, through/via Mr X, a sample of MF.*
• D'autre part, son réseau commercial distribue ces produits **par les canaux de** droguerie, des grands magasins et des supermarchés. - *. . . distributes its products through/via hardware shops, department stores and supermarkets.*

candidat -e *nmf* applicant, candidate
• Si donc vous cherchez toujours quelqu'un susceptible de diriger vos affaires françaises, c'est un **candidat** qui pourrait être intéressant. - *. . . someone to manage your business in France, he is an applicant who could be suitable.*

car *conj* because, for
USAGE *The clause introduced by 'car', expressing cause or justification, always follows the main clause. This restriction does not apply to its synonyms 'comme', 'étant donné', 'parce que' and 'puisque'. In spite of this, 'car' is used as often in business letters as all these other expressions put together.*
• Il n'y a pas de déformation de matière, **car** le couteau ne tourne qu'à 255 tours/minute. - *There is no deforming of the material, because the blade revolves at only 255rpm.*
• Nous vous prions de nous préciser quel est le nom du transitaire, **car** il est anormal que la marchandise mette autant de temps à arriver à Paris. - *Please tell us the name of the forwarding agent, because/for it is unusual for the goods to take so long to reach Paris.*

caractère *nm* character, nature

• Nous nous permettons d'insister sur le **caractère** d'indépendance et la polyvalence de notre bureau. - *May we emphasize the independent **nature** and the comprehensiveness of our consultancy.*

caractéristique *nf* characteristic, feature

• Les **caractéristiques** de ces pneumatiques sont les suivantes: ... - *The **characteristics** of these tyres are the following: ...*

carte *nf* card

• Faites l'essai de cette étonnante lame en nous retournant la **carte** ci-jointe. - *Try this astonishing blade by returning to us the enclosed **card**.*

carton *nm* cardboard, cardboard box, carton

• A noter que l'emballage caisse **carton** est compris dans ce tarif. - *Please note that packing in **cardboard** cases is included in this price.*

• Nous pouvons également vous fournir un excellent hydromel en **cartons** d'exportation de 12 bouteilles de 70cl. - *... an excellent mead in export **cartons**/**cardboard boxes** containing twelve 70cl bottles.*

cas *nm* case, event, instance, [under no circumstances, on no account, if the need arises, if so]

• Il ne s'agit pas d'un **cas** unique mais de plusieurs réclamations qui semblent bien prouver une insuffisance d'emballage. - *We are not dealing with an isolated **case**/**instance** but with several complaints which certainly seem to prove that the packing is inadequate.*

• Le mieux serait que vous envisagiez de vous présenter à notre bureau central à 9h.. Un chauffeur de notre Société se présenterait **dans ce cas** à votre hôtel vers 8h30. - *...a*

*chauffeur from our Company would present himself **in that case**/**in that event** at your hotel about 8.30.*

• **Au cas où** vous-même ne seriez pas intéressé à la vente de nos produits en Angleterre, pourriez-vous nous indiquer une personne susceptible de s'intéresser à celle-ci. - *In the event of you yourself not being interested in the sale of our products in England, could you ...*

• Nous vous précisons qu'**en cas de** commande les poids pourraient être modifiés en fonction des quotas impartis par le gouvernement tunisien. - *... in the event of an order being placed, the weights could be modified ...*

• **Dans le cas de** votre acceptation de cette solution, ... - *In the event of your accepting this solution, ...*

• J'ai cru bien faire en vous adressant la notice documentaire ci-jointe **pour le cas où** ces locaux seraient susceptibles de retenir votre attention. - *... in case these premises might be of interest to you.*

• Bien entendu, nous ne pouvons **en aucun cas** accepter votre facture sur la base annoncée. - *Of course, **under no circumstances**/**on no account** can we accept your invoice ...*

• Nous pourrions vous faire prendre à Metz: il suffirait, **le cas échéant**, de nous indiquer l'adresse de l'hôtel où vous aurez passé la nuit. - *We could have you picked up in Metz: it would be sufficient, **in such an event**/**if the need arose**/**if so**, for you to let us know the address of the hotel ...*

catalogue *nm* catalogue

• Dès que votre nouveau **catalogue** sera paru, je vous serais reconnaissant de bien vouloir nous l'adresser. - *As soon as your new catalogue appears, ...*

cause *nf* cause; [because of, owing to, on account of; in question, concerned]

• **A cause des** mauvais résultats de la livraison précédente, nous n'avons pas la commande. - *Because of/Owing to/On account of the poor results of the previous delivery, ...*

• ... nous faire savoir si nous pouvons procéder à la réexpédition de l'article **en cause**. - *... the article in question.*

CCP *See* compte

ceci *pro* this

• ... votre lettre précisant que vous êtes d'accord pour remplacer le matériel qui nous a été fourni, et **ceci** sous tous frais à votre charge. - *... your letter indicating that you agree to replace the material supplied to us, and (this) entirely at your expense.*

céder *vt* assign, hand over, let have
TENSES Pres *1,3 cède 4 cédons 6 cèdent* Imp *cédais* Fut *céderai* PP *cédé, -ée* Pres Part *cédant* Subj *1,3 cède 4 cédions 6 cèdent*

• Nous sommes prêts à vous **céder** les droits de traduction en langue anglaise pour les ouvrages qui pourraient vous intéresser. - *We are ready to assign to you/let you have translation rights ...*

• Nous sommes disposés à vous **céder** notre légitime profit si vous avez une perte personnelle. - *We are prepared to hand over to you our legitimate profit ...*

cela *pro* that

• ... mais je pourrai vous voir le mardi 11 si **cela** vous convient. - *... if that suits you.*

centaine *nf* hundred (or so)

• Il ne reste plus qu'**une centaine de** tonnes. - *There are only a hundred tons or so left.*

• Nous disposons encore de **quelques centaines de** cartons de cerneaux. - *We still have a few hundred boxes of half-shelled walnuts.*

cependant however

• Nous avons participé à cette Foire l'année dernière ... **Cependant**, cette année ... ne présente pour l'industrie mécanique qu'une importance tout à fait relative. - *We exhibited at this Fair last year ... However, this year ... is of minimal importance to the mechanical industry.*

• Il me paraît **cependant** que cela ne puisse se réaliser. - *It appears to me however that this cannot be done.*

certain *-e adj* certain; assured, positive, sure

• Les directeurs régionaux attendront d'avoir recueilli un **certain** nombre de commandes avant de nous les transmettre. - *The regional managers will wait until they have assembled a certain number of orders ...*

• **Certaines** planches étaient collées les unes contre les autres. - *Certain planks were stuck together.*

• Il est **certain** que notre stock de départ nous manque beaucoup. - *It is certain that we are greatly in need of our starting stock.*

• **Soyez certain que** nous ferons tous les efforts pour régler cette question. - *Rest assured that we will do our utmost to settle this question.*

certainement *adv* assuredly, certainly, definitely

• Ils pourront **certainement** vous mettre en rapport avec les différents

responsables. - *They will **assuredly/
certainly** be able to put you in
touch* ...

certificat *nm* certificate
• Nous avons bien noté toutes les
indications relatives au marquage
des cartons et aux divers **certificats** à
obtenir. - *We have noted all the
instructions regarding the marking of
the cartons and the various
certificates to be obtained.*

certifier *vt* certify
• Inclus: facture **certifiée** en 6
exemplaires No 123.

c'est-à-dire that is (to say), i.e.
• Nous enregistrons cette
commande pour exécution dans un
délai de 3 semaines, **c'est-à-dire**
pour le 16 prochain. - *... for
execution in 3 weeks, **i.e.** for the 16th
of next month.*

chambre *nf* room, accommodation
• Pouvez-vous me faire retenir **une
chambre** à l'Hôtel X pour le mardi 28
et le mercredi 29 septembre. - *Can
you book me **a room/
accommodation** ...*

chance *nf* chance
• Il n'y a aucune **chance** d'obtenir
une commande.
• Il y a de fortes **chances** pour que
la hausse des prix reprenne. - *The
chances are that the rise in prices will
resume.*

changer *vt & i* change, vary
TENSES Pres *1,3 change 4 changeons 5
changez 6 changent* Imp *1 changeais 4
changions 5 changiez 6 changeaient*
Fut *changerai* PP *changé, -ée* Pres
Part *changeant* Subj *1,3 change 4
changions 5 changiez 6 changent*
• Nous supposons qu'il vous serait
difficile de **changer** la forme
standard. - *We suppose it would be*

difficult for you to **change** the standard
shape.
• ... les formats des briques **ont
changé**. - *... the sizes of the bricks
have changed.*

changement *nm* change
• Attention, **changement**
d'adresse! - *NB **Change** of address!*

charge *nf* load; charge, [chargeable
to, payable by, bear, take care of]
• La **charge** moyenne par palette
serait de 1.500kg. - *The average **load**
per pallet* ...
• Toutefois les frais d'envoi de
moins de 5.000 pièces sont à la
charge du client. - *... are chargeable
to/payable by/to be borne by the
customer.*
• L'usine est d'accord pour **prendre
à sa charge** la différence de frais de
transport, soit F.123. - *The factory
agrees **to bear/to take care of** the
difference in transport charges,
namely 123 francs.*

chargement *nm* loading
• **Chargement** sur palettes: les
briques seraient expédiées sur
palettes de 1m par 1m. - ***Loading** on
pallets:* ...

charger *vt* load, embark; charge,
entrust, instruct
TENSES See *charger*
• Les marchandises **chargées** par
vos soins dans les remorques
arrivent telles quelles à destination.
- *The goods **loaded** by you in the
trailers* ...
• Ces remorques peuvent **être
chargées** directement dans vos
magasins. - *These trailers can **be
loaded** directly in your warehouses.*
• Nous **sommes chargés par** notre
client, CIE, de l'expédition des
marchandises référencées ... - *We
are charged by our customer, CIE,*

with the shipment of the above-referenced goods . . .

se **charger de** *vpro* take on, take charge of, undertake
• Si vous décidez finalement de participer à cette Foire, nous sommes en mesure de **nous charger de** toute l'organisation matérielle. - *. . . we are able to* **take charge of** *all the practical organization.*

chef *nm* head, manager; principal
USAGE *'Chef' is grammatically masculine even when used to refer to a woman.*
• Je vous remercie de l'intervention que vous avez faite auprès du **chef** de publicité de cette société. - *Thank you for your intercession with the advertising* **manager** *of that firm.*

chemin de fer *nm* railway, railroad
• Je vous confirme que je voyagerai par **chemin de fer.**

chèque *nm* cheque
• Nous vous demandons de bien vouloir nous adresser un **chèque** de 123 livres dès réception de ces documents. - *. . . send us a* **cheque** *for £123 on receipt of these documents.*

cher, chère *adj* costly, dear, expensive
• Les pinceaux sont **chers.** - *The brushes are* **dear/expensive.**

cher *adv* dear, a lot
• Cette opération nous coûte déjà passablement **cher.** - *This operation is already costing us rather* **a lot.**

chercher (à) *vt* look for, seek (to)
• Vous savez que je n'ai jamais **cherché à** concurrencer les confrères belges chez les utilisateurs. - *. . . I have never* **sought to** *compete with our Belgian colleagues . . .*
• CIE **cherche** un représentant en Belgique pour ses engins de

transport. - *CIE* **is looking for/is seeking** *a representative in Belgium . . .*

chez *prep* at, to, with, etc
• Cette marchandise sera livrée **chez** notre transitaire de Bordeaux, le 28 février. - *These goods will be delivered* **to** *our forwarding agent in Bordeaux . . .*
• Nous vous prions de vouloir bien transférer par le débit de notre compte **chez** vous la somme de F10.000.000 . . . - *Please transfer by debiting our account* **with** *you the sum of 10,000,000 francs.*

chiffre *nm* figure, [turnover]
• Les **chiffres** demandés n'étaient pas immédiatement disponibles. - *The* **figures** *requested were not immediately available.*
• Ces différents services pourront être rémunérés sur la base d'un pourcentage du **chiffre d'affaires.** - *. . . on the basis of a percentage of the* **turnover.**

choix *nm* choice, selection; grade, quality
• Vos prix devront être établis CIF Dunquerque, Anvers et, éventuellement, un autre port de votre **choix.** - *. . . another port of your* **choice.**
• Nous sommes acheteurs de slabs, de tôles et de ronds, **en premier et second choix.** - *. . . slabs etc, in first and second quality.*

chose *nf* thing, matter; [above all, first and foremost]
• **Si la chose vous intéresse** encore, nous pouvons vous offrir . . . - **If** *you are* **still** **interested**, *we can offer you . . .*
• **Avant toute chose**, nous vous rappelons que l'an dernier l'envoi a

été effectué le 5 juin. - *Above all/ First and foremost*, may we remind you that ...

ci- *prefix*
USAGE *As a prefix, 'ci-' corresponds to 'here' as in the old-fashioned English expression 'hereunder'. It has two rather distinct functions: (a) It makes a link with a later part of the text of the letter ('ci-après'/'ci-dessous' 'below') or with an earlier part ('ci-dessus' 'above'); (b) It makes a link with an attachment or enclosure ('ci-joint, -e'/ 'ci-inclus, -e'/'ci-annexé,-e' 'attached', 'enclosed'). 'Ci-joint' and 'ci-inclus' are interchangeable, the former being somewhat the more common. 'Ci-annexé' is much less common than either. The rules regarding their agreement or non-agreement with the noun to which they refer are very complex and seem to baffle a large proportion of native-speakers of French. The following provides a reasonable rule of thumb: (a) If 'ci-joint' (etc) occurs at the beginning of a sentence, use the unmarked form, i.e. masculine singular, even if the following noun is feminine or plural (as in our last example); (b) Otherwise, always make it agree, whether it comes before or after the noun to which it refers.*

• J'ai le plaisir de vous communiquer **ci-après** le nom et l'adresse d'une firme allemande de parfumerie. - *I have pleasure in passing on to you* **below** *the name ...*

• Nous avons le plaisir de vous communiquer **ci-dessous** nos prévisions pour l'année 19--. - *... to give you* **below/hereunder** *our forecasts for 19--.*

• Sans nouvelles de vous depuis l'échange de télex cité **ci-dessus,**

nous vous prions ... - *Having no news from you since the exchange of telex messages cited* **above,** *...*

• Vous trouverez **ci-incluse** une lettre de CIE concernant la palette No 43. - *You will find* **enclosed** *a letter ...*

• Nous vous prions de trouver **ci-joints** notre catalogue et notre tarif de vente métropole hors taxes locales. - *Please find* **enclosed** *our catalogue and our home price list ...*

• Nous vous demandons de bien vouloir ajouter à notre commande No 123 la commande **ci-jointe**. - *... the* **enclosed** *order.*

• **Ci-joint** vous trouverez une note qui expose brièvement les buts ... - **Enclosed** *you will find a note which sets out in brief the objectives ...* NB *See* **Usage** regarding agreement or non-agreement with the noun.

-ci *suffix* latter, last few, next few
• Ce petit travail aurait dû être fait par notre imprimeur, mais **celui-ci** n'a pas dû faire le nécessaire. - *This little job should have been done by our printer, but* **the latter** *cannot have done what was necessary.*

• Nous avons bien reçu **ces jours-ci** votre lettre du 2 août, qui nous a surpris. - *In the last few days we have received your letter, ...*

• Nous allons faire, **ces jours-ci,** notre première soumission ... - *In the next few days we are going to make our first tender ...*

CIF *See* coût

circonstance *nf* circumstance
• Étant donné ces **circonstances,** nous sommes d'accord que cet article nous soit retourné. - *Given these* **circumstances,** *...*

citer *vt* quote, cite

CLASSER column:

• Nous avons bien reçu votre lettre **citée** en référence. - ... *your letter quoted above.*

classer *vt* file
• Nous regrettons de vous prier de **classer** sans suite ce dossier. - ... *to file this dossier without follow-up./... to close this file.*

cliché *nm* block, negative
• Par courrier séparé nous vous adressons les 6 **clichés** d'images nécessaires à l'illustration de cette notice. - ... *the 6 negatives of pictures needed to illustrate this leaflet.*

client, -e *nmf* customer, client
• Dans ce cas le **client** pourra bénéficier des conditions de FOB. - ... *the customer will be able to enjoy FOB terms.*
• Il serait intéressant que ma **cliente** connaisse le produit dont vous pourriez lui concéder la licence. - *It would be worthwhile for my (lady) client to know about the product for which you could grant her a licence.*

clientèle *nf* customers, clientele
• Notre **clientèle** n'a pas spécialement apprécié les modèles que nous avons mis en vente. - *Our customers did not particularly like the models ...*

colis *nm* parcel
• Nous vous envoyons par **colis** séparé un échantillon de 12 bocaux de cornichons en tranches. - *We are sending you in a separate parcel ...*
• A partir du 10 décembre les **colis postaux** subiront une augmentation de 10%. - ... *parcel post will go up by 10%.*

colisage *nm* [packing note]
• Pour chaque envoi, vous recevrez un dossier de transit complet

COMMANDE column:

comportant: 1° ... 2° copie des **bordereaux de colisage** ... - ... *2) copy of the packing notes ...*

collaborateur, -trice *nmf* colleague
• J'ai demandé à mes **collaborateurs**, MM. X et Y, de vous recevoir à ma place. - *I have asked my colleagues, Messrs X and Y, to receive you on my behalf.*

collaboration *nf* collaboration
• ... renforçant l'heureux climat de **collaboration** dans lequel évoluent les relations de nos établissements. - ... *strengthening the favourable climate of collaboration ...*

collègue *nmf* colleague
• En mon absence, mes **collègues** prendront soin de vous et du Dr X. - *In my absence, my colleagues will look after Dr X and yourself.*

coller *vt* stick
• D'autre part, la plaque-étiquette de CIE ne devrait pas être **collée** sur les appareils. - ... *should not be stuck on the machines.*

commande *nf* order, indent
COLLOCATES *adresser, ajouter à, annuler, confirmer, enregistrer, expédier, livrer, maintenir, noter, obtenir, passer, perdre, recevoir, satisfaire, transmettre; annulation, confirmation, copie, double, duplicata, exécution, expédition, réception, reliquat, solde, suspension; en cours, éventuelle, export, ferme, grosse, importante, précédente, précitée, régulière, sous rubrique, supplémentaire; en cas de, (faire l') objet de, relative à, (faire) suite à*
• Suite à notre **commande** sous rubrique, nous vous prions de noter que ... - *Further to our above-mentioned order, ...*

• Nous avons le plaisir de vous **passer commande** pour 3 tonnes de crème MF. - *We have pleasure in* **placing an order** *with you for 3 tons of MF cream./. . . in* **ordering** *from you 3 tons of MF cream.*

• Nous vous prions de nous faire savoir quand vous comptez expédier les aciers faisant l'objet de notre susdite **commande**. - *. . . the steels covered by our above-mentioned* **order**.

• Les CIE demandent que l'expédition de leur **commande** soit faite avant le 21 avril. - *. . . the dispatch of their* **order** *be made before 21 April.*

• Délai: environ 10 jours, départ nos usines, à dater de la réception de votre **commande** ferme. - *. . . dating from receipt of your firm* **order**.

• La livraison sera à faire à notre magasin en même temps que le reliquat de la **commande** en cours. - *. . . at the same time as the remainder of the current* **order**.

commander *vt* order, indent

• Nous souhaitons que les matelas que vous avez bien voulu nous **commander** vous donnent entière satisfaction. - *. . . the mattresses which you were good enough to* **order** *from us . . .*

comme as, like; since
USAGE *When, as in the fourth example, 'comme' introduces a clause expressing cause or justification, this clause always precedes the main clause.*

• Nous nous présentons **comme** importateurs de miels de toutes provenances. - *May we introduce ourselves* **as** *importers of honeys . . .*

• CIE a été, **comme** nous, étonnée du contenu de cette lettre. - *CIE was,* **like** *us, astonished . . .*

• **Comme** nous vous l'avons déjà indiqué, nous sommes spécialisés dans le matériel de grandes cuisines. - *As we have already informed you, . . .*

• **Comme** l'assistance technique de Monsieur X est très importante pour nous, nous vous prions de bien vouloir nous confirmer cette nouvelle. - *As/Since the technical support of Mr X is very important to us, would you kindly confirm this report.*

commencer (à) *vi* begin (with), commence, start (with)
TENSES See *placer*

• Je m'empresse de vous faire parvenir **pour commencer** une documentation technique sur CIE. - *I will without delay send you* **to begin/ start with** *a set of technical literature about CIE.*

• Ces clients **commencent à** trouver que leur consommation de crème devient d'un prix quelque peu élevé. - *These customers* **are beginning/starting to** *find that their consumption of cream is becoming rather costly.*

commentaire *nm* comment

• Nous serions heureux de recevoir vos **commentaires** sur cette situation. - *. . . to have your* **comments** *on this situation.*

commerce *nm* trade, commerce

• Le **commerce** avec le Paraguay est actuellement au point mort. - *Trade with Paraguay is currently at a standstill.*

commercial -e *adj* commercial, trade, trading

• CIE est à la recherche d'une organisation **commerciale** susceptible de distribuer ses produits en Allemagne. - *CIE is looking for a **commercial** organization able to distribute its products in Germany.*

• ... si vous cherchez à développer vos relations **commerciales** avec la Côte d'Ivoire. - *... your **trade** relations with the Ivory Coast.*

commission *nf* commission
• Nous pourrions vous consentir sur le prix ci-dessus une **commission** de £50 par 1.015kg. - *We could allow you on the above price a **commission** of £50 per 1015kg.*

commun, -e *adj* common, joint, mutual, shared
• Nous ferons tous les efforts pour régler cette question dans le sens de nos intérêts **communs**. - *... to settle this question in the direction of our **common/mutual** interests.*
• Cependant **d'un commun accord** CIE et son correspondant allemand viennent de décider de se séparer. - *However, **by mutual agreement**, CIE and their German associates have just decided to sever relations.*

communication *nf* communication, message, call, [pass on]
• Comme suite à notre récente **communication** téléphonique, nous avons le plaisir de vous passer commande ... - *Further to our recent telephone **call/message**, ...*
• Nous venons de recevoir une lettre de CIE que nous vous **envoyons en communication**. - *... which we **are passing on** to you.*

communiquer *vt* communicate, impart, pass on
COLLOCATES *adresse, conditions, cotation, demande, informations, nom, précisions, prix, réclamation, renseignements, réponse*

• Nous lui **communiquerons** votre réponse dès sa rentrée au bureau. - *We will **communicate/pass on** your reply to him as soon as he returns to the office.*
• Le début et les cadences à respecter vous **seront communiqués** au plus tard à 14 heures ... - *The start and rates to be observed **will be communicated** to you no later than 14.00 hours ...*

compagnie *nf* company, [together with]
• La détérioration de l'ensemble du risque automobile oblige les **compagnies** d'assurance à une surveillance accrue de ces contrats. - *... insurance **companies** ...*
• Je serais heureux de vous rencontrer **en compagnie du** Dr X. - *... **together with/in company with** Dr X.*

comparatif, -ive *adj* comparative
• J'ai indiqué à M. X la nature des informations dont j'avais besoin pour procéder à mon étude **comparative**. - *... to carry out my **comparative** study.*

compétitif, -ive *adj* competitive
• Nous exportons aussi dans de nombreux pays étrangers, ce qui nous prouve que nos prix sont **compétitifs**. - *... which proves to us that our prices are **competitive**.*

complément *nm* addition, complement
• **En complément du** rapport que vous recevrez prochainement de M. X, nous vous adressons ... - ***In addition to/To complement** the report which you will be receiving soon ...*

complémentaire *adj* additional, complementary, further

- Pour tous renseignements **complémentaires**, veuillez vous adresser à M. X. - *For any* *additional/further information, . . .*

complet, -ète *adj* complete, full
USAGE *Compare 'entier'. 'Complet' is not used more frequently in business letters than 'entier', but it is more versatile, as the examples show. It virtually always follows the noun and emphasizes that the object or process in question is not short of any of its component parts (first and second examples). Sometimes it translates English. 'full' (third example).*
- Nous demandons au transitaire de vous faire parvenir le jeu **complet** de connaissements ainsi que les factures douanières. - *. . . the* *complete set of bills of lading.*
- Serait-il possible que CIE procède à la fabrication **complète** de la crème MF? - *Would it be possible for CIE to undertake the complete manufacture of MF cream?*
- Rien n'est changé en ce qui concerne les commandes représentant un wagon **complet**. - *Nothing has changed as regards orders representing a full/complete wagonload.*

complètement *adv* completely
- Nous vous demandons donc de nous adresser trois ou quatre par avion, car nous en sommes **complètement** démunis. - *. . . for we are completely out of stock.*

compléter *vt* complete, complement, supplement
TENSES See *céder*
- Les documents devront vous être adressés afin de **compléter** vos dossiers. - *. . . in order to complete your files.*

- Ma cliente recherche des produits qui **complètent** les siens. - *My client is looking for products which complement her own.*

comporter *vt* comprise, be composed of, consist of; include, involve
- Vous recevrez un dossier de transit complet **comportant**: 1° copie de nos instructions à CIE; 2° copie des bordereaux de colisage; 3° . . . - *You will receive a complete transit file comprising: 1) copy of our instructions to CIE; 2) . . . ; 3) . . .*
- Votre commande précitée **comportait** l'indication 'FOB le Havre'. - *Your above-mentioned order included the instruction . . .*
- On nous demande de faire une offre **comportant** si possible un délai n'excédant pas 2 mois. - *. . . an offer involving if possible delivery not exceeding 2 months.*

composer *vt* compose, make up
- Nous disposons d'un important personnel **composé de** 215 personnes dont 60 ingénieurs civils,. . . - *We have a large staff composed of/made up of 215 persons including 60 civil engineers, . . .*

compréhension *nf* indulgence, understanding
- Nous comptons sur votre **compréhension** et nous espérons que vous nous garderez votre confiance et votre amitié. - *We are relying on your understanding . . .*

comprendre *vt* understand; include, [inclusive of]
TENSES See *prendre*
- Devons-nous **comprendre** que le prix est le même . . .? - *Are we to understand that . . .*
- Livraison FOB port d'embarquement, emballage

maritime **compris**. - . . ., *seaworthy packing included*/. . ., *inclusive of seaworthy packing.*

• Serait-il possible que la Société CIE procède à la fabrication complète de la crème MF, **y compris** le produit mère? - . . ., *including the basic product?*

• Pour gouverne, les prix que nous avons faits **comprennent** l'assurance contre tous risques, sauf rouille. - *For your guidance, the prices we have given include insurance against all risks, except rust.*

comptable *adj* accounts

• Effectivement, le chèque de règlement de vos calendriers a bien été reçu par notre service **comptable**. - . . . *the cheque . . . has been received by our accounts department.*

comptant cash

• Nous vous accordons un escompte de 2% pour règlement **comptant**. - *We will give you a discount of 2% for cash payment.*

compte *nm* account, [charge for; behalf]

• Nous vous prions de vouloir bien transférer par le débit de notre **compte** chez vous la somme de F10.000.000 (dix millions de francs) en faveur de notre **compte** auprès de l'agence locale d'Eccloo de la Banque X. - . . .*transfer by the debit of our account with you the sum of . . . in favour of our account with the local branch of the Bank X at Eccloo.*

• Nous vous prions donc de bien vouloir nous faire parvenir celui-ci par chèque bancaire, ou versement à notre **CCP** Paris 123. - . . ., *or by payment to our Giro account (Compte Chèques Postaux) Paris 123.*

• Nous pensons qu'il serait équitable que nous puissions **porter en compte** les débours provenant de ce retard. - *We think it would be equitable for us to pass to account/ charge for the outlays arising from this delay.*

• **D'ordre et pour compte de** CIE nous continuerons donc avec vous les agréables relations que nous avons entretenues dans le passé. - *By order and for account of CIE therefore we shall continue. . . .*

• Nous construisons un réseau de représentants sur l'ensemble de la France **pour le compte** d'un tissage. - *We are setting up a sales force throughout France on behalf of a weaving mill.*

se rendre **compte** (de) *vpro* appreciate, ascertain, see for oneself, realize
TENSES See *rendre*

• Mais Monsieur X, votre Directeur Technique, a pu **se rendre compte** sur place qu'il n'y avait pas tellement de secrets dans la préparation. - *But Mr X . . . was able to ascertain/see for himself on the spot that there were not many secrets in the preparation.*

tenir **compte** de *vt indir* take account of, allow for, bear in mind, consider, [disregard, ignore]
TENSES See *venir*

• Le descriptif des travaux a donc été rectifié plusieurs fois pour **tenir compte de** ces changements. - . . . *to allow for/take account of these changes.*

• **Compte tenu de** l'importance de votre firme, nous estimons, en effet, pouvoir maintenir ce prix. - *In consideration of/Bearing in mind the size of your firm, we think we can in fact maintain this price.*

• Pour le cas où votre règlement, déjà transmis, n'aurait pas encore été enregistré dans nos livres, vous voudrez bien **ne pas tenir compte de** cette lettre. - *In the event of your payment, already sent, not yet having been recorded in our accounts, please* **disregard/ignore** *this letter.*

compter *vt & i* count; allow, reckon on; anticipate, count on, plan to; [as from]
• Nous apprenons que Monsieur X ne fera plus partie de votre Société **à compter du** 1er janvier 19--. - *. . . Mr X will no longer work for your company* **as from** *1 January 19--.*
• N'oubliez pas que nous devons **compter** encore 4 ou 5 jours pour le dédouanement. - *. . . we have to* **count/allow/reckon on** *another 4 or 5 days for customs clearance.*
• Nous aimerions savoir quand vous **comptez nous expédier** ces aciers. - *. . . when you* **anticipate/ count on dispatching/plan to dispatch** *these steels to us.*
• **Comptant** vous lire par retour du courrier . . . - *Counting on hearing from you by return . . .*

compter sur *vt indir* count on, depend on, rely on
• Aussi je **compte sur** votre intervention pour faire hâter les expéditions en cours. - *I am* **counting on** *your intervention to speed up the current shipments.*
• Nous **comptons sur** vous pour que ce transfert soit effectué. - *We are* **counting on** *you for this transfer to be made.*

concéder *vt* concede, grant
TENSES See *céder*
• Nous ne leur **avons concédé** aucune exclusivité ni représentation. - *We* **have** *not*

granted them any exclusive rights or representation.

concernant *prep* about, concerning, regarding
• Nous avons bien reçu votre lettre **concernant** la Foire Internationale de Lyon.

concerne re., subject
• **Concerne**: N/commande No 123 du 18 mars 19--. - *Re:/Subject: Our order . . .*

concerner *vt* concern, regard; as regards, with regard to
• **En ce qui concerne** les emballages, ils devraient être en votre possession très rapidement. - *As* **regards/With regard to** *the packing materials, . . .*

conclure *vt* conclude, gather, infer; clinch
TENSES Pres 1 *conclus* 3 *conclut* 4 *concluons* 6 *concluent* Imp *concluais* Fut *concluerai* PP *conclu, -ue* Pres Part *concluant* Subj 1,3 *conclue* 4 *concluions* 6 *concluent*
• Nous n'avons pas encore de réponse, . . . et nous en **concluons** que votre client n'a pas été intéressé. - *. . . and we* **conclude/ gather/infer** *that your customer was not interested.*
• Toutes mes remarques n'ont qu'un seul but, c'est d'arriver à **conclure** des affaires dans l'intérêt du groupe. - *All my remarks have only one objective, namely* **to clinch/ conclude** *some deals . . .*

conclusion *nf* conclusion
• Nous espérons que la rédaction de ce procès-verbal reflétera bien les **conclusions** des débats . . . - *We hope the wording of these minutes will properly reflect the* **conclusions** *of the discussions . . .*

• Nous sommes tout disposés à envisager la **conclusion** de nouveaux accords ... - *We are quite prepared to contemplate the conclusion of new agreements ...*

se **concrétiser** (par) *vpro* come to something, lead to; materialize, take shape

• J'espère que ces contacts finiront par se **concrétiser** de façon intéressante pour l'ensemble des parties en cause. - *I hope these contacts will in the end come to something to the advantage of all concerned.*

• ... relations d'affaires suivies avec vous, qui pourraient se **concrétiser par** l'ouverture d'un compte à terme à votre nom dans nos livres. - ... *regular business relations with you, which could lead to our opening a credit account in your name in our books.*

concurrence *nf* competition, competitors

• Les articles **en concurrence avec** nos MF sont ... - *The articles in competition with our MF are ...*

• Ils prétendent que la **concurrence** donne de telles garanties. - *They claim that the competion/our competitors give such guarantees.*

concurrencer *vt* compete with, be in competition with
TENSES See *placer*

• A l'heure actuelle les réfrigérateurs se **trouvent concurrencés par** les appareils français. - ... *the refrigerators are in competition with French appliances.*

concurrent, -e *nmf & adj* competitor; competing

• CIE pourrait éventuellement être intéressé à absorber des **concurrents**

de bonne qualité. - *CIE might be interested in taking over good quality competitors.*

• Veuillez nous dire si nous avons un produit **concurrent**. - ... *a competing product.*

condition *nf* condition, proviso; terms; [provided that]

• ... et avec l'espoir que la marchandise arrivera en parfaite **condition** à son destinataire, ... - ... *the goods will reach their consignee in perfect condition, ...*

• Le délai contractuel du navire ne sera pas affecté **à condition qu'**une décision soit prise d'ici fin août. - ... *on condition that/provided that/ with the proviso that a decision is taken by the end of August.*

• Nous vous fournirons les marchandises spécifiées aux **conditions** générales de vente reprises aux verso et aux **conditions** spéciales suivantes: ... - ... *on the general terms of sale overleaf and on the following special terms: ...*

• Veuillez nous adresser vos meilleures **conditions** de prix et délai pour la fourniture de: ... - ... *your best terms for price and delivery for the supply of: ...*

conditionnement *nm* packaging
• Ses installations industrielles permettent tous types de **conditionnement** pour ces produits. - ... *allow all kinds of packaging for these products.*

conditionner *vt* package
• 3 tonnes de crème MF **conditionnées** en bidons de fer de 10 litres. - *3 tons of MF cream packaged in 10 litre tins.*

confiance *nf* confidence, trust
• Nous vous remercions de la **confiance** que vous nous témoignez.

- ... the **confidence** which you are showing in us.

confidentiel, -ielle *adj* confidential
• Je voudrais que vous considériez cette lettre comme **confidentielle** vis-à-vis de cette maison de Gand. - ... as **confidential** vis-à-vis this firm in Ghent.

confidentiellement *adv* confidentially, in confidence
• Nous avons pu obtenir **confidentiellement** les prix auxquels la commande a été passée. - *We have been able to obtain in confidence the prices at which the order was placed.*

confier (à) *vt* entrust
• Faisant suite à la commande que vous avez bien voulu nous **confier**, ...

confirmation *nf* confirmation
• Nous vous remercions de votre **confirmation** de commande ci-dessus.
• **En confirmation de** notre conversation téléphonique avec Monsieur X, nous vous demandons ... - ***Confirming** our telephone conversation ...*

confirmer *vt* confirm, corroborate
• Vous voudrez bien nous **confirmer** votre accord pour ce choix. - *Please **confirm** your agreement to this choice.*
• Je vous **confirme que** je voyagerai par chemin de fer. - *I **confirm that I** shall travel by train.*

conforme (à) *adj* in accordance/ conformity with, matching
• Votre fourniture sera **conforme aux** conditions de fabrication reprises au cahier des charges. - *Your supply will be **in accordance/ conformity with** the manufacturing conditions.*

• Nous pourrions vous fournir des flasques **conformes à** ceux reproduits sur les plans que vous nous avez transmis. - ... hub caps **matching** those shown on the drawings ...

conformément à as per, in accordance/conformity with, conforming to, pursuant to
• Nous avons bien reçu votre lettre du 9 crt nous passant commande pour mille kilos de haricots verts Princesses **conformément à** notre offre du 7 crt. - ... for 1000 kilos of 'Princess' French beans **as per/in accordance with/conforming to** our offer of the 7th inst..

se conformer à *vpro* comply with, conform to, fulfil
• L'intéressé **s'est** donc **conformé à** ses obligations contractuelles. - *The interested party **has** therefore **complied with/fulfilled** his contractual obligations.*

confrère *nm* colleague
• Dans ce programme d'offres, tous nos **confrères** étrangers qui voudront y coopérer seront les bienvenus.

congé *nm* holiday; notice to quit
• Comme nous serons fermés pour **congés** annuels du 11 au 29 août, il serait préférable ... - *As we shall be closed for annual **holidays** ...*
• Notre bail étant expiré, notre propriétaire **nous a donné congé**. - *Our lease having expired, our landlord **has given us notice to quit.***

conjoncture *nf* economic climate/ conditions, state of the market
• Je sais qu'actuellement la **conjoncture** n'est pas très favorable. - ... the **economic climate** is not very favourable.

• Notre prix de F85 CIF est le minimum que nous puissions faire dans la **conjoncture** actuelle. - ... *in the current state of the market.*

connaissance *nf* knowledge, acquaintance; attention, notice, [learn of, note, meet]
• **Ayant eu connaissance de** la constitution de votre Société, nous nous permettons de ... - *Having learnt of the formation of your Company, ...*
• **J'ai pris connaissance de** l'argumentation de CIE. - *I have noted CIE's line of argument.*
• Nous nous permettons de **porter à votre connaissance** que nous sommes toujours en mesure de vous fournir des meubles de rangement ... - ... *to bring to your attention/ notice that we can still supply ...*
• Je voudrais vous dire combien j'ai été heureux de **faire votre connaissance**. - ... *how happy I was to make your acquaintance/to meet you.*

connaissement *nm* bill of lading
• Nous avons prévu de faire présenter à votre banque une traite à vue, accompagnée du jeu de **connaissements** et de 6 factures certifiées. - ... *a sight draft, together with a set of bills of lading and 6 certified invoices.*

connaître *vt* know, be familiar with, [well-known;let know, inform]
TENSES Pres 1 *connais* 3 *connaît* 4 *connaissons* 6 *connaissent* Imp *connaissais* Fut *connaîtrai* PP *connu, -ue* Pres Part *connaissant* Subj *1,3 connaisse* 4 *connaissions* 6 *connaissent*
• Nous aimerions **connaître** votre point de vue à ce sujet.

• Il s'agit d'une firme assez **connue**. - ... *quite a well-known firm.*
• Voulez-vous bien **nous faire connaître** les marques à apposer sur la caisse. - ... *let us know the marks to put on the case.*
• Nous nous empressons de vous **faire connaître** que nous pourrions vous fournir ... - *We hasten to inform you that we could supply you with ...*

consacrer *vt* devote
• Cette première semaine de lancement **a été consacrée** à l'organisation de notre réseau. - *This first week of the launch has been devoted to organizing our sales network.*

conseil *nm* advice
USAGE *English 'advice' is a* Mass *noun and hence not used in the plural. French 'conseil' is a* Count *noun and therefore can be pluralized, as in the example. A single 'piece of advice' is simply 'un conseil'.*
• Monsieur X, lui-même, nous a toujours donné d'excellents **conseils** pour l'emploi de ses machines. - ... *has always given us excellent advice for the use of his machines.*

conseiller (de) *vt* advise, recommend, urge
• M. X nous a vivement **conseillé de** nous mettre en rapport avec vous. - *Mr X has strongly advised/ urged us to get in touch with you.*
• Le prix de revente **conseillé** de nos panneaux MF est de F.2.300 le m². - *The recommended resale price of our MF panels is 2,300 francs per square metre.*
• CIE **conseille** maintenant l'utilisation de briques de magnésie. - *CIE now advises/ recommends the use of magnesia bricks.*

CONSENTIR

consentir *vt* allow, give, grant
TENSES See *sentir*
COLLOCATES *commission, conditions, crédit, investissement, prêt, remise, rémunération*
• Nous pourrions **consentir** des remises à des clients d'une telle importance. - *We could **allow** discounts to such big customers.*

conséquence *nf* consequence, repercussions, [consequently, therefore, accordingly, in view of this]
USAGE *'En conséquence', like 'aussi' but unlike 'donc' and 'par conséquent', is almost always used sentence-initially. This gives particularly great prominence to the consequential nature of what follows.*
• Nous avons décidé de prendre entièrement à notre charge l'augmentation de 6%. **En conséquence** notre tarif de vente reste inchangé. - ... *In consequence our price list remains unchanged.*
• Ces trois faits ont pour **conséquence** que les glissières glissent mal. - *These three facts have as a **consequence** that the slides slide badly.*

par conséquent consequently, therefore, accordingly
USAGE *'Par conséquent', like 'donc', is rarely used sentence-initially. However, unlike 'donc', it is usually preceded by 'et' (first and second examples) or is set off by a pair of commas (third example). These positions result in 'par conséquent' having rather stronger force than 'donc'.*
• Nous disposons de remorques fermées et remorques plateaux complètement bâchées et **par conséquent** étanches. - ... *flat*

CONSIDÉRER

trailers completely sheeted and **consequently** *watertight.*
• ... un tarif dont la lecture permettra à votre client de situer le prix moyen et **par conséquent** la classe des produits de CIE. - ... *a price list which will enable your customer to get an idea of the average price and* **consequently** *of the quality of CIE's products.*
• Je ne pourrai, **par conséquent**, pas vous accueillir ce jour-là à la Chambre Syndicale. - *I shall not,* **consequently**, *be able to welcome you that day at the Trade Federation.*

conserver *vt* keep, preserve, retain
• ... il vous suffira de **conserver** notre caisse d'emballage qui les contient. - ... *all you will need to do is* **keep/retain** *our packing case containing them.*
• L'adresse télégraphique pourrait sans doute être **conservée**. - *The telegraphic address could no doubt be* **kept/preserved/retained**.

considérable *adj* considerable
• Nos services ministériels ont pris un temps très **considérable** pour nous accorder le remboursement des droits et taxes. - *Our government departments took a very* **considerable** *time to grant us a refund of the duties and taxes.*

considération *nf* consideration
• Pour être prise en **considération**, votre offre devra nous parvenir au plus tard le 1er août 19--. - *To be taken into* **consideration**, ...

considérer (comme) *vt* consider, treat
TENSES See *céder*
• J'ai, dès l'abord, **considéré** le prix de vos services comme exorbitant. - *I have, from the outset,* **considered** *the price of your services to be exorbitant.*

• Mais je voudrais que vous-même et M.X **considériez** cette lettre comme confidentielle ... - *But I should like Mr X and yourself to **treat** this letter as confidential ...*

consister en/à *vt indir* consist of/in
• La fourniture **consisterait en** tubes en bronze ... - *The supply **would consist of** bronze tubes ...*
• Une solution **consisterait à demander** à tous les souscripteurs de joindre le montant de leur fourniture à la demande. - *A solution **would consist in requesting/would be to request** all subscribers. ...*

constater *vt* note, observe
COLLOCATES *amélioration, bien fondé, défaut, détérioration, différence, erreur, fait*
• Le client **constate** deux défauts principaux: ... - *The customer **notes** two main faults: ...*
• Nous **constatons que**, malgré ce rappel, notre facture reste toujours impayée. - *We **note that**, despite this reminder, our invoice remains unpaid.*

constituer *vt* constitute, create, establish, form, set (up)
• Cette puissante organisation commerciale **a été constituée** pour vendre des articles de consommation. - *... **has been constituted/has been set up** to sell consumer goods.*
• Cette façon d'agir ne peut **constituer** un précédent pour d'autres affaires similaires. - *This procedure cannot **create/set** a precedent for similar transactions.*

constitution *nf* establishment, formation, setting up
• Apprenant la **constitution** de votre Société, c'est un plaisir pour nous de vous présenter nos sincères souhaits de réussite et de

prospérité. - *Hearing of the **establishment** of your Company, ...*

construction *nf* building, construction
• Nous allons faire, ces jours-ci, notre première soumission pour la **construction** d'un hôpital important dans cette région. - *Within the next few days we are going to put in our first tender for the **building/construction** of a large hospital in this region.*

consulter *vt* consult
• A la suite de cette offre préliminaire, nous espérons **être consultés** de façon plus détaillée. - *... we hope **to be consulted** in greater detail.*

contact *nm* contact, touch
COLLOCATES *prendre ... avec*
• A l'heure actuelle j'ai peut-être un **contact** intéressant pour cette affaire. - *... a useful **contact** ...*
• Nous **prenons contact** ce jour **avec** cet éventuel client. - *We are contacting/are getting in touch with this prospective customer today.*

contacter *vt* contact, approach
• Nous **avons été contactés** par les sociétés suivantes: ... - *We **have been contacted/approached** by the following companies: ...*

conteneur *nm* container

contenir *vt* contain, hold
TENSES See *venir*
• Nous vous avons fait parvenir un paquet postal recommandé **contenant** un bidon vide en plastique. - *... a parcel **containing/holding** an empty plastic flask.*

contenu *nm* contents
• Nous vous accusons réception de votre lettre du 12 août, dont le

contenu nous surprend beaucoup. -
... *your letter of 12 August, whose*
contents are very surprising to us.

contestation *nf* dispute, objection
• De plus, il est opportun de visiter
les lots avant de remettre des offres,
car aucune **contestation** sur le
matériel ne sera admise par la
SNCF. - ..., *since no **dispute/***
***objection** about the equipment taken*
away will be countenanced by the
SNCF.

continuer (à) *vt & i* carry on,
continue
• ..., afin de nous permettre de
pouvoir **continuer** notre travail. -
..., *in order to allow us to be able to*
*carry on/**continue** our work.*
• Veuillez **continuer à** nous
remettre une photocopie du permis
d'importation. - *Please **continue to***
send us a photocopy of the import
licence.

contractuel, -elle *adj* contractual
• Il apparaît clairement que
l'installation actuelle dépasse
largement les obligations
contractuelles. - ... *the present*
installation far exceeds the
contractual obligations.

contraire (à) *adj & nm* contrary,
reverse, [otherwise]
• Tout ceci est **contraire à** nos
accords. - *All this is **contrary to** our*
agreements.
• **Dans le cas contraire**, vous nous
dédommageriez des frais encourus.
- *Should it be otherwise, you will*
indemnify us for the expenses incurred.
• **Sauf avis contraire de votre part**,
c'est de la première façon que nous
procéderons. - *Unless we hear from*
you to the contrary, ...
• Comme, **au contraire**, la caisse est
en souffrance depuis mai dernier, il

semble qu'il y ait un des
renseignements qui soit faux. -
*Since, **on the contrary**, the crate has*
been on demurrage since last May, it
seems that one of the pieces of
information is wrong.

contrairement à contrary to
• **Contrairement aux** indications
portées sur cet imprimé, le montant
de votre souscription n'était pas
joint à votre envoi. - *Contrary to the*
instructions on that form, ...

contrat *nm* contract
• Monsieur X a résilié les trois
contrats par lettre du 24 février 19--.
- *Mr X cancelled the three **contracts***
...

contre against, as against,
compared with, [on the other hand]
• Paiement: **contre** documents à la
première présentation. - *Payment:*
against documents ...
• La production journalière n'était
que de 270kg **contre** 350kg, chiffre
couramment obtenu autrefois. -
Daily production was only 270 kilos,
as against/compared with 350 kilos,
the figure regularly achieved before.
• La machine à laver, **par contre**, est
bon marché. - *The washing machine,*
on the other hand, is cheap.

contretemps *nm* contretemps,
hitch
• Nous nous excusons vivement de
ce **contretemps**.

contrôle *nm* check, checking,
control, inspection
• **Au contrôle de** nos écritures nous
constatons qu'une erreur s'est
glissée dans notre facture No 123. -
On checking our accounts ...
• Dans un lot de 500 barres il se
pourrait que 10 barres puissent

avoir subi un accident et qu'elles échappent au **contrôle**. - ... *it would be possible for 10 bars to suffer an accident and escape* **inspection**.

convenable *adj* acceptable, adequate, appropriate, correct, suitable
• ... et nous verrons si nous pouvons placer la bande sur un magnétophone **convenable**. - ... *and we will see whether we can put the tape on a* **suitable** *recorder*.

convenance *nf* convenience (See also *tôt*)
• Je suis à votre disposition pour vous voir à votre meilleur **convenance**. - *I am at your disposal to see you at your* **convenience**.

convenir à *vt indir* be acceptable to, be convenient to, suit
TENSES See *venir*
• La qualité de ces vanilles pourrait certainement **convenir à** vos clients. - *The quality of these vanillas could well* **suit/be acceptable to** *your customers*.
• Je suis très heureux que la date du 2 novembre vous **convienne** pour ma visite. - ... *that 2 November is* **convenient to** *you for my visit*.

convenir de *vt indir & impers* admit, agree (to), arrange; [advisable, appropriate, proper, right]
TENSES See *venir*
USAGE *In the sense 'agree to/that', 'convenir' is sometimes found with the auxiliary 'être' (second example). However, the contexts which allow 'être' are rather restricted, whereas 'avoir' is acceptable in all contexts.*
• Nous **avions convenu** avec Monsieur X **de** différer le paiement. - *We* **had agreed/arranged** *with Mr X to defer payment*.

• Nous **étions convenus** que je retournerais le voir le vendredi suivant. - *We* **had agreed/arranged** *that I would go back to see him* ...
• **Comme convenu**, j'ai rendu visite ce matin à M. X. - **As agreed**, ...
• Cette fréquence est, vous en **conviendrez**, anormale. - *This frequency is, you* **will admit**, *abnormal*.
• Il **conviendrait que** la correspondance soit adressée directement au propriétaire de cette firme. - *It* **would be appropriate/ advisable for** *correspondence to be addressed* ...

coopération *nf* cooperation
• Nous comptons sur votre **coopération** dans le domaine de la négociation avec ...

copie *nf* copy
USAGE *English. 'copy' corresponds to both 'copie' and 'exemplaire' in French, but these are not synonymous. As the first example shows, the original of a document, although not 'une copie', is nevertheless 'un exemplaire'. When, as in the second example, the writer is drawing attention to a copy of a document (a letter, an order etc) enclosed with the present letter, the article is regularly omitted before 'copie(s)'.*
• Vous voudrez bien nous donner votre accord en nous remettant votre offre en deux exemplaires (original et une **copie**). - ... *by sending us your offer in duplicate (original and one* **copy***)*.
• Vous trouverez ci-joint **copie** de notre lettre du 9 janvier à l'usine de Contes.

correspondance *nf* correspondence
• Nous vous référons à notre **correspondance** antérieure et

notammant à votre lettre du 5 courant. - *We refer you to our previous* **correspondence** . . .

correspondant, -e *nmf & adj* correspondent; corresponding
• Voulez-vous nous faire savoir si nous pouvons satisfaire la demande de ce **correspondant**.
• Cette différence vous serait facturée par le **correspondant** de CIE à Londres. - . . . *by CIE's London* **correspondent**.
• Nous vous retournons ci-jointe cette pièce, accompagnée d'une photocopie du bordereau de chargement **correspondant**. - . . . *together with a photocopy of the* **corresponding** *cargo list*.

correspondre à *vt indir* be consistent with, correspond to, match, meet, tally with
TENSES See *rendre*
• Si aucune de ces propositions ne **correspond** à vos besoins, n'hésitez pas à nous intérroger en nous précisant . . . - *If none of these proposals* **corresponds to/meets** *your requirements*, . . .

cotation *nf* quotation
USAGE *'Offre' is the more usual word in this sense.*
• Nous vous serions reconnaissants de bien vouloir nous adresser une **cotation** pour une éventuelle fourniture. - . . . *a* **quotation** *for a possible supply*.

cote *nf* dimension, measure
• Nous serions en particulier intéressés par des tubes aux **cotes** anglo-saxonnes et métriques. - . . . *tubes in Anglo-Saxon and metric* **dimensions**.

côté *nm* part, side

• Nous comptons sur vous pour que **de votre côté** vous fassiez le maximum pour éviter toutes les dépenses inutiles. - *We are relying on you,* **for your part***, to do your utmost to avoid all unnecessary expenses.*

coter *vt* quote
USAGE *'Indiquer' and 'proposer' are more usual words in this sense.*
• Nous pensons **coter** un prix qui serait environ de F67/69, en fonction de la quantité. - *We are thinking of* **quoting** *a price which would be approximately 67/69 francs depending on the quantity.*

coup (de fil, de téléphone) *nm* call, ring
• Je vous passerai dès mon arrivée un **coup de fil** pour convenir d'un rendez-vous. - *I'll give you a* **ring** *as soon as I arrive* . . .

couramment *adv* regularly, commonly; fluently
• Il serait peut-être utile que nous recevions **couramment** les doubles de toutes correspondances. - *It would perhaps be useful for us to receive* **regularly** *copies of all correspondence.*
• Nous vous remettons ci-joint plan des roues qui sont les plus **couramment** usitées dans cette dimension. - . . . *the wheels which are most* **commonly** *used in this dimension.*
• Il est Alsacien et de ce fait parle **couramment** allemand. - *He is from Alsace and consequently speaks German* **fluently**.

courant, -e *adj* current; of this month, inst.; of this year
• Nous avons bien reçu votre lettre du 6 **courant**. - . . . *letter of the 6th* **inst./of this month**.

• Nous aimerions avoir livraison de cet ordre le 25 novembre **crt**. - ... *on 25 November (of this year)*.

courant *nm* course, [informed, in the picture. up to date]
USAGE *'Dans le courant de' is practically always followed by an expression of time, e.g. 'mois', 'semaine', 'année', whereas 'au cours de' is more often followed by an expression denoting an activity, e.g. 'voyage', 'fabrication', 'visite'.*
• Nous pourrions vous livrer **dans le courant du** mois de mars 50 à 100 cartons de ... - *We could deliver to you **in the course of** the month of March ...*
• Etes-vous **au courant**? - *Are you **in the picture**?/Do you know about this?*
• Je vous tiendrai **au courant des** résultats de ce premier contact. - *I shall keep you **informed of**/up to date **with** the results of this first contact.*

courrier *nm* mail, post; letter
• Dans l'attente de vous lire par un prochain **courrier**. - *... **by an early post**.*
• Une réponse par retour du **courrier** est indispensable. - *... **by return (of post)** ...*
• Par même **courrier** nous vous faisons parvenir: ... - *By the same **post** ...*
• Nous répondons à vos **courriers** du 21 et 27 mai. - *We are replying to your **letters** ...*

cours *nm* course, progress; [hand, pipeline]
USAGE See *'courant'*.
• Je dois voir également **au cours de** ce voyage un autre de nos fournisseurs. - *I am also to see **in the course of** this trip another of our suppliers.*
• En effet, la quantité de distributeurs actuellement en

magasin ne nous permet pas d'assurer les commandes **en cours**. - *... to service the orders which are **in hand/in progress/in the pipeline.***
• Les avaries surviennent **en cours d'**expédition par chemin de fer. - *The damage occurs **in the course of** dispatch by rail.*

court, -e *adj* short, early
• Veuillez nous remettre prix et délai **le plus court** pour la fourniture éventuelle de tubes ... - *Please send us your price and **earliest** delivery ...*

coût *nm* cost
USAGE *'Coût, assurance et fret' can be abbreviated 'CAF', but it is more usual to use the English 'CIF', as in the first example.*
• Toutefois, nous remarquons que le prix **CIF** Dunkerque est maintenant de 123 livres par 1.000kg.
• Vos prix doivent s'entendre FOB ou, si possible, **coût**, assurance et fret Tunis. - *Your prices should be FOB or, if possible, **cost**, insurance and freight Tunis.*

coûter *vt* cost
• Cette opération nous **coûte** déjà passablement cher. - *This operation is already **costing** us rather a lot.*

couvrir *vt* cover
TENSES See *offrir*
• Nous n'**avons** pas **couvert** l'assurance, le client devant faire le nécessaire lui-même. - *We **have not covered** the insurance, ...*
• Nous pourrons ainsi **couvrir** tout juste nos frais généraux. - *We can in this way just **cover** our overheads.*

craindre *vt* be afraid, fear
TENSES Pres 1 *crains* 3 *craint* 4 *craignons* 6 *craignent* Imp *craignais* Fut *craindrai* PP *craint, -e* Pres Part

craignant Subj *1,3 craigne 4 craignions 6 craignent*
USAGE *'Craindre que'* + Subjunctive.
• Ils **craignent que** cette structure ne puisse tenir encore longtemps. - *They fear that this structure cannot last much longer.*
• Je **crains de** perdre beaucoup dans cette affaire. - *I am afraid of losing a great deal over this business.*

crédit *nm* credit, letter of credit
• Nous avons transmis à CIE votre note de **crédit** du 24 février. - *...your credit note ...*
• Paiement: par **crédit** irrévocable, divisible, transmissible et transférable, confirmé par une banque de Londres de premier ordre. - *Payment: by irrevocable, divisible, transmissible and transferable letter of credit, ...*

créditer *vt* credit

• Nous pensons que vous serez bien d'accord pour **créditer** la CIE de cette différence par tonne. - *... to credit CIE for this difference per ton.*

croire *vt* believe, think
TENSES Pres *1 crois 3 croit 4 croyons 6 croient* Imp *croyais* Fut *croirai* PP *cru, -ue* Pres Part *croyant* Subj *1,3 croie 4 croyions 6 croient*
• Je **crois** utile de vous faire parvenir dès à présent une note ... - *I think it useful to send you right now a note ...*
• J'**ai cru bien faire en** vous donnant cette indication ... - *I thought it right to give you this information ...*

se croiser *vpro* cross
• Votre lettre du 5 courant et la nôtre du 4 courant ont dû **se croiser**. - *... must have crossed.*

D

date *nf* date, [dated]
• Veuillez nous préciser à quelle **date** est parti le premier MF. - *... on what date the first MF left.*
• Nous accusons réception de votre lettre **en date du** 14 février 19--. - *... your letter dated 14 February, 19--.*

dater (de) *vt & i* date, date from, [counting from, old]
• Ces plans **sont datés** du 1er octobre. - *These drawings are dated 1 October.*
• Ce dépliant **date de quelques années**. - *This leaflet dates from some years ago/is some years old.*

• Délai de livraison: 4/5 mois environ **à dater du** jour où nous aurons reçu le crédit. - *Delivery: about 4/5 months (counting) from the day we receive the letter of credit.*

débit *nm* debit
• Nous vous prions de vouloir bien transférer **par le débit de** notre compte chez vous la somme de F10.000.000 ... - *... to transfer by the debit of our account with you ...*
• Pouvez-vous établir une **note de débit** à CIE des frais correspondants? - *Can you raise a debit note on CIE for the corresponding costs?*

DÉBITER

débiter *vt* debit
• Notre facture du 3 décembre 19--, vous **débitant** de cette fourniture pour la somme nette convenue de F123, vous a été transmise sous pli fermé. - ... *debiting you for this supply in the sum of 123 francs nett as agreed*, ...

débouché *nm* outlet, market
• Préparation des collections en fonction des **débouchés** – grossistes, detaillants, grands magasins. - ... *according to the outlets – wholesalers, retailers, department stores.*
• Le Marché Commun, tout en ouvrant des **débouchés** nouveaux, ... - *The Common Market, although it has opened new markets*, ...

début *nm* beginning, start
USAGE *The expressions 'au début de' and 'à la fin de' are often shortened to 'début' and 'fin' with names of months (second example), but not otherwise.*
• J'espère avoir le plaisir de vous rencontrer **au début de** la semaine prochaine. - ... *at the beginning of next week.*
• Les deux commandes seront expédiées dès la réouverture de notre usine **début** septembre. - ... *as soon as our factory reopens at the beginning of September.*
• Cette maison nous a acheté 200 MF depuis le **début** de nos relations. - ...*since the start of our dealings with them.*

décembre *nm* December

déchargement *nm* unloading
• Il a été observé au **déchargement** des emballages déchirés, ... - *Torn packaging was noted during unloading*, ...

décharger *vt* unload

DÉCOULER DE

TENSES See *changer*
• Vos ouvriers **ont déchargé** ces matériaux sur notre chantier sans autorisation préalable. - *Your men unloaded these materials on our site* ..

décider (de) *vt* decide, resolve
• Nous avons **décidé de** prendre entièrement à notre charge l'augmentation de 6%. - *We have decided to bear in full the increase of 6%.*

décision *nf* decision, ruling
• Nous avons pris la **décision** suivante.

(se) déclarer *vt & pro* declare (oneself)
• Nous **nous déclarons** en parfait accord avec les termes de votre lettre - *We declare ourselves to be in full agreement with the terms of your letter*

décliner *vt* decline
• Nous devons **décliner** la fourniture de cette marchandise pour laquelle les usines françaises sont totalement hors marché. - *We have to decline to supply these goods* ...

décomposer *vt* break down, itemize
• Votre offre **sera à décomposer de** la manière suivante: 1° frais ... 2° .. - *Your offer should be broken down in the following way:* ...

décompte *nm* breakdown, detailed account
• Pouvez-vous également nous établir le **décompte** des frais que vous avez payés ... - *Can you do us a breakdown of the charges you paid* ..

découler de *vt indir* arise, ensue, result from
• En raison des difficultés et inconvénients importants **découlant de** cette livraison erronée, nous vous

concédons que ... - *Because of the serious difficulties and inconveniences arising from this wrong delivery, ...*

décrire *vt* describe
TENSES See *écrire*
• Nous pourrions vous livrer la marchandise **décrite** dans votre lettre du 6 juillet au prix de ... - *We could deliver you the goods **described** in your letter ...*

dédouanement *nm* customs clearance
• Le **dédouanement** serait effectué par nos soins. - *Customs clearance would be taken care of by ourselves.*

dédouaner *vt* clear (through customs)
• Pour que CIE puisse **dédouaner** ces échantillons, il faudrait que vous lui envoyiez au plus vite une facture pro-forma en trois exemplaires. - *For CIE to be able **to clear** these samples, you would have to send them ...*

déduction *nf* allowance, deduction, [less]
• Paiement: sous 10 jours de réception de facture par virement bancaire, **sous déduction** d'un escompte à débattre. - *... **less a discount** to be discussed.*

déduire *vt* deduct, take off
TENSES Pres 1 *déduis* 3 *déduit* 4 *déduisons* 6 *déduisent* Imp *déduisais* Fut *déduirai* PP *déduit, -e* Pres Part *déduisant* Subj 1,3 *déduise* 4 *déduisions* 6 *déduisent*
• Cependant, si vous décidez de couvrir l'assurance vous-mêmes, nous **déduirons** de notre prix 0,25%. - *... we **will deduct/take off** 0.25% from our price.*

défaut *nm* defect, fault, flaw; [alternatively, failing that, for want of]

• Notre responsabilité se limite au remplacement pur et simple de tôles reconnues défectueuses à la suite de **défauts** cachés. - *... sheets found to be defective due to hidden **flaws**.*
• Veuillez demander à cette firme un plan du mécanisme ou, **à défaut**, un échantillon. - *... a drawing of the mechanism or, **alternatively/failing that**, a sample.*

défectueux, -euse *adj* defective, faulty
• Nous avons dû conclure que l'usinage était **defectueux**. - *We had to conclude that the machining was **defective/faulty**.*

définitif, -ive *adj* definitive, final
• Nous vous ferons parvenir en temps utile notre facture **définitive** concernant cette réparation. - *... our **final** invoice for this repair.*
• Nous vous envoyons ci-joints 2 exemplaires du plan **définitif** de la ventilation. - *... 2 copies of the **definitive** drawing of the ventilation.*

définitivement *adv* definitively, finally, once and for all, permanently
• Afin de tirer **définitivement** cette affaire au clair, nous vous serions obligés de ... - *In order to clear this matter up **once and for all**, ...*
• Nous ne pouvons pas encore **vous fixer définitivement** sur notre programme 19--. - *We cannot yet **put you fully in the picture** regarding our programme for 19--.*

en dehors (de) outside
COLLOCATES *de la France, des heures habituelles*
• Cet échange de pièce n'a pu se faire qu'**en dehors de** nos usines. - *This replacement can only have been made **outside** our works.*

déjeuner *nm & vi* lunch

• L'objet de cette lettre est de vous remercier personnellement pour l'agréable **déjeuner** auquel j'ai pu assister hier en votre présence.

délai *nm* time allowed, [delivery]
USAGE *'Un délai' is a period of time which elapses, or which is expected to elapse, before some action is taken or completed. Almost always the action in question is delivery of goods ('délai de livraison') but other things are possible, e.g. 'délai de fabrication'. When 'délai' is not qualified in any way the context usually makes it clear that it relates to delivery. NB 'délai' can carry the implication of an unwelcome postponement, e.g. 'sans délai', 'demander un délai', thus corresponding to English 'delay', but it very rarely does so. (See retard.)*

• Aussi, pouvez-vous m'indiquer quel serait normalement le **délai de livraison** pour . . . - *Consequently, can you indicate what **delivery** would normally be for . . .*

• **Délai**: 8 jours à réception de commande. - *Delivery: 8 days from receipt of order.*

délégué, -ée *nmf* representative
• Nous nous référons à la récente visite de notre **délégué**, Monsieur X, et vous remercions pour votre commande.

demande *nf* application, demand, inquiry, request
• Nous nous permettons de rappeler à votre bonne attention notre **demande** de prix rappelée sous rubrique. - *. . . our **request** for prices referred to above.*

• **A la demande de** M. X, nous vous prions de trouver ci-joint un exemplaire des différentes publicités MF. - *At the **request of** Mr X, . . .*

• Si notre offre vous intéresse, nous vous ferons parvenir **sur votre demande** nos cotations et échantillons. - *. . ., we will send you on application/demand/request our quotations and samples.*

• Suite à une publicité parue dans une revue spécialisée française, nous recevons une **demande** de CIE, que vous trouverez ci-jointe. - *. . ., we have received an **inquiry** from CIE, . . .*

demander (de) *vt* ask, request; ask for; inquire; [in demand]
USAGE *'Nous vous demandons de + Infinitive' (second example) is a no-nonsense way of making a request. It could be softened by adding 'bien vouloir' or substituting 'prier' for 'demander'.*

• Je me permets de vous écrire pour vous **demander** des renseignements sur une firme américaine d'électronique. - *. . . to **ask** you for some information . . .*

• Nous vous **demandons de** limiter le poids total de vos caisses à environ 120/130kg. - *We **must ask** you to limit the total weight of your crates . . .*

• CIE **demande que**, dans la mesure du possible, l'expédition de leur commande soit faite avant le 21 avril. - *CIE **requests that** . . . dispatch of their order be made before 21 April.*

• . . . nous venons vous **demander si** vous seriez intéressés par des cédrats de Corse . . . - *. . . we are approaching you to **inquire whether** you would be interested in Corsican citrons . . .*

• Cette machine est **peu demandée** de notre clientèle. - *This machine is **little in demand** by our customers.*

démarche *nf* step, effort, approach
• Nous vous saurions gré de vouloir bien effectuer les **démarches** nécessaires afin que des retards de ce

genre soient évités à l'avenir. - *We should be obliged if you would kindly take the necessary **steps** so that such delays are avoided in future.*

• Nous regrettons de vous dire, après 4 mois de **démarches**, que ces thermostats ne sont pas réimportables. - *..., after 4 months of **efforts/trying**, that these thermostats cannot be reimported.*

• Il a sans doute négligé d'effectuer sa demande d'exportation en temps utile, pensant **que cette démarche vous incombait**. - *... thinking **that this was up to you/that this was your responsibility.***

• Nous allons nous arranger pour que vous **n'ayez aucune démarche à faire**; tout sera fait par un transitaire sur place. - *We are going to see to it that you **have nothing to do**; everything will be done by a forwarding agent on the spot.*

démarrage *nm* starting up
• Bien entendu, la période de **démarrage** peut être un peu longue étant donné le genre de clientèle dans laquelle nous avons à vendre. - *Of course, the **starting-up** period can be a little long, given the type of customer we have to sell to.*

démonstration *nf* demonstration
• Nous serions heureux de vous rencontrer pour assister à une **démonstration** de son fonctionnement. - *... to see a **demonstration** of how it works.*

démuni, -e (de) *adj* out of (stock)
• Nous vous demandons de nous adresser 3 ou 4 paquets, car nous **en sommes** complètement **démunis**. - *..., for we **are** completely **out of them.***

dépannage *nm* emergency supply
• Nous vous serions reconnaissants de vouloir bien nous adresser de

toute urgence un **dépannage** de 250 appareils et, le plus rapidement possible, les 500 restant. - *... to send us urgently an **emergency supply** of 250 appliances ...*

dépanner *vt* help out, bail out
• Nous espérons pouvoir **dépanner** ce client en empruntant 2 tonnes de MF à CIE. - *We hope to be able **to help** this customer **out** ...*

départ *nm* beginning, outset, start; departure, sailing; [ex-works]
• Il est important que le montant de votre rémunération soit nettement indiqué **dès le départ/au départ**. - *... that the amount of your remuneration should be clearly indicated **from the outset/start**.*
• Le prix exportation du MF est de FF 1.500 **départ usine**. - *The export price of the MF is 1,500 French francs **ex-works**.*

dépasser *vt* exceed
• Cependant, l'humidité observée de 18% est élevée et nous désirons qu'elle ne **dépasse** pas 12%. - *... and our wish is that it should not **exceed** 12%.*

dépendre de *vt indir* depend on
TENSES See *rendre*
• Nous pensons que, du point de vue technique, la décision **dépendra** pour beaucoup **de** l'avis de Monsieur X de Nancy. - *..., the decision **will depend** largely **on** the opinion of Mr X of Nancy.*

dépense *nf* expenditure, outgoings
• Il y a lieu d'envisager une **dépense** supplémentaire minimum de F123. - *There is reason to expect a minimum additional **expenditure** of 123 francs.*

déplacement *nm* trip; travel, travelling

• Malheureusement, il ne m'est pas possible de faire ce **déplacement** à l'heure actuelle. - ... *to make this **trip** at the moment.*

• Nous sommes tout à fait d'accord que ces frais de **déplacement** sont extrèmement élevés. - ... *these **travelling** expenses are extremely high.*

dépliant *nm* leaflet (folded), folder
• Je vous envoie ci-joint un **dépliant** donnant un aperçu des principales présentations fabriquées par CIE. - ... *a **leaflet/folder** giving an idea of the main presentations manufactured by CIE.*

dépourvu, -e (de) *adj* out of (stock)
• Nous avons regretté qu'à ce moment nous étions **dépourvus de** gentiane. - ... *we were **out of** gentian.*

depuis (que) for, since
USAGE *Notice that in the first example, whereas English has the* Present Perfect *tense ('since we **have been**'), French has the* Present *('depuis que nous **sommes**'). The same applies to the second and third examples. Why then does French as well as English have the* Present Perfect *in the fourth example ('a monté' – 'has risen')? The reason would appear to be as follows. In the first three examples the state of affairs being described still holds good – 'we' are **still** the agent; 'the crate' is **still** on demurrage; 'the customer' is **still** manufacturing and distributing her household materials. In the fourth example, however, although the market has been rising recently ('cette année'), it is now no longer doing so. In the next sentence of the letter from which this example is taken the writer says explicitly that the market has now levelled off. If the market were still rising, he would write 'Le marché **monte**' and in English we would signal*

this nuance by writing '**has been rising**' in place of '**has risen**'. The same contrast is available when attention is focused on some point in the past: 'Le marché **avait monté** (**had risen**) depuis le début de cette année-là' versus 'Le marché **montait** (**had been rising**) depuis le début de cette année-là'. When, however, in French the verb is made negative, one of the* Perfect *tenses is preferred in all cases, as in the fifth example.*

• Nous venons de réaliser le client le plus important **depuis que** nous sommes agent de votre maison. - *We have just secured our biggest customer **since** we have been the agent of your company.*

• La caisse est en souffrance à Mombasa **depuis** mai dernier. - *The crate has been on demurrage **since** last May.*

• Ma cliente fabrique et distribue en France **depuis** des années des produits d'entretien destinés à la ménagère. - *My client has been manufacturing and distributing in France **for** many years cleaning materials for the housewife.*

• Le marché de la vanille a beaucoup monté **depuis** le début de l'année. - *The vanilla market has risen considerably **since** the beginning of the year.*

• Mais malheureusement **depuis** le 27 octobre nous n'avons eu aucune nouvelle de vous. - *But unfortunately **since** 27 October we have had no other news from you.*

dérangement *nm* bother, disturbance, inconvenience, trouble
• Avec mes excuses pour le **dérangement** que je vous cause.

déranger *vt* bother, disturb, inconvenience, trouble
TENSES See *changer*

• Pour ne pas avoir à vous relancer continuellement et pour ne pas vous **déranger**, nous aimerions que vous joigniez 300 catalogues MF à l'expédition de notre commande No 123. - *So as not to have to pester you continually and so as not to have to **bother**/**trouble** you, ...*

dernier, -ière *adj* last, (most) recent, latest, final
USAGE *'Dernier' follows the noun when it refers to a day, week, etc viewed as the last in a **series** leading up to the present moment (first example). Otherwise, it is normally placed before the noun (other five examples).*
• Nous avons participé à cette Foire **vendredi dernier/la semaine dernière/le mois dernier/en septembre dernier/le 11 septembre dernier/l'année dernière**. - *We participated in that Fair **last Friday/last week/(etc)**.*
• Ayant eu **ces derniers jours/ces dernières semaines/ces derniers mois/ces dernières années** de longues conversations avec diverses personnalités de CIE, ... - *Having had **these last few days/weeks/(etc) | in recent days/weeks/(etc)**. long conversations ...*
• Nous vous adressons notre **dernier** catalogue français qui est beaucoup plus complet. - *... our **latest** French catalogue ...*
• Faisant suite à notre **dernier** entretien téléphonique, ... - *Further to our **last/most recent** phone conversation, ...*
• Nous voudrions que vous nous confirmiez que les 4 carabines des deux **derniers** postes de votre commande ne doivent pas être équipées d'une plaque anti-recul. - *... that the 4 rifles forming the **last/final** two items of your order ...*

• Cette offre s'entend sous réserve que votre accord définitive soit reçu le 18 crt **dernier délai**. - *... subject to your final agreement being received on the 18th inst. **at the latest**.*

ce dernier, cette dernière *nmf* latter
• Lors de la transmission de ce chèque à notre service comptable, **ce dernier** nous signale que votre compte n'est pas régularisé. - *..., **the latter** points out that your account is not clear.*

dernièrement *adv* recently
• Prière nous donner également les instructions pour les 100 cartons vendus **dernièrement**. - *Please also give us instructions for the 100 cartons sold **recently**.*

dès (que) as soon as, immediately, right from, [straight away]
• **Dès que** votre nouveau catalogue sera paru, je vous serais reconnaissant de bien vouloir nous l'adresser. - *As soon as/Immediately your new catalogue comes out, ...*
• **Dès** réception de ce document nous procéderons à l'envoi. - *As soon as/Immediately we receive this document, we will proceed with the dispatch.*
• **Dés** le début de nos conversations nous étions d'accord pour estimer nécessaire cette clarification préalable. - *Right from the start of our conversations we agreed in considering this prior clarification to be necessary.*
• Vous avez donc intérêt à commander **dès maintenant**. - *It is therefore in your interests to order **straight away/immediately**.*

désigner (comme) *vt* appoint, designate
• Nous **avons été désignés** par CIE **comme** correspondants de cette

Société pour les relations avec ses fournisseurs en dehors de la Gambie.
- *We **have been appointed/designated** by CIE **as** the sole correspondents of that company* . . .

désir *nm* desire, wish
• Nous tenons à votre disposition un échantillon que nous vous enverrons, si vous en manifestez le **désir**. - *. . ., if you signify your **wish** for it./. . ., **if so desired**.*

désirer *vt* desire, want, wish
USAGE See *'souhaiter'*. *'Désirer que'* + Subjunctive.
• Toutefois nous vous signalons que notre client **désire** du fil extrudé.
- *. . . our customer **wants** extruded wire.*
• Nous **désirons** procéder à une série d'essais comparatifs. - *We **wish/desire** to conduct a series of comparative tests.*
• Il y a longtemps que je **désirais** vous écrire. - *I **had been wanting/wishing** to write to you for a long time.*
• Monsieur X **désire que** son fils fasse un stage en Angleterre de quelques semaines. - *Mr X **wants** his son to get work experience in England for a few weeks.*
• Nous sommes à votre entière disposition pour vous fournir tous les renseignements complémentaires que vous pourriez **désirer**.
• Nous nous étonnons que l'intéressé ait attendu si longtemps avant de signaler que la précision **laissait à désirer**. - *. . . that the accuracy **left something to be desired**.*

désireux, -euse de *adj* anxious to, desirous of
• Toutes ces maisons seraient naturellement **désireuses d'**obtenir cette agence. - *. . . **anxious to get** this agency.*

se **désister** *vpro* drop out, withdraw

• Nous craignons de ce fait ne pas pouvoir vous rentrer une offre judicieusement établie et préférons dès lors **nous désister**. - *. . . and we consequently prefer **to withdraw**.*

désolé, -e (de) *adj* (very) sorry
USAGE *'Etre désolé que'* + Subjunctive.
• Nous avons bien reçu votre lettre du 6 courant et sommes **désolés de** ne pouvoir vous satisfaire. - *. . . and are **very sorry that** we cannot oblige you.*

désormais *adv* henceforth, from now on
• Nous avons pris nos dispositions pour que **désormais** vous receviez toute la documentation que nous pourrions éditer. - *. . . so that **henceforth/from now on** you will receive all the literature we produce.*

dessous below (*See also* ci-dessous)
• La classe des produits de cette maison se situerait plutôt **en dessous de** ce que vous recherchez. - *The standard of this firm's products would seem to be somewhat **below** what you are looking for.*

dessus (on) top, on it/them (*See also* ci-dessus)
• Dès que ces connaissements vous sont parvenus, vous avez pu lire **dessus**: Messieurs CIE à Mombasa. - *As soon as these bills of lading reached you, you were able to read **on them**: . . .*

destinataire *nmf* addressee, consignee
• Si le **destinataire** conteste avoir reçu un pli, . . . - *If the **addressee** claims not to have received a letter, . . .*

destination *nf* destination, (bound for)
• Les marchandises chargées par vos soins dans les remorques arrivent telles quelles **à destination**. -

*The goods . . . arrive undisturbed **at their destination.***
• Les 30 pistolets ont été embarqués sur le XBATEAU parti d'Anvers le 21 crt **à destination de** Port Soudan. - *. . . **bound for** Port Sudan.*

destiner (à) *vt* intend (for/to), mean (for/to), [designed for/to]
• Le prix de la commande No 25 **destinée à** cette usine était en novembre dernier de 123 livres. - *The price of order No. 25 **intended/meant for** that factory was . . .*
• A la recherche permanente de nouveautés et d'informations techniques **destinées à** rendre plus vivante notre revue, . . . - *. . . **intended to** make our magazine more lively, . . .*

détail *nm* detail, [thoroughly]; breakdown, detailed account; retail
• Nous vous prions de nous donner le plus de **détails** possible afin de nous permettre de vous remettre notre prix le plus juste. - *Please give us as many **details** as possible . . .*
• Nous avons examiné toutes les autres pièces **en détail**. - *. . .in detail/ thoroughly.*
• Nous vous prions de bien vouloir lire ci-dessous le **détail** des présentoirs MF que nous avons livrés pour votre compte. - *Please see below a **breakdown/detailed account** of the MF displays . . .*
• Nos représentants visitent chaque magasin **de détail** de façon régulière. - *Our representatives call on each **retail** shop regularly.*

détaillant -e *nmf* retailer
• Préparation des collections en fonction des débouchés – grossistes, **détaillants**, grands magasins. - *. . . wholesalers, **retailers**, department stores.*

détailler *vt* detail; break down, itemize, set out; retail
• Dans l'affirmative, nous vous enverrons une spécification **détaillée** et un plan d'ensemble du bateau. - *. . ., we will send you a **detailed** specification . . .*
• Votre offre doit **être détaillée** de la façon indiquée à ces extraits . . . - *Your offer should **be broken down/be set out** as shown in these extracts . . .*

déterminer *vt* determine, work out
• Vous nous fournirez toutes précisions nous permettant de **déterminer** les taxes, droits de douane, frais de port. - *You will give us all information enabling us to **determine/work out** the taxes, customs duties, carriage charges.*

deuxième *adj* second

devant before, faced with, facing
• . . . et je pense que tout le monde, **devant** le même problème, serait du même avis. - *. . . and I think everyone, **faced with** the same problem, would be of the same opinion.*

développement *nm* development, growth
• Nous possédons toutes les données financières concernant le **développement** de cette Société.

développer *vt* boost, develop
• Il semble que nous ayons la possibilité de **développer** nos ventes très rapidement. - *. . . the possibility of **boosting/developing** our sales very quickly.*

devenir *vi* become
TENSES See *venir*

devis *nm* estimate
• Je pense principalement aux administrations où les **devis** ne sont pas immédiatement suivis de

commandes. - . . . *government departments in which* **estimates** *are not followed immediately by orders.*

devoir *vt & aux* owe; must, have to, ought to; be due to
TENSES Pres 1 *dois* 3 *doit* 4 *devons* 6 *doivent* Imp *devais* Fut *devrai* PP *dû, due* Pres Part *devant* Subj *1,3 doive* 4 *devions* 6 *doivent*
• Notre service comptabilité nous signale que, sauf erreur, vous restez nous **devoir** la somme de F390, montant de notre facture . . . - . . . *you still* **owe** *us the sum of 390 francs, . . .*
• La destination finale **doit** nous être indiquée avant fin juin 19--. - *The final destination* **must** *be given us . . .*
• Pour être prise en considération, votre offre **devra** nous parvenir au plus tard le 1er août 19--. - . . ., *your offer* **must/will have to** *reach us . . .*
• En conséquence, nous **avons dû** renoncer à l'exécution de votre commande. - *Consequently, we* **have had to** *decline to process your order.*
• . . . et vous **avez dû** recevoir entretemps une réponse de M. X. - . . . *and you* **must have** *received meanwhile a reply from Mr X.*
• . . . ce qui **aurait dû** permettre au destinataire d'effectuer sa demande d'exportation. - . . . *which* **should have/ought to have** *enabled the consignee to make his export application.*
• **Devons-nous comprendre** que le prix est le même . . .? - *Are we to understand that the price is the same . . .?*
• Le retard à vous adresser les documents **est dû** à un oubli du transitaire. - *The delay in sending you the documents* **is due** *to an oversight on the part of the forwarding agent.*
• Monsieur X **doit** rentrer de voyage très prochainement. - *Mr X*

will/is due to return from a trip very shortly.

dévoué, -ée (à) *adj* devoted
• Restant **dévoués à** vos ordres, . . .

différence *nf* difference
• CIE demande si vous ne pourriez pas participer à une partie de ces frais supplémentaires en prenant à votre charge la **différence** de frais de transport entre Dunkerque/Contes et Paris/Contes. - . . . *by bearing the* **difference** *in carriage charges between Dunkerque/Contes and Paris/Contes.*

différent, -e (de) *adj* various; different
• Ils ont également des ateliers de construction dans **différents** pays. - *They also have construction workshops in* **various** *countries.*
• Les tonnages disponibles dans les **différents** dépôts sont vraiment trop faibles. - *The tonnages available at the* **various** *depots are really too small.*
• Le parfum du cédrat est **différent de** celui du citron. - *The fragrance of the citron is* **different from** *that of the lemon.*

différer de *vt indir* differ from, vary from
• Ce message **diffère du** précédent sur les deux points suivants: . . . - *This message* **differs from** *the previous one . . .*

différer *vt* defer, postpone, put off
TENSES See *céder*
• Nous avions convenu avec M. X de **différer** le paiement de la facture sous rubrique jusqu'au 15 décembre. - *We had agreed with Mr X* **to defer** *payment . . .*

difficile *adj* difficult
• Il nous est **difficile** de prévoir aujourd'hui quelles seront les

réactions de nos clients. - *It is difficult for us to foresee* ...
• Certes, nous n'ignorons pas que la circulation devient **de plus en plus difficile**, mais ... - *Certainly, we are not unaware that driving is becoming more and more difficult, but* ...

difficulté *nf* difficulty, obstacle
COLLOCATES *avoir, éprouver, être en, faire face à, se heurter à, rencontrer, surmonter; éviter, faire, mettre en, poser, présenter; se présenter, survenir*
USAGE *Usually* Plural.
• ... mais la Société précitée a des **difficultés** à se procurer ce matériel. - *... is having difficulties in obtaining this material.*
• Aucune **difficulté** n'est survenue à ce jour. - *No difficulty/obstacle has arisen so far.*

diffuser *vt* distribute, market
• Nous viendrons en Angleterre afin d'examiner avec vous quels sont les appareils les plus intéressants à **diffuser** en Belgique. - *... which are the appliances which it would be most worthwhile to distribute/market in Belgium.*

diffusion *nf* distribution, marketing
• Au cours de ma récente visite à Londres, j'ai eu l'occasion de vous donner quelques renseignements sur les possibilités éventuelles de **diffusion** en France de votre système MF. - *... to give you some information on the prospects for distributing/marketing your MF system in France.*

dimanche *nm* Sunday (*See* lundi)

dimension *nf* dimension, size
• ... car nous avons en projet l'exécution d'outillage pour des écrous de toutes **dimensions**. - *... of tooling for nuts of all sizes.*

diminution *nf* reduction

• ... la pression que la clientèle exerce sur nous pour une **diminution** des prix. - *... for a price reduction.*

dire *vt* say, state
TENSES Pres *1 dis 3 dit 4 disons 6 disent* Imp *disais* Fut *dirai* PP *dit, -e* Pres Part *disant* Subj *1,3 dise 4 disions 6 disent*
• ... alors que votre price list **disait** 123 livres 'on customer's pallets'. - *...whereas your price list stated £123 'on customer's pallets'.*
• Pour les raisons déjà **dites** dans notre lettre du 26 octobre, ... - *For the reasons already stated* ...
• ... l'installation actuelle dépasse largement les obligations contractuelles reprises au **dit** descriptif. - *... the contractual obligations set out in the said description.*

direct, -e *adj* direct, through
• ... en nous communiquant des adresses nous permettant une prospection **directe**. - *... enabling us to do direct canvassing.*
• L'on ne peut pas faire de connaissement **direct** pour les Seychelles. - *We cannot do a through bill of lading for the Seychelles.*

directement *adv* direct, straight
• Nous vous prions d'adresser ces éléments **directement** à CIE à Hayange. - *Please send this information straight to CIE at Hayange.*
• Nous pensons que vous pourrez nous facturer soit **directement** soit par l'intermédiaire de CIE. - *... you can invoice us either direct or through CIE.*

directeur, -trice *nmf* manager, manageress
• Avec l'avis favorable de notre **directeur** du Service Tennis, nous avons le plaisir de renouveler notre

publicité . . . - *With the approval of the*
manager *of our Tennis Division,* . . .

direction *nf* management;
department, office
• Nous avons reçu une commande
d'équipement de CIE (à **direction**
américaine) . . . - *We have received an
order for equipment from CIE (under
American* **management**) . . .
• Le 16 courant, nous avons
rencontré à CIE Monsieur X
(**Direction** Technique) et Monsieur Y
(**Direction** Commerciale). - . . . *we
met Mr X (Technical* **Department**) *and
Mr Y (Commercial* **Department**).
• . . . une formule de bon de
commande à remplir et à renvoyer à
votre **Direction Régionale**. - . . . *an
order form to fill in and return to your
Regional Office.*

diriger *vt* direct, guide, manage,
run
TENSES See *changer*
• Si donc vous cherchez toujours
quelqu'un susceptible de **diriger** vos
affaires françaises, . . . - . . . *someone
suitable to* **manage/run** *your French
operations,* . . .

discrètement *adv* discreetly
• Afin de nous permettre de **nous
renseigner discrètement**, . . . - *In
order to enable us* **to make discreet
inquiries**, . . .

discrétion *nf* discretion
• J'ai rencontré des interlocuteurs
éventuellement intéressés à étudier
avec la **discrétion** nécessaire le
dossier CIE. - . . . *who may be interested
in looking at the CIE file , with the
necessary* **discretion**.

discussion *nf* discussion, talk;
argument, dispute
• De plus, lors des **discussions**
antérieures à l'élaboration du bon de

commande 123, CIE a exigé . . . -
Moreover, at the time of the **discussions**
prior to drawing up order form 123, . . .
• Afin d'éviter toute **discussion**
ultérieure, je pense que . . . - *In order
to avoid any subsequent* **argument/
dispute**, . . .

discuter (de) *vt & i* discuss, have
discussions (about)
• Afin de vous être agréables, nous
sommes disposés à **discuter** la
question avec votre délégué. - . . . *we
are prepared* **to discuss** *the question
with your representative.*
• Nous vous préviendrons lorsque
nous serons en mesure de **discuter
de** votre offre avec le représentant de
votre Société. - . . . *when we are in a
position to* **have discussions about**
your offer . . .

disponible *adj* available, in stock
• Veuillez noter que les trois articles
référence 123 ne sont pas
disponibles actuellement.
• . . . nous avons actuellement **en
disponible** un tonnage relativement
important de tomates . . . - . . . *we have
now* **available/in stock** . . .

disposé, -e **à** *adj* prepared to, ready
to, willing to, disposed to
• . . . et nous vous demandons si
vous êtes **disposés à** nous donner
l'exclusivité de vente de vos articles
pour notre pays. - . . . *if you are
prepared to give us the sole selling
rights* . . .

disposer de *vt indir* dispose of, have
available, have in stock, hold, [spare]
• Nous **disposons** encore **de**
quelques centaines de cartons . . . -
We still **have available/have in stock/
hold** *a few hundred cartons* . . .
• Je ne sais pas si vous **disposez du**
temps nécessaire pour nous rendre

ce service, mais ... - *I don't know if you **can spare** the time....*

disposition *nf* arrangement, step; disposal, service
• Je lui signale ces malfaçons, en lui demandant de **prendre des dispositions** pour améliorer la fabrication. - *... asking him to make arrangements/to take steps to improve manufacture.*
• Nous mettons à votre **disposition** notre organisation efficace et rapide, ... - *We are placing at your **disposal** our efficient and speedy organization, ...*
• Nous restons à votre **disposition** pour tous renseignements complémentaires. - *We remain at your **disposal** for any further information.*
• Nous nous tenons à votre **disposition** pour vous faire visite à votre meilleure convenance. - *We are holding ourselves at your **disposal/service** to call on you at your convenience.*

distribuer *vt* distribute
• Étant fabricant de pâtes de protection **distribuées** directement dans les usines et ateliers par un réseau de représentants, nous ... - *As manufacturers of protective creams **distributed** direct to factories and workshops ...*

distributeur, -trice *nmf* distributor, dealer
• Nous vous confirmons que nous sommes **distributeurs** exclusifs pour la France du matériel MF. - *We confirm that we are the sole **distributors** for France of MF material.*

distribution *nf* distribution
• Ayant appris que vous seriez peut-être intéressés par une **distribution** systématique sur l'ensemble de la France de votre

production, ... - *Having learnt that you might be interested in the systematic **distribution** of your products throughout France, ...*

dito ditto
• Nous disposons des 10 pistolets MF et 10 gaines pour **dito** faisant l'objet de la commande sous rubrique. - *We have ready the 10 pistols and 10 holsters for **dito** ...*

divers, -ses *adj pl* diverse, varied, [a variety of]; various
• Il y a longtemps que je voulais vous écrire, mais des occupations **diverses** m'en ont empêché. - *... but a **variety of/diverse** tasks prevented me from doing so.*
• Je vais maintenant essayer de répondre aux **diverses** questions que vous posez dans votre lettre. - *I will now try to answer the **various** questions ...*

dizaine *nf* (about) ten
• Les marchandises seront expédiées dans **une dizaine de** jours. - *The goods will be dispatched in **about ten** days.*
• Vous en avez très certainement apprécié l'objectivité et l'abondante documentation comme **des dizaines de** milliers de lecteurs. - *... like **tens of thousands** of readers.*

docteur *nm* doctor
USAGE *Notice the obligatory use of the article, 'le', and the absence of a capital letter in 'docteur'. A more formal variant would be 'Monsieur le docteur X' or 'Madame le docteur X'. In the latter case the article is still 'le' not 'la', since 'docteur' is a grammatically masculine noun. 'Doctoresse' would not be used. The same remarks apply to other titles e.g. 'professeur', though for some it is normal to use the corresponding female title, e.g. 'directrice'.*

• Je serais heureux de vous rencontrer, ainsi que votre collègue **le docteur** X. - ... *together with **Dr** X.*

document *nm* document, [records]
• Nous vous serions obligés de bien vouloir à l'avenir nous envoyer vos notices, circulaires et, en général, tous **documents** techniques ... - ... *send us your instruction leaflets, circulars and, in general, all technical documents* ...
• Nous tenons à votre disposition photocopie des **documents** douaniers en notre possession. - ... *photocopies of the customs **documents** in our possession.*
• Je suppose que vous avez dû le garder dans vos **documents**. - *I presume you must have kept it (a sales report) in your **records**.*

documentation *nf* literature, information, documentation; [for reference (purposes)]
USAGE *'Documentation' is a* Count *noun. (See 'conseil' for the* Count/Mass *distinction)*
• Il nous serait très agréable de recevoir **une documentation** en langue française. - *We should be very pleased to receive **some literature** in French.*
• Je vous adresse ci-joint **deux documentations** sur des systèmes de construction à base de tubes carrés. - *I enclose **two sets of literature** on square-tube construction systems.*
• Pourriez-vous nous faire parvenir un exemplaire de chacune de ces feuilles **pour notre propre documentation**. - ... *one copy of each of these sheets **for reference/for reference purposes**.*

documenter *vt* fill in, [give information to]

• Vous seriez bien aimables de **nous documenter** au sujet des desiderata de cette firme. - *It would be very kind of you **to fill us in** regarding this firm's requirements.*
• Dans le but de **vous documenter**, nous vous adressons notre catalogue ... - *In order to **give you the information you require**, ...*

domaine *nm* domain, field, realm, sphere
• ... les problèmes touchant plus particulièrement au **domaine** de la recherche. - ... *problems concerned more particularly with the **field** of research.*

dommage *nm* damage, injury; [pity, unfortunate]
• Vous restez responsables de **tout dommage matériel et/ou corporel** que vous pourriez causer. - *You remain responsible for **any material damage and/or personal injury** which you might cause.*
• **C'est bien dommage** que cet accident soit arrivé. - *It is a great pity/It is most unfortunate that this accident should have happened.*

donc *adv* so, therefore
USAGE *'Donc' always comes straight after a verb, either the main verb (first example), even when negative (second example), or the auxiliary verb if there is one (third example). It is used much more frequently than 'aussi', 'par conséquent' and 'en conséquence' and therefore puts rather less emphasis on the consequence concerned.*
• Je vous serais **donc** reconnaissant si vous pouviez me faire parvenir le catalogue général. - *So I should be grateful if you could send me a general catalogue.*
• Le couteau ne tourne qu'à 255 tours/minute: il n'y a **donc** pas

d'échauffement. - *The blade revolves at only 255 rpm : so there is no overheating.*
• Nos services ont **donc** opéré comme ils le font pour toutes les commandes export. - *Our departments have therefore proceeded as they do for all export orders.*

données *nf pl* data, particulars
• Nous vous enverrons un plan d'ensemble du bateau mis à jour par rapport aux **données** qui étaient en votre possession ... - ... *brought up to date in relation to the data/ particulars which were in your possession ...*

donner *vt* give, [given]
• **Étant donné** la destination, nous pensons que le mieux serait de faire une proposition CIF Marseille. - *Given the destination, ...*
• Les droits de douane sont applicables à ces thermostats, **étant donné** qu'ils sont d'origine étrangère. - *Customs duties are applicable to these thermostats, given that they are of foreign origin.*

dont *rel pro* whose, of/for which
USAGE *'Dont' always as it were includes 'de'. So, the first example is related to 'la représentation de ce matériel' and the second example to 'vous remercier de votre offre'. In both these contexts, 'dont' refers back to a specific noun ('matériel', 'offre') and could be replaced equally well by 'duquel,/de laquelle'. In the third example, however, the connection is not with a specific noun but with the whole of the expression 'donner satisfaction à notre client commun', hence the use of 'ce dont' rather than simply 'dont'.*
• Seul l'agent peut exposer le matériel **dont** la représentation lui a été confiée pour la Belgique. - *Only the agent may display the material for*

which the representation has been entrusted to him for Belgium.
• Nous avons bien reçu votre susdite offre **dont** nous vous remercions. - ... *your above-mentioned offer for which we thank you.*
• Nous espérons qu'il vous sera possible de donner satisfaction à notre client commun, **ce dont** nous vous remercions par avance. - *We hope it will prove possible for you to give our mutual customer satisfaction, and we thank you for this in anticipation.*

dossier *nm* dossier, file
• En examinant le **dossier** en question, nous constatons que ...

douane *nf* customs, [bond]
• Nous vous laissons le soin d'adresser à Bulawayo une facture pour les besoins de la **douane**. - ... *an invoice for customs purposes.*
• CIE devra mettre les marchandises à votre disposition en entrepôt **sous douane** - *CIE will place the goods at your disposal in the warehouse in bond.*

douanier, -ière *adj* customs
• Nous tenons à votre disposition photocopie des documents **douaniers** en notre possession.

double *nm* duplicate, copy
• Je vous prie de trouver ci-joint le **double** du contrat de distributeur, ... - ... *the duplicate/copy of the distributor's contract, ...*

double *adj* double, [in duplicate]
• Nous vous adressons sous ce pli, **en double exemplaire**, les factures régulières correspondantes. - *We enclose, in duplicate, ...*

doute *nm* doubt; [doubtless, no doubt]
• Il résulte de tout ceci qu'il n'y a aucun **doute** que les CIE ne peuvent

prétendre plus longtemps à l'existence des contrats. - . . . *there is no **doubt** that CIE cannot claim any longer that the contracts exist.*

• Cet article devrait, **sans aucun doute**, soulever l'intérêt de ceux de nos lecteurs qui ne le connaissent pas encore. - *This article should, **without any doubt**, arouse the interest . . .*

• Votre retard à nous en effectuer le règlement est **sans doute** le fait d'un oubli. - *Your delay in effecting payment is **no doubt/doubtless** due to an oversight.*

droit *nm* right, [entitled to]

• Nous nous réservons le **droit** de résilier le contrat . . . - *We reserve the **right** to terminate the contract . . .*

• Aucun avis de souffrance ne nous ayant été signalé, nous étions **en droit de** penser que la marchandise vous était parvenue en son temps. - *. . ., we were **entitled to** think that the goods had reached you promptly.*

droits *nm pl* dues, duties

• Vous nous fournirez toutes précisions nous permettant de déterminer les taxes, **droits** de douane, . . . - *. . . to determine the taxes, customs **duties**, . . .*

dûment *adv* duly

• Pour la bonne règle, nous vous prions de nous retourner le double de la présente commande, **dûment**

signé pour accord. - *. . ., please return the duplicate of the present order, **duly** signed to signify agreement.*

duplicata *nm* (Plural *invariable*) duplicate

• Vous trouverez ci-inclus le **duplicata** de cette facture.

durant *prep* during

USAGE *According to some grammarians, 'durant' and 'pendant' should not be used interchangeably. If their distinction is observed, then our example implies that the writer is planning to spend the whole of March with his representatives. If he had meant a shorter period within that month, he would have used 'pendant' instead. In practice, the distinction is often ignored and we therefore cannot be sure which interpretation is the correct one here. 'Durant' is less frequently used than 'pendant'.*

• J'ai prévu **durant** le mois de mars de tourner avec chacun des représentants pour essayer de confirmer leur méthode de vente. - *I plan **during** March to accompany each of the representatives in order to try to consolidate their sales technique.*

durée *nf* duration, length (of time)

• Option: la présente offre est valable **pour une durée** d'un mois prenant cours aujourd'hui. - *. . . valid **for** one month from today.*

E

écart *nm* difference, gap
• Entre ce tarif et celui que nous avons proposé en dollars australiens il y a environ **5% d'écart**. - ... *there is about 5% difference.*

échange *nm* exchange
• Nous vous confirmons notre **échange** de télex du 16 août: ...

échanger *vt* change, exchange
TENSES See *changer*
• ... nous ne trouvons pas trace en nos dossiers d'une correspondance que nous **aurions échangée** récemment avec CIE. - ... *correspondence which we **are said to have exchanged** recently with CIE.*
• Nous sommes d'accord que ce pistolet nous soit retourné pour l'**échanger** contre un autre du calibre 7,65 mm. - ... *to **change/exchange** it for a 7.65 mm one.*

échantillon *nm* sample
• Nous nous réserverions la faculté de prélever des **échantillons** en vue de leur vérification. - *We should reserve the right to take **samples** ...*
• Suivant votre demande, nous vous adressons par même courrier **échantillons types** des marchandises suivantes ... - ... ***type samples** of the following goods ...*

échapper (à) *vi* escape, [beyond]
• ... mais cet échange de pièce n'a pu se faire qu'en dehors de nos usines et par conséquent de façon **échappant au** contrôle. - ... *and consequently **beyond** our control.*

échéance *nf* due date, settlement date
• L'**échéance** de ce compte se situe donc à fin septembre prochain.

(s')échelonner *vt & pro* space out, spread (out), stagger

• Le problème consiste maintenant à savoir s'il entreprendra simultanément ces trois fabrications ou s'il préfère les **échelonner** dans le temps. - ... *or if he prefers **to space them out/to stagger** them.*
• Les 150 premiers appareils ont été livrés il y a une semaine et la livraison du solde **s'échelonnera** sur une quinzaine de mois. - ... *and delivery of the balance **will be spread out** over about fifteen months.*

échoir *vi* expire, fall due (*Espec. in* échu, -e; le cas échéant)
• Pouvez-vous refaire le point de la situation des produits dont la date de péremption **est échue**. - ... *the situation regarding products whose sell-by date **has expired**.*
• Ces renseignements nous permettront, **le cas échéant**, de régulariser votre compte et de donner suite à votre dernière commande. - *This information will enable us, **if the need arises/in such an event**, to regularize your account ...*

éclaircir *vt* clarify, clear up
• Nous mettons tout en oeuvre pour que ceci **soit éclairci**, tant en France que, surtout, aux États-Unis. - *We are making every effort to ensure that this **is clarified/is cleared up**, both in France and, above all, in the USA.*

économique *adj* economic
• Ventes France: cette année la situation **économique** en France est défavorable.

écoulé, -ée *adj & nm* last month, ultimo
• J'ai bien reçu votre lettre **du 12 écoulé** et vous en remercie.
• Nous avons bien reçu votre lettre du 29 **de l'écoulé** ...

écouler *vt* clear, dispose of, get rid of, move

• Nous avons dû supporter des démarques importantes afin d'**écouler** le plus rapidement possible un stock d'été qui perd toute sa valeur l'année suivante. - *We have had to bear substantial markdowns in order to* ***clear*** *as quickly as possible summer stock* ...

écrire *vt* write
TENSES Pres 1 *écris* 3 *écrit* 4 *écrivons* 6 *écrivent* Imp *écrivais* Fut *écrirai* PP *écrit, -e* Pres Part *écrivant* Subj 1,3 *écrive* 4 *écrivions* 6 *écrivent*

écrit *nm* writing

• Je me demande si l'occasion ne serait pas venue de préciser **par écrit** vos intentions en ce qui le concerne. - *... to make clear* ***in writing*** *your intentions in his regard.*

écritures *nf pl* accounts, books

• Au contrôle de nos **écritures** notre service comptable nous signale que, sauf erreur, vous restez nous devoir la somme de F123 ... - *On checking our* ***accounts/books*** *our accounts department informs us* ...

éditer *vt* publish, produce

• En ce qui concerne l'exportation la maison CIE **édite** deux documents (documents de couleur jaune).

édition *nf* edition, version

• Nous profitons de cette occasion pour vous demander si vous n'avez pas une **édition** plus récente de cette brochure que la publication No 85. - *... a more recent* ***edition/version*** *of this brochure* ...

effectivement *adv* indeed, as you say

• Dès réception de votre lettre, nous avons enquêté auprès de nos services comptables qui, **effectivement**, ont

omis de nous signaler, en temps opportun, que notre facture a fait l'objet d'un double règlement. - *...we questioned our accounts department, who,* ***indeed/as you say****, had omitted to advise us...*

(s')effectuer *vt & pro* do, effect, make, carry out, perform, execute
COLLOCATES *analyse, dédouanement, demande, démarche, envoi, expédition, fourniture, livraison, modification, opération, paiement, règlement, remplacement, transaction, transfert, travail, vente, versement, visite, voyage* USAGE *All sorts of operations can be 'effectués'. Among the most common are: 'règlement', 'expédition', 'livraison' and 'travail'. A larger representative selection is given under* Collocates. *The English verb which comes closest to matching 'effectuer' in all contexts is 'to effect', but usually some other verb sounds more natural, e.g.* '*to make a shipment', 'to* ***carry out/execute*** *work'. Alternatively, the French* Verb + Noun Phrase *may best be rendered in English by a* Verb *alone, e.g. 'votre retard à nous en* ***effectuer le règlement****', 'your delay in* ***paying us for it****'.*

• Nous sommes à votre disposition pour effectuer la création, la remise en état, la toilette ou l'entretien de parcs, jardins ... - *... to effect the creation, restoration, cleaning or maintenance of parks, gardens ...*

• Vous aurez à attendre la réception de la facture correspondante pour nous en **effectuer** le règlement. - *... to* ***make*** *the payment of it to us.*

• Les transports ont dû s'effectuer partiellement de nuit pour atteindre le départ. - *Transport had* ***to be effected/to be carried out*** *partly at night to catch the sailing.*

effet *nm* effect; fact; end, purpose; [indeed]

USAGE *The expression 'en effet' signals an explanation or justification of what has gone before. It has the same force as 'car' or 'parce que', namely 'because', 'in view of the fact that'. Unlike them, however, 'en effet' can begin a new sentence as in the first two examples. It should not be confused with 'en fait', which signals an idea which is opposed to what has gone before, and which is therefore akin to 'mais'. Both 'en effet' and 'en fait' can in many contexts be rendered in English by 'in fact', hence the likelihood of confusion.*

• Nous sommes désolés de ce long délai de livraison que vous nous donnez. **En effet,** nos stocks sont pratiquement à zéro. - ... *Our stocks are **indeed/in fact** practically exhausted.*

• Nous avons bien reçu votre lettre du 6 courant et sommes désolés de ne pouvoir vous satisfaire. **En effet**, nous ne possédons la licence MF que pour la France. - ... ***In fact/The fact is** we have the MF licence only for France.*

• Nous sommes, dès à présent, décidés à utiliser les assemblages MF dans nos propres fabrications et, **à cet effet**, il nous serait agréable d'avoir le prix des différentes pièces. - ... *and, **to that end/for that purpose**, we should like to have the price of the various components.*

efficace *adj* effective, efficient
• Son organisation a demandé beaucoup de peine pour la rendre la plus **efficace** possible. - *Organizing it required a big effort to make it as **effective/efficient** as possible.*

effort *nm* effort
• Soyez certains que nous ferons **tous les efforts** pour régler cette question dans le sens de nos intérêts communs. - ... *we shall make **every effort** to settle this question ...*

également *adv* also, equally, likewise
USAGE *In the firstexample, but not in the second, 'également' could be replaced by 'aussi'. In business letters, however, 'également' is much preferred to 'aussi' in those contexts where, in theory, either would do. 'Aussi' does of course have other senses not shared by 'également' (See aussi).*

• Pourriez-vous **également** nous confirmer la date de livraison prévue pour fin décembre 19--.

• Un deuxième document, **également** jaune, donne le prix de la série MF, qui est une production de luxe. - *A second document, **also/ likewise** yellow, gives the prices of the MF series, ...*

égard *nm* regard, respect, [considering]
• Nous avons réalisé un bénéfice plus élevé que normalement, mais nullement exagéré **eu égard** à nos frais et à nos prestations. - ... *but in no way excessive, **having regard to/ considering** our expenses and services.*

• En vue d'améliorer les services de notre établissement **à l'égard de** notre honorable clientèle, nous ... - *With a view to improving our establishment's services **with regard/ respect to** our esteemed customers, ...*

s'égarer *vpro* go astray, be mislaid
• Nous n'avons pas reçu vos cotations pour les susdites demandes et nous supposons que le pli **s'est égaré**. - ... *and we suppose the letter **has gone astray**.*

élément *nm* fact, factor
• ... et, en réponse, vous résumons ci-dessous les **éléments** que nous possédons sur cette affaire. - ... *the **facts** which we have regarding this matter.*

• Le délai de livraison le plus court sera un des **éléments** d'appréciation. - *The quickest delivery will be one of the* **factors** *to be considered.*

élevé, -e *adj* high
• En raison du prix très **élevé** des haricots blanches de Madagascar, nous . . . - *Because of the very* **high** *price of Madagascar butter beans, . . .*

s'élever à *vpro* amount to, come to
TENSES See *acheter*
COLLOCATES *bénéfice, facture, frais, montant, prix, total*
• Nous vous confirmons que le montant de sa remise en état **s'élèverait à** F.B.123. - *. . . the total for its repair* **would amount/come to** *123 Belgian francs.*

éliminer *vt* eliminate
• Cette solution, de toute évidence, **éliminerait** en totalité les inconvénients mentionnés plus haut. - *Clearly, this solution* **would** *completely* **eliminate** *the drawbacks mentioned above.*

émarger *vt* sign, initial (in the margin)
TENSES See *changer*
• Nous vous retournons ci-jointe cette pièce, accompagnée d'une photocopie du bordereau de chargement correspondant, **émargé** par vos services de Sandouville. - *. . . together with a photocopy of the corresponding cargo list,* **initialled/signed** *by your staff in Sandouville.*

emballage *nm* packing, wrapping
• Si nous devons assurer un **emballage** maritime, celui-ci vous sera facturé en sus. - *If we are to provide seaworthy* **packing**, *. . .*
• Nous vous prions de nous indiquer, en temps utile, les marques à apposer sur la caisse **d'emballage**. -

. . . the marks to be put on the **packing** *case.*

emballer *vt* pack, wrap
• Nous vous signalons que la marchandise est **emballée** en une caisse bois et zinc, pesant . . . - *. . . the goods are* **packed** *in a timber and zinc crate, weighing . . .*

embarquement *nm* loading
• L'**embarquement** a eu lieu le 30 juin sur le SS X. - **Loading** *took place . . .*

embarquer *vt* load
• Nous nous permettons d'insister auprès de vous afin que les 500 appareils soient **embarqués** sur le prochain navire en partance. - *. . . that the 500 appliances should be* **loaded** *on the next ship due to sail.*

empêcher (de) *vt* hinder, prevent, restrain
• Nous nous excusons de ne pas y avoir répondu plus tôt, la période des vacances nous en ayant **empêchés**. - *. . ., the holiday period having* **prevented** *us from doing so.*

emploi *nm* employment, job; use; [schedule, timetable]
• Durant le mois de mars nous pourrons confirmer chacun de ces représentants dans leur **emploi**. - *. . . we shall be able to confirm each of these reps in their* **employment/jobs**.
• Monsieur X, lui-même, nous a toujours donné d'excellents conseils pour l'**emploi** de ses machines . . . - *. . . excellent advice on the* **use/employment** *of his machines . . .*
• S'il vous était possible de modifier en conséquence votre **emploi du temps**, le mieux serait que . . . - *. . . to modify your* **timetable/schedule**, *. . .*

employer *vt* employ, use
TENSES See *payer*

• Les clients sont toujours libres d'**employer** un produit de leur choix. - *Customers are always free to **employ**/ **use** a product of their choosing.*

s'empresser de *vpro* hasten; [delay]
• Notre directeur, Monsieur X, vient de nous transmettre votre lettre du 2 septembre à laquelle **nous nous empressons de** répondre. - *...to which **we hasten to** reply/we reply **without delay***

emprunter (à) *vt* borrow (from)
• Nous espérons pouvoir le dépanner en **empruntant** 2 tonnes de MF à CIE. - *We hope to be able to help him out by **borrowing** 2 tons of MF from CIE.*

encore *adv* still, yet; again; [another, further; even]
• Existe-t-il **encore** une possibilité pour nous d'être mêlés à cette affaire? - *Is there **still** a possibility for us to get involved?*
• Le dossier n'est pas **encore** à l'étude. - *The file is not **yet** under consideration.*
• Nos ventes ayant **encore** sensiblement augmenté, ... - *Our sales having **again** increased appreciably, ...*
• Nous aurions la possibilité de livrer **encore** 50 caisses ... - *... to deliver **another**/a **further** 50 cases ...*
• Nous envisageons d'améliorer **encore** nos ventes. - *We anticipate improving our sales **still further**.*
• Nous serons **encore plus** attentifs à éviter ces inconvénients. - *We shall be **even**/**still**/**yet more** careful to avoid these problems.*

encourir *vt* incur
TENSES Pres 1 *encours* 3 *encourt* 4 *encourons* 6 *encourent* Imp *encourais* Fut *encourrai* PP *encouru, -ue* Pres Part *encourant* Subj 1,3 *encoure* 4 *encourions* 6 *encourent*

• Dans le cas contraire, vous nous dédommageriez des frais **encourus** ... - ..., *you would compensate us for the expenses **incurred** ...*

endommager *vt* damage
TENSES See *changer*
• Plusieurs appareils ont été **endommagés.**

enfin *adv* finally, lastly; at (long) last
• Nous précisons **enfin** que le démarrage de nos fournitures ne pourrait intervenir ... - ***Finally/ Lastly**, we should point out that ...*
• Il serait vraiment souhaitable que cette affaire soit **enfin** tirée au clair. - *... that this matter should be cleared up **at last**.*

engagement *nm* commitment, obligation, undertaking
• En tout cas, c'est sans **engagement** de votre part que nous vous rendrions visite ... - *In any case, it is without **obligation**/**commitment** on your part that ...*

s'engager à *vpro* commit oneself to, undertake to
TENSES See *changer*
• Nous nous **engageons** par avance à ne pas divulguer ces résultats, sauf accord de votre part. - *We **undertake** in advance not **to** divulge these results, ...*

enlever *vt* collect, remove, take away
TENSES See *acheter*
• Il vous appartiendra d'**enlever** les marchandises dans les meilleurs délais pour transport jusqu'à Malines. - *It will be your responsibility to **collect** the goods ...*

ennui *nm* trouble, bother, worry
• ... car si les mêmes **ennuis** devaient se reproduire, le client retournerait l'ensemble. - *... for if the*

*same **troubles** were to recur, the customer would return the lot.* [This refers to mechanical devices which have not functioned satisfactorily.]

enquête *nf* inquiry, investigation
• J'ai fait une **enquête** approfondie sur la qualité des sections MF, . . . - *I have conducted a thorough **inquiry/investigation** into. . . .*

enquêter (sur) *vi* inquire (into), investigate
• Je serais très heureux d'avoir un entretien avec la personne qui viendra **enquêter sur** les possibilités de diffusion de MF. - *. . . the person who comes to **inquire into/investigate** the prospects for marketing MF . . .*

enregistrement *nm* booking, recording, registration
• Voulez-vous nous adresser le montant de votre souscription afin de nous permettre l'**enregistrement** régulier de votre ordre. - *. . . in order to enable us **to book/register** your order correctly.*

enregistrer *vt* book, record, register
• Nous avons **enregistré** votre ordre pour livraison dans 4 à 5 mois. - *We have **booked/registered** your order . . .*
• Indépendamment des sérieuses pertes de temps **enregistrées** au cours de la fabrication, . . . - *Independently of the serious hold-ups **recorded/which occurred** during manufacture, . . .*

ensemble *nm* whole, range
• Nous allons construire un réseau de représentants sur l'**ensemble de** la France. - *. . . a sales force covering **the whole** of France.*
• L'**ensemble de ces opérations** nécessitera donc un tirage de 10.000 exemplaires. - *These operations as a*

whole will require a run of 10,000 copies.
• Il est bien entendu que ce stand présentera l'**ensemble** de nos matériels: meubles, rayonnages et chariots. - *. . . this stand will display the **complete range** of our materials: furniture, shelving and trolleys.*

ensemble *adv* together
• Nous aurons plusieurs problèmes à étudier **ensemble**. - *We shall have several problems to examine **together**.*

ensuite *adv* afterwards, then
• Les articles comportent un emballage individuel en papier Kraft, et sont **ensuite** placés dans de grands sacs papier. - *The articles are packed individually in Kraft paper, and are **then** put in large paper bags.*

entamer *vt* begin, enter into, open, start
• CIE aimerait **entamer** avec vous des négociations en vue d'un contrat d'importation. - *CIE would like **to begin** negotiations with you . . .*

entendre *vt* hear; believe, understand (*See also* bien entendu)
TENSES See *rendre*
• Le fait que vous n'avez pas répondu à cette lettre nous laissait **entendre** que vous étiez entièrement d'accord à ce sujet. - *. . . led us **to believe/understand** that you were entirely in agreement.*
• Il est **entendu** que cette fourniture vous sera facturée par nos soins. - *It is **understood** that . . .*

s'entendre *vpro* be (understood)
TENSES See *rendre*
• Le prix **s'entend** pour marchandise enballée départ Doment. - *The price **is** for goods packed, ex-Doment.*

entier, -ière *adj* entire, whole

ENTIÈREMENT

USAGE *'Entier' usually qualifies abstractions such as 'disposition', 'responsabilité' and 'satisfaction' and precedes the noun, as in the first example. When qualifying a physical object, 'entier' follows the noun and emphasises that the object is whole and intact, as it should be. For example, 'une tomate entière' has not been peeled, chopped up, etc. 'Entier' occurs mainly in the expression 'à votre entière disposition', 'entirely at your disposal'.* (Compare *'complet'*)

• Nous espérons que les deux produits en question donneront **entière** satisfaction à vos clients. - *. . . will give entire satisfaction to your customers.*

• . . . vous avez probablement toute l'année des visiteurs **du monde entier**. - *. . . visitors from the whole world/all over the world.*

entièrement *adv* entirely, in its entirety

• Nous regrettons de n'avoir pu satisfaire votre récente demande téléphonique, notre stock de vente étant à ce moment **entièrement** épuisé. - *. . . entirely exhausted.*

• Nous avons décidé de prendre **entièrement** à notre charge l'augmentation de 6%. - *We have decided to bear entirely/in its entirety the increase of 6%.*

entraîner *vt* bring about, entail, involve, lead to

• Le non-respect de cette clause **entraînerait** la suspension de tout paiement. - *Non-respect of this clause would entail suspension of all payments.*

entre between

• . . . et j'espère que nous pourrons mettre au point tous les problèmes existant **entre** nous.

ENTRETENIR

• Je dois m'absenter pour un voyage aux États-Unis **entre** le 11 et le 22 avril.

entremise *nf* intervention; [through]

• CIE pourrait certainement se satisfaire de la qualité que nous lui offrons **par votre entremise**. - *. . . which we are offering them through you/through your agency.*

entrepôt *nm* warehouse

• Le correspondant de CIE devra mettre ces marchandises à votre disposition en **entrepôt** sous douane. - *CIE's correspondent will place these goods at your disposal in a bonded warehouse.*

entreprendre *vt* embark on, take on, undertake

TENSES See *prendre*

• Nous sommes en mesure d'**entreprendre** l'étude complète de bâtiments industriels, . . . - *We are able to undertake the complete design of industrial buildings, . . .*

entreprise *nf* concern, enterprise, firm, undertaking

• Si le retard était de nature à exercer une influence sur le délai d'exécution de l'**entreprise** générale, . . . - *If the delay were such as to affect the completion date of the overall enterprise/undertaking, . . .*

• Je passerai la journée du 13 avril à Grenoble dans une **entreprise** industrielle. - *. . . with an industrial firm.*

entre-temps (*or* entretemps) *adv* meanwhile, in the meantime

• **Entre-temps**, nous avons eu plusieurs entretiens avec la direction générale de CIE à Paris.

entretenir *vt* talk to; have, maintain

TENSES See *venir*

• L'occasion nous sera d'ailleurs donnée d'**en entretenir Monsieur X.** - *We shall moreover be given the opportunity **to talk to Mr X about it.***

• Afin que nous puissions continuer d'**entretenir** des relations commerciales, . . . - *So that we can continue to **have/maintain** commercial relations, . . .*

entretien *nm* conversation, discussion, meeting, talk

• Je serais très heureux d'avoir un **entretien** avec la personne qui viendra enquêter sur les possibilités de diffusion de MF . . . - *I should be very happy to have a **meeting/talk** with the person . . .*

• Suite aux **entretiens** téléphoniques que nous avons eus avec Messieurs X et Y, . . . - *Further to the telephone **conversations** . . .*

environ *adv* about, approximately

• Nous vous demandons de limiter le poids total de chacune de vos caisses à **environ** 120/130kg. - *Please restrict the total weight of each of your crates to **about/approximately** 120/ 130kg.*

• Les marchandises de vos ordres sous rubrique seront expédiées dans une dizaine de jours **environ.** - *The goods . . . will be dispatched in **about** ten days.*

envisager (de) *vt* envisage; consider, contemplate, think of
TENSES See *changer*

• Il y a lieu d'**envisager** une dépense supplémentaire minimum de F123. - *There is reason to **envisage** a minimum additional expenditure of 123 francs.*

• J'ai été heureux d'apprendre que vous **envisagez** de revenir à Paris au mois de mai prochain. - *. . . that you are **considering/contemplating/ thinking of** coming back to Paris next May.*

envoi *nm* dispatch, [sending]; consignment, shipment

• Nous vous remercions vivement pour l'**envoi de** cette documentation. - *. . . for **sending** this literature.*

• Quant à l'**envoi** des documents, nous pourrons vous les faire adresser par notre transitaire. - *As for the **dispatch** of the documents, we can have them sent to you by our forwarding agent.*

• Bien entendu, il n'est ici question que des **envois** de faible tonnage. - *Of course, this only applies to **consignments** of small tonnage.*

envoyer *vt* send, mail
TENSES See *payer*

• Voulez-vous bien **envoyer** votre devis directement à notre Société. - *Please **send** your estimate . . .*

• Nous vous **envoyons** par colis séparé un échantillon de 12 bocaux de cornichons en tranches. - *We **are sending** you in a separate parcel a sample of 12 jars of sliced gherkins.*

épaisseur *nf* thickness

• Toutefois, les largeurs extrêmes ne sont pas compatibles avec les **épaisseurs** extrêmes. - *However, the extreme widths are not compatible with the extreme **thicknesses**.*

épreuve *nf* proof; test

• Nous vous adressons ci-inclus pour accord les **épreuves** du message d'information relatif à la distribution du calendrier 19--. - *We enclose for your approval the **proofs** of the notification regarding distribution of the 19-- calendar.*

• Monsieur X préférerait sans doute **mettre à l'épreuve** des écrous de 8mm. - *Mr X would no doubt prefer **to test** some 8mm nuts.*

épuiser *vt* exhaust, use up

• . . . notre stock de vente étant à ce moment entièrement **épuisé.** - *. . .*

since our sales stock is at the moment entirely **exhausted**.

équiper (de) *vt* equip
• Ce réseau est assisté d'une administration moderne, **équipée** d'ordinateurs ... - *This sales-force is backed up by a modern administration,* **equipped with** *computers ...*
• Nous ne sommes pas **équipés** pour recevoir et manutentionner des caisses de 200 à 300kg. - *We are not* **equipped** *to receive and handle crates weighing 200 to 300kg.*

équitable *adj* equitable, fair
• En conclusion, nous pensons qu'il serait **équitable** que nous puissions porter en compte les débours provenant de ce retard. - *... we think it would be* **equitable/fair** *for us to be able to pass to account the outlays arising from this delay.* (NB 'être équitable' que' + Subjunctive.)

équivalent *nm & adj* equivalent
• Je vous confirme que nous faisons le nécessaire pour vous virer l'**équivalent** de 2.500 livres. - *... we are arranging to transfer to you the* **equivalent** *of £2,500.*

erreur *nf* error, mistake
COLLOCATES *commettre, éviter, induire en, rectifier; se produire, provenir*
• C'est **par erreur** que nous avons envoyé au client notre exemplaire du plan No 123. - *Mistakenly/By* **mistake**, *we sent the customer our copy of drawing No 123.*
• Sauf **erreur** ou omission, vous restez nous devoir la somme de F123 ... - *Errors and omissions excepted, you still owe us ...*
• Suite à notre commande sous rubrique, nous vous prions de noter qu'une **erreur de frappe** s'est glissée dans le délai demandé. - *... a* **typing**

error has crept into the delivery requested.

erroné, -e *adj* erroneous, wrong
• Le prix unitaire de F8,87 que nous avions appliqué sur notre facture 123 du 5 juillet 19-- était **erroné**, car ... - *The unit price ... was* **erroneous/ wrong**, *because ...*

escompte *nm* discount
• ... notre facture, sur le montant de laquelle nous vous accordons un **escompte** de 2% pour règlement comptant. - *... we allow you a* **discount** *of 2% for cash payment.*

espérer *vt* hope (for), trust
TENSES See *céder*
USAGE *'Espérer que'* + Indicative.
• **Espérant** que ces conditions vous conviendront et toujours à votre disposition, ... - **Hoping/Trusting** *that these terms will suit you ...*
• Nous ne pourrons pas **espérer** de nouvelle commande à CIE tant que nous n'aurons pas de meilleure qualité de MF à proposer. - *We shall not be able to* **hope for** *any new order from CIE so long as we do not have a better quality of MF to offer.*

espoir *nm* hope
• Dans l'**espoir** que notre article pourra convenir pour le marché anglais, ...

essai *nm* trial
• En effet, l'**essai** de nos briques n'a pas été un succès.

essayer (de) *vt* attempt, endeavour, try; test
TENSES See *payer*
• Il **essaiera** de se renseigner concernant l'affaire en question. - *He* **will attempt/endeavour/try to** *find out about the matter in question.*
• Nous avons dû conclure que ces mâchoires n'**avaient** pas **été essayées**

avant leur expédition. - *We had to conclude that these jaws **had** not **been tested** before dispatch.*

essentiel, -elle *adj & nm* essential; main
• L'**essentiel** est que vous ayez pu avoir avec ces messieurs des entretiens intéressants pour les deux parties. - *The **main thing** is that you should have been able to have with these gentlemen discussions which were useful for both parties.*

estimée *nf* esteemed letter
• Nous avons bien reçu votre **estimée** du 17 courant et ...

estimer *vt* esteem; assess, estimate; consider
• Nous vous remercions pour votre **estimée** demande du 31 écoulé. - ... *your **esteemed** inquiry of the 31st of last month.*
• En fait, le client **estime** les frais à 123 livres. - ... *the customer **assesses/estimates** the costs at £123.*
• Nous **estimons que** 150 bidons assureront très aisément les livraisons à prévoir d'ici fin 19--. - *We **estimate that** 150 tins will cover quite easily the shipments ...*
• Il faudrait donc peut-être que vous précisiez vous-mêmes la durée que vous **estimez** normale. - ... *the life that you **consider** to be normal.*

établir *vt* draw up, fix, make out, prepare, work out
COLLOCATES *bilan, budget, chèque, comparaison, compte, conditions, connaissement, décompte, devis, dossier, facture, note de crédit, note de débit, pièce, prix, procès-verbal, tableau, versement*
• En effet la maison CIE vous a écrit le 6 avril pour vous informer qu'elle **établissait** les connaissements pour Mombasa au nom de Messieurs X. -

... *that they **were drawing up/preparing** the bills of lading for Mombasa ...*
• Devrons-nous **établir** des prix CIF Londres ou FOB Rouen, Boulogne, Dieppe, etc? - *Are we to **fix/work out** prices CIF London or ...*

établissement *nm* drawing up, preparation; establishment
• Nous vous confirmons qu'une erreur, dont nous nous excusons, s'est glissée dans l'**établissement** du devis No 123 du 26 février 19--. - ... *an error crept into the **drawing up/preparation** of estimate No 123 of 26 February, 19--.*
• En vue d'améliorer les services de notre **établissement** à l'égard de notre honorable clientèle, nous ... - *With a view to improving the services of our **establishment** ...*

état *nm* condition, state, [the way things are, as things are, as matters stand]
• Elle nous offre d'acheter l'ensemble des immeubles, qui sont **en bon état**. - *She is offering to purchase all our buildings, which are **in good condition**.*
• **Dans l'état actuel des choses** cela nous permet de couvrir tout juste nos frais généraux. - *In the present state of affairs/The way things are, this just enables us to cover our overheads.*

(s')étendre *vt & pro* expand, extend, increase
TENSES See *rendre*
• ... et nous avons actuellement en France 80% du marché, qui ne cesse de s'**étendre**. - ..., *which **is** still **expanding**.*

étendue *nf* extent
• ... et nous avons constaté l'**étendue** de votre programme de fabrication.

étiquette *nf* label
• ... vos conditions pour 500 exemplaires d'une **étiquette** auto-collante applicable sur bois et métaux, établie suivant le croquis ci-inclus. - ... *a self-adhesive* **label** *for use on wood or metals,* ...

étonner *vt* astonish
• Nous ne vous cacherons pas que cette demande d'annulation, introduite par vos clients, nous **étonne**. - ... *this request for cancellation* ... **astonishes us.**
• Nous **sommes étonnés de** ne pas encore avoir reçu cette pièce.

étranger, -ère *adj* foreign
• Nous exportons aussi dans de nombreux pays **étrangers**.

à l' **étranger** abroad
• ... M. X étant en voyage **à l'étranger** pour le moment.

être *vi* be
TENSES Pres *1 suis 3 est 4 sommes 5 êtes 6 sont* Imp *étais* Fut *serai* PP *été* Pres Part *étant* Subj *1 sois 3 soit 4 soyons 6 soient*

étude *nf* study, planning stage, (market) research; consideration
• L'**étude** à laquelle nous nous sommes livrés fait apparaître que le marché anglais est actuellement très calme. - *The* **market research** *which we have done shows* ...
• Le dossier n'est pas encore **à l'étude**. - *The file is not yet* **under consideration/being examined.**

étudier *vt* consider, investigate, look into, study
• Toutes ces maisons seraient naturellement désireuses d'obtenir cette agence, mais nous avons pour le moment réservé notre réponse et **étudions** leurs propositions. - ... *and*

are studying/considering their proposals.
• CIE nous demande d'**étudier** la possibilité de livrer ces postes en même temps que la fourniture NP8. - *CIE is asking us to* **investigate/look into** *the possibility of delivering these items* ...

éventuel, -elle *adj* possible, potential, prospective, [prospect, possibility, if any]
USAGE *Although French Noun + 'éventuel' can be rendered by English 'possible' + Noun, it is often more idiomatic for English to have 'the possibility of' + Verb. So, in example 1, 'concernant une fourniture* **éventuelle**' *might be better translated as 'concerning* **the possibility of** *supplying'.*
'Éventuel' usually follows the noun, but can also precede it with no change in the sense, e.g. 'cet **éventuel** *client'.*
• ... la demande que nous avons reçue de Monsieur X concernant une fourniture **éventuelle** de cornière pour le Soudan. - ... *concerning a* **possible** *supply of angle iron for the Sudan.*
• Nous prenons contact ce jour avec ce **client éventuel**. - ... *this* **prospective/potential customer/this prospect.**
• Frais consulaires: **éventuels**, en sus, à votre charge. - *Consular fees:* **if any**, *in addition, at your expense.*

éventuellement *adv* possibly; if necessary, if need be, should the occasion arise
USAGE *The sense of this word is difficult to pin down, but note that it is in no way equivalent to that of English 'eventually'. 'Éventuellement' draws attention to the uncertain, contingent nature of some future event.*
• Je pense qu'il peut être intéressant pour vous de connaître ces deux

systèmes et, **éventuellement**, d'entrer en rapport avec leur fabricant. - . . . *and, **possibly**, to make contact with their manufacturer.*
• Cependant, la question se pose de savoir si CIE pourrait **éventuellement** être intéressés à absorber des concurrents de bonne qualité. - . . . *whether CIE might **possibly** be interested in taking over good quality competitors.*
• Vos prix devront être établis CIF Dunkerque, Anvers et, **éventuellement**, un autre port de votre choix. - . . . *and, **if necessary**/**if need be**, another port of your choosing.*
• Nous avons bien noté que c'est à vous que nous nous adresserons **éventuellement** pour les commandes, les expéditions et les règlements. - . . . *it is you that we should approach, **if necessary**/**if need be**/**should the occasion arise**, for orders . . .*

évidemment *adv* clearly, obviously, of course
• **Évidemment**, dans un lot de 500 ou 1000 barres, il se pourrait que 10 ou 20 barres puissent avoir subi un accident . . .
• Le client, **évidemment** fort mécontent, maintiendra l'annulation de la commande . . . - *The customer, **obviously** very displeased, will stand by the cancellation of the order . . .*

évident, -e *adj* apparent, clear, obvious
• Il est **évident que** les chiffres demandés n'étaient pas immédiatement disponibles. - *It is **apparent that**/**Clearly** the figures requested were not available immediately.*

éviter *vt* avoid, prevent, spare, save
• En vue d'**éviter** des difficultés à votre client, nous avons . . . - *In order*

*to **avoid** difficulties for your customer, . . .*
• Vous m'aviez prêté votre magnétophone portatif afin de m'**éviter d**'avoir à prendre des notes. - . . . *in order to **spare**/**save** me having to take notes.*
• Nos membres nous ont demandé d'intervenir auprès de vous à ce sujet pour **éviter que** se reproduisent à l'avenir de tels faits. - . . . *to **prevent**/**avoid** such things recurring in future.* (NB 'éviter que' + Subjunctive.)

évoluer *vi* develop, advance, progress
• Pourriez-vous nous dire si cette affaire **a évolué** depuis votre lettre du 12 février. - *Could you tell us whether this matter **has developed**/**advanced** . . .*

évolution *nf* development(s), progress
• Nous suivrons donc l'**évolution** de ce marché. - *We shall therefore keep an eye on the **development** of this market.*
• Nous vous remercions de suivre cette affaire et nous tenir au courant de l'**évolution**. - . . . *and keep us informed of **developments**/**progress**.*

exact, -e *adj* accurate, exact; correct, right; punctual
• Toutefois, la spécification **exacte** n'est pas encore rédigée. - *However, the **accurate**/**exact** specification has not been drawn up yet.*
• Nous vous serions néanmoins reconnaissants de nous confirmer que notre interprétation est **exacte**. - . . . *that our interpretation is **correct**/**right**.*

exactement *adv* exactly
• Sans vous demander de vous aligner **exactement** sur les prix de la

concurrence, ... - *Without asking you to match the competition's prices exactly*, ...

exagéré -ée *adj* excessive, unreasonable
• Nous avons réalisé un bénéfice ... nullement **exagéré** eu égard à nos frais et prestations. - *We made a profit ... in no way **excessive/unreasonable** considering our expenses and services.*

examen *nm* examination, inspection, scrutiny
• La meilleure solution serait que l'article nous soit renvoyé **pour examen**. - ... *that the article be returned to us **for examination/ inspection**.*

examiner *vt* examine, go into, inspect, investigate, look into, scrutinize
• En même temps, je demande à notre inspecteur d'**examiner** spécialement le fini des surfaces lors des prochaines réceptions. - ... *to **examine/inspect** especially the finish of the surfaces* ...
• Nous sommes en train d'**examiner** ce problème et ... - *We **are investigating/are looking into** this problem and* ...

excellent, -e *adj* excellent, superb
• Je n'ai pas oublié votre **excellent** accueil lors de ma visite en juin 19--. - *I have not forgotten your **superb** welcome* ...

exceptionnel, -elle *adj* exceptional, outstanding, remarkable
• ... et il faut que vous fassiez un effort **exceptionnel** pour nous aider à ce sujet.

exceptionnellement *adv* exceptionally, as an exception, in this particular instance
• Nous avions convenu avec Monsieur X de différer le paiement de la facture sous rubrique jusqu'au 15 décembre, ceci **exceptionnellement** pour vous permettre de faire face à vos difficultés financières du moment. - ... *to defer payment ... **in this particular instance** to enable you to cope with your present financial difficulties.*

exclure *vt* exclude, rule out
TENSES See *conclure*
• Nous attirons votre attention sur le fait qu'**il n'est pas exclu que** l'Office des Licences nous demande également un document complémentaire. - ... *that **it cannot be ruled out that** the Licence Office may also ask us for a further document.*

exclusif, -ive *adj* exclusive, sole
• Nous vous confirmons que nous sommes distributeurs **exclusifs** pour la France du matériel MF. - ... *we are the **sole** distributors* ...

exclusivement *adv* exclusively, solely
• ... une notice concernant notre aplatisseur mobile de voitures, fabriqué et distribué **exclusivement** par notre Société. - ... *manufactured and distributed **exclusively/solely** by our company.*

exclusivité *nf* (exclusive/sole) rights
• Nous aimerions avoir votre accord écrit de l'**exclusivité de l'agence** jusqu'à fin 19--. - ... *your written agreement to our having the **sole/exclusive agency** until the end of 19--.*

excuses *nf pl* apologies
• Avec nos **excuses** pour ce contretemps, ... - *With our **apologies** for this hitch,* ...

(s')excuser (de) *vt & pro* excuse, forgive; apologize

• Nous vous écrivons en français afin de mieux exprimer notre pensée. Veuillez nous en **excuser**. - *Please excuse us.*

• Nous **nous excusons de** l'erreur qui s'est produite. - *We apologize for the mistake which occurred.*

exécuter *vt* carry out, execute, make, process

• Nous insistons également pour que les envois de granules **soient exécutés** comme demandé. - *... that the shipments of granules be carried out/executed/made as requested.*

exécution *nf* carrying out, execution, fulfilment, performance, [against]

• Nous vous avons adressé hier une nouvelle commande de 75 tonnes pour **exécution** à la suite de celle-ci. - *... for execution/fulfilment following this one.*

• L'article dont il est question a été expédié le 8 décembre 19-- **en exécution de** votre ordre No 123. - *... in fulfilment of/against your order No 123.*

• L'**exécution** de ce travail nous étant demandée d'urgence, ... - *Since we are being asked to carry out/execute/perform this work urgently, ...*

exemplaire *nm* copy, [in duplicate, in triplicate, etc]
USAGE *Not to be confused with 'copie'. See Usage Note for 'copie'. 'Exemplaire' is* Singular *in the expessions 'en double/triple exemplaire'. Thereafter, it is* Plural *in 'en 4/5/6/etc exemplaires'.*

• Nous vous confirmons avoir reçu en son temps votre commande de 200 **exemplaires** du calendrier MF 19--.

• Nous joignons, en annexe, le contrat No 123 **en double exemplaire**. - *... in duplicate.*

exemple *nm* example, instance

• Je préférerais vous recevoir le vendredi 14 avril, **par exemple** à 15h.. - *... for example/instance at 3pm.*

• Plusieurs clients sont actuellement revenus à nos fabrications grâce aux services rapides que nous effectuons en Belgique, pour vous citer un **exemple**: CIE. - *..., to give you an example: CIE.*

exercer *vt* exercise, exert, carry on
TENSES See *placer*
COLLOCATES *activité, contrôle, droit, fonction, influence, monopole, pression, profession*

• Il s'agit d'un emplacement où CIE **exerce** un monopole. - *... where CIE exercises/has a monopoly.*

• En tenant compte de la pression que la clientèle **exerce** auprès de nous pour une diminution des prix nous vous prions ... - *Taking account of the pressure which our customers are exerting on us ...*

exigences *nf pl* requirements
COLLOCATES *conforme aux, en fonction des, répondre aux, satisfaire aux, selon les*

• Votre offre doit être conforme aux **exigences** des extraits du cahier de charges et des plans joints à la présente. - *Your offer must conform to the requirements of the enclosed extracts from the specifications and drawings.*

exiger *vt* demand, insist on, require
TENSES See *changer*

• Je ne crois pas que l'on puisse **exiger** une telle inspection pour plus de 1/10 des pièces. - *I don't think we can demand such an inspection ...*

existant, -e *adj* existing, in existence
• Ce dernier tarif vient s'ajouter à la série de tarifs et barèmes déjà

existante. - ... *the series of price lists and scales already in existence.*

existence *nf* existence
• Les CIE ne peuvent prétendre plus longtemps à l'**existence** des contrats. - *CIE can no longer lay claim to the existence of the contracts.*

exister *vi* exist
• ... et j'espère que nous pourrons mettre au point tous les problèmes **existant** entre nous. - *... and I hope we can settle all the problems existing between us.*

exorbitant, -e *adj* exorbitant
• J'ai, dès l'abord, considéré le prix de vos services comme **exorbitant**.

expédier *vt* dispatch (despatch), ship, consign
USAGE *Used of dispatches by land, sea or air, of any size, but normally not smaller than a parcel.* Compare *adresser, envoyer.*
• Nous vous **expédions** par colis séparé un échantillon de notre gelée de pommes de reinette. - *We are dispatching to you in a separate parcel a sample of our pippin jelly.*
• Nous accusons réception de 12 briques MF **expédiées** par le SS X le 27 septembre. - *... 12 bricks shipped/ consigned on the SS X ...*

expéditeur, -trice *nmf & adj* sender, consignor
• L'**expéditeur** trouve dans l'attestation d'une lettre recommandée la preuve que ce pli a bien été envoyé. - *The sender has, in the certificate for a registered letter, the proof that this letter was actually sent.*

expédition *nf* dispatch (despatch), shipment, consignment, [forwarding, shipping]
• Nous vous prions de ne faire aucune **expédition** pour cette

commande avant les vacances. - *Please make no dispatch/shipment against this order before the holidays*
• Comme demandé, nous vous enverrons la facture en même temps que l'**avis d'expédition**. - *... at the same time as the forwarding advice/ advice of dispatch.*
• Voulez-vous bien nous faire connaître les marques à apposer sur la caisse ainsi que vos instructions d'**expédition**. - *... together with your forwarding/shipping instructions.*

expérience *nf* experience; experiment
• Guidés par l'**expérience** des années précédentes, nous vous signalons que ... - *Guided by the experience of previous years, ...*
• L'**expérience** que nous avons faite cet été n'a pas été très concluante. - *The experiment which we undertook this summer was not very conclusive.*

expirer *vi* expire
• Le délai prévu pour la fourniture est à présent **expiré**. - *The planned delivery period for the supply has now expired.*

expliquer *vt* explain, account for
• Il serait également souhaitable de pouvoir **expliquer** au client pourquoi les formats ont changé. - *... to be able to explain to the customer why the formats have changed.*
• Ces différences techniques pourraient **expliquer** nos moins bons résultats. - *These technical differences could account for our less good results.*

exportateur, -trice *nmf & adj* exporter: export, exporting
• Je leur ai demandé de nous faire connaître les industriels **exportateurs** qui désireraient prendre contact avec le groupe CIE. - *I have asked them to*

make known to us the **exporting** *manufacturers . . .*
• Rabais **exportateur**: 3%. - *Export discount: 3%.*

exportation *nf* export, exporting
COLLOCATES *demande d', licence d', prix, tarif*
• . . . correspondance concernant la fourniture éventuelle de marchandises pour **exportation** vers le Nigéria. - *. . . of goods for export/ exporting to Nigeria.*
• Veuillez trouver ci-joint notre tarif **exportation** 19--. - *Enclosed please find our export price list 19--.*

exporter *vt* export
• Notre correspondant à Paris nous fait savoir que son client, CIE, désirerait **exporter** ces matériels vers la Belgique. - *. . . would like to export these materials to Belgium.*

exposé *nm* account, outline, statement (of facts)
• Ces inconvénients, dont l'**exposé** détaillé dépasserait le cadre d'une lettre, ont été étudiés attentivement par nos soins. - *These difficulties, of which a detailed account would exceed the scope of a letter, . . .*

exposer *vt* display, exhibit; give, set out
• Nous avons eu connaissance qu'une entreprise britannique **exposait**, lors de la dernière Exposition de la Manutention à Londres, un nouveau procédé . . . - *. . . that a British company was exhibiting, at the last Materials Handling Exhibition in London, a new process . . .*
• Nous sommes extrêmement pressés de recevoir ces plateformes, pour les raisons que nous vous **avons** déjà **exposées**. - *. . . for the reasons which we have already given/set out.*

exposition *nf* exhibition; [showroom]
• Nous pensons plutôt que des **expositions** plus spécialisées dans l'hydraulique ou la mécanique doivent être plus intéressantes. - *. . . exhibitions more specialized in. . . .*
• Notre **salle d'exposition**, située au coeur de la ville, permettra à votre clientèle de trouver son choix. - *Our showroom, . . .*

exprès, -esse *adj* express
• Cette demande pourrait être satisfaite sous la réserve **expresse** de la régularisation de votre compte dans nos livres. - *. . . with the express reserve that your account with us is regularized.*

exprimer *vt* express
COLLOCATES *étonnement, gratitude, opinion, pensée, regret*
• Toutefois, **nous vous exprimons notre étonnement le plus complet** concernant le contenu de cette lettre. - *However, we are utterly astonished by the contents of this letter.*

extraire *vt* extract, take
TENSES Pres 1 *extrais* 3 *extrait* 4 *extrayons* 6 *extraient* Imp *extrayais* Fut *extrairai* PP *extrait, -e* Pres Part *extrayant* Subj 1,3 *extraie* 4 *extrayions* 6 *extraient*
• Prix **extrait** de notre tarif gros actuel. - *Price taken from our current wholesale price list.*

extrait *nm* extract
• Comme vous le remarquerez sur l'**extrait** du bulletin que nous vous envoyons, le cours d'ouverture était de . . . - *As you will see from the extract from the bulletin, which we are sending you, the opening rate was . . .*

extrêmement *adv* extremely
• Nous vous signalons que notre client a un besoin **extrêmement** urgent de ces aciers.

F

fabricant *nm* maker, manufacturer
• Il a passé dix ans à vendre des freins aux **fabricants** de cycles de qualité. - *He has spent ten years selling brakes to **makers/manufacturers** of high-quality cycles.*

fabrication *nf* manufacture, production, fabrication; *Plural* manufactured goods, products
• Nous allons installer une nouvelle usine pour la **fabrication** de vêtements de travail. - *... for the manufacture of work clothes.*
• Cette marchandise n'est pas encore **en fabrication**. - *... in production.*
• Nous nous permettons d'insister sur la précision et le fini de nos **fabrications**. - *... on the precision and finish of our **products**.*

fabriquer *vt* manufacture, produce, fabricate
• La Société X **fabrique** un refroidisseur de lait de 200 litres.

faire face à face, face up to, meet
TENSES See *faire*
• ... ceci exceptionnellement pour vous permettre de **faire face** à vos difficultés financières du moment. - *... to enable you to **face (up to)/meet** your present financial difficulties.*

façon *nf* manner, way, [periodically; anyway, at any rate, in any case; so as to, in order that, so that; with the result that]
USAGE *Most occurrences of 'façon' form part of a longer grammatical expression; in Adverbial Phrase e.g. 'de façon régulière', 'de toute façon' (second and third examples), the compound Preposition 'de façon à' (fourth*

example), or the compound Conjunctions *'de façon que'* and *'de façon à ce que' (fifth example). Notice that in the fifth example 'de façon que' expresses purpose, hence the* Subjunctive *of 'recevoir'. 'De façon que', but not 'de façon à ce que', may instead express consequence ('with the result that'), in which case it takes the* Indicative, e.g. *'Il est très sportif, **de façon qu'il est** toujours en bonne santé'. (See also manière.)*
• Donc, pour l'instant nous ne changeons rien à notre **façon** de procéder. - *... we are making no change in our **way** of proceeding.*
• Nos représentants visitent chaque magasin **de façon régulière**. - *... regularly/periodically.*
• **De toute(s) façon(s)**, j'espère avoir le plaisir de vous rencontrer au début de mai. - *Anyway/At any rate/In any case, ...*
• Les bâches seraient tendues **de façon à** éviter leur contact avec les briques. - *The tarpaulins would be stretched **so as to** avoid contact with the bricks.*
• Veuillez nous adresser les paquets par avion **de façon que/de façon à ce que** nous les recevions de suite. - *... **in order that/so that** we may receive them straight away.*

facturation *nf* invoicing, billing
• Paiement: 30% à la commande, le solde à 30 jours de la **facturation** - *..., the balance at 30 days from invoicing.*

facture *nf* invoice, bill
COLLOCATES *certifiée, commerciale, consulaire, correspondante, définitive, douanière, originale, pro-forma,*

provisoire, rectificative, régulière, de remplacement
USAGE *'Facture' is the normal translation equivalent of English 'invoice', 'bill' for goods and services in commerce and industry. A hotel bill would be 'une note' and a restaurant bill 'une addition'.*
• Nous établirons une **facture** pour les frais comme stipulé à votre lettre précitée. - *We will make out an **invoice** for the costs ...*
• Vous trouverez ci-joint notre **facture** No 123 en 3 exemplaires. - *... our **invoice** No 123 in triplicate.*
• Nos règlements s'effectuent par accréditif bancaire sur **facture pro-forma**. - *Our payments are made by letter of credit against **pro-forma invoice**.*

facturer *vt* charge for, invoice, bill
• Les articles de cette commande vous **seront facturés** aux anciens prix.

faculté *nf* option, right
• Nous nous réserverions la **faculté** de prélever des échantillons. - *We would reserve the **right** to take samples.*

faible *adj* low, poor, small, slight
COLLOCATES *chance, demande, différence, écart, épaisseur, marge, poids, pouvoir d'achat, remise, rendement, revenu, tonnage*
USAGE *'Faible' precedes the noun except in the sense of 'weak' (third example).*
• Au sujet du prix spécial que j'avais demandé, la remise est vraiment très **faible**. - *... the reduction is really very **poor/small/slight**.*
• Bien entendu, il n'est ici question que des envois de **faible** tonnage. - *Of course, this only concerns shipments of **low/small** tonnage.*
• Ces brasures ont multiplié les points **faibles** dans le câble. - *These*

*brazed joints have multiplied the **weak** points in the cable.*

faire *vt* do, make, etc.
TENSES Pres 1 *fais* 3 *fait* 4 *faisons* 5 *faites* 6 *font* Imp *faisais* Fut *ferai* PP *fait -e* Pres Part *faisant* Subj 1,3 *fasse* 4 *fassions* 6 *fassent*

fait *nm* fact, [because of, due to, in consequence (of); in actual fact, in practice, actually]
USAGE *'En fait' should not be confused with 'en effet'. (See effet.)*
• Nous attirons votre attention sur le **fait** que vous n'avez pas répondu
• On envisage une baisse du prix **du fait de** la suppression des droits de douane. - *... **because of/due to/in consequence of/resulting from** the abolition of customs duties.*
• Ce monsieur est Alsacien. **De ce fait** il parle couramment allemand. *... **Because of this/Due to this/In consequence** he speaks German fluently.*
• Les glissières glissent mal. Or, **en fait**, le client désire qu'elles coulissent très librement. - *The slides slide badly, whereas, **in actual fact/in practice/actually**, the customer wants them to run very freely.*

falloir *v impers* must, need (to), be necessary
TENSES Pres *faut* Imp *fallait* Fut *faudra* PP *fallu* Subj *faille*
USAGE *'Falloir que'* + Subjunctive.
• **Il faut que vous fassiez** un effort exceptionnel pour nous aider à ce sujet. - *You must make a special effort to help us in this matter.*
• D'autre part, si nous décidons de travailler ensemble, **il vous faudra** une collection complète. - *Moreover, if we decide to cooperate, **you would need** a complete collection.*

faute *nf* fault, [without fail]

• Pour expédition avant le 3 mars 19-- **sans faute** - ... *without fail.*

faveur *nf* favour
• Ce contrat fait ressortir une commission de 3.000F **en faveur de** la Sté X. - ... *a commission of 3000 francs in favour of Messrs X.*
• Espérant que **ces conditions nous vaudront la faveur de** votre commande. - *Hoping that on these terms you will favour us with your order.*

favorable *adj* favourable
USAGE *For 'favourable prices', see 'avantageux'.*
• Je suis enchanté d'apprendre la réaction **favorable** de vos amis américains.

favorablement *adv* favourably
• Avec l'espoir que cette requête sera accueillie **favorablement** ... - *Hoping that this request will be received favourably* ...
• Nous sommes **favorablement** impressionnés par votre dynamisme.

favoriser (de) *vt* favour
• Espérant **être favorisés de** votre ordre à l'exécution de laquelle nous apporterons nos meilleurs soins. - *Hoping to be favoured with your order* ...

féliciter (de) *vt* congratulate (**on**)
• Nous vous **félicitons** vivement **de** cette heureuse initiative ...

fer *nm* iron; rail
• Ce paquet, acheminé par **fer** et mer, est certainement parvenu à destination ... - *This packet, forwarded by rail and sea,* ...

ferme *adj* firm
• C'est seulement maintenant que nous sommes en mesure de vous faire une offre **ferme**.

• Les prix sont **fermes** pour toute l'année 19-- et seront revus le 1er janvier.

fermer *vt & i* close, shut

fermeture *nf* closure (for holidays), close-down
• Nous vous précisons que nos dates de **fermeture** sont: – du 30 juillet au 30 août.

feuille *nf* leaf, sheet, leaflet
• Nous vous prions de trouver ci-joints une **feuille** de caractéristiques techniques et ... - ... *a sheet of technical characteristics and* ...

feuillet *nm* sheet, leaflet
• Nous vous serions reconnaissants de bien vouloir nous expédier 20 **feuillets** techniques No 23.

février *nm* February

figurer *vi* figure, appear, be listed
• La référence BJ254 **figure** sur l'insertion à paraître le 1er novembre. - *The reference BJ254 figures in the insertion (of an advertisement) to appear on 1 November.*
• Parmi ces équipements **figure** un article qui ressemble fort aux vérins MF. - *Among these pieces of equipment is listed an article which strongly resembles the MF jacks.*

filiale *nf* subsidiary (company)

fin *nf* end; [information; stop]
USAGE See *Usage Note for 'début'.*
• Mon adjoint sera à Genève à la **fin** de la semaine.
• Je suis tout à fait d'accord pour vous rencontrer **fin** février. - ... *at the end of February.*
• Les factures sont payables à 30 jours **fin de mois** de réception de facture. - *Invoices are payable at 30 days from the end of the month in which the invoice is received.*

• ... trop tard pour les ventes **de fin d'année**. - ... *too late for the end-of-year sales.*

• Je vous signale, **à toutes fins utiles**, que je passerai la journée du 13 avril à Grenoble. - ..., *for your information, ...*

• Je souhaite vivement que la conclusion de ces accords ne **mette** pas **fin** à nos rencontres. - *I very much hope that the conclusion of these agreements will not put an end to our meetings.*

final, -e (*mpl* -aux) *adj* final, ultimate
• Nous vous confirmons également que la destination **finale** doit nous être indiquée avant fin juin 19--. - ... *the final/ultimate destination must be given us ...*

finalement *adv* eventually, finally, in the end, at long last, ultimately
• Je viens **finalement** d'obtenir un rendez-vous pour le mercredi 31 courant. - *At long last I have just got an appointment for Wednesday the 31st of this month.*

financier, -ière *adj* financial
• Néanmoins notre situation **financière** actuelle est fort instable. - *Nevertheless our present financial situation is highly unstable.*

firme *nf* firm, company
• Parmi nos références figurent des **firmes** de réputation mondiale. - ... *firms/companies with a world-wide reputation.*

fixe *adj* fixed
• Nous pourrions réaliser ces modifications moyennant un prix **fixe** de F123. - *We could make these modifications for a fixed price of 123 francs.*

fixer *vt* fix, put in the picture

• Je vous **fixerai** un peu plus tard la date exacte de ce voyage. - *I will fix the exact date of this trip a little later.*

• Étant donné la date de livraison, nous vous demandons de **nous fixer** le plus rapidement possible. - *Given the delivery date, we would ask you to put us in the picture as quickly as possible.*

FOB *See* franco

foire *nf* (trade) fair

fois *nf* time; both ... and; [twice, three times, etc]
COLLOCATES *l'autre, cette, chaque, deux (trois, etc), de nombreuses, une nouvelle, plusieurs, la première (deuxième, etc)*
• M. X s'est plaint **plusieurs fois** à moi de n'avoir jamais eu rien d'écrit de votre part. - *Mr X has complained to me several times that he has never had anything from you in writing.*
• Notre offre devra être **à la fois** technique et commerciale. - *Our offer will have to be at the same time/both technical and commercial.*

fonction *nf* [in accordance with, depend on]
• Les poids pourraient être modifiés **en fonction des** quotas impartis par le gouvernement tunisien. - *The weights could be altered in accordance with/depending on the quotas allowed by the Tunisian government.*
• Nous ne pouvons vous indiquer le prix maintenant, car **il est fonction de** la quantité de matériel commandée. - ..., *since it depends on the quantity of material ordered.*

forfaitaire *adj* fixed, all-in, (all-)inclusive
• Nous confirmons pouvoir mettre à votre disposition notre salle de conférences pour **le prix forfaitaire**

de F1.600. - *We confirm we can place our meeting room at your disposal for the all-inclusive price of 1,600 francs.*

formalité *nf* formality
• Dans l'affirmative, nous vous ferons connaître les **formalités** à remplir. - *..., we will let you know the formalities to be completed.*

format *nm* size, format
• Pouvez-vous nous fournir des briques de **format** standard que l'on pourrait tailler à ces dimensions? - *Can you supply us with bricks of standard size which we could trim to these dimensions?*

forme *nf* form, shape
• Nous vous demandons de bien vouloir établir ces conditions **sous forme de** factures pro-forma. - *... to draw up these terms in the form of pro-forma invoices.*
• Je reçois ce jour des nouvelles de M. X **sous la forme de** la lettre dont je vous envoie ci-joint copie. - *... news from Mr X in the shape of the letter of which I enclose a copy.*

formule *nf* form; arrangement, method
• Vous avez dû recevoir récemment un message d'information auquel était annexée une **formule** de bon de commande ... - *... to which was attached an order form ...*
• Ces différents services pourront être rémunérés selon une **formule** à déterminer. - *These various services can be remunerated in accordance with a method/arrangement to be decided.*

formuler *vt* formulate, make, put in
COLLOCATES *demande, indication, obligation, plainte, réclamation, requête, sentiment, souhait*
• Il vous appartient de **formuler** une réclamation auprès de la SNCF à

Cholet. - *It is up to you to put in a claim to the SNCF at Cholet.*

fort, -e *adj* large, big, high, strong, good
COLLOCATES *augmentation, baisse, chance, consommation, différence, hausse, influence, quantité, somme* (Compare *grand, gros, important*)
• Nous disposons de **fortes** quantités de bois à Anvers. - *We have large quantities of timber available at Antwerp.*
• Il y a **de fortes chances** pour que la hausse des prix reprenne d'ici un ou deux mois. - *There is a good chance/a strong possibility that the rise in prices will resume within one or two months.*

fort *adv* very, highly
• L'importance de nos achats nous permet de vous faire des prix **fort** avantageux. - *The size of our purchases enables us to offer you very favourable prices.*
• Vous avez été assez aimable de m'entretenir de ce dossier **fort** intéressant. - *... to speak to me about this highly interesting dossier.*

fournir (à) *vt* provide, supply (to); [furnish with]
USAGE NB The construction is 'fournir quelque chose à quelqu'un' not '*fournir quelqu'un de quelque chose'. In the second example therefore, 'des références' is the Direct Object. (Compare *approvisionner*.)
• Monsieur X s'inquiète de savoir si l'huile **est fournie** par nous. - *Mr X is anxious to know whether the oil is provided/supplied by us.*
• ... et si vous le désirez, nous pouvons vous **fournir** des références. - *... we can furnish/provide you with references.*

fournisseur, -euse *nmf* supplier

FOURNITURE

• La commande est annulée au bénéfice du **fournisseur** précédent qui est à même d'en assurer la fabrication - ... *in favour of the previous **supplier** who is in a position to undertake the manufacture.*

fourniture *nf* supply; consignment, shipment
• Nous vous prions de nous remettre vos meilleurs prix et délai pour la **fourniture** éventuelle de: acier inoxydable type 316. - *Please send us your best prices and delivery for the possible **supply** of: stainless steel ...*
• Le client se plaint de ce que les briques de cette **fourniture** n'ont plus les mêmes dimensions que la **fourniture** précédente. - *The customer complains that the bricks of this **consignment** do not have the same dimensions as the previous **consignment**.*

frais *nm pl* costs, charges, expenses, overheads
COLLOCATES *consulaires, de déplacement, de douane, élevés, d'envoi, généraux, de port, supplémentaires, de téléphone, de transport*
• En ce qui concerne les **frais** de téléphone, nous avons laissé au budget une somme de 600 livres. - *As regards telephone **expenses**, ...*
• Les **frais** de transport de Dunkerque à Lille sont de ... - *The carriage **charges** ...*
• Nous avons décidé à prendre à notre compte les **frais** occasionnés par cette réparation. - *We have decided to bear the **costs** arising from this repair.*
• Cet envoi se fera **à nos frais**. - *This consignment will be made **at our expense**.*
• Ce client nous demande de participer aux **frais** pour la moitié. -

This customer is asking us to pay half the costs.

franco *adv* free, FOB
• Nous sommes chargés par notre client, CIE, de l'expédition des marchandises référencées, vendues **FOB** Marseille. - *We are instructed by our customer, CIE, with the dispatch of the above goods, sold **FOB** (free on board) Marseille.*
• Les prix doivent être établis **franco** gare et, dans le cas d'exportation, les prix s'entendent **franco** frontière. - *The prices are to be worked out **free** to the station and, in the case of export, the prices are **free** to the frontier.*
• Ces prix s'entendent pour marchandise rendue **franco de port et d'emballage**. - *These prices are for goods delivered **carriage and packing free**.*

fréquent, -e *adj* frequent
• Nous sommes en rapport **fréquent** avec M. X.

fret *nm* freight charge
• Le **fret** d'Anvers à Londres est de 123 livres par 1000kg. - *The **freight** (charge) from Antwerp to London ...*

frontière *nf* border, frontier

au **fur et à mesure** as (and when)
• Nous vous serions obligés de bien vouloir à l'avenir nous envoyer, **au fur et à mesure de** leur parution, vos notices, circulaires ... - *... send us, **as and when** they appear, your announcements, circulars ...*
• Je ne manquerai pas de vous tenir au courant des développements de cette affaire **au fur et à mesure que** j'en aurai moi-même connaissance. - *... **as** I get to know about them myself.*

G

gagner *vt* gain, save, win
• Essayer cet article: vous avez tout à **gagner** et rien à perdre. - ...: *you have everything to gain and nothing to lose.*
• Ne serait-il pas possible d'expédier par Boulogne, si on peut **gagner** quelques jours par ce port? - ..., *if we can save a few days by this port?*

gain *nm* saving
• Inversement, tout **gain** de temps fait bénéficier de 50F. dans les mêmes conditions. - *Conversely, any saving of time attracts a bonus of 50 francs.*

gamme *nf* range
• CIE et son correspondant allemand viennent de décider de se séparer, leurs **gammes** respectives de produits ne relevant pas exactement du même réseau de distribution. - ..., *since their respective product ranges do not quite correspond to the same distribution channels.*

garantie *nf* assurance, guarantee, warranty
• Il faut faire une demande d'exportation au service des douanes pour remplacement **sous garantie**. - ... *for replacement under guarantee/ warranty.*
• Nous ne désirons faire l'effort et les frais nécessaires pour lancer votre article qu'avec la **garantie** que tout ce travail ne sera pas inutile. - ... *only with the assurance/guarantee that all this work will not be in vain.*

garantir *vt* guarantee, vouch for
• Tous nos miels **sont garantis** 100% d'abeilles. - *All our honeys are guaranteed 100% from bees.*

• Nous pouvons vous **garantir que** l'installation actuelle donnera satisfaction. - *We can guarantee that the present installation will give satisfaction.*

gare *nf* station

général, -e *adj* general; top; [as a rule]
COLLOCATES *assemblée, budget, catalogue, conditions, directeur, direction, documentation, information, renseignements, secrétariat, tarif; en, d'ordre, d'une façon/manière*
• ... et joignons à cette lettre notre documentation **générale**. - ... *and enclose with this letter our general literature.*
• Nous avons eu plusieurs entretiens avec la **direction générale** de CIE à Paris. - *We have had several meetings with the top management of CIE in Paris.*
• ... vos notices, circulaires et, **en général**, tous documents techniques pouvant servir à notre documentation. - ... *your information sheets, circulars and, in general, all technical documents ...*

genre *nm* kind, sort, type
• Afin que des retards **de ce genre** soient évités à l'avenir, nous vous demandons .... - *In order that delays of this kind may be avoided in future, ...*

se glisser (dans) *vpro* creep (into), slip (into)
• Au contrôle de nos écritures nous constatons qu'une erreur **s'est glissée dans** notre facture No 123 du 30 novembre 19--. - .... *we notice that an error has crept into our invoice ...*

global, -e *adj* global, lump, total
• . . . augmenter les quantités afin que la commande atteigne la somme **globale** de mille livres. - . . . *so that the order may reach the global/total amount of £1000.*

pour (votre) **gouverne** for (your) guidance
• **Pour (votre) gouverne**, le prix exportation du refroidisseur MF est de FF 123 départ usine.

grâce à thanks to
• Plusieurs clients sont actuellement revenus aux appareils MF **grâce aux** services rapides que nous effectuons en Belgique. - . . . *thanks to the quick service we give in Belgium.*

grand, -e *adj* big, great, large, [large scale]
COLLOCATES *attention, confiance, format, honneur, importance, intérêt, magasin, maison, modèle, nombre, plaisir, regret, risque, société, soin, taille.* (Compare *fort, gros, important.*)
• A mon **grand** regret, il me sera impossible de me rendre libre le 10 avril. - *To my **great** regret, . . .*
• Nous fournissons en France la plupart des **grandes** sociétés de produits chimiques. - . . . *the majority of the **big/large** chemical products companies.*
• . . . mais l'ampleur même des investissements nécessaires pour lancer **en grand** cette fabrication rend les dirigeants de l'affaire extrêmement hésitants. - . . . *but the very size of the investments necessary to launch this production **on a large scale** . . .*

grandeur *nf* size
• Il conviendrait que nous sachions l'**ordre de grandeur** des investissements que vos clients

seraient en mesure de consentir. - *We should like to know at least the **approximate size** of the investments . . .*

gratuit, -e *adj* complimentary, free
• Échantillon **gratuit** sur demande de nos clients en champignons secs. - *Complimentary/free sample on demand . . .*

gratuitement *adv* free of charge
• Veuillez donc nous adresser **gratuitement**, le plus rapidement possible, 50 nouveaux manuels.

grave *adj* serious
• En fait cela n'est pas extrêmement **grave**. - *In actual fact this is not very serious.*

gré *nm* (*In* 'savoir gré de') [be grateful for/if]
• En conséquence, nous vous **saurions gré de** nous adresser au plus tôt vos instructions d'expédition et, . . . - *Consequently, we **should be grateful if** you would send us . . .*

grève *nf* strike
• Sauf cas de force majeure indépendante de notre volonté (**grève**, inondation, incendie, . . .) - *Except in the case of force majeure beyond our control (**strike**, flood, fire, . . .)*

gros *nm* wholesale; [broadly, roughly]
• Voulez-vous avoir l'amabilité de nous dire si vous pouvez vous occuper de la **vente en gros**. - . . . *if you can handle the **wholesale**.*
• Il conviendrait donc de proposer un appareil qui comprendrait **en gros** les éléments du MF, mais avec la modification demandée par CIE. - *It would be appropriate therefore to offer an apparatus having **broadly** the characteristics of the MF, . . .*

gros, grosse *adj* big, large, great
COLLOCATES *acheteur, affaire, bénéfice, commande, dégâts, demande, dimension, difficulté, effort, ennui, erreur, industrie, intérêt, oeuvre, problème, progrès, société, somme, succès.* (Compare *fort, grand, important.*)
• J'avais fait un très **gros** effort publicitaire pour le lancement des étaux MF. - *I had made a **big/great** advertising effort for the launch of the MF vices.*
• Nous pensons que vous pourrez nous donner 200 exemplaires en même temps que les deux **grosses** commandes ci-dessus rappelées. - *... at the same time as the two **large** orders referred to above.*

gros *adv* a lot
COLLOCATES *coûter, donner, rapporter, risquer*
• Si vous coupez des tubes en acier, la machine vous **rapportera gros**. - *..., the machine **will yield a handsome profit**.*

grossiste *nmf* wholesaler

groupe *nm* group
• J'ai l'honneur de vous informer que je suis chargé, par un **groupe** de mes clients, de la réalisation d'un bail commercial portant sur des locaux importants. - *I have been instructed, by a **group** of my clients, to arrange a commercial lease ...*

groupement *nm* group, grouping
• J'ai adressé une copie de votre notice d'information aux deux **groupements** professionnels industriels du Havre: la Chambre Syndicale des Industries Métallurgiques,Mécaniques et Connexes, ainsi que ...

grouper *vt* group, combine
• Cependant, veuillez ne nous faire qu'un seul envoi, **à grouper** si possible avec notre commande 123 du 26 avril 19--. - *... a single consignment, **to be combined** if possible with our order 123 ...*

H

habitude *nf* habit; [usually, normally; as usual]
• Nous avons naturellement redit que CIE **n'avait pas l'habitude d'accepter** ce genre de formule. - *... that CIE **did not usually accept/was not in the habit of accepting** this sort of arrangement.*
• **Comme d'habitude,** nous vous laissons le soin d'aviser votre client de cet envoi. - *As usual, we leave it to you ...*

habituel, -elle *adj* usual

• Nous vous remercions à l'avance de votre obligeance **habituelle**. - *... for your usual kindness.*

habituellement *adv* usually, routinely
• L'expédition a été effectuée par nos transporteurs comme ils le font **habituellement** pour les envois de faible poids outre-mer. - *The shipment was made by our carriers as they do **usually/routinely** with small shipments overseas.*

hasard *nm* chance; [at random]

• **Le hasard fait donc que** notre intervention arrive précisément à un moment particulièrement propice. - *So by chance our intervention comes precisely at a particularly opportune time.*

• Nous casserions en plusieurs morceaux des échantillons prélevés **au hasard**. - *We would break in pieces samples taken at random.*

hausse *nf* rise, increase
• Il y a de fortes chances pour que la **hausse** des prix reprenne d'ici un ou deux mois. - *It is very likely that the rise in prices will resume in a month or two.*

haut, -e *adj & nm* high, above; top
• Cette solution, de toute évidence, éliminerait en totalité les inconvénients mentionnés **plus haut**. - *... the drawbacks mentioned above.*

hauteur *nf* height

hésiter (à) *vi* hesitate, be reluctant
• **N'hésitez pas à** m'écrire si vous avez besoin d'un renseignement complémentaire. - *Do not hesitate to write to me ...*

heure *nf* hour, time
• ... et notre stock sera à néant dans 48 **heures**. - *... and our stocks will be exhausted in 48 hours.*
• Malheureusement il ne m'est pas possible de faire ce déplacement **à l'heure actuelle**. - *... to go at the present time.*
• Je vous confirme que j'arriverai le 2 novembre à 9h.10 (**heure anglaise**). - *... .at 9.10 (English time).*

heureux, -euse *adj* glad, happy, pleased
USAGE *'Etre heureux que'* + Subjunctive.
• Je suis très **heureux que** la date du 2 novembre vous convienne

pour ma visite. - *I am very glad/ pleased that November 2 suits you ..*
• Nous vous félicitons vivement de cette **heureuse** initiative. - *We congratulate you on this happy initiative.*

hier *adv* yesterday
• Comme indiqué au téléphone, nous vous avons adressé **hier** une nouvelle commande de ... - ..., *we sent you yesterday a new order for ..*
• Comme suite à votre rappel téléphonique **d'hier**, nous pouvons à présent vous informer que ... - *Further to your telephone reminder of yesterday's date, we can now inform you that ...*

honneur *nf* [beg]
• **Nous avons l'honneur de** vous informer que nous disposons de fortes quantités de ... - *We beg to inform you that we have available large quantities of ...*

honorable *adj* esteemed
• En vue d'améliorer les services de notre établissement à l'égard de notre **honorable** clientèle, nous ... - *With a view to improving the services of our company to our esteemed customers, we ...*

honorer *vt* honour, favour
• Nous vous remercions par avance de bien vouloir **honorer** ces factures lorsque vous en aurez la possibilité. - *... kindly to honour these invoices ...*
• Espérant **être honorés de** vos ordres auxquels le meilleur soin sera apporté. - *Hoping to be favoured with your orders ...*

hors exclusive of
• Vos prix seront indiqués **hors** taxes. - *Your prices should be shown exclusive of taxes.*

hôtel *nm* hotel

ici *adv* here; now; [within]
USAGE *In business letters 'ici' more often refers to a point in time ('now') than in space ('here'), and is used particularly in the expression 'd'ici' (second and third examples).*
• Nous désirons faire l'effort pour lancer votre article **ici**. - . . . *to launch your article **here**.*
• Il ne reste plus qu'une centaine de tonnes à vendre **d'ici la fin de l'année**. - . . . *to sell **between now and the end of the year**.*
• Il y a de fortes chances pour que la hausse des prix reprenne **d'ici un ou deux mois**. - . . . *that the rise in prices will resume **within the next month or two**.*

identique (à) *adj* identical (to)
• Nous aurions la possibilité de placer chez CIE des briques **identiques à** celles des commandes citées en références. - . . . *bricks **identical to** those of the orders quoted above.*

ignorer *vt* not know, be unaware, [be aware]
• J'**ignore si**, de votre côté, vous êtes toujours intéressé à le voir. - *I **do not know whether**, for your part, you are still interested in seeing him.*
• Certes, nous **n'ignorons pas que** la circulation devient de plus en plus difficile. - *Certainly, we **are not unaware that**/**are aware that** driving is becoming more and more difficult.*

immédiatement *adv* at once, directly, immediately, straight away
• Nous prenons contact **immédiatement** avec Monsieur X . . .

immeuble *nm* building
USAGE *'Bâtiment' is the general word. 'Immeuble' denotes specifically a multi-storey building, e.g. a block of flats.*

impayé, -e *adj* unpaid, outstanding, unsettled
• Nous constatons que, malgré ce rappel, notre facture reste **impayée**. - . . ., *our invoice is still **unpaid**.*

impératif *nm* demand, pressure, requirement
• Ce retard est dû aux **impératifs** de notre pleine période d'activité. - *This delay is due to the **demands**/**pressures** of our peak period.*

(s')implanter *vt & pro* establish, establish oneself
• En effet, nous n'avons pas encore réussi à **implanter** cet appareil, même après votre campagne de publicité. - *We have not yet succeeded in **establishing** this device (on the market), even after your advertising campaign.*
• Nous pensons être en mesure de devenir l'agent et le diffuseur de firmes de votre pays, désireuses de **s'implanter** sur le marché français. - . . . *firms wishing to **get established** in the French market.*

impliquer *vt* entail, imply, involve
• Tout dépend à vrai dire des conditions financières relatives à ces trois projets et notamment des immobilisations qu'ils **impliquent**. - . . . *notably on the capital expenditure which they **entail**/**imply**/**involve**.*

importance *nf* importance; size, extent

USAGE See *important*

• Il est inutile de souligner auprès de vous l'**importance** d'une préparation soignée de cette opération. - *It is hardly necessary to emphasize to you the **importance** of preparing this operation carefully.*

• L'**importance** de nos achats nous permet de vous faire des prix fort avantageux. - *The **size** of our purchases enables us to ...*

important, -e *adj* important, significant, [matter]; big, large, substantial, considerable
COLLOCATES *affaire, assistance, caractéristiques, chose, client, commande, débouché, délai, dépense, distributeur, effort, fabricant, firme, frais, information, inconvénient, marché, nombre, opération, point, quantité, réduction, remise, retard, somme, stock, tonnage* (Compare *fort, grand, gros*)
USAGE *French 'important' does sometimes correspond straightforwardly to English 'important' (first three examples). More often, in business French, it is not evaluative but merely conveys the notion of quantity or size (fourth and fifth examples). Nevertheless, since big things tend to be important by virtue of their sheer size (customers for instance), it is frequently impossible to separate these notions clearly (sixth example). The same remarks apply to the Noun 'importance'. Regardless of its precise sense, 'important' usually follows the noun, but may precede it when the noun is postmodified, for instance by a relative clause, as in the fifth example. NB 'Il est important que' + Subjunctive (second example).*

• Objet: écrous MF – Peu de choses **importantes** depuis ma dernière

lettre. - *Re: MF nuts – Few **important**/**significant** developments since my last letter.*

• Si la pièce n'est pas partie, il est très **important** que vous l'apportiez avec vous. - *... it is very **important** that you bring it with you.*

• De plus, je me permets de vous rappeler les points qui me sont très **importants** pour le lancement MF. - *Further, may I remind you of the points which **matter a lot to me** for the launch of MF: ...*

• Nous avons actuellement en disponible un tonnage relativement **important** de tomates entières. - *... a relatively **large** tonnage of whole tomatoes.*

• Vous voyez donc l'**important** effort que nous avons organisé pour vous aider. - *... the **big**/**considerable** effort which we have made to help you.*

• Nous venons de réaliser le client **le plus important** depuis que nous sommes agent de votre maison. - *We have just won the **biggest**/**most important** customer since we have been your company's agent.*

importateur, -trice *nmf & adj* importer, importing

importation *nf* import, importation

importer *vt* import

imposer *vt* impose, lay down
COLLOCATES *condition, date, décision, droit, interdiction, obligation, prix, règle, taxe*

• Vous vous substituez complètement à l'entrepreneur quant aux obligations **imposées** dans la description des matériaux à utiliser. - *... as regards the obligations **laid down** in the description of the materials to be used.*

impossibilité *nf* impossibility, [find it impossible to, be unable]
• Elle **se trouve dans l'impossibilité de** nous donner le moindre renseignement. - *She finds it impossible/is unable to give us any information at all.*

impossible *adj* impossible
• Nous sommes au regret de vous informer qu'il nous est **impossible** de vous faire offre dans ces articles. - ... *it is **impossible** for us to make you an offer as regards these articles.*

imprévu, -e *adj & nm* unexpected, unforeseen, [accident]
• L'objet de cette lettre est de vous tenir au courant d'un contact **imprévu** que je viens d'avoir ... - ... *to inform you of an **unexpected** contact I have just had ...*
• ... le second sera prêt – **sauf imprévu** – vers la fin de cette semaine. - ... *the second (order) will be ready – **barring accidents/barring unforeseen circumstances** – towards the end of this week.*

imprimé *nm* form; leaflet, printed matter
• La facture douanière était absolument conforme au type d'**imprimé** destiné à la République Sud-Africaine. - *The customs invoice was in complete conformity with the type of **form** ...*
• Nous joignons à la présente un petit **imprimé**, qui vous permettra de noter les caractéristiques des valves. - *We enclose a small **leaflet**, ...*

imprimer *vt* print
• Nous pourrions vous fournir ces marchandises à nos conditions générales de vente **imprimées** au verso de la présente. - ... *on our general terms of sale **printed** overleaf.*

incessamment *adv* at any moment, very shortly, very soon
• ... et vous recevrez **incessamment** notre note de crédit pour un montant de F123.

inchangé, -e *adj* unaltered, unchanged
• En conséquence notre tarif de vente reste **inchangé**.

incidence *nf* effect, incidence
• Nous vous saurions gré de nous signaler quelle est l'**incidence** de ces modifications sur le prix de l'installation. - ... *what the **effect** of these modifications is on the price of the installation.*

incident *nm* incident
• Nous nous sommes rendu compte que l'**incident** pouvait à la rigueur se produire à la suite de manipulations extrêmement brutales. - ... *the **incident** could just possibly take place as a result of extremely rough handling.*

inclure *vt* include, [inclusive of] (See also *ci-*)
TENSES See *conclure*
• Cet ordre **inclut** 2.200 appareils destinés à la France.
• Ces prix s'entendent T.V.A. **incluse**, marchandises rendues à votre usine de Lunéville. - *These prices are **inclusive of** VAT, ...*

incomber à (de) *vt indir* be incumbent on, be the responsibility of, be up to: [onus]
• Il a négligé d'effectuer sa demande d'exportation, pensant que **cette démarche vous incombait**. - ..., *thinking that **this was incumbent on you/this was your responsibility/the onus was on you**.*

inconvénient *nm* disadvantage, drawback, inconvenience, problem, risk

• Afin d'éviter de pareils **inconvénients**, nous vous demandons de nous adresser dès maintenant les 1.250 appareils restant à livrer. - *In order to obviate such problems/inconvenience* (i.e. inability to supply a customer because of lack of stock), *please send us immediately the 1,250 appliances remaining to be delivered.*

• Je pense que la procédure entamée pour le brevet américain est suffisamment avancée à présent pour qu'il n'y ait aucun **inconvénient** à ce que vos amis américains aient connaissance de tout. - *I think that the procedure which has been put in hand for the American patent is now sufficiently far advanced for there to be no disadvantage/risk in your American friends knowing everything.*

incriminer *vt* complain about, [offending]

• Nous avons procédé à la reprise des deux roues **incriminées** pour examen. - *We have taken back the two offending wheels/the two wheels complained about for examination.*

indépendant, -e (de) *adj* independant, [beyond one's control]

• Il ne nous a malheureusement pas été possible de respecter la seconde clause ci-avant pour des raisons **indépendantes de notre volonté**. - *... for reasons beyond our control.*

indicatif, -ive *adj* (In 'à titre indicatif' for information only, as a rough guide)

• **A titre indicatif** et sans engagement de notre part, nous vous communiquons que les frais de transport sont d'environ 123FB

par tonne. - *As a rough guide and without commitment on our part, ...*

indication *nf* information, guidance, direction, [showing]

• D'après les **indications** que nous avons, les frais de transport, par wagon de 20 T., sont de ... - *According to our information, transport charges ...*

• **A titre d'indication**, j'ai actuellement en stock sauf vente: ... - *For your information/ guidance, ...*

• Nous avons bien noté toutes les **indications** relatives au marquage des cartons et aux divers certificats à obtenir. - *... all the directions concerning the marking of cartons and the various certificates to be obtained.*

• Sur votre demande, nous pourrions vous adresser une proposition de prix **avec l'indication du** délai de livraison. - *... showing delivery time.*

indiquer *vt* indicate, inform, point out, quote, show, tell
USAGE *This word is very characteristic of business letters and is used much more often than its English cognate 'indicate', hence the large number of translation equivalents given here.*

• ... et nous pouvons vous confirmer que les prix **indiqués** dans notre dernière liste de prix sont toujours valables. - *... the prices shown in our last price list are still valid.*

• Veuillez donc nous **indiquer** le prix et le délai pour une commande (normalement entre 40 et 60 paires). - *Please therefore quote us the price and delivery for ...*

• Il vous suffirait de nous **indiquer** l'adresse de l'hôtel où vous aurez passé la nuit. - *It would be sufficient* *for you to **tell**/**give** us the address of the hotel ...*

• Pourriez-vous nous **indiquer** parmi vos relations une personne susceptible de s'intéresser à la vente de nos produits en Angleterre? - *Could you **indicate**/**point out** to us among your connections a person who might be interested in ...*

• Nous vous **avions indiqué** que nous étions extrêmement pressés de recevoir ces plateformes. - *We had **indicated**/**had pointed out** to you that we were in a great hurry to receive these platforms.*

• Veuillez m'**indiquer** si cette période vous convient. - *Kindly **inform** me/**let** me **know** whether that period suits you.*

indispensable *adj* essential, indispensable

• Une réponse par retour du courrier est **indispensable**.

• Notre équipement industriel est à même de vous apporter les garanties **indispensables** pour l'exécution dans les meilleurs conditions de vos commandes en France. - *Our plant has the capacity to give you the guarantees **essential** for the efficient servicing of your orders in France.*

industrie *nf* industry

• En réponse, nous devons vous informer que notre Société ne peut vendre dans l'**industrie** du pétrole, attendu que ... - *... our company cannot sell in the oil **industry**, since ...*

industriel, -elle *adj* industrial

• Je passerai la journée du 13 avril à Grenoble dans une entreprise **industrielle**.

industriel *nm* industrialist, manufacturer

• Je leur ai demandé de nous faire connaître les **industriels** exportateurs qui désireraient prendre contact avec le groupe CIE. - *... the exporting **manufacturers** who would like to contact the CIE group.*

inférieur, -e *adj* lower, less

• C'est pourquoi il ne nous est pas possible de vous demander une note de crédit pour un nombre de briques **inférieur à** celui de 174 mentionné à l'origine. - *... a credit note for a number of bricks **less/lower than** the 174 mentioned originally.*

infiniment *adv* infinitely, extremely, [very much indeed]

• Je vous remercie **infiniment** de l'amabilité avec laquelle vous m'avez reçu à Londres. - *Thank you **very much indeed** ...*

information *nf* information
COLLOCATES *donner, fournir; absence d', circulaire d', demande d', message d', notice d', réunion d', stage d'*
USAGE *In French, 'information' is a* Count Noun. *We can say 'une information', 'deux informations' etc In English, 'information' is not countable. Instead we may, if the context requires it, say 'piece(s) of information', as in the third example, though this is normally unnecessary. In French, the plural may still be preferred even when reference is not being made specifically to a single piece of information, as in the fourth example.*

• Copie à CIE pour **information**. - *Copy to CIE for **information**.*

• L'envoi à CIE de la circulaire d'**information** a été effectué le 5 juin. - *The **information** circular was sent to CIE on June 5.*

• L'**information** importante est que CIE conseille maintenant ... - *The important piece of information is that CIE now advises ...*

• ... et nous vous remercions pour les **informations** que vous nous communiquez. - *... and we thank you for the information you have sent us.*

informer (de) *vt* inform, acquaint

• Nous vous **informons que** nous expédions la commande ci-dessus à CIE au Havre.

• J'ai été **informé de** la cessation d'activité de la CIE à Milan.

• Je ne manquerai pas de vous **tenir informé de** la suite qui pourra être donnée à cet offre. - *I shall not fail to keep you acquainted/informed of any developments from this offer.*

initial, -e (mpl *-aux*) *adj* initial, original

• J'espère donc que notre stock **initial** nous parviendra avant la fin du mois.

initialement *adv* initially, originally

• ... un nombre de clichés beaucoup plus important que celui **initialement** prévu. - *... a much larger number of blocks than that initially/originally expected.*

initiative *nf* initiative

• Nous espérons que notre **initiative** sera de nature à vous donner toute satisfaction. - *We hope our initiative (an improvement in the method of accounting) will give you every satisfaction.*

(s')inquiéter *vt & pro* concern, disturb, worry

• Cette fréquence est, vous en conviendrez, anormale et de nature à **inquiéter** tout assureur

consciencieux. - *This frequency is, you will agree, unusual and such as to concern/disturb/worry any conscientious insurer.*

inscription *nf* inscription

• ...en boîte lithographiée avec **inscription** en anglais et en français.

insérer *vt* insert, place
TENSES See *céder*

• Veuillez nous faire parvenir l'exemplaire de votre facture à **insérer** dans le colis. - *Please send us the copy of your invoice to be inserted/placed in the parcel.*

insertion *nf* insertion

• Espérant recevoir prochainement vos instructions pour une **insertion** dans ce numéro. - *... for an insertion (of an advertisement) in this number.*

insister (sur) *vi* emphasize, insist (on), press for
USAGE *'Insister pour que'* + Subjunctive.

• Nous nous permettons d'**insister sur** la précision et le fini de nos fabrications. - *May we emphasize the precision and the finish of our goods.*

• Nous **insistons pour que** la livraison se fasse immédiatement. - *We insist that delivery should be made immediately.*

installation *nf* installation

• Cette plateforme a été affectée à la Société CIE, et il s'agit d'une **installation** spéciale sur un de nos tracteurs. - *This platform was allocated to CIE, and it is a special installation on one of our tractors.*

(s')installer *vt & pro* establish (oneself), install, set up; equip

• Cette affaire pourrait intéresser une entreprise désireuse de **s'installer** à Levallois. - *This business*

would interest an enterprise wishing to
set up/establish itself at Levallois.
• Nous venons attirer votre
attention sur les activités de notre
firme, qui est spécialement **installée**
pour le vernissage de papiers et
cartons. - . . ., *which is specially*
equipped for varnishing papers and
boards.

en **instance de** about to, on the point
of; ready to/for, waiting to
• Ce dépliant **est en instance d'être**
supplanté par un document plus
récent. - *This leaflet is about to be/is*
on the point of being replaced by a
more recent document.
• Nous vous rappelons que les 1300
boîtes sont toujours **en instance de**
départ. - . . . *are still ready/waiting*
to go.

à l'**instant** just now, just this
instant/minute
• P.S. Je reçois **à l'instant** une
réponse de l'hôtel: réservation OK -
I have just now received a reply from
the hotel: . . .

pour l'**instant** for the moment, for
the time being
• Donc, **pour l'instant** nous ne
changeons rien à notre façon de
procéder.

instructions *nf pl* instructions
• Nous nous permettons de vous
rappeler notre lettre du 9 novembre
19--, dans laquelle nous vous
demandions des **instructions** pour
l'expédition de la commande ci-
dessus. - . . . *in which we asked you for*
instructions for shipping the above
order.
• Nous passons les **instructions**
voulues dans ce sens à notre service
facturation. - *We are conveying the*
necessary instructions to this effect to
our invoicing department.

insuffisance *nf* inadequacy,
insufficiency, shortage, shortfall
• Nous nous réservons le droit de
résilier le contrat dans le cas où il y
aurait **insuffisance** répétée de
qualité ou de quantité. - . . . *in the*
event of there being repeated
inadequacy of quality or quantity.

insuffisant, -e *adj* inadequate,
insufficient
• L'emballage unitaire des paquets
de cornière MF est **insuffisante** pour
ce mode de transport. - *The*
individual packaging of the bundles of
MF angle is inadequate for this means
of transport.

intention *nf* intention, [intend to,
mean to]
• En ce qui concerne les **intentions**
de CIE, elles sont extrêmement
simples: . . .
• Nous **avons l'intention d'**envoyer
la collection par voie maritime. - *We*
intend/mean to send the collection by
sea.
• Nous avons décidé d'expédier
par avion **à l'intention de** M. X
un mécanisme . . . - *We have decided*
to dispatch by air to Mr X a
mechanism . . .

intéressant, -e *adj* interesting,
promising; useful, valuable,
worthwhile, worth it; attractive,
favourable
• Cette notice nous semble très
intéressante. - *This leaflet seems very*
interesting to us.
• Nous pourrions vous assurer par
la suite des commandes
intéressantes et . . . - *We could secure*
for you subsequently some useful
orders and . . .
• Je pense qu'il peut être
intéressant pour vous de connaître
ces deux systèmes et, . . . - *I think it*

may be worth it for you/be worth your while to acquaint yourself with these two systems and . . .

• Aussi je vous serais reconnaissant de bien vouloir m'indiquer si, pour une telle commande, des prix **intéressants** pourraient nous être accordés. - . . . *if, for such an order, **attractive/favourable** prices could be allowed us.*

intéressé, -e *nmf* interested party
• Notre firme possède des références de tout premier ordre qui sont évidemment à la disposition des **intéressés**. - *Our firm possesses first-rate references which are, of course, available to **interested parties**.*

(s')intéresser (à) *vt & pro* interest, [interested]
USAGE *'(S')intéresser' is found very frequently in business letters in a variety of constructions. Our examples are given in approximate order of importance. Notice the structures in question:* 1. quelque chose *intéresse* quelqu'un; 2. quelqu'un *est intéressé* par quelque chose; 3. quelqu'un *est intéressé* à + Infinitive; 4. quelqu'un *s'intéresse* à quelque chose; 5. il *intéresse* à quelqu'un de + Infinitive. *'S'intéresser' is not normally used to translate 'We should be interested to know/receive/etc'. Alternatives are: 'Veuillez nous faire savoir . . .' and 'Nous aimerions recevoir. . .' etc*
• Je pense que cet offre pourrait **intéresser** diverses usines de votre pays.
• Nous serions très **intéressés par** l'importation de ce matériel pour la France.
• Cependant la question se pose de savoir si vous pourriez éventuellement **être intéressés à** absorber des concurrents de bonne

qualité. - . . . *if you might be interested in taking over good quality competitors.*

• Enfin nous **nous intéressons à** tous vos autres appareils de bar tels que . . . - *In short we **are interested in** all your other bar appliances such as . . .*

• **Il nous intéresserait** vivement **de** connaître les longueurs maxima que vous pouvez fournir dans les différents diamètres. - *It **would interest us** very much to know the maximum lengths . . .*

intérêt *nm* interest; advantage, benefit
• Nous tenons à vous confirmer l'**intérêt** que nous portons au système d'assemblage MF que vous nous avez présenté. - . . . *our **interest** in the MF assembly system which you showed us.*

• **En cas d'intérêt** nous vous enverrons prix et échantillons. - *If **you are interested** . . .*

• Je suis très satisfait de la visite de votre usine qui m'a été **d'un grand intérêt**. - . . . *which was **of great interest** to me.*

• Toutes mes remarques n'ont qu'un seul but, c'est d'arriver à conclure des affaires **dans l'intérêt du** groupe. - . . ., *to clinch some deals **in the interests of/for the benefit of** the group.*

• **Vous avez** donc **intérêt à** commander dès maintenant. - *Therefore **it is in your interest to/it is to your advantage to** order straight away.*

• Nous vous saurions gré de vouloir bien effectuer les démarches nécessaires . . . afin de garantir nos **intérêts communs**. - . . . *in order to safeguard our **common interests**.*

INTERLOCUTEUR

• Nous vous proposons de payer les **intérêts** qui seront dûs ... - *We propose to pay you the interest which will be due* ...

interlocuteur, -trice *nmf* interlocutor, person spoken to
• Parmi **nos interlocuteurs récents** s'est trouvé l'ingénieur dirigeant les hauts fourneaux de CIE. - *Among the people we have spoken to recently was the engineer* ...

intermédiaire *nmf* intermediary, agency, medium, [offices, through]
• Nous n'accepterons plus aucune commande par **intermédiaire**. - *We shall accept no more orders through an intermediary.*
• Nous n'avons évidemment pas tenu compte, dans ces prévisions, des quantités qui pourraient être vendues **par l'intermédiaire de** la firme CIE. - *... through the agency/medium of CIE.*
• Nous avons entre-temps fait visiter ce client **par l'intermédiaire d'**un de nos inspecteurs de notre succursale de Lyon. - *We have meanwhile had this customer visited through the offices of one of our inspectors from our Lyon branch.*

international, -e *adj* international

interprétation *nf* interpretation, understanding
• Nous vous serions néanmoins reconnaissants de nous confirmer que notre **interprétation** est exacte. - *... that our interpretation/understanding (of a quotation) is correct.*

interroger *vt* consult, question
TENSES See *changer*
• Nous accusons réception de votre appel d'offres No 123 du 18 mai, et vous remercions de nous **avoir**

INTRODUCTION

interrogés. - *... and thank you for consulting us.*

intervenir *vi* intervene, approach, involve oneself; take place
TENSES See *venir*
• Nous tenons à vous faire savoir que nous **sommes intervenus** de nombreuses fois dans des cas semblables. - *... we have intervened on numerous occasions in similar cases.* (cases of unprofessional conduct at a trade fair)
• Nous pensons qu'il serait souhaitable que CIE **intervienne auprès du** transitaire à Mombasa afin de lui préciser où se trouve la caisse. - *... it would be as well for CIE to approach the forwarding agent at Mombasa* ...
• Nous vous demandons de bien vouloir faire le nécessaire pour que l'expédition de la première tranche de 25 tonnes **intervienne** immédiatement. - *... so that shipment of the first batch of 25 tons takes place immediately.*

intervention *nf* intervention, involvement, intercession
• Aussi je compte sur votre **intervention** pour faire hâter les expéditions en cours. - *I am counting on your intervention to expedite* ...
• Nous avons le plaisir de vous informer qu'à la suite de nos **interventions** les CIE viennent de ramener le surfret pour Glasgow de 230 francs à 110 francs par unité payante. - *... following our intercessions CIE has just reduced the freight surcharge for Glasgow* ...

introduction *nf* introduction
• De toutes façons, je vous remercie infiniment de l'**introduction** que vous m'avez ménagée auprès de Monsieur X.

inutile (de) *adj* pointless, unnecessary, wasted; [hardly, scarcely]

• Il est **inutile de** nous envoyer séparément les 'auto-feed boosters'. - *It is **pointless to** send us the 'auto-feed boosters' separately.*

• Nous vous serions très obligés de bien vouloir faire le maximum pour éviter toutes dépenses **inutiles**. - *... to avoid all **unnecessary** expenditure.*

• ... avec la garantie que tout ce travail ne sera pas **inutile**. - *... will not be **wasted**.*

• **Inutile** de souligner l'intérêt que présente pour nos clients cette fabrication leur permettant une marge bénéficiaire plus élevée ... - *We **hardly/scarcely** need to emphasize the advantage for our customers of this product which gives them a bigger profit margin ...*

inversement *adv* conversely, vice versa

• **Inversement**, tout gain de temps fait bénéficier de F50 dans les mêmes conditions. - *Conversely, any saving of time attracts a bonus of 50 francs under the same conditions.* (i.e. as opposed to a 50 franc penalty for lost time)

inviter (à) *vt* invite; request, instruct

• Nous avons bien reçu votre aimable lettre du 27 octobre 19-- nous **invitant à** remettre prix pour l'affaire sous rubrique. - *... inviting us to submit a price ...*

• Pour la bonne règle nous **invitons** nos services comptables à reporter d'un mois l'échéance de notre facture prérappelée. - *We are requesting/instructing our accounts department to postpone the due date of the above invoice.*

irrévocable *adj* irrevocable

• Paiement: par crédit **irrévocable** et confirmé en Belgique par un banquier belge. - *Payment: by irrevocable letter of credit ...*

issue *nf* close, conclusion; outcome

• Il est bien entendu qu'**à l'issue de** cette matinée M. X se fera un plaisir de déjeuner en votre compagnie. - *It goes without saying that at the close/conclusion of that morning session Mr X ...*

• Vous serez, bien entendu, tenus au courant de l'**issue** de nos pourparlers avec Messieurs CIE. - *... the outcome of our talks with CIE.*

J

janvier *nm* January

jeu (*Plural* jeux) *nm* set; play, stake
• Nous vous remettons, ci-inclus, un nouveau **jeu** en six exemplaires de la facture modèle 42. - . . . *a fresh set of six copies of invoice model 42.*
• . . . mais nous espérons que vous comprendrez que notre réputation est **en jeu**. - . . . *our reputation is at stake.*

jeudi *nm* Thursday (*See* lundi)

joindre (à) *vt* enclose, include (*See also* -ci)
TENSES Pres 1 joins 3 joint 4 joignons 6 joignent Imp *joignais* Fut *joindrai* PP *joint, -e* Pres Part *joignant* Subj 1,3 joigne 4 joignions 6 joignent
USAGE With 'joindre' what is 'included' is always a physical object, whereas with 'inclure' it may also be an abstraction such as a cost, a question or a tax., e.g. 'Ces prix s'entendent TVA *incluse*' - *'including VAT'*.
• Nous **joignons** un document à remettre à CIE. - *We enclose a document to give to CIE.*
• Veuillez noter que les trois cendriers référence 123 ne sont pas disponibles actuellement et **n'ont pas été joints** à votre ordre. - . . . *and have not been included with your order.*

jour *nm* day; [today, today's date, to date; update]
USAGE *The expression 'ce jour', as in the first three examples, is extremely common in business letters, being the normal translation equivalent of 'today' (rather than 'aujourd'hui'). See also 'journée'.*
• Nous prenons contact **ce jour** avec cet éventuel client. - *We are today contacting this prospective customer.*
• Nous vous confirmons les termes de notre communication téléphonique **de ce jour** . . . - *We confirm the terms of our telephone message of today's date . . .*
• Nous vous informons que, malheureusement, **à ce jour**, nous n'avons jamais reçu la commande de la maison CIE. - . . ., *unfortunately, to date, we have never received the order from CIE.*
• Nous vous suggérons, de plus, qu'un contrôle sérieux soit organisé la veille ou **le jour même** de l'ouverture de la Foire. - . . . *proper supervision should be organized on the day before or on the actual day the Fair opens.*
• Cette spécification **a été mise à jour** le 15 février 19--. - *This specification was updated/was brought up to date . . .*
• Paiement: 30% à la commande, le solde **à 30 jours** de la facturation. - . . ., *the balance at 30 days from invoicing.*
• Le mécanisme destiné à M. X sera expédié **dans quelques jours**. - . . . *in a few days.*
• Nous avons bien reçu **ces jours-ci** votre lettre du 2 août . . . - *We have received in the last few days your letter . . .*
• Nous allons faire, **ces jours-ci**, notre première soumission . . . - *We are going to submit, in the next few days, our first tender . . .*

journée *nf* day, working day
USAGE *'Journée' is preferred to 'jour' when the day is being regarded as a day's activities ('une longue journée',*

'une journée de travail'), rather than simply as one in a succession of 24-hour periods.

• Je passerai la **journée** du 13 avril à Grenoble dans une entreprise industrielle.

• ... et je pense, si tout va bien, arriver à Toulouse en fin de **journée**. - ... *towards the end of the* **day**.

• Le rythme est calculé sur un débit de 600m^2 par **journée** de 12 heures. - *The rate is calculated on an output of 600 square metres per 12 hour* **day**.

juger *vt* consider, find, think
TENSES See *changer*

• Nous **avons jugé** opportun **de** vous poser certaines questions, car ... - *We* **thought** *it advisable* **to** *ask you certain questions, because* ...

• ... ils nous autorisent à satisfaire votre commande, si toutefois vous la **jugez** toujours valable. - ..., *if, that is, you still* **consider** *it valid.*

juillet *nm* July

juin *nm* June

jusqu'à (ce que) till, until, up to
USAGE *'Jusqu'à ce que'* + Subjunctive.

• **Jusqu'à** présent je n'ai pas insisté outre mesure pour entrer en relation directe avec ces affaires. - **Until now** *I have not pressed too hard to deal direct with these businesses.*

• Adresse provisoire **jusqu'au** 20 septembre: ... - *Provisional address* **until** *September 20:* ...

• Le client, évidemment fort mécontent, maintiendra l'annulation de la commande **jusqu'à ce que** vous ayez pris

position. - *The customer, obviously very displeased, will stand by the cancellation of the order* **until** *you have come to a decision.*

• Dimensions: largeur **jusqu'à** 350mm – épaisseur de 4 à 0,1mm. - ...: *width* **up to** *350mm* ...

juste *adv* just

• Pour vous, nous avons **juste** passé quelques ordres pour retourner la livraison erronée chez CIE. - ..., *we have* **just** *given orders* ...

juste *adj* fair, low

• En cas de demande, nous vous prions de nous donner le plus de détails possible afin de pouvoir vous remettre notre prix **le plus juste**. - ... *so we can send you our* **lowest** *price.*

justificatif, -ive *adj & nm* justificatory; proof, [checking]

• ... votre lettre relative à une demande de **justificatif de livraison** pour les marchandises ... - ... *your letter concerning a request for* **proof of delivery** *for the goods* ...

• Notre succursale de Reims nous a transmis en communication un **exemplaire justificatif** des insertions parues dans la page agricole de votre édition du 25 octobre 19--. - ... *a* **checking copy** *of the insertions (i.e. advertisements) which appeared on the agricultural page* ...

justifier *vt* justify

• Monsieur X ne m'a jamais dit quelles étaient les raisons qui **justifiaient** cette demande. - ... *the reasons which* **justified** *this request.*

L

laisser *vt* allow, leave, let; [give]
COLLOCATES *marge, possibilité, profit, soin*
• Cela nous **laisserait** très peu de profit sur les affaires réalisées avec l'Australie. - *This would leave/allow us really very little profit . . .*
• Comme d'habitude, nous **vous laissons le soin** d'aviser votre client de cet envoi. - *As usual, we leave it to you to advise your customer of this dispatch.*
• Le fait que vous n'avez pas répondu à cette lettre **nous laissait entendre** que vous étiez entièrement d'accord à ce sujet. - *. . . gave us to understand that you were entirely in agreement.*
• Celui-ci m'a fait savoir qu'il désirait **laisser passer** un délai de quelques mois . . . - *The latter gave me to understand that he wished to let a few months elapse . . .*

lancement *nm* launch, launching
• J'ai bien reçu, en son temps, votre lettre du 17 décembre 19-- concernant l'éventuel **lancement** d'une nouvelle cornière perforée. - *. . . concerning the possible launching of a new slotted angle.*

lancer *vt* introduce, launch, [put]
TENSES See *placer*
• La maison CIE **lance** sur le marché les équipements hydrauliques MF. - *CIE is introducing/launching MF hydraulic equipment on the market.*
• Voulez-vous tenir compte de ces indications pour **lancer en fabrication** la dernière plateforme MF . . . - *Would you take these instructions into account in putting into production the last MF platform . . .*

largeur *nf* breadth, width
• Quantité: 20 à 30 tonnes par mois. Épaisseurs: 2 à 10mm. **Largeur**: 200mm.

lettre *nf* letter

libellé *nm* wording
• Le **libellé** du bon de commande annexé à ce message diffère du précédent sur les deux points suivants: . . . - *The wording of the order form . . .*

libeller *vt* word; [read, run]
• Nous nous permettons de vous confirmer les termes de notre câble de ce jour **ainsi libellé**: . . . - *. . . the terms of our cable of today's date worded/which reads/which runs as follows: . . .*

libre (de) *adj* free
• A mon grand regret, il me sera impossible de me rendre **libre** le 10 avril. - *. . ., it will be impossible for me to be free on April 10.*
• . . . les clients sont toujours **libres** d'employer un produit de leur choix. - *. . . free to use a product of their choosing.*

licence *nf* licence
• Ce document nous permettra d'obtenir notre **licence** d'exportation pour le fusil. - *. . . to obtain our export licence for the rifle.*
• Ces chaînes de fabrication sont équipées de votre MF, fabriqué **sous licence** par CIE. - *. . . your MF, manufactured under licence by CIE.*

lieu (Plural -*x*) *nm* place; [last resort; give rise to; be a good thing/ necessary/as well; if need be; instead (of)]
• L'embarquement **a eu lieu** le 30 juin sur le S/S X. - *Loading took place . . .*

• Cette éventualité est à envisager **en dernier lieu**. - *This possibility is to be considered only as a last resort.*

• Nous espérons que ce document reflétera bien les conclusions des débats auxquels la réunion **a donné lieu**. - *... will reflect the conclusions of the discussions to which the meeting gave rise.*

• Si des bris de l'espèce se produisaient encore, **il y aurait lieu** pour vos clients **de** faire intervenir l'assurance. - *If such breakages happened again, it would be a good thing/be necessary/be as well for your customers to involve the insurance company.*

• Je me permettrai de vous téléphoner pour que nous échangions, **s'il y a lieu**, nos impressions. - *... so that we can, if necessary/if need be, exchange our impressions.*

• Nous essaierons d'orienter certains acheteurs à prendre CIF Boulogne **au lieu de** CIF Dunkerque. - *... instead of CIF Dunkirk.*

• ... nous consulter avant de faire des réexpéditions, **au lieu de** nous mettre devant le fait accompli. - *... instead of presenting us with a fait accompli.*

ligne *nf* line
COLLOCATES *maritime, téléphonique, de crédit, de chemin de fer, de navigation*
• Nous avons remarqué que CIE mettait un nouveau bateau sur la **ligne** Boulogne/Goole.

limite *nf* limit
COLLOCATES *atteindre, dépasser, étendre, fixer, franchir, observer*
• Nous pourrions consentir des remises à des clients d'une telle importance sans dépasser cette **limite**. - *... without exceeding this limit.*

(se) limiter (à) *vt & pro* confine, keep down, limit, restrict
• Nous vous demandons de **limiter** le poids total de vos caisses à environ 120/130kg. - *Please keep down/limit/restrict the total weight of your crates to about 120/130kg.*

• Notre programme **se limite** actuellement à la fabrication de feuillards d'acier ... - *Our programme is confined/limited/restricted at present to the manufacture of steel strip ...*

lire *vt* hear from, read
TENSES Pres 1 *lis* 3 *lit* 4 *lisons* 6 *lisent* Imp *lisais* Fut *lirai* PP *lu, lue* Pres Part *lisant* Subj 1,3 *lise* 4 *lisions* 6 *lisent*
• Dans l'attente du plaisir de vous **lire**, ... - *Awaiting the pleasure of hearing from you, ...*

• ... et nous serions heureux de vous **lire** à ce sujet. - *... to hear from you on this matter.*

liste *nf* list, schedule
• Vous trouverez ci-joint la **liste** exacte des produits de notre fabrication.

litige *nm* dispute, contention
• En effet, nous ne sommes pas du tout au courant d'un **litige** sur un règlement, ... - *We are totally unaware of any dispute over a payment, ...*

livrable *adj* deliverable
• Nous attirons votre attention sur les quelques pièces non **livrables** indiquées dans le bas de notre confirmation. - *... the various non-deliverable items shown at the bottom of our confirmation.*

livraison *nf* delivery
• Nous avons enregistré votre ordre pour **livraison** dans 4 à 5 mois.
• Délai de **livraison**: 4/5 mois env. à dater du jour où nous aurons reçu le crédit. - *Delivery: 4/5 months approx. from our receiving the credit.*

• Nous ne pourrons donc plus effectuer de **livraison** avant le 20 septembre. - *We shall therefore not be able to make any further **delivery** before 20 September.*

• ... mais nous insistons beaucoup pour que vous teniez rigoureusement les dates de **livraison** indiquées sur votre lettre. - *... but we stress that you should keep strictly the **delivery** dates given in your letter.*

• ... votre correspondance du 15 octobre nous indiquant la cadence probable de **livraisons** pour le solde de notre ordre. - *... giving us the probable rate of **delivery** for the balance of our order.*

livre *nm* book, accounts

• Cette demande, quoique bien tardive, pourrait être satisfaite sous la réserve expresse de la régularisation de votre compte dans nos **livres**. - *... the regularization of your account in our **books**.*

livre *nf* pound (sterling or weight)

livrer *vt* deliver
• Les 150 premiers appareils **ont été livrés** il y a une semaine.

local, -e (*mpl* -aux) *adj* local

local (*Plural* -aux) *nm* premises
USAGE *Occasionally found in the* Singular, *but usually the* Plural *is preferred even when, as here, it refers to a single location.*
• Notre Société occupe **des locaux/ un local** de 800 mètres carrés environ.

location *nf* rent; let, letting: hire; hiring out
USAGE *'Location' and the corresponding verb, 'louer', are used of land and buildings (which in English are either 'rented' or 'let', depending on whose*

point of view is being taken). They are also used of cars, equipment, etc (which in English are either 'hired' or 'hired out', again depending on the point of view).*

• Nous ne pensons pas, étant donné le coût de la **location** du stand, que cet effort soit justifié cette année. - *..., given the cost of **renting** the stand (at a trade fair), ...*

• Nous sommes chargés de la **location** et de la vente des propriétés dont description en annexe. - *We are responsible for the **letting** and sale of the properties of which description herewith.*

loger *vt* pack
TENSES See *changer*
USAGE *A much less common word in this sense than 'emballer'.*
• Nous sommes en mesure de vous fournir des piments au vinaigre **logés** en bordelaises de 110kg environ. - *... peppers in vinegar **packed** in barrels of approximately 110kg.*

long, -ue *adj* lengthy, long
• Ayant eu ces derniers jours de **longues** conversations avec diverses personnalités de CIE, ...
• ... transférer l'atelier dans le nouveau bâtiment de 90ms de **long** et 16ms de large. - *... transfer the workshop into the new building , which is 90m **long** by 16m wide.*

longtemps *adv* long, a long time
• D'autre part, nous nous étonnons qu'il ait attendu si **longtemps** avant de signaler que ... - *... that he waited so **long**/such **a long time** before indicating that ...*

longueur *nf* length
• La quantité porterait sur environ 40 à 50 tubes, **longueurs** comprises entre 25 et 40mm. - *..., **lengths** ranging from 25 to 40mm.*

• Nous avons fourni gratuitement à CIE 10 **longueurs** MF en remplacement. - . . . *10 lengths of MF as replacements.*

lors de at the time of, on the occasion of, [when]
• **Lors de** l'affaire MF, vous avez coté 123 livres . . . - *At the time of the MF deal, you quoted £123 . . .*
• Je n'ai pas oublié votre excellent accueil **lors de** ma visite en juin 19--. - . . . *on the occasion of my visit in June 19--.*
• Vous auriez pu, et dû, faire cette observation **lors de la réception de** la commande officielle. - . . . *when you received the official order.*

lorsque *conj* when
USAGE *Notice firstly that 'lorsque' corresponds to* Eng *'when' only as a* Conjunction *and not as an* Adverb. *(See 'quand' adv.) Secondly, although 'lorsque' is used more frequently than 'quand' conj in business letters, it is nevertheless relatively infrequent compared with the* Preposition *'lors de'. Hence, in the above 'lors de' examples, 'lors de ma visite' is preferred to 'lorsque je vous ai rendu visite' and 'lors de la réception de la commande' is preferred to 'lorsque vous avez reçu la commande'. Finally, when the clause introduced by 'lorsque' (or 'quand' conj) refers to the future, as in the two examples below, French requires the* Future *or* Future Perfect *tense, not as in English the* Present *or* Perfect.
• Nous vous préviendrons, **lorsque** nous serons en mesure de discuter de votre offre . . . - *We shall advise you, when we are in a position to discuss your offer.*
• Nous vous demandons de grouper les MF avec les autres appareils, **lorsqu**'ils seront disponibles. - *Please combine the MF*

with the other appliances, when they are available.

lot *nm* batch
• Évidemment, dans un **lot** de 500 ou 1.000 barres, il se pourrait que 10 ou 20 barres aient subi un accident lors de l'extrusion. - *Of course, in a batch of 500 or 1000 bars, it could be that 10 or 20 bars suffered an accident during extrusion.*

louer *vt* rent; let: hire; hire out
USAGE See *'location'.*

lundi *nm* Monday
USAGE *Like the other days of the week, 'lundi' is used without the* Definite Article *in translating* Eng *'on Monday' (first example), unless the date is specified (second example). The article is also omitted in translating 'next Monday' and 'last Monday' (third and fourth examples) and when 'lundi' is placed in apposition to 'ce matin', 'ce soir', etc (fifth example). Otherwise, the article is needed, as shown in the remaining examples. Notice that the habitual 'on Mondays' is rendered by the* Singular *'le lundi' (last example).*
• Je l'ai rencontré **lundi** à Paris. - *I met him on Monday in Paris.*
• Je vous confirme que nous nous rencontrerons **le lundi 10 avril** à la Chambre Syndicale. - *I confirm that we shall meet on Monday April 10. . .*
• Je retournerai le voir **lundi prochain**, 17 avril, à la même heure. - . . . *next Monday, April 11, at the same time.*
• Je vous confirme donc l'ensemble des entretiens que nous avons eus **lundi dernier** à Londres. - . . . *the talks we had last Monday in London.*
• Nous avons reçu **ce matin, lundi 20**, un coup de téléphone de Monsieur X. - *We received this morning, Monday 20, a phone call from Mr X.*

- Toutefois, **le lundi 13 avril** ne me convient pas bien. - *However, Monday April 13 does not suit me well.*
- Date d'arrivée: **le lundi 3**. - *Arrival date: Monday 3rd.*
- Je pense pouvoir le faire **dans la journée du lundi 29 septembre**. - *... some time on Monday September 29.*

- Je viens finalement d'obtenir un rendez-vous **pour le lundi 30 septembre 19--** - *I have finally managed to get an appointment for Monday September 30 19--.*
- Les locaux sont ouverts **le lundi** jusqu'à 20 hrs. - *The premises are open on Mondays till 8 o'clock.*

M

magasin *nm* shop, warehouse, [stock]
- Ces remorques peuvent être chargées directement dans vos **magasins** ou vos usines, ... - *These trailers can be loaded directly in your warehouses or works, ...*
- Nous avons déjà des accords pour la fourniture des **magasins** hors taxes dans cette région. - *We already have agreements to supply the duty-free shops in this region.*
- En effet, la quantité de distributeurs actuellement **en magasin** ne nous permet pas d'assurer les commandes en cours. - *..., the quantity of dispensers now in stock ...*

mai *nm* May

main *nf* hand, [available, at one's disposal]
- Pour nous permettre d'avoir tous les éléments **en main**, je vous serais reconnaissant de bien vouloir me faire parvenir le texte complet de la lettre. - *So that we may have all the facts at our disposal,...*
- Je pense que le problème est **en bonne main** avec M. X. - *... in good hands with Mr X.*

main-d'oeuvre *nf* labour (force), work-force
- ... employant à cet effet une **main-d'oeuvre** exclusivement spécialisée en ce domaine. - *... employing a work-force specializing exclusively in this field.*

maintenant *adv* now, [straight away, forthwith]
USAGE *'Maintenant' is **not** the normal translation equivalent of 'now, 'at present'. See 'actuellement'. 'Maintenant' carries the implication 'now as opposed to earlier', as demonstrated by the first two examples.*
- C'est seulement **maintenant** que nous sommes en mesure de vous faire une offre ferme. - *It is only **now** that we are in a position to make you a firm offer.*
- C'est nous **maintenant** qui sommes en difficultés. - *It is we **now** who are in difficulties.*
- Vous avez donc intérêt à commander **dès maintenant**. - *It is therefore in your interest to order **straight away**.*

(se) maintenir *vt & pro* maintain, hold, stick to, uphold
TENSES See *venir*

• Comme vous pourrez le remarquez, nous avons pu **maintenir** l'ancien prix de F.28,50 - . . ., *we have been able to maintain/hold the old price of 28.50 francs.*

• . . . et nous espérons que la bonne entente, qui a régné au cours de cette journée, pourra **se maintenir** et, si possible, s'améliorer encore. - . . . *and we hope that the good understanding, . . ., can be maintained and, if possible, be improved further.*

• Nous **maintenons** absolument notre point de vue, c'est-à-dire . . . - *We are maintaining/are sticking to our point of view, namely . . .*

maison *nf* company, firm
• Toutes ces **maisons** seraient naturellement désireuses d'obtenir cette agence, mais . . .
• Nous avons eu ce jour une communication téléphonique du représentant de la **maison** CIE concernant . . .

majoration *nf* increase, rise
• Les prix de revente conseillés de nos panneaux MF standard sur le marché belge (avec **majoration** de 15% pour les panneaux découpés) sont de 230Frs le m^2. - *The recommended resale price. . . (with an increase of 15% for cut panels) is . . .*

majorer *vt* increase, put up, raise
• Nous **avions** alors **majoré** le prix car nous savions que CIE feraient de toutes façons l'essai de cette brique. - *We had then increased the price since we knew . . .*

mal *adv* badly; [misunderstand; a lot of]
• Les glissières glissent **mal**. - *The slides slide badly.*
• Nous pensons que vous avez **mal compris**. - *We think you have misunderstood.*

• Néanmoins, ces difficultés m'ont occasionné **pas mal d'**ennuis. - *Nevertheless, these difficulties have caused me a lot of trouble.*

malentendu *nm* misunderstanding
• Tout ce que vous pourrez faire à Washington pour éclaircir ce **malentendu** ne pourrait que faire progresser la question. - *Anything you can do in Washington to clear up this misunderstanding could not fail to give an impetus to this matter.*

malgré *prep* despite, in spite of, notwithstanding, [after all]
• Nous constatons que, **malgré** ce rappel, notre facture reste toujours impayée. - *. . ., in spite of this reminder, . . .*
• Bien qu'il reste encore des sociétés d'importance non négligeable, vous aurez **malgré tout** une vue d'ensemble de la sidérurgie lourde française. - *. . ., you will have after all an overall view of the French iron and steel industry.*

malheureusement *adv* unfortunately
USAGE *'Malheureusement' is usually placed at the beginning of its clause as in the first example. However, as the second example shows, it can occur elsewhere, especially in conjunction with 'pouvoir' and 'être possible', when they are used in the negative.*
• **Malheureusement**, je ne serai pas libre le 12 avril au matin comme vous me le proposez.
• Il ne nous est **malheureusement** pas possible de vous envoyer actuellement les quantités que vous demandez.

mandat-poste *nm* money order, postal order
• P.J. Un **mandat-poste**. - *Encl. A money order.*

manière *nf* manner, way, [similarly]

USAGE *'Manière' and 'façon' are almost interchangeable. In principle, 'façon' could be substituted for 'manière' in these three examples and, equally, 'manière' could be substituted in all the examples given under 'façon'. (See 'façon') However, in practice, 'façon' is rather more frequent. Also, in Adverbial Phrases, there is a tendancy for 'façon' to occur without an article, e.g. 'de façon régulière/imminente' and for 'manière' to occur with one, as in the three examples given below.*

• Ces difficultés sont en voie de règlement, et d'une **manière** très favorable pour moi. - *These difficulties are being resolved, and in a very favourable manner for me.*

• Votre offre sera à décomposer de la **manière** suivante: ... - *Your offer should be broken down in the following manner: ...*

• Je lui ai proposé pour les règlements à venir d'opérer de la même **manière** qu'avec vous-même. - *... to operate in the same way as with yourself.*

manifester *vt* indicate, show

• Nous tenons à votre disposition un échantillon que nous vous enverrons, si vous en **manifestez** le désir. - *..., if you indicate a wish for it/ if you so desire.*

• J'ai noté l'intérêt de principe que vous **avez manifesté** concernant l'affaire CIE. - *I have noted the interest you have shown in principle/I have noted that you are interested in principle in the CIE business.*

manquer *vt* miss

• Croyez que je regrette cette occasion **manquée** d'une visite ... - *Believe me, I do regret this missed opportunity for a visit.*

manquer *vi & impers* be missing, [lack, be in need of, be short of]

• Je viens d'avoir la désagréable surprise de constater qu'**il manque** les vis de fixation de la base et de la tige des cendriers. - *... to discover that the fixing screws for the base and stem of the ashtrays are missing.*

• Monsieur X nous signale qu'**il lui manque** les pièces suivantes: ... - *... that he lacks/that he is short of the following parts: ...*

• Il est certain que notre stock de départ **nous manque** beaucoup pour produire les premiers résultats. - *... that we are greatly in need of our starting stock ...*

manquer de *vt indir* fail to, forget to, hesitate to, neglect to, [without fail, be sure to]

• Nous **ne manquerons pas de** vous aviser quand le colis quittera nos usines. - *We shall not fail to advise you/We shall advise you without fail when the parcel leaves our works.*

• **Ne manquez pas de** nous consulter dès que vous aurez des besoins. - *Be sure to/Don't forget/ hesitate to consult us ...*

• X **n'a pas manqué**, je le vois, **de** vous tenir au courant des difficultés que nous rencontrons ... - *X hasn't forgotten/neglected, I see, to keep you informed ...*

manutention *nf* (materials) handling

• Ces réclamations semblent bien prouver une insuffisance d'emballage pour le mode de **manutention** auquel il est soumis. - *These claims certainly seem to prove that the packing is inadequate for the type of handling to which it is subjected.*

manutentionner *vt* handle

• Nous vous confirmons à nouveau que nous ne sommes pas équipés pour recevoir et **manutentionner** des caisses de 200 à 300kg. - ... *we are not equipped to receive and **handle** crates weighing 200 to 300kg.*

marchandise *nf* goods, commodity, merchandise
USAGE *'Marchandise' is used commonly in both the* Singular *and the* Plural *without any difference in meaning.*
• La **marchandise** est prête à être expédiée par colis postaux avion, comme vous le souhaitez. - *The **goods** are ready to be dispatched ...*
• Les **marchandises** ont été embarquées à Bordeaux le 10 novembre 19--. - *The **goods** were loaded ...*

marché *nm* market, sale; bargain, contract
• La maison CIE **lance sur le marché** les équipements hydrauliques MF. - *CIE is **launching on the market/putting on sale** MF hydraulic equipment.*
• Nous connaissons parfaitement le **marché** français et en particulier le **marché** des tissus pour vêtements féminins. - ... *the French **market** and in particular the **market** in fabrics for ladies' wear.*
• ... et d'autre part, le **Marché Commun** ne fait que rendre le problème plus vivant. - ... *and furthermore, the **Common Market** only makes the problem more pressing.*
• Nous allons prendre contact avec cette maison pour voir si elle est décidée à passer un **marché** plus important. - ... *if they are prepared to conclude a bigger **bargain/contract**.*
• ... nous donner les 1.250 appareils restant à livrer sur le **marché** en cours. - ... *remaining to be delivered against the current **contract**.*

mardi *nm* Tuesday *See* lundi

marge *nf* margin
• Inutile de souligner l'intérêt que présente pour nos clients cette fabrication, leur permettant une **marge** bénéficiaire plus élevée. - *We hardly need stress the importance which this product has for our customers, allowing them a larger profit **margin**.*

maritime *adj* marine, sea, [shipping]
COLLOCATES *agence, assurance, caisse, commerce, droit, emballage, fret, gare, ligne, navigation, port, risque, trafic, transport, voie*
• Nous avons l'intention d'envoyer la collection **par voie maritime** ... - ... ***by sea** ...*
• Nous avons demandé les prix de transport **maritime** à notre affréteur. - ... *the prices of **marine** transport/ transport **by sea** ...*

marquage *nm* marking
• Nous savons que Monsieur X de notre Service Courses s'occupe du **marquage** des pneus. - *We know Mr X of our Racing Department is taking care of the **marking** of the tyres.*

marque *nf* mark; brand, make
• De votre côté, voulez-vous bien nous faire connaître les **marques** à apposer sur la caisse ... - ... *the **marks** to be put on the crate ...*
• Nous vous prions de noter que ces pièces devront porter obligatoirement en creux votre **marque de fabrique** et notre repère. - ... *these items should be impressed with your **trade mark** and our identification mark.*
• Ainsi que la plupart des sociétés productrices de pneumatiques, nous ne garantissons pas les produits de notre **marque** en cours d'usage. - *Like most tyre manufacturers, we do not guarantee the products of our **make/ brand** while in use.*

marquer *vt* mark, record, register, signify

• Nous vous laissons donc toutes facultés pour **marquer** les paquets comme bon vous semblera. - ... *to mark the bundles as you see fit.*

• Nous **marquons** notre accord sur les différents points soulevés. - *We hereby signify/register our agreement regarding the various points raised.*

• **Nous vous marquons notre étonnement** de n'avoir pas encore reçu le règlement de ces articles. - *We are very surprised not to have received payment yet for these articles.*

mars *nm* March

matériau *nm* (construction) material
USAGE *'Matériau' is used of building materials (stone, cement, etc), i.e. materials to be used specifically in building and civil engineering. 'Matière' is the general word for raw materials. 'Matériel' nm, on the other hand, usually corresponds to* Eng *'equipment' rather than 'material', except in the restricted sense of the tools of someone's trade, e.g. 'matériel de bureau/d'artiste'* ('office/artist's *materials').*

• Vos **matériaux** seront agréés par le représentant du maître de l'oeuvre. - *Your materials will be approved by the representative of the main contractor.*

matériel *nm* equipment, plant
USAGE See *'matériau'.*

• Nous sommes spécialisés dans le **matériel** de grandes cuisines. - *We specialize in equipment for large kitchens.*

matière *nf* material; [as regards]
USAGE See *'matériau'.*

• Le couteau ne tourne qu'à 255 tours/minute; il n'y a donc pas d'échauffement, pas de perte de

matière non plus. - *The blade revolves at only 255 rpm; there is therefore no overheating, no loss of material either.*

• Nos activités se bornent à l'exportation de **matières premières** pour la fabrication de l'acide tartrique. - *Our activity is limited to exporting raw materials for the manufacture of tartaric acid.*

• Nous pensons tout spécialement à CIE dont nous connaissons les goûts **en matière de** vanille. - ... *whose tastes we know as regards vanilla.*

matin *nm* morning
USAGE *For 'matin' versus 'matinée', see Usage Note for 'journée'.*

• Nous avons reçu **ce matin**, lundi 20, un coup de téléphone de M. X.

• Puisque vous arriverez **le matin du 8** par le train de nuit, - *Since you will arrive on the morning of the 8th by the night train, ...*

• Malheureusement, je ne serai pas libre le 12 avril **au matin** ... - *Unfortunately, I shall not be free on the 12th April in the morning ...*

• Je vous enverrai chercher vers **10h du matin**. - *I will send a car for you about 10 o'clock in the morning.*

• M. X serait à votre disposition dès **lundi matin**. - ... *from Monday morning.*

matinée *nf* morning
USAGE *For 'matinée' versus 'matin' see Usage Note for 'journée'.*

• Il nous serait possible par contre de vous recevoir au cours de la **matinée** de ce même vendredi 14 avril. - ... *to receive you in the course of the morning of that same Friday, 14 April.*

maximum (*Plural* -ums *or* -a) *nm & adj* maximum, utmost

• Nous vous serions très obligés de bien vouloir faire **le maximum** pour éviter toutes dépenses inutiles. - ...

*to do **your utmost** to avoid unnecessary expenses.*

• . . . et, en 6mm de largeur, l'épaisseur **maximum** ne sera que de 2 à 2,5mm. - . . . *the **maximum** thickness will be only 2 to 2.5mm.*

• Il nous intéresserait vivement de connaître les longueurs **maxima** que vous pouvez fournir . . . - . . . *the **maximum** lengths you can supply . . .*

• Nous vous demandons de bien vouloir réduire **au maximum** la livraison des MF. - . . . *to reduce **as much as possible** delivery of the MF's.*

mécontent, -e *adj* displeased, dissatisfied

• Le client, évidemment fort **mécontent**, maintiendra l'annulation de la commande . . . - *The customer, obviously very **dissatisfied**, will stand by the cancellation of the order . . .*

meilleur, -e *adj* better, best, lowest
COLLOCATES *attention, conditions, convenance, délai, offre, prix, souhaits, soin, solution*
USAGE *The context sometimes dictates that 'meilleur' is to be taken in the sense of 'keenest', 'most competitive', etc, for example with 'prix' or 'conditions'. Elsewhere, it simply adds a note of politeness or deference, as in the second example.*

• Nous nous tenons à votre entière disposition pour vous adresser nos **meilleurs** prix . . .

• Je suis à votre disposition pour vous voir **à votre meilleure convenance**. - . . . *to see you **at your convenience**.*

membre *nm* member

même *pro & adj & adv* same; very, even; [similarly, likewise, in a position to]

• Vous voudrez bien nous faire savoir si le texte précédent, accepté

par vous, restera **le même** cette année. - . . . *whether the preceding text, accepted by you, will remain **the same** this year.*

• Si les **mêmes** ennuis devaient se reproduire, le client retournerait l'ensemble. - *If the **same** difficulties were to arise again, . . .*

• Pour cette raison **même**, ces miels sont fort appréciés par le consommateur belge. - *For that **very** reason, these honeys are very popular with Belgian consumers.*

• En effet, nous n'avons pas réussi à implanter cet appareil, **même** après votre campagne de publicité. - *We have not succeeded in establishing this appliance on the market, **even** after your advertising campaign.*

• **De même**, vous vous substituez complètement à l'entrepreneur . . . - *Similarly/Likewise, you substitute completely for the contractor . . .*

• Si vous croyez être **à même de** prendre des ordres sur cette base, veuillez nous le faire connaître. - *If you think you are **in a position to** take orders on this basis, . . .*

mémoire *nf* memory; [for your information]

• Je vous envoie enfin, **pour mémoire**, la liste des différentes capacités des présentations de la maison CIE. - *Finally I am sending you, **for your information**, the list . . .*

mention *nf* annotation, mark, mention

• Ces plans ne portent désormais plus la **mention** 'provisoire'. - *These drawings no longer bear the **annotation**/are no longer marked 'provisional'.*

• Nous n'avons jamais reçu la commande dont votre lettre **fait mention**. - *We have never received the order which your letter **mentions**.*

mentionner *vt* mention
• En effet, nous sommes parfaitement d'accord pour acquitter les frais que vous **mentionnez** dans votre lettre. - ... *to pay the costs which you mention* ...

merci *inter* thanks, thank you
• J'aimerais vous lire. **Merci d'avance**. - ... *Thank you in anticipation.*

mercredi *nm* Wednesday *See* 'lundi'

mesure *nf* measure; [in a position to, extent, as far as, in so far as, insomuch as]
• Monsieur X veut d'autre part établir des comparaisons entre les **mesures** anglaises et françaises de résistance à l'abrasion. - ... *to make some comparisons between the English and French measures for resistance to abrasion.*
• Nous vous préviendrons lorsque nous serons **en mesure de** discuter de votre offre ... - ... *when we are in a position to have discussions about your offer* ...
• La spécification nous sera soumise pour voir **dans quelle mesure** nous pourrons aider à l'approvisionnement des matériaux nécessaires. - ... *to see to what extent we shall be able to assist in providing the necessary materials.*
• Pour éliminer ce risque, **dans (toute) la mesure du possible**, nous avons intercalé dans l'emballage une protection supplémentaire. - *To eliminate this risk, as far as possible, we have inserted* ...
• **Dans la mesure où** nous pouvons vous aider, pourquoi ne pas avoir recours à nous? - *In so far as/ Insomuch as we can help you, why not call upon our assistance?*

méthode *nf* method
• Monsieur X, qui s'occupera de l'industrie, va passer la journée de mercredi à l'usine pour confirmer ses **méthodes** de vente. - ... *to consolidate his sales methods.*

mettre *vt* place, put, take
TENSES Pres 1 *mets* 3 *met* 4 *mettons* 6 *mettent* Imp *mettais* Fut *mettrai* PP *mis, -e* Pres Part *mettant* Subj *1,3 mette 4 mettions 6 mettent*
• ... car il est anormal que la marchandise **mette** autant de temps à arriver à Paris. - ... *for it is unusual for goods to take so long to reach Paris.*

mieux *adv* better
• Nous vous adressons notre catalogue qui vous permettra de **mieux situer** les articles de notre fabrication. - ... *which will enable you to get a better idea of the articles we manufacture.*

mieux *nm* best, the best thing
• En ce qui concerne CIE, **le mieux serait** évidemment d'écrire à M. X. - *As regards CIE, clearly the best thing would be/it would be best to write to Mr X.*

minimum (*Plural* -ums *or* -a) *nm & adj* minimum
• Notre prix de F85 CIF est le **minimum** que nous puissions faire dans la conjoncture actuelle. - ... *is the minimum we can manage in the current state of the market.*
• ... et le remboursement des droits et des taxes va demander au **minimum** 6 mois. - ... *and the reimbursement of the duties and taxes will require at least 6 months.*
• Il y a lieu d'envisager une dépense supplémentaire **minimum** de F123. - *We need to reckon on a minimum additional expenditure of 123 francs.*

• Il est bien entendu que ces chiffres sont approximatifs et considérés comme des **minima**. - *These figures are of course approximate and considered as **minima**.*

modalité nf method, mode
COLLOCATES *de livraison, de paiement*
USAGE *A synonym of 'mode' nm, the latter being much the commoner of the two.*

• Vous trouverez ci-joint les caractéristiques de nos panneaux, ainsi que les **modalités** de livraison. - *... together with the **methods** of delivery.*

mode nm method, mode
COLLOCATES *de coopération, d'emploi, d'expédition, de livraison, de manutention, de preuve, de recouvrement, de transport*
• Nous vous prions de bien vouloir nous indiquer votre **mode** de règlement. - *... your **method** of payment.*

modèle nm design, model, pattern, type
• La marchandise serait expédiée sur palettes de 1m par 1m d'un **modèle** agréé par la SNCF. - *... on pallets 1m by 1m of a **design/pattern/ type** approved by the SNCF.*
• Malheureusement ce **modèle**, dont nous équipions les sièges MF, se trouve abandonné. - *Unfortunately this **model** (of slide bars), with which we used to fit the MF car seats, has been discontinued.*

modification nf alteration, modification
• ... il ne nous est plus possible d'accepter la **modification** demandée par votre client en ce qui concerne la longueur des canons. - *... the **alteration/modification** requested by*

your customer as regards the length of the barrels.
• ... certaines **modifications** ont été apportées au cahier des charges initial. - *... certain **modifications** have been made to the original specification.*

modifier vt adjust, alter, modify
• Nous restons dans l'attente des contrats **modifiés**. - *We await the **modified** contracts.*

moindre adj lesser, least, slightest
• La comparaison est évidemmement faite avec des machines de **moindre** importance. - *Clearly the comparison is being made with machines of **lesser** size.*
• ... car nous ne voyons pas la **moindre** chance pour cette firme de négocier la vente de nos produits. - *... for we cannot see the **slightest** chance for this firm to negotiate the sale of our products.*

moins less, fewer, [at least]
USAGE *'Moins de' introduces an expression of quantity and means 'up to but excluding', as in the first example. 'Moins que' introduces a comparison, as in the second example.*
• Toutefois les frais d'envoi de **moins de** 5.000 pièces sont à la charge du client. - *However the forwarding costs for **less/fewer than** 5000 are chargeable to the customer.*
• Ce lot est nettement **moins** beau **que** le précédent. - *This batch is distinctly **less** fine **than** the previous one.*
• Ces prix s'entendent F.O.B. Bordeaux **moins** escompte 3¹/₄. - *These prices are FOB Bordeaux **less** discount 3¹/₄.*
• Durée de validité de votre offre, **au moins** 2 mois. - *Duration of validity of your offer **at least** 2 months.*

mois nm month

- Délai de livraison: 4/5 **mois** env. à dater de . . . - *Delivery: 4/5 **months** approx. from . . .*
- J'ai été heureux d'apprendre que vous envisagez de revenir à Paris **au mois de mai prochain**. - *. . . to return to Paris **next May**.*

moitié *nf* half
- Nous prenons à notre charge plus de la **moitié** de votre commission. - *We are bearing the cost of more than **half** of your commission.*
- Il serait souhaitable que pour une prochaine commande ces délais soient réduits au moins **de moitié**. - *. . . that these times should be reduced at least **by half**.*

moment *nm* moment, time, [at present, now; ripe]
- En conséquence, CIE est **en ce moment** à la recherche d'une organisation commerciale . . . - *Consequently, CIE is **at present/at the moment/just now** looking for a commercial organization . . .*
- Il était **à ce moment** trop tard pour enregistrer régulièrement votre commande. - *It was **at that time/by then** too late to book your order properly.*
- Nous vous demandons donc **pour le moment** de bien vouloir patienter encore quelque temps . . . - *We ask you therefore **for the moment/for now/ for the time being** to wait a little longer . . .*
- En examinant le dossier en question, nous constatons qu'**au moment où nous vous écrivons** cette affaire n'a plus eu de suite. - *. . ., we note that **at the time of writing** this matter has come to nothing.*
- Nous vous serions reconnaissants de bien vouloir nous indiquer **à quel moment** vous pensez nous faire expédier notre commande citée plus

haut. - *. . . inform us **when you are** expecting to dispatch our abovementioned order.*
- **Le moment venu**, il nous sera facile de vous donner des références de tout premier ordre. - ***When the time comes/is ripe**, we can easily give you first-class references.*

momentanément *adv* temporarily, for the moment
- . . . et d'autre part notre bureau technique est **momentanément** fort surchargé par d'importantes commandes . . . - *. . . and furthermore our technical department is **temporarily/for the moment** very overloaded with large orders . . .*

monde *nm* world; [everybody, everyone]
- Étant donné la grande importance de votre firme, vous avez probablement toute l'année des visiteurs du **monde entier**. - *. . . visitors from **all over the world**.*
- Je pense que **tout le monde** doit s'en féliciter. - *I think **everybody** must be pleased.*

mondial, -e (*mpl* -iaux) *adj* world, world-wide
- Présentée pour la première fois sur le marché **mondial** par notre maison, cette fabrication est . . . - *Presented for the first time on the **world** market by our company, this product is . . .*
- Parmi nos références figurent des firmes de réputation **mondiale**, notamment CIE, . . . - *Among our references are firms enjoying a **world-wide** reputation, notably CIE, . . .*

monnaie *nf* currency
- . . . car nous croyons que cette **monnaie**-là n'a pas suivi la dévaluation de la livre sterling. - *. . . since we do not think that **currency** has*

followed the devaluation of the pound sterling.

monsieur (*Plural* messieurs) *nm* gentleman

• . . . et l'essentiel est que vous ayez pu avoir avec ces **messieurs** des entretiens intéressants pour les deux parties. - *The main thing is that you should have been able to have with these **gentlemen** talks which were useful for both parties.*

montant *nm* amount, value
USAGE *'Montant' and 'somme' are not fully interchangeable. Whereas 'somme' denotes simply a quantity of money, 'montant' denotes the total value of something, for example an order, invoice or goods. The following example brings out the contrast: 'Sauf erreur, vous restez nous devoir la **somme** de F.390, **montant** de notre facture No 123 du 31 janvier 19--.'.*

• Nous vous accusons également réception de votre chèque bancaire de F.800 réglant le **montant** de votre souscription. - *. . . settling the **amount** of your subscription.*

• Au contrôle de nos écritures, nous constatons que le **montant** de cette facture était de F.1700, alors que votre versement s'est élevé à 1100. - *On checking our accounts, we find that the **amount/value** of this invoice was 1700 francs, whereas . . .*

• Nous accusons réception de votre virement susmentionné dont le **montant** a été porté au crédit de votre compte. - *We acknowledge receipt of your above-mentioned transfer, the **value** of which has been credited to your account.*

montage *nm* assembly

monter *vt* assemble, put together

moyen *nm* means

• Veuillez avoir l'obligeance de nous adresser rapidement cet arriéré par le **moyen** à votre convenance: chèque bancaire, . . . - *Please be so good as to send us these arrears quickly by the **means** which suit your convenience: cheque, . . .*

moyen, -enne *adj & nf* average, medium

• La charge **moyenne** par palette serait de 1.500kg. - *The **average** load per pallet . . .*

• Par le truchement d'une société spécialisée dans le contact avec les affaires de **moyenne** importance, j'ai vraisemblablement la possibilité de . . . - *With the help of a company specializing in contact with businesses of **medium** size. . .*

moyennant *prep* for, in return for
• Nous nous efforcerons de nous rapprocher au maximum des cotes demandées par votre client avec une tolérance d'environ 3mm, **moyennant** un supplément de Frs.B.123. - *. . . **for** a supplement of 123 Belgian francs.*

multiple *adj* multiple
• . . . il désirait ne pas brouiller ses propres cartes en ayant de **multiples** contacts en même temps. - *. . . he did not wish to get his cards mixed up by having **multiple** contacts (with prospective business partners) at the same time.*

mutuel, -elle *adj* mutual
• En espérant que cette formule nous permettra de raffermir une collaboration **mutuelle** efficace. - *Hoping that this arrangement will permit us to strengthen an efficient **mutual** collaboration.*

N

nature *nf* nature, [such as to]
• J'ai indiqué à M. X la **nature** des informations dont j'avais besoin . . . - . . . *the **nature** of the information . . .*
• . . . une offre qui pourrait être **de nature à intéresser** un des membres de votre compagnie. - *. . ., an offer which could be **such as to interest/ which could interest** one of the members of your company.*

naturellement *adv* naturally
• De ce fait certaines de ces maisons risquent peut-être d'être un peu montées contre nous et il y aura lieu **naturellement** de faire preuve de beaucoup de diplomatie dans cette affaire. - *Because of this, some of these firms may be a little annoyed with us and **naturally** it will be as well to be very diplomatic in this matter.*

navire *nm* boat, ship, vessel
• Pour votre gouverne, nous vous prions de bien vouloir noter que le prochain **navire** au départ de Marseille est le SS X du 18 novembre 19--. - *. . . the next **ship** leaving Marseille . . .*

navré, -ée (de) *adj* annoyed, (very) sorry
• Nous sommes évidemment extrêmement **navrés de** ces ennuis . . . parce qu'ils nous font perdre une commande . . . - *We are obviously extremely **annoyed by** these difficulties . . .*
• Nous sommes **navrés de** ce malentendu: en effet, nous sommes parfaitement d'accord pour acquitter les frais que vous mentionnez dans votre lettre. - *We are **very sorry about** this misunderstanding and are perfectly agreeable to paying the costs mentioned in your letter.*

néanmoins *adv* nevertheless, nonetheless, yet
• Nous savons que vous vous êtes mis d'accord avec vos représentants. **Néanmoins**, pour la bonne règle, nous aimerions avoir une confirmation de votre part. - *We know that you have reached an agreement with your agents. **Nevertheless**, to keep everything above board. . . .*
• Il m'est donc impossible d'établir une offre raisonnable mais, **néanmoins**, je me permets de souligner les points suivants: . . . - *It is therefore impossible for me to put together a reasonable offer but, **nevertheless**, I should like to emphasize the following points: . . .*

nécessaire *adj & nm* necessary, needed; [arrange, ensure]
USAGE *Notice 'nécessaire **à** + Noun Phrase' (first example) versus 'nécessaire **pour** + Infinitive' (second example). The impersonal 'il est nécessaire' introduces either 'de + Infinitive' or 'que + Subjunctive' (third example). 'Faire le nécessaire' introduces either 'pour + Infinitive' or 'pour que + Subjunctive' (fourth example).*
• Nous vous adressons ce jour les bandes-adresses **nécessaires à** l'expédition de ces imprimés. - *. . . the addressed wrappers **necessary/needed for** the dispatch of this printed matter.*
• Ces factures pro-forma sont **nécessaires pour** faire établir le paiement préalable par notre banque. - *These pro-forma invoices are **necessary for** having payment arranged in advance by our bank.*

• Faisant suite à votre demande, nous vous signalons qu'**il n'est pas nécessaire de** retourner/**il n'est pas nécessaire que** vous nous retourniez les deux photos. - *. . . it is not necessary for you to return . . . .*

• Veuillez prévenir votre assurance et **faire le nécessaire** pour effectuer le remplacement. - *Please advise your insurers and **arrange/do what is necessary** to make the replacement./ **ensure** the replacement is made.*

nécessité *nf* necessity

• L'expérience du chantier déterminera la **nécessité** de l'application de cette clause. - *Experience on site will decide whether this clause **need** be applied.*

nécessiter *vt* call for, necessitate, require

• Les derniers appareils que vous nous avez envoyés fonctionnent, mais leur utilisation **nécessite** des précautions toutes particulières. - *. . ., but their use **calls for/necessitates/requires** quite exceptional precautions.*

négatif, -ive *adj* negative

• Peu de jours après nous avons reçu de CIE une réponse **négative**.

négociation *nf* negotiation

• Crédit ouvert pour la durée totale de l'embarquement plus 15 jours pour nous permettre la **négociation** des documents. - *Credit open for the full duration of loading plus 15 days to allow us **to negotiate** the documents.*

négocier *vt* negotiate

• . . . car nous ne voyons pas la moindre chance pour cette firme de **négocier** la vente de nos produits. - *. . . for we cannot see the slightest chance for this firm to **negotiate** the sale of our products.*

net, nette *adj & adv* net, nett

• Poids **net** du produit: 790 grammes. - *Net weight of the product: 790 grammes.*

• Nous avons vendu à Messieurs CIE sur la base d'un prix **net**, alors que nous devons encore vous réserver 11% de commission sur ces prix. - *We sold to CIE on the basis of a net price, . . .*

• Notre facture du 3 décembre 19--, vous débitant pour la somme **nette** convenue de F.1.650, vous a été transmise sous pli fermé. - *. . ., debiting you for the agreed net sum of 1650 francs, . . .*

nettement *adv* clearly, distinctly; markedly, decidedly

• Il est important que le principe du montant de votre rémunération soit **nettement** indiqué dès le départ. - *It is important that the principle of the value of your remuneration should be **clearly** stated at the outset.*

• . . . nous pouvons vous offrir un article de remplacement **nettement** supérieur comme suit: . . . - *. . . an alternative article which is **markedly** superior as follows: . . .*

neuf, -ve *adj* new; [overhaul, recondition(-ing), refurbish(-ment), repair]

USAGE *The normal translation equivalent of Eng 'new' is 'nouveau'. 'Neuf' is used only in the sense of 'brand new or hardly used; in mint condition'. It follows the noun, e.g. 'une voiture neuve', 'a (brand) new car'.*

• Après avoir examiné soigneusement cette arme, nous vous informons que le montant de sa **remise à neuf** s'élèverait à FrB.123 . . . - *. . . we have to inform you that its **overhaul** would cost 123 Belgian francs . . .*

niveau (*Plural* -aux) *nm* level

• Le marché anglais est actuellement très calme, ce qui motive un **niveau** de prix relativement bas. - *The UK market is at present very quiet, resulting in a relatively low **level** of prices.*

nom *nm* name; [make out to]
• Par un prochain courrier nous vous indiquerons **leurs nom et adresse**. - . . . *we shall inform you of their name and address.*
• Ce règlement pourra s'effectuer: soit par chèque bancaire **au nom de** CIE, soit . . . - . . . *either by cheque in the name of/made out to CIE, or . . .*

nombre *nm* number, quantity
COLLOCATES *bon, certain, grand* (all before the noun); *élevé, important, (non) négligeable, raisonnable, suffisant* (all after the noun)
USAGE See '*numéro*'.
• . . . mais nous aimerions connaître au préalable le **nombre** d'appareils qui vous seraient nécessaires. - . . . *the number of appliances which you would need.*
• Anciens catalogues MF: nous notons que vous avez retrouvé **un certain nombre de** ces exemplaires et . . . - *Old MF catalogues: we note that you have discovered **a quantity of** these copies and . . .*

nombreux, -euses *adj* many, numerous
USAGE '*De nombreux*', rather than '*beaucoup de*', is the usual translation equivalent of Eng '*many*' in business letters.
• Nous exportons aussi dans **de nombreux** pays étrangers, . . . - *We also export to **many** foreign countries, . . .*

nomenclature *nf* list, nomenclature
• Vous aurez à joindre à votre offre une **nomenclature** précisant les

types et nombres de briques nécessaires. - . . . *a **list** of the types and quantities of bricks needed.*

non *adv* not; [excluding; either, neither]
• Il s'agissait d'un prix CIF Durban et **non** d'un prix FOB le Havre. - *It involved a price CIF Durban and **not** FOB le Havre.*
• Voulez-vous avoir l'obligeance de nous faire savoir s'il y a lieu d'assurer ou **non** la marchandise. - . . . *whether we are to insure the goods or **not**.*
• Prix: veuillez nous remettre des prix pour marchandise rendue franco frontière française, **non** dédouanée, . . . - . . . *for goods delivered free to the French frontier, **not** cleared through customs, . . .*
• Nos conditions sont les suivantes: . . . votre commission **non comprise**. - *Our terms are the following: . . . your commission **not included/excluding** your commission.*
• Il n'y a donc pas d'échauffement, pas de perte de matière **non plus**. - *There is no overheating* (in a cutting process), *and no loss of material **either**.*

normal, -e (*mpl* -aux) *adj* normal, usual
• . . . prestations partiellement en dehors des heures **normales**. - . . . *services rendered partly outside **normal** hours.*

normalement *adv* normally, usually
• Aussi, pouvez-vous m'indiquer quel serait **normalement** le délai de livraison pour . . . - . . . *what would delivery **normally/usually** be for . . .*
• Après remontage, cet outillage semblait fonctionner **normalement**. - *After reassembly, this equipment appeared to be working **normally**.*

norme *nf* standard
• Votre offre doit être . . . et répondra en outre aux **normes** suivantes: . . . - *Your offer should be . . . and will furthermore comply with the following* **standards:** *. . .*

notamment *adv* notably, in particular
• Nous vous référons à notre correspondance antérieure et **notamment** à votre lettre du 5 courant concernant . . .

note *nf* note
COLLOCATES *de colisage, de crédit, de débit*
• Ci-joint, vous trouverez une **note** qui expose brièvement les buts et les activités de notre organisation européenne. - *. . . a* **note** *setting out in brief. . . .*
• . . . et vous recevrez incessamment notre **note** de crédit pour un montant de F123. - *. . . and you will receive shortly our credit* **note** *to the value of 123 francs.*
• Nous vous remercions de votre lettre du 10 octobre et vous assurons que nous **avons pris bonne note** de son contenu. - *. . . that we* **have taken good note** *of its contents.*

noter *vt* note, take note of
• Nous **avons bien noté** toutes les indications relatives au marquage des cartons et . . . - *We* **have taken good note of** *all the instructions regarding the marking of the cartons and . . .*
• Veuillez **noter que** le client annule provisoirement sa commande.

notice *nf* information sheet, instructions sheet, leaflet
• J'ai également bien reçu votre **notice** concernant les casiers-palettes. - *. . . your* **information sheet** *concerning the pallet racks.*

nouveau, -elle (*mpl* -eaux) *adj* new, fresh, further, repeat; [again]
USAGE *'Nouveau' takes the form 'nouvel' before a masculine Noun beginning with a vowel or a 'mute h', e.g. 'un* **nouvel** *hôtel'. 'Nouveau' occasionally follows the Noun, without any change in the sense, but it much more often precedes it. In the second example, post-position of the Adjective points up the contrast between new companies and those which have gone bankrupt.*
• Nous vous serions obligés de bien vouloir nous envoyer quelques échantillons de la **nouvelle** brique MF. - *. . . if you would send us a few samples of the new MF brick.*
• En Belgique, pour l'année 19--, il a été enregistré 1.100 faillites et il s'est constitué plus de 1.200 sociétés **nouvelles**. - *. . . and more than 1200 new companies were set up.*
• Dès que votre **nouveau** catalogue sera paru, je vous serais reconnaissant de bien vouloir nous l'adresser. - *As soon as your new catalogue comes out, . . .*
• Comme indiqué au téléphone, nous vous avons adressé hier une **nouvelle** commande de 75 tonnes . . . - *. . ., we sent you yesterday a new/ further order for 75 tons . . .*
• Nous vous remercions **à nouveau** pour votre ordre. - *Thank you* **again** *for your order.*

nouvelle *nf* (piece of) news
• Cette **nouvelle** m'a beaucoup surpris, et profondément déçu. - *This* **piece of news** *surprised me greatly, and disappointed me profoundly.*
• Dans l'attente de **vos nouvelles**, . . . - *Looking forward to* **hearing from you**, *. . .*

novembre *nm* November

nul, nulle *adj* null (and void)

• En conséquence nous vous prions de considérer comme **nulle** la facture précitée, laquelle doit être remplacée par celle rectificative incluse. - *Consequently please consider the aforementioned invoice as **null and void**, . . .*

nullement *adv* in no way, not in the least, by no means; [what(so)ever]

• Nous avons réalisé un bénéfice sur ce transport plus élevé que normalement, mais **nullement** exagéré eu égard à nos frais et prestations. - *We made a profit on this transport, which was higher than usual but **in no way** excessive having regard to the costs and the services we provided.*

• Vous comprendrez facilement donc que nous n'avons **nullement** l'intention de renouveler cette expérience dans les jours à venir. - *So you will readily understand that we have no intention **what(so)ever** of repeating the experience. . .*

numéro *nm* number; issue

USAGE *'Numéro' is used in phrases such as '**numéro** de téléphone/du compte/de la rue/du journal', viz where it identifies one member of a set of things. 'Nombre', on the other hand, means 'number', in the sense of 'a quantity', e.g. 'un grand* **nombre** de pièces'.

• A propos de cette affaire, nous constatons que nous lui avons affecté par erreur deux **numéros** de référence NP73 et NP80. - *. . . that we have mistakenly given it two reference **numbers** NP73 and NP80.*

• Le dernier **numéro**, qui devait être mis en vente le 9 courant, est arrivé le 14 dans l'après-midi. - *The last **issue**. which should have been put on sale on the 9th, arrived on the 14th in the afternoon.*

numéroter *vt* number

• En vue d'éviter des difficultés à votre client, nous **avons numéroté** cet ensemble 847, soit le même numéro que celui de la carabine originale. - *. . ., we **have numbered** this set of parts 847, i.e. the same number as that of the original rifle.*

O

objet *nm* object, purpose, subject; re.; [covered by]

• L'**objet** de cette lettre est de vous mettre au courant d'un contact imprévu que je viens d'avoir . . . - *The purpose/object of this letter is to tell you about an unexpected contact I have just made . . .*

• **Objet**: notre demande de prix 123. - *Re:/Subject: our request for prices no 123.* (Placed at the head of a letter.)

• Nous avons le plus urgent besoin des matériels **objet de/faisant l'objet de** notre commande 123 du 3 octobre dernier. - *. . . the materials covered by our order . . .*

• . . . notre facture des calendriers 19-- **a fait l'objet d'un double règlement**. - *. . . our invoice for the 19--calendars has been paid twice.*

• Quoiqu'il en soit, votre courrier **a fait l'objet de** toute notre attention et . . . - *Be that as it may, your letter has been given our closest attention and . . .*

obligation *nf* obligation
COLLOCATES s'acquitter de, avoir, se conformer à, contracter, dépasser, se faire, faire honneur à, remplir; se soustraire à: imposer; délier de, libérer de

• Aussi, est-ce dans cet ordre d'idées que nous nous voyons **dans l'obligation de** vous alerter. - *Therefore, it is in this connection that we find ourselves obliged to alert you.*

obligatoire *adj* compulsary, obligatory

• Vous comprendrez qu'il est absolument **obligatoire** que vous nous expédiiez au moins une plate-forme au plus tard le 20 avril. - *. . . it is absolutely obligatory/imperative that you dispatch at least one platform on 20 April at the latest.*

obligeance *nf* kindness, consideration, [be so kind, be so good, oblige]

• Nous vous remercions à l'avance de votre **obligeance** habituelle. - *. . . for your usual kindness/consideration.*

• **Veuillez avoir l'obligeance de** nous faire savoir si vous désirez remettre offre pour ce navire. - *Please oblige us by/Please be so kind as to inform us whether you wish to tender for this vessel.*

obliger (de/à) *vt* oblige, [grateful]; compel, force, oblige, [bound to]
TENSES See *changer*

• Nous vous serions **très obligés** de nous faire parvenir votre offre au plus tôt. - *We should be very grateful/much obliged if you would send us your offer as soon as possible.*

• Cette affaire étant très urgente, vous nous **obligeriez** en nous faisant parvenir votre cotation par retour du courrier, si possible. - *. . ., you would oblige us by sending us your quotation by return, if possible.*

• Une prompte réponse nous **obligerait**.

• Cependant, je **suis obligé de** vous tenir au courant de certaines difficultés . . . - *However, I am bound/compelled/obliged to keep you informed of certain difficulties . . .*

• Vous savez que la détérioration de l'ensemble du risque automobile **oblige** les compagnies d'assurance à une surveillance accrue de ces contrats. - *You know that the deterioration of the whole of the motor vehicle risk is compelling/forcing/obliging insurance companies to keep a close watch on these contracts.*

observation *nf* observation, remark
• Nous vous retournerons un de ces exemplaires muni de notre cachet ou de nos **observations** éventuelles. - *We will return to you one of these copies with our stamp signifying agreement or with any **observations/remarks** we may have.*

observer *vt* observe
• Cependant, l'humidité **observée** de 18% est élevée et nous désirons qu'elle ne dépasse pas 10 à 12%. - *However, the **observed** humidity of 18% is high and ...*

obtenir *vt* get, obtain, secure
TENSES See *venir*
• Si vous pouvez proposer ce prix, nous essaierons d'**obtenir** une commande d'essai de 20 à 40 tonnes. - *..., we shall try to **get/secure** a trial order ...*
• ... et je suis de plus en plus persuadé que nous **obtiendrons** de bons résultats car l'intérêt des clients est certain. - *... and I am more and more convinced that we **shall get** good results ...*
• Le client serait prêt à payer un petit supplément pour **obtenir** satisfaction. - *... to **obtain** satisfaction.*

occasion *nf* occasion; opportunity, chance; bargain, [second-hand, used]
COLLOCATES *se présenter; avoir, laisser passer, manquer, profiter de, saisir; donner*
• Je retournerai le voir vendredi prochain. J'espère avoir **à cette occasion** le plaisir de vous rencontrer. - *... I hope **on that occasion** to have the pleasure of meeting you.*
• Néanmoins, nous serons heureux d'avoir votre visite **à l'occasion d'**un

de vos voyages en France. - *... **on the occasion of** one of your trips to France.*
• Aurez-vous l'**occasion** de venir en France cette année? - *Will you have the **opportunity/chance** to come to France this year?*
• Nous profitons de cette **occasion** pour vous demander si vous n'avez pas une édition plus récente ... - *We take this **opportunity** of asking you ...*
• ... une insertion publicitaire dans le bulletin mensuel des véhicules d'**occasion**. - *... an advertisement in the monthly bulletin of **second-hand/used** vehicles.*

occasionner *vt* cause, give rise to, occasion
COLLOCATES *dégâts, dérangements, difficultés, ennuis, frais, retard, risque*
• Nous vous signalons que nous avons pris à notre compte les frais **occasionnés** par le remplacement de ces deux pièces. - *... we have borne the costs **arising from** replacing these two parts.*

occuper *vt* occupy, [busy, engaged in]
• Notre Société **occupe** un local de 800 mètres carrés environ, ... - *Our company **occupies** premises measuring 800 square metres approximately, ...*
• Nous sommes actuellement **occupés** à mettre ce plan à jour pour les petits détails. - *We are at present **busy/engaged in** bringing this drawing up to date as regards the small details.*

s'occuper de *vpro* attend to, concern oneself with, deal with, handle, look after, see to, take care of, take on
• Nous **nous occupons** uniquement de la vente sur Paris. - *We just **attend to/concern ourselves with** sales in Paris.*

• Nous savons que Monsieur X de notre Service Courses **s'occupe du** marquage des pneus. - *We know Mr X of our Racing Department is attending to the marking of the tyres.*

octobre *nm* October

oeuvre *nf* (*In* 'mettre tout en oeuvre' do one's best/utmost)
• Soyez assurés que nous **mettrons tout en oeuvre** afin de vous satisfaire. - *Rest assured that we shall do our utmost to satisfy you.*

officiel, -ielle *adj* official
• J'ai besoin que vous me fassiez parvenir de toute urgence une lettre **officielle** précisant que vous êtes d'accord pour remplacer le matériel ... - ... *an official letter stating that you agree to replace the material* ...

offre *nf* offer, quotation, [quote]
COLLOCATES *adresser, confirmer, établir, faire, remettre, soumettre; accepter, décliner, recevoir*
• Veuillez nous faire votre meilleure **offre** pour le matériel selon spécification ci-après.
• Il m'est donc impossible d'établir une **offre** raisonnable.
• ... si nous pouvions lui **faire une offre au prix de** 300 Fr. français les 1.000kg, il pourrait nous passer commande. - ... *if we could quote him 300 French francs per 1000kg, he could order from us.*

offrir *vt* offer, quote
TENSES Pres *1,3* offre *4* offrons *6* offrent Imp *offrais* Fut *offrirai* PP *offert, e* Pres Part *offrant* Subj *1,3* offre *4* offrions *6* offrent
• Nous pouvons vous **offrir** un article de remplacement nettement supérieur ... - *We can offer you an alternative article* ...
• Il s'agit évidemment du lot No 14 mais je crains que le prix **offert** est

erroné. - ... *but I am afraid the price offered/quoted is wrong.*

omettre (de) *vt* neglect, omit
TENSES See *mettre*
• ... nous avons **omis de** rectifier le numéro d'origine de cette pièce ... - ... *we neglected/omitted to correct the original number of this gun* ...

omission *nf* omission, oversight
• Cette **omission** ne nous permet pas de suivre le rendement de nos insertions, ce qui est regrettable. - *This omission* (of a reference number) *is preventing us from gauging the effectiveness of these advertisements.* ...

(l')**on** *pro* they, we
• **On** nous a promis la prochaine commande. - *They have promised us the next order.*
• Je ne crois pas qu'**on** puisse exiger une telle inspection pour plus de 1/10 des pièces. - *I do not think we can demand such an inspection* ...

onéreux, -euse *adj* costly, expensive
• Ce mode de transport vous permet d'éviter des emballages maritimes souvent très **onéreux**. - *This means of transport enables you to dispense with seaworthy packing which is often very costly/expensive.*

opération *nf* operation, transaction
• Ces dispositions permettent de renforcer le contrôle de la comptabilisation des **opérations** que vous nous confiez. - *These arrangements enable us to exercise a tighter control when posting the transactions which you entrust to us.*

opérer *vi* operate, proceed
TENSES See *céder*
• Je lui ai d'ailleurs proposé pour les règlements à venir, d'**opérer** de la même manière qu'avec vous-mêmes,

ce qu'il a accepté. - . . . *that, for future payments, we should* **operate/proceed** *in the same way as with yourselves, . . .*

opinion *nf* opinion, view
• Il nous serait agréable de connaître votre **opinion**.

opportun, -e *adj* opportune, timely; advisable, appropriate, expedient, right, ripe
USAGE *'Il est* **opportun** *que'* + Subjunctive.
• Veuillez nous dire si, à votre avis, il est **opportun** que nous transmettions ces indications à l'usine de Mondeville. - *Please tell us if, in your opinion, it is* **opportune/advisable** *for us to. . . .*
• Nous reprendrons contact avec vous **en temps opportun**. - *We will contact you again* **at the right time/when the time is ripe**.

opportunément *adv* opportunely
• Votre lettre du 17 décembre me **rappelle opportunément** la précédente tombée, je le reconnais, dans l'oubli . . . - *Your letter of December 17* **served as a timely reminder** *of the previous one which, I admit, had been forgotten . . .*

option *nf* option
• **Option**: la présente offre est valable pour une durée d'un mois prenant cours aujourd'hui. - *Option: the present offer is valid for one month from today.*

or however, whereas
USAGE *Unlike 'cependant' and 'toutefois', 'or' must always be the first word in the clause. In practice it is almost always sentence-initial. However, in the example below, the full-stop could be replaced by a comma or semi-colon, in which case* Eng *'whereas' or 'but' would be the appropriate translation.*

• M. X avait prévu qu'il fallait disposer de 500kg de ce matériel. **Or**, la commande que vous nous avez envoyée ne mentionne que 254kg. - *Mr X had envisaged that 500 kilos of this material would be required.* **However**, *the order you have sent us mentions only 254kg.*

ordinaire *adj* ordinary

ordre *nm* order; notice; nature; connection; region; [payable]
COLLOCATES See *commande*
USAGE *Although 'ordre' does often refer to an order for goods or services (first example), 'commande' is more usual. Unlike 'commande', 'ordre' has a wide range of other senses, as shown by the number and variety of the remaining examples.*
• Nous aimerions avoir livraison de cet **ordre** le mercredi 25 novembre courant. - *We should like to take delivery of this* **order** *. . .*
• Restant dévoués à vos **ordres**, . . .
• . . .notre lettre suspendant **jusqu'à nouvel ordre** de notre part la commande sous référence. - *. . . our letter suspending* **until further notice** *from us our above-mentioned order.*
• . . . et vous prions de bien vouloir adresser à notre attention un chèque de F.1.500 **établi à l'ordre de** CIE. - *. . . a cheque . . .* **payable to/made out to the order of** *CIE.*
• Nous profitons de ce cas particulier pour vous poser une question **d'ordre générale**. - *. . . to ask you a question* **of a general nature**.
• Aussi, est-ce **dans cet ordre d'idées** que nous nous voyons dans l'obligation de vous alerter. - *Therefore, it is* **in this connection** *that we find ourselves obliged to alert you.*
• Nous vous serions obligés de nous adresser rapidement vos possibilités et conditions de

fourniture de naphtaline pour une consommation annuelle **de l'ordre de** 300/500 tonnes. - . . . *for an annual consumption of the order of/in the region of 300/500 tons.*
• Il conviendraient que nous sachions au moins **l'ordre de grandeur** des investissements . . . - *We should like to know at least the order of magnitude of the investments . . .*

organisation *nf* organization, organizing
• En conséquence, CIE est en ce moment même à la recherche d'une **organisation** commerciale susceptible de distribuer ses produits en Allemagne. - *Consequently, CIE is at this very moment seeking a commercial organization able to distribute its products in Germany.*
• Cette première semaine de lancement MF a été consacrée à l'**organisation** de notre réseau. - *This first week of launching MF has been devoted to organizing our sales force.*

organiser *vt* organize, arrange
• Pour me permettre de bien **organiser** votre visite, puis-je vous demander de me préciser . . . - *In order to enable me to organize/arrange your visit properly, . . .*

organisme *nm* body, organism, organization
• Vous nous obligeriez en nous faisant savoir si votre **organisme** peut nous mettre en rapport avec des tissages. . . - . . . *if your organization* (a Chamber of Commerce) *can put us in touch with some weaving mills . . .*

original, -e (*mpl* -aux) *adj & nm* original
• Vous voudriez bien nous donner votre accord en nous remettant votre offre en 2 exemplaires (**original** et

une copie). - . . . *by sending us your offer in duplicate (original and one copy).*
• Nous vous prions de trouver ci-joint jeu de connaissements **originaux** concernant une expédition . . . - . . . *a set of original bills of lading concerning a shipment . . .*

origine *nf* origin, [originally]
• . . . étant donné que les thermostats contenus dans cette caisse sont d'**origine** étrangère. - . . . *given that the thermostats contained in that crate are of foreign origin.*
• . . . une note de crédit pour un nombre de briques inférieur à celui de 174 mentionné **à l'origine**. - . . . *a credit note for a quantity of bricks less than the 174 mentioned originally.*

où *adv* where, [situation]
• A ce sujet, j'aimerais bien savoir **où en est** le problème de l'usine du Havre. - *In this connection, I should very much like to know where we are with/what the present situation is with the factory at le Havre.*

oubli *nm* oversight
• Nous vous précisons que le retard à vous adresser les documents est dû à un **oubli** du transitaire. - . . . *the delay in sending you the documents is due to an oversight on the part of the forwarding agent.*

oublier (de) *vt* forget, overlook
• N'**oubliez** pas que nous devons compter encore 4 ou 5 jours pour le dédouanement. - *Don't forget we must allow another 4 or 5 days for customs clearance.*

(en) **outre** in addition, besides, furthermore, moreover
• Notre société fabrique, **outre** les meubles de rangement et les blocs-éviers, des hottes filtrantes . . . - *Our*

*company makes, **besides/in addition to** cupboards and sink-units, filter hoods . . .*
• Notre atelier bois peut, **en outre**, apporter une aide précieuse dans les périodes de pointe . . . - *Our carpentry workshop can, **moreover/in addition**, give invaluable assistance at busy periods . . .*

outre-mer *adv* abroad, overseas
• En effet, nous ne possédons la licence MF que pour la France et les pays d'**outre-mer** d'expression française. - *We in fact have the MF licence only for France and French-speaking countries **abroad/overseas**.*

ouverture *nf* opening
• Livraison: 15 jours environ après la commande et l'**ouverture** de

l'accréditif. - . . . *after the order and the **opening** of the letter of credit.*

ouvrable *adj* working
• Pour la bonne règle, nous joignons en annexe le détail du coût des frais généraux de chantier **par jour ouvrable**. - . . ., *we enclose a breakdown of the cost of the site overheads **per working day**.*

ouvrir *vt* open
TENSES See *offrir*
COLLOCATES *accréditif, compte, crédit, débouché, magasin, souscription, succursale*
• Nous avons l'honneur de revenir à notre lettre du 12 juillet 19-- par laquelle nous vous avons demandé d'**ouvrir** ce compte . . . - . . . *asking you to **open** this account . . .*

P

page *nf* page

paiement *nm* payment
• **Paiement**: à la réception de la marchandise.
• Nous nous excusons beaucoup pour ces **paiements** qui n'ont pas été effectués en leur temps. - . . . *payments which were not made at the right time.*

paire *nf* pair

palette *nf* pallet
• La charge moyenne par **palette** serait de 1.500kg. - *The average load per **pallet** would be 1500kg.*

paquet *nm* packet, package, bundle
• P.S. Prière de ne commander pour essai qu'un seul **paquet** de 10 lames. - *P.S. For trial purposes please order only a single **packet** of 10 blades.*

parce que *conj* because, since
USAGE See *'car'*.
• Nous n'avons rien pu faire **parce que** M. X considérait que les deux produits étaient de qualité sensiblement égale. - *We could do nothing **because/since** Mr X considered the two products to be virtually identical in quality.*

paraître *vi* appear, seem, [place, publish]
TENSES See *connaître*
USAGE *'Il paraît que'* + Subjunctive.
• Dans son principe, l'idée leur **paraît** séduisante mais . . . - *In principle, the idea **appears** attractive to them, but . . .*
• Il me **paraît** cependant que cela ne puisse se réaliser. - *It **appears** to me however that this cannot come about.*

• Comme suite à votre rubrique 116-70 **parue** dans cette revue, ... - *Further to your column 116-70 which **appeared** in that journal ...*

• Suite à la publicité que nous **faisons paraître** dans diverses revues françaises ... - *As a result of the advertisements which we **are placing/are publishing** in various French journals ...*

pareil, -eille *adj* similar, such

• Toutefois, afin d'éviter de **pareils** inconvénients, nous vous demandons de nous adresser dès maintenant les distributeurs ... - *However, in order to avoid **similar** difficulties (lack of stock), please send us ...*

• ... il désirait, comme il est normal **en pareil cas**, ne pas brouiller ses propres cartes ... - *... he wished, as is only natural **in such a situation**, not to get his own cards mixed up ...*

parfait, -e *adj* perfect

• Avec l'espoir que la marchandise arrivera en **parfaite** condition à son destinataire, ... - *Hoping that the goods will reach their consignee in **perfect** condition ...*

parfaitement *adv* perfectly, completely

• Nous sommes **parfaitement** d'accord avec vous sur le processus d'envoi de factures. - *We are **perfectly** in agreement with you as to the procedure for sending invoices.*

parmi among

• **Parmi** nos interlocuteurs récents s'est trouvé l'ingénieur dirigeant les hauts fourneaux de CIE. - ***Among** the people we have talked to recently was the engineer who manages CIE's blast furnaces.*

part *nf* part, behalf, [from, in return; furthermore, moreover; hand; communicate, inform of]

• Je pense **pour ma part** aller en Angleterre vers septembre – octobre. - *... **for my part** ...*

• ... et l'organisation a demandé beaucoup de peine **de la part de** nos collaborateurs pour la rendre le plus efficace possible. - *... and the organization (of a sales campaign) required a big effort **on the part of** our colleagues ...*

• Il s'agit des échantillons que nous vous demandions **de la part de** M. X. - *These are the samples we were asking you for **on behalf of** Mr X.*

• Nous étions en effet surpris de ne pas encore avoir reçu de réponse **de votre part**. - *We were in fact surprised not to have received a reply **from you/in return**.*

• **D'autre part**, si nous décidons de travailler ensemble, il vous faudra une collection complète. - ***Furthermore/moreover**, ...*

• Nous vous adressons en annexe **d'une part** notre catalogue et, **d'autre part**, notre tarif vente métropole. - *We are enclosing **on the one hand** our catalogue and, **on the other hand**, our home sales price list.*

• Elle vous **a** peut-être **fait part de** mon appel téléphonique. - *She **has** perhaps **informed** you **of** my phone call.*

participation *nf* participation, share

• Je vous confirme notre accord pour que ce soit CIE qui lui adresse directement le montant de sa **participation** aux frais, soit £1.500. - *I confirm our agreement that it should be CIE who send him direct the amount of their **participation/share** in the costs, namely £1500.*

participer à *vt indir* participate in, share in, take part in

• Nous vous signalons que nous **avons participé à** cette Foire l'année dernière. - . . . we *participated in that trade fair last year.*

particulier, -ière *adj* particular, special
• Un problème **particulier** me fait vous écrire aujourd'hui. - *A particular problem . . .*
• Or, dans votre lettre du 19 juin 19-- aucune indication **particulière** n'était formulée. - *. . ., no special instruction was given.*
• Quelques points **en particulier** ont retenu notre attention. - *Certain points in particular attracted our attention.*

particulièrement *adv* particularly, especially, specially
USAGE *In the second and third examples, 'tout' and 'plus' are optional. They serve simply to strengthen the force of 'particulièrement'. In the third example, 'plus' makes explicit the comparison between small ships in general and ones belonging to 'non-Conference' lines in particular. Neither 'tout' nor 'plus' would be appropriate when, as in the first example, 'particulièrement' premodifies an* Adjective.
• Le hasard fait donc que notre intervention arrive à un moment **particulièrement** propice. - *So by chance our intervention comes at a particularly/especially opportune time.*
• Nous attirons **tout particulièrement** votre attention sur nos conditions générales d'achat . . . - *May we draw your attention particularly to our general conditions of purchase . . .*
• Il s'agit ici de petites unités pour lesquelles 50 tonnes de plus ou de moins sont importantes, **plus particulièrement** avec une ligne hors Conférence. - *We are dealing with small ships for which 50 tons on either*

side is important, ***particularly*** *with a non-Conference line.*

partie *nf* part, proportion, [partly]; party, [belong to]
• Nous nous référons à votre lettre du 15 avril 19-- nous priant d'examiner la possibilité de récupérer une **partie** des frais de transport pour le lot sous rubrique. - *. . . asking us to look into the possibility of recovering a part/proportion of the transport costs for the above batch.*
• . . . car nous devrons éliminer certaines bottes, en totalité ou **en partie**. - *. . . since we shall have to eliminate some bundles (of wire), entirely or partly/in part.*
• A nos conditions générales de vente reprises au verso et **faisant partie intégrante** de la présente, . . ., nous vous offrons: . . . - *In accordance with our general conditions of sale reproduced overleaf and forming an integral part of this letter, . . .*
• L'essentiel est que vous ayez pu avoir avec ces messieurs des entretiens intéressants pour les deux **parties**. - *. . . talks which were useful for both parties.*
• Nous apprenons que Monsieur X **ne fera plus partie de** votre Société à compter du 1er janvier 19--. - *. . . that Mr X will no longer belong to/work for your company . . .*

partiel, -ielle *adj* partial, part
• Expéditions **partielles** autorisées. - *Part shipments allowed.*

partiellement *adv* partly, partially
• Les transports ont dû s'effectuer **partiellement** de nuit pour atteindre le départ. - *The goods had to be transported partly at night to catch the sailing.*

partir *vi* depart, leave, set off; [as from, on and after, from . . . onwards; basis, working from]

TENSES Pres 1 *pars* 3 *part* 4 *partons* 6 *partent* Imp *partais* Fut *partirai* PP *parti, -ie* Pres Part *partant* Subj 1,3 *parte* 4 *partions* 6 *partent*

• Comme convenu, je **partirai de Paris** le vendredi 6 avril vers 5 ou 6 heures. - *As agreed, I shall leave Paris/depart/set off from Paris* ...

• Les livraisons peuvent être effectuées **à partir du** 1er septembre 19--. - *Deliveries can be made as from Sept. 1st 19--./from Sept. 1st 19-- onwards*.

• En **partant de** notre plan PR 1466 ci-joint, vous aurez à nous préciser les différentes quantités de briques ... - *On the basis of/Working from our drawing PR 1466 enclosed, you will specify* ...

parution *nf* publication, appearance, [appear]

• Nous vous serions obligés de bien vouloir à l'avenir nous envoyer, au fur et à mesure de **leur parution**, vos notices, circulaires, ... - ... *send us in future, as and when they appear, your information sheets, circulars,* ...

parvenir à *vt indir* reach; contrive to, manage to, succeed in; let have, send

TENSES See *venir*

USAGE *The expression 'faire parvenir' has lost its literal sense of 'cause to reach' and is used very frequently as a synonym of 'adresser'. The objects sent are letters, documents and small parcels (third example).*

• ..., nous vous indiquions que les connaissances vous **parviendraient** par notre banquier. - ..., *we informed you that the bills of lading would reach you via our bank.*

• ... votre sous-traitant chauffagiste n'**est** jamais **parvenu à** poursuivre son installation en fonction de l'avancement des

travaux de gros oeuvre. - ... *your heating sub-contractor never contrived to/managed to/succeeded in keeping his installation abreast of the construction work.*

• Pourriez-vous **nous faire parvenir** une vingtaine de chacune de ces fiches. - *Could you let us have/ send us twenty of each of these cards.*

passage *nm* visit

• Nous vous serions obligés de prendre rendez-vous avec nous lors de votre prochain **passage** à Paris. - ... *to arrange to meet us on your next visit to Paris.*

passé *nm* past

• Les marchandises seront, comme dans le **passé**, livrées par nos soins à CIE. - *The goods will, as in the past, be delivered by us to CIE.*

passer *vi* go by, pass

• ... car chaque jour qui **passe** ... vous coûte de l'argent. - ... *for each day which goes by/passes ... is costing you money.*

se **passer** *vpro* happen, go (off)

• ... duquel j'ai surtout retenu que rien ne **se passerait** vraisemblablement avant le mois de septembre prochain. - ... *from which (a message) I mainly gathered that probably nothing would happen before next September.*

• De mon côté tout **s'est bien passé**. - *For my part everything went (off) well.*

passer *vt* pass, spend; place

COLLOCATES *annonce, assurance, commande, contrat, coup de fil/ téléphone, instructions, journée, marché, nuit, ordre, vacances*

• Il **a passé** dix ans chez CIE à vendre des freins ... - *He spent ten years with CIE selling brakes* ...

• Nous avons le plaisir de vous **passer commande** pour: 3 tonnes de crème MF. - *We have pleasure in placing an order with you for: ...*

payable *adj* payable
• La facture s'entendait **payable** à réception, comme spécifié sur notre commande. - *The invoice was payable on receipt, ...*

payer *vt* pay (for)
TENSES Pres *1,3 paie* or *paye 4 payons 6 paient* or *payent* Imp *payais* Fut *paierai* or *payerai* PP *payé, -ée* Pres Part *payant* Subj *1,3 paie* or *paye 4 payions 6 paient* or *payent*
• Peu de clients veulent **payer** un prix supérieur pour une marchandise similaire. - *Few customers are willing to pay a higher price ...*
• D'ailleurs, vous ne la **payez** pas, vous avancez son prix d'achat, ... - *Furthermore, you do not pay for it (a machine), you advance its purchase price, ...*

pays *nm* country
• En effet, nous ne possédons la licence MF que pour la France et les **pays** d'outremer d'expression française. - *In fact, we have the MF licence only for France and French-speaking countries overseas.*

peine *nf* trouble; [on pain of]
• Les caractéristiques fournies par les résultats des essais devraient être respectées **sous peine du** rebut de la totalité de la fourniture. - *The characteristics supplied by the test results should be respected on pain of rejection of the entire consignment.*

pendant (que) *prep* during, for, while
• J'ai beaucoup regretté de n'avoir pu vous rencontrer **pendant** ces vacances. - *... during these holidays.*

• Nous avons fabriqué **pendant** plusieurs années des glissières de sièges ... - *We manufactured for several years seat slides ...*
• Un hasard malencontreux a voulu que je sois moi-même en Allemagne **pendant que** vous étiez en visite à Paris. - *As luck would have it, I was myself in Germany while you were visiting Paris.*

penser *vt* believe, consider, think (of)
USAGE *'Ne pas penser que'* takes the Subjunctive, *as in the third example.*
• Nous avons pris la décision suivante qui, nous le **pensons**, est propre à donner satisfaction à notre client CIE. - *We have taken the following decision which, we believe/ think, will satisfy our customer CIE.*
• Je **pense que** les brevets MF doivent être tombés en désuétude. - *I believe/think that the MF patents must have expired.*
• Nous **ne pensons pas que** cet effort soit justifié. - *We do not consider/think that this effort is justified.*
• Au point de vue prix nous **pensons** pouvoir vous proposer F.20 le bocal. - *As regards price we believe/ think that we can offer you 20 francs a jar.*
• Je **pense** toujours vous rendre visite à Londres dans la troisième semaine de septembre. - *I am still considering/thinking of visiting you ...* (NB Contrast *with the last example* for *'penser à'* **vt indir** 'think to' below.)

penser à *vt indir* think about, think of; think to, remember to
• Je **pense** principalement **aux** administrations où les devis ne sont pas immédiatement suivis de commandes. - *I am thinking mainly*

of government departments where estimates are not followed immediately by orders.

• Pour nous permettre de **penser à** ce problème avec le maximum de chances d'arriver à une solution, il conviendrait ... - *To allow us to* **think about** *this problem* ...

• Or, ce n'est que le 6 décembre que vous **avez pensé à** donner suite à cette proposition. - ... *that you* **thought to/remembered to** *act on this proposal*. (NB Contrast *with the last example for 'penser'* **vt** *'consider, think of' above*.)

penser de *vt indir* think about/of, [opinion]

• Donc, quoi que vous en **pensiez**, notre facture est raisonnable et CIE doit l'accepter. - *So, whatever you* **may think about/of** *it,/So whatever* **your opinion** *of it, our invoicing is reasonable.*

perdre *vt* lose, waste
TENSES See *rendre*

• Ces ennuis nous font **perdre** une commande d'équipement de CIE de 150.000 livres. - *These difficulties are causing us* **to lose** *an order* ...

• Prix: 520 livres les 1.000kg CIF Dunkerque, non dédouané, hors taxes, sur palettes **perdues**. - ... *on* **non-returnable** *pallets.*

période *nf* period
COLLOCATES *creuse; d'activité, des congés, de démarrage, d'essai, des fêtes, de pointe, des vacances*

• C'est donc ce taux qui est appliqué à votre compte pendant la **période** allant du 28 septembre au 31 décembre 19--. - *It is therefore this rate which is applied to your account for the* **period** *running from 28 September to 31 December 19--.*

périodiquement *adv* periodically

• Néanmoins je crois utile de faire **périodiquement** le point pour vous et pour ... - *Nevertheless I think it is useful to take stock of the situation* **periodically** *for you and for* ...

permanence *nf* manning, staffing

• Nous sommes en mesure d'assurer sur place la **permanence** indispensable. - *We are in a position to undertake the necessary* **staffing** *(of a stand at a trade fair).*

permettre (de) *vt* allow, enable, make possible, permit
TENSES See *mettre*
USAGE *Although 'permettre' is by far the most frequent translation equivalent of Eng 'allow', 'permit', it is almost always followed by 'de/que' + Verb, rarely by a Noun. See also 'laisser', 'consentir' and 'accorder'.*

• Crédit ouvert pour la durée totale de l'embarquement plus 15 jours pour nous **permettre** la négociation des documents. - ... *to* **allow** *us to negotiate the documents.*

• L'importance de nos achats nous **permet de** vous faire des prix fort avantageux. - *The size of our purchases* **allows** *us* **to** *offer you very attractive prices.*

se **permettre de** *vpro* take the liberty of, [would, wish to]
TENSES See *mettre*

• Nous **nous permettons de** vous rappeler notre échange de correspondance ... - *We* **are taking the liberty of** *reminding you* ...

• Nous **nous permettons de** vous faire remarquer que tout ceci est contraire à nos accords. - *We* **wish to/would** *point out that all this is contrary to our agreements.*

personne *nf* person, people

• Je vous propose de prendre contact avec **les personnes**

suivantes: ... - *I suggest you get in touch with the following: ...*

personnel *nm* staff, personnel
• Nous disposons d'un important **personnel** composé de 215 personnes ... - *We have a large **staff** comprising 215 persons ...*

personnel, -elle *adj* personal
• Ils désirent en acheter un pour leur utilisation **personnelle**. - *They wish to buy one (a soap dispenser) for their own **personal** use.*

personnellement *adv* personally
• L'objet de cette lettre est de vous remercier **personnellement** pour l'agréable déjeuner ... - ... *to thank you **personally** for the enjoyable lunch ...*

perspective *nf* outlook, prospect
• Nos ventes ayant encore sensiblement augmenté, et les **perspectives** d'avenir paraissant très bonnes, ... - ..., *and future **prospects** appearing very good, ...*

persuader (de) *vt* convince, induce, persuade, [certain, convinced, confident, sure]
• Je suis de plus en plus **persuadé** que nous obtiendrons de bons résultats ... - *I am more and more **certain** that we shall get good results ...*

perte *nf* loss
• ... finis aussi tous les frais et toutes les **pertes de production** qui en découlent. - ... *finished too all the costs and all the **lost production** which result from them* (from broken components).

peser *vt & i* weigh
TENSES See *acheter*
• La marchandise est emballée en une caisse bois et zinc **pesant** brut: 18.500kgs. - *The goods are packed in a wood and zinc crate **weighing** gross: 18,500kg.*

petit, -e *adj* small, minor
USAGE Compare *'faible'*
• Nous sommes actuellement occupés à mettre ce plan à jour pour les **petits** détails. - *We are at present busy updating this drawing as regards the **small/minor** details.*

peu *nm & adv* (a) little, (a) few, slightly; not very; [just, shortly, soon]
USAGE *The expression 'peu de temps', as well as referring **back** from a fixed point in time as in 'peu de temps **avant** les vacances' (sixth example), may also refer **forwards** – 'peu de temps **après** les vacances', 'shortly/soon **after** the holidays'. 'Sous peu', however, can only refer **forwards**, as in the last example.*
• Bien entendu, la période de démarrage peut être **un peu longue**, étant donné le genre de clientèle ... – *Of course, the starting-up period may be **a little long**, given the type of customers ...*
• Le prix à communiquer à CIE serait de F72, représentant pour nous une marge d'**un peu plus de** 12%. - ..., *representing for us a margin of **a little over/slightly over** 12%.*
• **Peu de** clients veulent payer un prix supérieur pour une marchandise similaire. - ***Few** customers are willing to pay a higher price ...*
• En fait, dans ce maquis auquel je ne connais que **peu de chose**, je me fie complètement à Monsieur X. - *In actual fact, in this complex area about which I know **little**, I place my trust completely in Mr X.*
• Le marché de la vanille, à la suite d'une récolte **peu abondante** en 19-- a beaucoup monté. - *The market in vanilla, following a **not very good/poor** harvest in 19--, has risen sharply.*
• Ce document, arrivé **peu de temps avant** les vacances de Pâques,

s'est trouvé enfoui sous d'autres papiers. - *This document, having arrived just/shortly before the Easter holiday, got buried under other papers.*
• Un plan corrigé vous sera envoyé **sous peu**. - *A corrected drawing will be sent to you **shortly/soon**.*

photo *nf* photograph (*See* photographie.)

photocopie *nf* photocopy
• Veuillez trouver ci-joint commande No 123 du 18 courant et **photocopie** d'une lettre de la même date.

photographie or **photo** *nf* photograph
• Bien entendu, nous accepterions volontiers également avec votre documentation une ou plusieurs **photographies** destinées à illustrer notre texte. - *... one or several **photographs** to illustrate our text.*

pièce *nf* part; document; [apiece, each]
USAGE *'P.J.', placed at the end of a letter, stands for 'pièce(s) jointe(s)', literally 'document(s) enclosed'. See third example.*
• Il s'est avéré qu'une de ces **pièces** a été mise hors d'usage par un serrage excessif des écrous de fixation. - *It transpires that one of these **parts** was put out of action by excessive tightening of the fixing nuts.*
• J'ai pu obtenir de CIE un petit dépannage de **pièces** me permettant la mise en place des trousses pour les représentants. - *CIE has been able to help me out with a few **documents** enabling me to make up the salesmen's kits.*
• **P.J.** 2 factures. - *Encl. 2 invoices.*
• Nous avons l'honneur de vous informer de ce que nous serions en mesure de fournir: mécanismes ...

au prix de F.B.900 **la pièce**. - *...: mechanisms ... at 900 Belgian francs apiece/each.*

pied *nm* (*In* 'mettre sur pied' inaugurate, set up)
• Nous sommes en train de **mettre sur pied** une série de tests. - *We are **inaugurating/setting up** a series of tests.*

place *nf* place, stead; spot; [establish, install, set up]
• J'ai demandé à mes collaborateurs, MM X et Y, de vous recevoir **à ma place**. - *..., to receive you **in my place/stead**.*
• Un courant de trafic déjà important est **en place**. - *An already large volume of traffic is **in place/ established** (a freight haulage service).*
• L'organisation **mise en place** est pour nous d'un prix de revient relativement élevé. - *The organization which has been **set up/established** is a relatively high-cost one for us.*
• Tout sera fait par un transitaire **sur place**, correspondant d'un transitaire français. - *Everything will be done by a forwarding agent **on the spot**, the correspondant of a French forwarding agent.*

placement *nm* installation; buyer
• ... un grand panneau publicitaire ... travail soigné, transports et **placement** compris, pour le prix de ... - *... a large advertising hoarding ... careful work, transport and **installation** included, for the price of ...*
• ... mais peut-être auriez-vous des **placements** en France ... - *... but perhaps you would have **buyers/outlets** in France ...*

placer *vt* place; sell, find a buyer/ outlet for

TENSES Pres *1,3 place 4 plaçons 6 placent* Imp *plaçais* Fut *placerai* PP *placé, ée* Pres Part *plaçant* Pres Part *plaçant* Subj *1,3 place 4 placions 6 placent*

• Les articles comportent un emballage individuel, mais sont ensuite **placés** dans de grands sacs papier. - *The articles are individually packed, but are then **placed** in large paper bags.*

• Nous aurions la possibilité de **placer** chez CIE des articles identiques ... - *It would appear we may be able to **sell** to CIE identical articles ...*

se **plaindre** (de) *vpro* complain
TENSES See *craindre*

• M. X **s'est plaint** plusieurs fois à moi de n'avoir jamais eu rien d'écrit de votre part. - *Mr X **has complained** to me several times **of** never having had anything from you in writing....*

plaisir *nm* pleasure

• Nous avons le **plaisir** de vous informer que ...

• Dans l'attente du **plaisir** de vous lire, ...

• C'est avec le plus grand **plaisir** que je vous recevrai à cette heure, ...

plan *nm* drawing, plan, blueprint; level, plane, [as regards]

• Nous vous envoyons ci-joints 2 exemplaires du **plan** définitif de la ventilation No 123. - *... 2 copies of the definitive **drawing/plan** of the ventilation No. 123.*

• En effet, les difficultés que nous allons avoir **sur le plan administratif** pour vous retourner ces 3 appareils sont délicates et longues. - *Indeed, the difficulties we are going to have **on the administrative level** in order to return these devices....*

• Nous pouvons obtenir ailleurs un matériel dont les résultats sont identiques **sur le plan utilisation** et qui ... - *We can obtain elsewhere equipment whose results are identical **as regards use/in use** and which ...*

pli *nm* cover, envelope; [herewith, enclosed]

• Nous vous adressons **sous ce pli** un duplicata de cette commande. - *We are sending you **herewith/enclosed** a duplicate of this order.*

• Nous vous faisons parvenir ce jour **sous pli séparé** un spécimen récent de notre revue. - *We are sending you today **under separate cover** a recent issue of our review.*

• La facture correspondante, payable à réception, vous a été adressée en son temps **sous pli fermé**. - *... was duly sent to you **in a sealed envelope**.*

la **plupart** *nf* bulk, majority, [most]

• Nous fournissons en France **la plupart des** grandes sociétés de produits chimiques, ...

plutôt *adv* rather, somewhat; instead

• Votre réponse ou **plutôt** vos instructions télégraphiques nous obligeraient. - *Your reply or **rather/instead** your telegraphic instructions would be appreciated.*

• La classe des produits de cette maison se situerait **plutôt** en dessous de ce que vous recherchez. - *The standard of this firm's products seems to be **rather/somewhat** below what you are looking for.*

plusieurs *pro & adj* several

poids *nm* weight

• L'emballage est prévu en cartons standards de 4 pièces. Dimensions des cartons: ... – **poids brut**: 9kg –

poids net: 7,5kg. - *Packing is provided in standard cartons of 4. Dimensions of the cartons*: ... – **gross weight**: 9kg – **net weight**: 7.5kg.

point *nm* point; [as regards; about to; take stock of, sum up; finalize, settle]

• Néanmoins je me permets de souligner les **points** suivants: ... - *Nevertheless I wish to emphasize the following **points**: ...*

• ... mais nous aimerions connaître votre **point de vue** à ce sujet. - *... but we should like to know your **point of view** on this matter.*

• ..., l'échantillon examiné ayant donné satisfaction **au point de vue** qualité. - *..., the sample examined having given satisfaction **from the point of view** of quality/**as regards** quality.*

• Nous attirons votre attention sur le fait que le délai extrême de 8 semaines est **sur le point** d'expirer. - *... the absolute time limit of 8 weeks is **about to** expire/**on the point of** expiring.*

• ... et afin de **faire le point de** nos commandes en cours, nous avons établi le tableau ci-dessous. - *... and in order to **take stock of** our current orders, we have drawn up the table below.*

• Vous recevrez une note de CIE **faisant le point** exact **de** la procédure entamée pour le brevet américain. - *You will receive a note from CIE **summing up** exactly the procedure begun for the American patent.*

• Dès que cette spécification sera **mise au point**, elle nous sera soumise ... - *As soon as this specification has been **finalized**/**settled**, it will be submitted to us ...*

police *nf* policy

• ...à couvrir sur la **police** flottante en rubrique. - *...to be covered by the above-mentioned floating **policy**.*

port *nm* port

• Livraison FOB **port** d'embarquement, emballage maritime compris. - *Delivery FOB loading **port**, seaworthy packing included.*

port *nm* carriage charge, postage

• Dans ce cas, le **port** et l'emballage seront facturés en sus. - *In this case, the **postage**/**carriage charge** and packing will be invoiced in addition.*

• Il est entendu que cette fourniture, qui vous sera adressée **en port dû**, vous sera facturée ... - *... this consignment, which will be sent to you **carriage forward**, ...*

• En effet, cette fourniture vous a été adressée le 25 juin dernier, par colis SNCF, **port payé**. - *... by SNCF parcel, **carriage paid**.*

porter *vt* bear, carry; exhibit, show; give, bring; increase, raise; pass, [charge]

• Ce dépliant **porte** la référence 123. - *This leaflet **bears**/**carries** the reference 123.*

• Nous vous remercions de **l'intérêt que vous portez** aux produits de notre fabrication. - *Thank you for the **interest you are showing** in the products we manufacture.*

• En vous remerciant bien vivement pour **l'attention que vous voudrez bien porter** à cette affaire. - *Thanking you very much for **the attention which you will kindly give**/**your kind attention** to this matter.*

• Nous nous permettons de **porter à votre connaissance** que nous sommes toujours en mesure de vous fournir des meubles ... - *We are taking the liberty of **bringing to your notice** that we can still supply you with furniture ...*

• Si vous désirez **portez votre commande** à 300 exemplaires, . . . - *If you wish to increase/raise your order to 300 copies, . . .*

• Nous accusons réception de votre virement susmentionné, dont le montant **a été porté au crédit de votre compte**. - *. . ., the amount of which has been passed to the credit of your account.*

• Tout préjudice que nous pouvons subir par suite de mauvaises fournitures **vous sera** donc **porté en compte**. - *Any loss we may suffer as a result of faulty consignments will therefore be charged to you.*

• Or, vous avez omis de respecter ces conditions, puisque votre commande **porte sur** 250 exemplaires. - *. . ., since your order refers to/is for 250 copies.*

poser *vt* ask, pose, put, raise
COLLOCATES *problème, question*

• Nous restons à votre disposition pour toute question que vous voudriez nous **poser**. - *. . . for any question you may wish to ask/put to/ raise with us.*

• Nous nous permettons de **poser la question de savoir** s'il vous est agréable d'avoir prochainement la visite de M. X. - *We should like to ask you whether you are agreeable to having Mr X visit you in the near future.*

• Nous aurions pu examiner ensemble le problème que vous nous **posez**. - *We could have examined together the problem which you are raising./are putting to us.*

se poser *vpro* arise, come up, crop up, present itself
COLLOCATES *problème, question*

• Cependant, **la question se pose de savoir si** CIE pourrait éventuellement être intéressés à

absorber des concurrents de bonne qualité. - *However, the question is/the question arises as to whether CIE might possibly be interested in . . .*

• Nous sommes à votre entière disposition pour vous aider dans n'importe quel problème qui **se poserait**. - *We are entirely at your disposal to assist you with any problem which might arise.*

positif, -ive *adj* positive
• Il semble qu'il ne faille pas fonder beaucoup d'espoir sur une réponse **positive**. - *It appears we must not pin too much hope on a positive reply.*

position *nf* position
• Nous tenons à vous préciser notre **position** en tant qu'agent import-export. - *We should like to clarify our position as import-export agent.*

posséder *vt* have, own, possess, be in possession of
TENSES See *céder*

• . . . il **possède** la carabine depuis l'année dernière. - *He has owned the rifle since last year.*

• Nous **possédons** toutes les données financières concernant le développement de cette société. - *We are in possession of/have all the financial data concerning the development of this company.*

possession *nf* possession
• En ce qui concerne les emballages, ils devraient être **en votre possession** très rapidement. - *As regards the packing materials, they should be in your possession very quickly.*

possibilité *nf* possibility, feasibility, potential; alternative
COLLOCATES *de diffusion, de distribution, d'exportation, de fourniture, d'investissements, de marché, de vente*

• En procédant comme cela, **nous aurions la possibilité de** fournir à CIE une machine correspondant aux caractéristiques demandées. - *By proceeding in this way, it would be possible for us to supply CIE with a machine having the required characteristics.*

• Nous offrons plusieurs **possibilités**: 1°... - *We offer several possibilities/alternatives: 1 ...*

• Je serais très heureux d'avoir un entretien avec la personne qui viendra enquêter sur les **possibilités de** diffusion de MF. - *... to have a meeting with the person who comes to look into the feasibility of/potential for distributing MF.*

possible *adj* possible, feasible
USAGE *'Il est possible que'* + Subjunctive, *as in the second example.*

• En réponse, nous regrettons de devoir vous informer qu'il ne nous est plus **possible d'**accepter la modification demandée par votre client. - *... it is no longer possible/feasible for us to accept the modification ...*

• ... et **il est possible que** cela corresponde à ce que recherche votre correspondant. - *... and it is possible that this corresponds to what your correspondent is looking for.*

• Nous vous serions obligés de nous envoyer le plus rapidement **possible** les indications demandées par Monsieur X. - *Please send us as quickly as possible the information requested by Mr X.*

• Vos prix doivent s'entendre FOB port d'embarquement ou, **si possible**, coût, assurance et fret Tunis. - *... FOB loading port or, if possible, CIF Tunis.*

• ... et si nous voulons arriver à un résultat positif, vous devez, **dans la**

mesure du possible, vous conformer aux données que je peux vous transmettre. - *..., you must, as far as possible, conform to the details which I can send you.*

postal, -e (*mpl* -aux) *adj* postal, [mailing, post]
COLLOCATES *carte, chèque, colis, paquet, récipissé, règlement, service, taux, versement, virement*

• C'est un document que nous laissons s'épuiser après utilisation pour nos campagnes **postales** professionnelles. - *... after it has been used for our professional postal campaigns/mailings.*

• ... nous vous indiquons vous adresser immédiatement, **par colis postal**, les 300 exemplaires du calendrier 19--. - *... that we are sending you immediately, by parcel post, the 300 copies of the 19-- calendar.*

poste *nm* heading, item
• Vous nous avez livré, en exécution du premier **poste** de notre commande susdite, 145 rouleaux ... - *..., against the first item of our above-mentioned order, 145 rolls ...*

poste *nf* post, [postal]
COLLOCATES *aérienne, avion, échantillons, ordinaire, séparée; administration des, service des*

• Nous vous saurions gré de vouloir bien effectuer les démarches nécessaires auprès de l'**administration des Postes** afin que des retards de ce genre soient évités à l'avenir. - *We should be grateful if you would kindly take the necessary steps with the postal authorities ...*

pourcentage *nm* percentage
• Rémunération: ces différents services pourront être rémunérés: soit sur la base d'un **pourcentage** du chiffre d'affaires – soit ... - *...: either*

*on the basis of a **percentage** of turnover or ...*

pourparlers *nm pl* discussions, negotiations, talks, [negotiate]
• La maison CIE à Melbourne, avec laquelle nous sommes **en pourparlers** concernant une affaire éventuelle, nous informe que ... - *The firm CIE in Melbourne, with which we **are negotiating** concerning a possible deal, ...*

pouvoir *vaux* be able, can

pratiquement *adv* almost, practically, virtually
• Le principal fournisseur est CIE, qui est **pratiquement** le seul fabricant français de ces articles. - *...., which is **almost** the only French supplier of these articles.*

préalable (à) *adj & nm* prior; [beforehand, first]
COLLOCATES *accord, autorisation, avis, clarification, condition, entretien, paiement, versement*
• ... vos ouvriers, qui ont déchargé sur notre chantier sans autorisation **préalable**. - *... your workmen, who unloaded on our site without **prior** authorization.*
• Nous aimerions connaître, **au préalable**, le nombre d'appareils qui vous seraient nécessaires. - *We should like to know, **beforehand/first**, ...*

précaution *nf* precaution
• Il n'est pas toujours possible de prendre de telles **précautions** dans une installation d'usine. - *It is not always possible to take such **precautions** in a factory installation.*

précédemment *adv* previously, earlier
• Veuillez nous envoyer un certain nombre de vos dépliants comme ceux que vous nous avez fait

parvenir **précédemment**. - *... like those which you sent us **previously**.*

précédent, -e *adj & nm* preceding, previous, earlier
• Nous constatons qu'il y a eu effectivement erreur de prix, mais dans la facture **précédente**, et pas dans la facture 123. - *...., but on the **previous/preceding** invoice, not on invoice 123.*
• Ce lot est nettement moins beau que le **précédent**. - *This batch is markedly inferior to the **previous/ earlier** one.*

précéder *vt* precede, [foregoing]
TENSES See *céder*
• Dans l'attente de vous lire par retour du courrier au sujet de **ce qui précède**, ... - *Looking forward to hearing from you by return regarding **the foregoing**, ...*

précieux, -ieuse *adj* invaluable
• Toutefois, nous vous prions de croire que votre aide nous a été **précieuse**. - *However, we assure you that your assistance has been **invaluable** to us.*

précis, -e *adj* precise
• Nous comptons y assister afin d'obtenir des renseignements plus **précis** sur la conduite des essais. - *... in order to obtain more **precise** information about the conduct of the trials.*

précisément *adv* in fact, as it happens
• Nous ne comprenons pas la raison que vos clients invoquent pour annuler deux des appareils alors que nous sommes en situation de les livrer avant la date qu'ils ont eux-mêmes fixée. Les quatre appareils restant à fournir viennent **précisément** d'être terminés. - *We do*

*not understand the reason your customers give for cancelling two of the machines when we are in a position to deliver them before the date which they themselves stipulated. The four machines still to be supplied have, **as it happens/ in fact**, just been finished.*

• Il va de soi que ce tonnage ne saurait être une réalité que dans la mesure où, **précisément**, vous accepteriez de modifier substantiellement nos conditions. - *It goes without saying that this tonnage can be achieved only insofar as you **do in fact** agree to modify our terms substantially.*

préciser *vt* make clear, specify, spell out, state specifically; be more precise
COLLOCATES *but, caractéristiques, conditions, date, délai, durée, faits, format, gare, intentions, nature, point, position, quantité, termes, type, usage, valeur*
USAGE *'Préciser' is found particularly often introducing an indirect question, ('si . . .', 'quel . . .', 'à quoi . . .', etc), as in the third and fourth examples.*

• Pour me permettre de bien organiser votre visite, puis-je vous demander de me **préciser** par avance les principaux points que vous aimeriez voir discuter. - *. . ., may I ask you to **make clear/specify** in advance. . . .*

• J'ai besoin que vous me fassiez parvenir de toute urgence une lettre officielle **précisant que** vous êtes d'accord pour remplacer le matériel . . . - *I need you to send me urgently an official letter **spelling it out/making it clear** that you agree. . .*

• Veuillez nous **préciser si** nous pouvons quand même assimiler ces briques au groupe de prix 1. - *Please **make it clear whether** we can include these bricks in price category 1.*

• P.S. – Veuillez nous **préciser à quelle date** est parti le premier MF. - *P.S. – Please **tell us the exact date on which** the first MF left.*

• Pour mémoire, ces frais seront pris en charge par X ou Y; nous vous **préciserons** ultérieurement. - *. . .; we **will be be more precise** later.*

précisions *nf pl* particulars, details
• . . . et vous nous fournirez toutes **précisions** nous permettant de déterminer les taxes, droits de douane et frais de transport. - *. . . and you will furnish us with all **particulars/ details** to enable us to determine the taxes, . . .*

précité, -e *adj* above, above-mentioned
• Si, contre toute apparence, vous avez réglé la facture **précitée**, . . . - *If, in spite of appearances, you have settled the **above-mentioned** invoice, . . .*

préférable *adj* preferable, to be preferred, best
USAGE *'Il est **préférable** que' +* Subjunctive.
• C'est la raison pour laquelle nous pensons qu'il est **préférable** que chaque année les collections nous soient retournées. - *That is why we think it **best/preferable** that each year the collections should be returned to us.*

préférence *nf* preference, [preferably]
• Auriez-vous la possibilité de nous faire obtenir une reproduction du texte de cet article, **de préférence** en microfilm? - *. . . a copy of the text of this article, **preferably** on microfilm?*

préférer *vt* prefer
TENSES See *céder*
• Je **préférerais** vous recevoir, si vous êtes encore à Paris, le vendredi 14 avril, par exemple à 14h.

préjudice *nm* loss
• Tout **préjudice** que nous pouvons subir ... vous sera donc porté en compte. - *Any loss which we may suffer* ....

préjugé *nm* prejudice; [consider]
• Nous devons cependant vous indiquer que nous sommes favorablement impressionnés par votre dynamisme et que vous **bénéficierez de notre préjugé favorable**. - *... and you will be favourably considered.*

préjuger de *vt indir* prejudge, [prejudice]
TENSES See *changer*
• Pour nous permettre d'examiner cette affaire en connaissance de cause et **sans préjuger de** la suite que nous pourrons y réserver, ... - *... and without prejudice to/without prejudging the response we might make to it, ...*

prélever *vt* withdraw, take
TENSES See *acheter*
• Nous nous réserverions la faculté de **prélever** des échantillons au hasard en vue de leur vérification. - *We should reserve the right to take samples at random for checking.*

premier, -ière *adj & nm* first, first-class/rate, top
USAGE *In dates, the ordinal numeral, 'le premier' (normally abbreviated 'le 1er'), is used for day one of the month but thereafter cardinal numerals, 'le 2', 'le 3', etc, are used, as in the first example.*
• Fermeture pour congés payés du **1er** au 23 août. - *Closed for paid holidays from 1st to 23rd August.*
• Notre firme possède des références **de tout premier ordre**. - *Our firm has first-rate references.*
• Vous nous garantiriez votre fourniture de toute **première** qualité.

- *You would guarantee your supply to be of top quality.*

prendre *vt* take, collect, pick up
TENSES Pres 1 *prends* 3 *prend* 4 *prenons* 6 *prennent* Imp *prenais* Fut *prendrai* PP *pris, -e* Pres Part *prenant* Subj 1,3 *prenne* 4 *prenions* 6 *prennent*
• Ce mode de transport permet également de **prendre** les marchandises chez vous, ... - *This means of transport also makes it possible to collect the goods at your premises, ...*
• Nous pourrions d'ailleurs vous faire **prendre** à Metz. - *We could moreover arrange for you to be picked up at Metz.*

préparation *nf* preparation
• Il est inutile de souligner l'importance d'une **préparation** soignée d'une opération aussi importante que celle que vous préparez. - *... the importance of careful preparation of an operation as big as the one you are planning.*

préparer *vt* prepare
• P.S. Prière me faire savoir si CIE **ont préparé** leur rapport ...

près (de) *adv & prep* near, close (to), [closely, keep tabs on]
USAGE Compare *'proche'*.
• Dans notre note relative à notre visite à l'usine de Mondeville **près de** Caen, ... - *In our note regarding our visit to the factory at Mondeville, near Caen, ...*
• Nous **suivons** cette affaire **de près** et vous tiendrons au courant. - *We are following this matter closely/We are keeping tabs on this matter and will keep you informed.*

présence *nf* presence, attendance
• Nous allons faire une visite sur place **en présence de** l'architecte. -

We are going to take a look **in the presence of** the architect.

présent, -e *adj & nm* present; [now; hitherto]

USAGE *'A présent' corresponds more closely to* Eng *'now' than to 'at present' (fourth and fifth examples).* Compare *'(en ce) moment'.*

• Option: la **présente** offre est valable pour une durée d'un mois. . . - *Option: the **present** offer is valid for one month. . .*

• **Par la présente** nous accusons réception de votre lettre du 10 février 19--. - *We **hereby** acknowledge/**By the present letter** we acknowledge receipt of your letter of 10 February, 19--.*

• Nous regrettons de ne pouvoir cette année être **présents** sous forme d'une insertion publicitaire dans votre bulletin. - *We regret we cannot this year be **present** in the shape of an advertisement in your bulletin.*

• Les délais prévus pour ces lots étant **à présent** expirés, nous comptons fermement vous lire par avis d'expédition. - *The agreed delivery periods for these batches having **now** expired. . . .*

• Je ne manquerai pas, comme je l'ai fait **jusqu'à présent**, de vous tenir au courant des développements de cette affaire. - *I shall not fail to keep you informed, as I have **until now/hitherto**, of the way this matter develops.*

présentation *nf* presentation; appearance

• Règlement, contre **présentation** de nos factures commerciales et du mate's receipt. - *Payment, against **presentation** of our commercial invoices and the mate's receipt.*

• Nos petits bocaux ont entretemps été remplacés par des bocaux plus grands d'une **présentation** meilleure. - *Our jars have meanwhile*

been replaced by larger jars with a better **appearance**.

présenter *vt* present, show; introduce; [wish]

• Si vous le préférez, un de nos collaborateurs pourra vous rendre visite pour vous **présenter** ce matériel. - *. . . in order to **show/present** this material to you.*

• D'autre part, comme vous nous le suggérez, nous ferons **présenter** une traite à vue à votre banque, CIE à Londres. - *. . . we will have a sight draft **presented** to your bank, CIE in London.*

• Cette note **présente** un certain nombre de lacunes . . . - *This note **presents/has** a certain number of gaps . . .*

• Permettez-moi, à l'occasion de cette nouvelle année, de vous **présenter mes voeux les meilleurs**. - *Allow me to **wish** you a **Happy New Year**.*

se **présenter** *vpro* arise, crop up, present itself; come, present oneself; introduce oneself

• Si l'occasion **se présente** à nouveau, nous ne manquerons pas d'avoir recours à vous. - *If the opportunity **arises/presents itself** again, we shall not fail to call on your assistance.*

• Dans ce cas un chauffeur de notre Société **se présenterait** vers 8h30 au lieu indiqué. - *In that event a driver from our company **would present himself/would come** about 8.30 to the appropriate place.*

• Nous **nous présentons** comme importateurs de miels de toutes provenances. - *We **introduce ourselves as/are** importers of honeys of all origins.*

presque *adv* almost, nearly

• Celui-ci m'a répondu **presque** par retour du courrier ... - *The latter replied to me **almost** by return of post ...*

prêt, -e (à) *adj* ready, prepared, willing
• Nous supposons que, lorsque toutes les pièces seront **prêtes**, nous pourrons les remettre à CIE ... - *..., when all the parts are **ready**, ...*
• Nous sommes **prêts à** vous céder des droits de traduction ... - *We are **prepared/ready/willing to** sell you translation rights ...*

prétendre *vt* assert, claim, contend, maintain, make out
TENSES See *rendre*
• Ils **prétendent** que la concurrence donne de telles garanties. - *They **assert** that the competition gives such guarantees.*

preuve *nf* proof, [show, display; prove itself, be tried and tested]
• Il y aura lieu de **faire preuve de** beaucoup de diplomatie dans cette affaire. - *We shall have to **show/display** great diplomacy in this matter.*
• La lame MF **a fait ses preuves** ... - *The MF blade **has proved itself/is tried and tested** ...*

prévenir (de) *vt* alert, forewarn, give notice, inform, warn
TENSES See *venir*
• Veuillez **prévenir** votre assurance ... - *Please **alert/inform** your insurers ...*
• Toutefois nous aimerions **être prévenus au moins un jour à l'avance de** l'heure de passage de ce dernier. - *However we should like **to be given at least one day's notice of** the time when the latter will call.*
• Quant à l'avenir, nous sommes évidemment **prévenus** maintenant. -

*As to the future, obviously we are now **forewarned**.*

prévision *nf* forecast
• Concerne: **prévisions** de vente pour 19--. - *Subject: sales **forecasts** for 19--.*

prévoir (de) *vt* anticipate, expect, foresee; plan, provide for
TENSES Pres 1 *prévois* 3 *prévoit* 4 *prévoyons* 6 *prévoient* Imp *prévoyais* Fut *prévoirai* PP *prévu*, *-ue* Pres Part *prévoyant* Subj 1,3 *prévoie* 4 *prévoyions* 6 *prévoient*
• Cette étude se révélant à vrai dire plus longue que je ne l'**avais prévu**, je crois utile de ... - *Since, to tell the truth, this investigation is turning out to be longer than I **anticipated** ...*
• Nous désirons que le contrat **prévoie** une amende en cas de retard de livraison. - *We wish the contract **to provide for** a penalty in the event of late delivery.*
• J'**ai prévu**, durant le mois de mars, **de** tourner avec chacun des représentants ... - *I **have planned**, during the month of March, **to** go round with each of the representatives ...*

prier (de) *vt* [kindly, please]; ask, request
USAGE *'Prier' is used almost exclusively in the expressions 'je vous prie de ...' and 'nous vous prions de ...', followed by an Infinitive and corresponds to Eng 'kindly', 'please', etc in making requests.*
• **Nous vous prions de** bien vouloir nous indiquer votre mode de règlement. - ***Kindly/Please** inform us as to your method of payment.*
• La société française qui a fait paraître l'annonce du 9 février me **prie de** répondre à votre lettre du 11 février. - *The French company which placed the advertisement of 9 February*

has asked me to reply to your letter of 11 February

prière *nf* [please]
• **Prière** nous donner également les instructions pour les 100 cartons vendus dernièrement. *Please also give us instructions...*

primo *adv* first, firstly
USAGE *'Primo' and similarly 'secundo', 'tertio', etc, are normally abbreviated '1°', '2°', '3°', etc. They are used when listing a number of points, either in separate paragraphs or sentences or within a single complex sentence, as in the following example.*
• Je crois que cette réadaptation de notre raison sociale doit tenir compte de trois impératifs: **1°)** conserver le caractère publicitaire de MF; **2°)** faire connaître CIE; **3°)** utiliser le stock de papier à lettre existant. - *I think this readjustment of our corporate name must take into account three requirements: **1)** to retain the brand image of MF; **2)** to make CIE known; **3)** to use up the existing stock of stationery.*

principal, -e *adj* leading, main, principal
• Nous serions même heureux si vous preniez des renseignements auprès des **principales** firmes de Belgique. - *... if you made inquiries with the **principal** firms in Belgium.*

principalement *adv* chiefly, mainly, mostly, principally
• Nous sommes spécialisés **principalement** dans les vannes ... - *We specialize **mainly** in lock gates ...*

principe *nm* principle
• J'ai noté l'intérêt **de principe** que vous avez manifesté concernant CIE. - *I have noted the interest **in principle** which you have shown in CIE.*

• ... et je fais retenir une chambre, **en principe** à l'hôtel X. - *... and I am arranging to book a room, **in principle** at the Hotel X.*

priorité *nf* priority, [as a matter of urgency]
• Cela nécessitera un tirage de 1000 exemplaires que vous voudrez bien livrer **en priorité** à Monsieur X. - *... which you will kindly deliver to Mr X as a priority/as a matter of urgency.*

prix *nm* price, charge, [at]
COLLOCATES *abordable, d'achat, actuel, avantageux, de base, compétitif, élevé, exact, ferme, fixe, forfaitaire, intéressant, juste, meilleur, minimum, moyen, net, prohibitif, raisonnable, réduit, de revient, supérieur, unitaire, de vente, en vigueur; augmenter, baisser, calculer, communiquer, confirmer, demander, diminuer, donner, s'entendre, établir, faire, hausser, indiquer, maintenir, modifier, monter, proposer, recevoir, remettre, revoir; groupe de, liste de; au ... de*
• Ces **prix** s'entendent nets – sans commission. - *These **prices/charges** are net – without commission.*
• **Prix**: veuillez nous remettre des **prix** pour marchandise rendue franco frontière française, ... - *Price: please quote us **prices** for goods delivered free to the French frontier, ...*
• ... et cette production étonnante, vous l'obtenez pour un **prix de revient** insignifiant. - *... and this astonishing production is achieved at an insignificant **cost price**.*
• Nous pourrions fournir 200kg **au prix de** F.850 le kg CIF Londres. - *We could supply 200kg **at** 850 francs per kg CIF London.*

probable *adj* probable, likely
USAGE *'Il est **probable** que' (unlike 'possible') + Indicative.*

• Cette affaire présente actuellement un caractère d'information et il est **probable** qu'elle évoluera favorablement. - ... *and it is **probable** that it will develop favourably.*

problème *nm* problem
COLLOCATES *avoir, discuter de, étudier, examiner, poser, régler, résoudre, soulever, apporter/trouver une solution à; se poser, surgir*
• Un **problème** particulier me fait vous écrire aujourd'hui. - *An exceptional **problem** causes me to write to you today.*

procédé *nm* process
• Nous avons eu connaissance que CIE y exposait un nouveau **procédé** de manutention sur coussin d'air. - *We have learnt that CIE displayed a new **process** for materials handling on an air cushion.*

procéder *vi* proceed
TENSES See *céder*
• Pour chaque extrusion, nous **procédons** toujours de la même façon. - *For each extrusion, we always **proceed** in the same way.*

procéder à *vt indir* carry out, conduct, go ahead with
TENSES See *céder*
• Veuillez me faire signe quand vous serez en mesure de **procéder** à la signature de ce contrat. - *Please contact us when you are in a position to **go ahead with** signing this contract.*
• Nous désirons **procéder** à une série d'essais comparatifs. - *We wish to **carry out**/**conduct** a series of comparative trials.*

processus *nm* procedure, modus operandi
• Nous sommes d'accord pour que cette opération exceptionnelle soit réalisée selon le **processus** que vous nous avez exposé. - *We agree to this exceptional operation being carried out in accordance with the **procedure**/**modus operandi** that you have explained to us.*

prochain, -e *adj* next; early, coming, forthcoming, approaching, imminent, impending
USAGE *'Prochain' follows the* Noun *when the latter refers to time, e.g. 'semaine', 'mois', 'année', 'lundi', 'janvier', as in the first two examples. In this use, 'la semaine prochaine' ('next week') contrasts with 'cette semaine' ('this week') and with 'la semaine dernière' ('last week'). Notice that 'la semaine prochaine/dernière' ('next/last week') also contrast with 'la semaine suivante/précédente' ('the following/previous week'). When 'prochain' precedes the* Noun*, it has a range of related senses, as in the last three examples.*
• Nous comptons expédier votre ordre No 123 dans le courant de la semaine **prochaine**. - *... in the course of **next** week.*
• Le Salon se tiendra du 8 au 19 octobre **prochain**. - *The Show will be held from 8 to 19 October **next**.*
• Le **prochain** navire au départ de Marseille est le S.S. X du 18 novembre 19--. - *The **next** boat leaving Marseille is the S.S. X ...*
• Nous attendons le plaisir de vous lire par tout **prochain** courrier. - *... hearing from you by a very **early** post/ very **soon**.*
• Monsieur X vient de m'annoncer votre **prochaine** visite à Paris ... – *Mr X has just informed me of your **forthcoming** visit to Paris.*

prochainement *adv* shortly, soon, in the near future
USAGE *'Prochainement' is usually preferred to 'bientôt' in business letters.*

• Monsieur X doit rentrer de voyage très **prochainement**. - *Mr X is due to return from a trip very **shortly/soon**.*

proche *adj* close, near
USAGE Compare *près*.
• Nous aimerions vous lire à ce sujet dans un **proche** avenir. - *We should like to hear from you in this connection in the **near** future.*
• Nous avons bien reçu, très **proche** l'un de l'autre, les deux premiers envois. - *We have received, very **close** together, the first two shipments.*

se procurer *vpro* acquire, get hold of, procure
• ... mais la société précitée a des difficultés pour **se procurer** ce matériel. - *... but the aforementioned company is having difficulties in **acquiring/procuring/getting hold of** this material.*

producteur, -trice *nmf & adj* producer, [produce]
• CIE ne peut vendre dans l'industrie du pétrole, attendu que ces fournitures sont assurées directement par les **producteurs**. - *..., since these supplies (of pipework) are made directly by the **producers**.*
• ... la plupart des sociétés françaises et étrangères **productrices** de pneumatiques. - *... most French and foreign companies **which produce/which are producers of** tyres.*

production *nf* production, output; products
• La **production** journalière n'était parallèlement que de 270kg contre 350kg. - *In the same way, daily **production/output** was only 270kg as against 350kg.*
• J'espère que ces quelques renseignements vous suffiront pour vous faire une première idée de la

production de CIE. - ... *for you to get a rough idea of the **products** of CIE/of what CIE produces.*

se produire *vpro* come about, happen, occur
TENSES See *déduire*
• C'est ce qui **s'est produit** le mois dernier après seulement 20.000 tonnes de marche. - *This (a machine breakdown) is what **came about/happened/occurred** last month after only 20,000 tons throughput.*

produit *nm* product
• Nous vous remercions de l'intérêt que vous portez aux **produits** de notre fabrication. - *Thank you for your interest in the **products** we manufacture.*

professionnel, -elle *adj* professional, trade
• ... nous indiquer les noms et adresses des journaux **professionnels** dans lesquels nous pourrions faire des annonces ... - *... tell us the names and addresses of the **trade** journals in which to advertise ...*

profit *nm* profit; benefit, favour
• Nous sommes prêts à vous céder notre légitime **profit** ... - *We are prepared to let you have our legitimate **profit** ...*
• Nous aimerions entamer avec vous l'étude d'un contrat d'importation **à notre profit**. - *We should like to look at the possibility of an import contract **in our favour/for our benefit**.*

profiter de *vt indir* avail oneself of, make the most of, take advantage of
• Nous **profitons de** cette occasion pour vous dire que l'essai des MF ne sera un succès que si ... - *We **take** this opportunity of telling you...*

pro-forma *adj invar* pro-forma

• Nous ajoutons qu'une facture **pro-forma** a été adressée au destinataire le 12 octobre 19-- en vue des démarches nécessaires au dédouanement de la marchandise. - *Furthermore a **pro-forma** invoice was sent to the consignee on 12 October, 19-- to facilitate the arrangements required to clear the goods through customs.*

programme *nm* programme
• Nous vous remercions du catalogue qui s'y trouvait joint et nous avons constaté l'étendue de votre **programme** de fabrication. - . . . *and we have noted the extent of your manufacturing **programme**.*

projet *nm* plan, project, proposal, scheme
• Je vous tiendrai, bien entendu, au courant des développements de nos **projets** dans ce secteur. - *I will, of course, keep you informed of the way our **plans** are developing in this area.*

promettre (de) *vt* promise
• Nous supposons qu'il s'agît des échantillons **promis**. - *We suppose that these are the **promised** samples.*
• Je vous **avais promis de** vous adresser très rapidement le travail que . . . - *I **had promised to** send you . . .*

prompt, -e *adj* prompt, expeditious, speedy
• Vous remerciant par avance d'une **prompte** réponse, . . .

propos *nm* connection; [about, concerning, regarding]
• **A ce propos**, nous vous prions de nous adresser 12 pamphlets MF. - *In **this connection**, please send us 12 MF pamphlets.*
• Nous reprenons les différents points des entretiens téléphoniques que nous avons eus **à propos de** cette

affaire. - . . . *of the phone conversations we have had **about** this matter.*

proposer (de) *vt* propose, put forward, suggest; offer, quote
• Devons-nous vous les retourner ou quelle autre solution nous **proposez**-vous? - . . . *or what other solution do you **propose/put forward/ suggest**?*
• Si vous pouvez **proposer** ce prix, nous essaierons d'obtenir une commande d'essai de 20 à 40 tonnes. - *If you can **offer/quote** this price, . . .*
• Pour ce qui est de la sidérurgie lourde, je vous **propose de** prendre contact avec les personnes suivantes: . . . - *As regards the iron and steel industry, I **suggest** you contact the following: . . .*

proposition *nf* proposition, proposal
• Si cette **proposition** vous intéresse, veuillez, je vous prie, m'adresser votre commande . . . - *If this **proposition** interests you, . . .*
• Si vous avez des remarques à suggérer ou des **propositions** constructives à servir, faites-les, je vous prie, par écrit. - *If you have some remarks to make or constructive **proposals** to put forward, please put them in writing.*

propre (à) *adj* own; appropriate, suitable
• Veuillez nous faire parvenir l'exemplaire de votre **propre** facture à insérer dans le colis. - *Please send us the copy of your **own** invoice to insert in the parcel.*
• Notre offre s'entend pour un travail fini comprenant tous les parachèvements **propres à** ces travaux. - *Our offer is for a finished job including all the finishing touches **appropriate to** such work.*

propriétaire *nmf* owner, proprietor
• Il conviendrait que la correspondance soit adressée au **propriétaire** de cette firme, le Dr.Ing. X.

prospecter *vt* canvass
• Nous envisageons d'améliorer encore nos ventes en engageant des représentants pour **prospecter** systématiquement et régulièrement toute la Belgique. - ... *by engaging representatives to canvass systematically*...

prospection *nf* canvassing
• Nous vous expédions ce jour 50 flacons échantillons de MF destinés à la **prospection** de votre clientèle. - ... *50 sample bottles of MF for canvassing your customers.*

provenance *nf* origin, provenance, source
• Il vient de nous rentrer de beaux lots de vanille **en provenance de** Madagascar. - *We have just received some very fine batches of vanilla from Madagascar.*

provenir de *vt indir* arise from, come from, be due to, originate from, result from
TENSES See *venir*
• L'erreur **provient du** fait que votre commande précitée comportait l'indication 'FOB le Havre' ... - *The mistake is due to/arose/resulted from the fact that your aforementioned order bore the instruction 'FOB le Havre'.*

provisoire *adj* provisional, temporary
• Ces plans ne portent plus la mention '**provisoire**' et sont datés du 1er octobre 19--. - *These drawings are no longer marked 'provisional'* ...
• Adresse **provisoire** jusqu'au 20 septembre: ... - *Temporary address until 20 September:* ...

provisoirement *adv* provisionally, temporarily, for the time being
• Veuillez noter que le client annule **provisoirement** sa commande. - *Please note that the customer is cancelling his order for the time being.*

P.S. P.S., post-script
• **P.S.** Bien entendu, il n'est ici question que des envois de faible tonnage. - **P.S.** *Of course, this only applies to small tonnage consignments.*

publicitaire *adj* advertising
• Il nous est difficile de prévoir aujourd'hui quelles seront les réactions de nos clients d'ici la fin de notre campagne **publicitaire**. - ... *what our customers' reactions will be between now and the end of our advertising campaign.*

publicité *nf* advertising, advertisement
• En effet, nous n'avons pas encore réussi à implanter cet appareil même après votre campagne de **publicité**. - *We have not yet succeeded in establishing this appliance on the market even after your advertising campaign.*
• Suite à une **publicité** parue dans une revue spécialisée française, ... - *Following an advertisement which appeared in a French specialized journal,* ...

puisque *conj* because, since
USAGE See *'car'*.
• Les emballages devraient être en votre possession très rapidement **puisque** l'expédition est maintenant en cours. - *The packing materials should be with you very quickly because/since they are now being dispatched.*
• Or, vous avez omis de respecter ces conditions **puisque** votre commande porte sur 250 exemplaires. - *However, you have failed to conform to these conditions because/since your order calls for 250 copies.*

Q

quai *nm* quay
- ... nos envois se font franco frontière française, ou franco près **quai** d'embarquement métropole. - ..., *or free on loading* **quay** *in metropolitan France.*

qualité *nf* quality, grade, standard; capacity, [as]
- ... l'échantillon examiné ayant donné satisfaction au point de vue **qualité**. - ... *the sample we examined having given satisfaction from the point of view of* **quality**.
- ... la **qualité** d'acier requise pour la susdite affaire est ... - ... *the* **grade** *of steel required for the above deal is* ...
- Vous nous garantiriez votre fourniture **de toute première qualité** du point de vue matière ... - *You would guarantee your supply to be* **of the highest standard** *as regards raw material* ...
- En votre **qualité** d'agent MF, vous avez dû recevoir ... - *As/In your* **capacity as** *a MF agent, you should have received* ...

quand *adv* when
USAGE *As an* **Adverb,** *'quand' is equivalent to 'à quel moment', 'à quelle date/heure'. It introduces an indirect question and therefore cannot be replaced by 'lorsque'. Contrast 'quand' conj in the next entry below.*
- Nous aimerions savoir **quand** vous comptez nous expédier ces marchandises. - *We should like to know* **when** (on what date) *you expect to despatch these goods to us.*

quand *conj* when
USAGE *As a* **Conjunction,** *'quand' is equivalent to 'au moment où'. It is little used in business letters. See lorsque.*

- Veuillez nous faire signe **quand** vous serez en mesure de procéder à la signature de ce contrat. - *Please get in touch with us* **when** (as soon as) *you are ready to go ahead and sign this contract.*

quant à as for, as to, in respect of
- **Quant à** l'envoi des documents, nous pourrons vous les faire adresser directement par notre transitaire. - *As for the dispatch of the documents,* ...
- Dès que nous aurons les renseignements **quant aux** quantités commandées, nous vous les ferons parvenir. - *As soon as we have the information* **as to** *the quantities ordered,* ...

quantité *nf* amount, quantity
- Cette maison nous a acheté par très petites **quantités**, 200 MF au total, ... - *This company has bought from us, in very small* **amounts/quantities**, *200 MF in all,* ...

quel, quelle *adj* which, what
- Nous vous serions reconnaissants de bien vouloir nous préciser à **quelle** expédition cette facture se rapporte. - ... *tell us to* **which** *shipment this invoice relates.*
- Nous vous prions de nous indiquer **quelles** quantités de MF nous devons vous réserver ... - *Please let us know* **what** *quantities of MF we should reserve for you.*
- Nous vous prions de nous indiquer **quel** aurait été le prix en MF. - *Please tell us* **what** *the price would have been for MF.*

question *nf* question, query; issue, matter, subject

COLLOCATES *se poser; discuter, évoquer, poser, régler, répondre à, reprendre, revenir sur, revoir, traiter de; de principe, d'ordre générale*

• Je vais maintenant essayer de répondre aux diverses **questions** que vous posez dans votre lettre. - *I will now try to reply to the various questions/queries which you raise in your letter.*

• Cependant, la **question** se pose de savoir si CIE pourrait éventuellement être intéressé à absorber des concurrents de bonne qualité. - *However, the **question** arises as to whether CIE might possibly be interested in taking over good quality competitors.*

• Nous espérons que les deux produits **en question** donneront entière satisfaction à vos clients. - *We hope the two products **in question** will give full satisfaction to your customers.*

• . . . il n'est absolument **pas question** pour nous **de** vous payer la différence. - *. . . **there is** absolutely **no question of** our paying you the difference.*

• Nous nous réservons donc de revenir très prochainement sur cette **question**. - *We therefore reserve the right to reexamine this **matter** very shortly.*

quinzaine *nf* (about) fifteen; fortnight

• . . . notre usine, qui se trouve à une **quinzaine** de kilomètres de la ville. - *. . . our factory, which is **about fifteen** kilometres from the town.*

• Cette année le message d'information ne pourra être diffusé que la première **quinzaine** de

septembre. - *This year the mailing cannot be sent out till the first **fortnight/half** of September.*

quitter *vt* leave, vacate

• Nous ne manquerons pas de vous aviser quand le colis **quittera** nos usines. - *We shall not fail to advise you when the parcel **leaves** our works.*

quoi *pro* what, whatever; [however]
USAGE *In examples 2 and 3, 'quoi que', written as two words, is not to be confused with 'quoique', meaning 'although'. See next entry below.*

• Nous vous proposons donc de nous donner l'exclusivité de vos MF pour une année, après **quoi** nous reverrons la chose ensemble. - *. . ., after **which** we will reexamine the matter together.*

• Donc, **quoi que** vous en pensiez, notre facturation est raisonnable . . . - *So, **whatever** you may think, our invoicing is reasonable . . .*

• **Quoi qu'il en soit**, nous vous laissons le soin de . . . - *However that may be*, we leave it to you to . . .

quoique *conj* although
USAGE *'Quoique'* + Subjunctive.

• **Quoique** vous ne soyez pas nos clients, nous sommes disposés à vous céder notre légitime profit . . . - *Although you are not our customer, we are prepared. . .*

quota *nm* quota

• Les poids pourraient être modifiés en fonction des **quotas** impartis par le gouvernement tunisien. - *The weights could be altered in accordance with the **quotas** granted by the Tunisian government.*

R

rabais *nm* discount, rebate
• **Rabais** exportateur: 3%. - *Export discount: 3%.*

raison *nf* reason; corporate name; [owing to, on account of]
• Il ne nous a malheureusement pas été possible de respecter la seconde clause ci-avant pour des **raisons** indépendantes de notre volonté. - . . . *for reasons beyond our control.*
• En effet, nos services ministériels ont pris un temps très considérable pour nous accorder le remboursement des droits et taxes et, pour cette **raison**, nous avons tellement tardé . . . - *Our government departments took a very long time to agree to pay back the dues and taxes and, for this reason, we have delayed so long . . .*
• Nous vous prions de trouver sous ce pli . . . la tête de lettre CIE repiquée à votre **raison sociale**. - . . . *the CIE letterhead with your corporate name inserted.*
• **En raison des** frais vraiment élevés de transport aérien, nous avons l'intention d'envoyer la collection par voie maritime. - *Owing to/On account of the really high cost of airfreight, . . .*

raisonnable *adj* reasonable, sensible
• Pourriez-vous nous soumettre une offre **raisonnable**? - *Could you make us a reasonable offer?*

ramener *vt* reduce
TENSES See *acheter*
• Or, entre-temps vous **avez ramené** ce nombre à 25 exemplaires. - *But, in the meantime you reduced this number to 25 copies.*

rapide *adj* fast, quick, rapid, speedy, swift
COLLOCATES *accord, décision, développement, examen, exécution, expédition, lecture, organisation, progrès, réponse, service, travail*
• Nous insistons auprès d'eux pour qu'une décision **rapide** soit prise. - *We are emphasizing to them that a quick decision should be taken.*

rapidement *adv* fast, promptly, quickly, rapidly
• Nous vous serions obligés de nous envoyer le plus **rapidement** possible les indications demandées par Monsieur X. - *Kindly send us as quickly as possible the information requested by Mr X.*
• Il semble que nous ayons la possibilité de développer nos ventes **rapidement**, . . . - *It seems to be possible for us to develop our sales rapidly.*

rappel *nm* reminder
• Nous regrettons vivement que vous ayez dû avoir recours à un second **rappel** concernant les factures. . . - *We very much regret that you should have had to resort to a second reminder about the invoices . . .*

rappeler *vt* remind; quote
TENSES See *appeler*
• Nous nous permettons de vous **rappeler** notre lettre du 15 février 19- -. - *May we remind you of our letter . . .*
• Nous vous **rappelons que** nos expéditions se font contre accréditif bancaire ou documents bancaires. - *May we remind you that our shipments. . .*
• Demande de prix No 123 à **rappeler** dans la réponse. - *Request for prices No. 123 to be quoted in your reply.*

rapport *nm* report; connection, dealings, relation; contact, touch; [approach, communicate with]
COLLOCATES *entrer en, être en, (se) mettre en ... avec*

• Suite à ces entretiens, je ne manquerai pas de vous adresser un **rapport** complet dans lequel ... - ..., *I shall not fail to send you a complete report in which ...*

• ... vous êtes en retard de livraison **par rapport aux** délais que nous vous avions demandés. - ... *you are behind with deliveries in relation to/with regard to the deadlines we asked for.*

• Notre principale activité nous permet d'**être en rapport avec** les plus importants fabricants en France, en Allemagne et en Scandinavie. - *Our principal activity enables us to have dealings/connections with the biggest manufacturers ...*

• Pourriez-vous nous **mettre en rapport avec** des fonderies de votre pays? - *Could you put us in contact/ touch with some foundries in your country?*

• ... nous **nous sommes mis en rapport avec** notre usine. - ... *we approached/communicated with/got in touch with our factory.*

se rapporter à *vpro* be applicable to, be connected with, relate to
• Nous accusons réception de votre lettre du 7 courant concernant des échantillons et la correspondance s'y **rapportant**. - *We acknowledge your letter of 7th inst. concerning some samples and the correspondence applicable to/connected with/related to them.*

réaction *nf* reaction, response
• De toutes façons, je vous serais reconnaissant de me tenir au courant des **réactions** de nos clients. - ... *keep me informed of our customers' reactions.*

réalisation *nf* achievement, carrying out, completion, fulfilment, implementation
USAGE *'Réalisation' and 'réaliser' have an extremely wide range of applications with the general sense of 'bringing something into existence' or 'bringing something to a successful conclusion'. The 'something' in question can be concrete, e.g. a building, or it can be abstract, e.g. a commercial operation. The examples below give a selection of the more common English translation equivalents.*

• Compte tenu du délai nécessaire à **la réalisation des outillages**, le démarrage de nos fournitures ne pourrait intervenir qu'environ 5 mois à dater de la réception de votre ordre ferme. - *Taking into account the time needed to complete the equipment/for tooling up, our supplies could only get under way ...*

• Veuillez nous informer de votre position et nous donner toutes précisions utiles à la **réalisation** de notre projet. - ... *and give us all information useful for the implementation of our project.*

réaliser *vt* achieve, carry out, complete, fulfil, implement, make
USAGE See *'réalisation' above.*
• Nous pourrions **réaliser** les modifications définies ci-dessus moyennant un prix supplémentaire ... - *We could carry out the modifications defined above for an additional charge ...*

• Aussi, nous convenons bien volontiers que nous **avons réalisé** un bénéfice sur ce transfert, plus élevé que normalement, ... - *Therefore, we quite agree that we made a profit on this transfer, bigger than usually, ...*

• Nous sommes cependant étonnés du délai qu'il a fallu pour **réaliser** cette commande. - *We are however astonished at the length of time that was needed to **fulfil** this order.*

réalité *nf* reality

• Le montant de ce devis, établi à la somme de 48.000F., devait **en réalité** s'élever à F.45.000 pour 15.000 exemplaires. - *The amount of this estimate, drawn up for 48,000 francs, should **in reality/in actual fact** have come to 45,000 francs for 15,000 copies.*

rebut *nm* scrap, scrapping

• Après un contrôle très sérieux, nous avons dû de ce fait éliminer et **mettre au rebut** les 174 briques de la palette No 43. - *After a very careful check, we had because of this to eliminate and **scrap** the 174 bricks of pallet No. 43.*

récemment *adv* lately, recently

• Nous avons **récemment** su que CIE avait des difficultés avec son four MF. - *We learnt **recently** that CIE was having some difficulties with its MF oven.*

récent, -e *adj* recent, up-to-date

• Nous vous confirmons les termes de notre **récente** communication téléphonique relative à . . .

• . . . et il est en instance d'être supplanté par un document plus **récent**. - . . . *and it (a leaflet) is about to be replaced by a more **recent/up-to-date** document.*

réception *nf* receipt, [receive]

• Nous accusons **réception** de votre lettre du 14 octobre qui a retenu toute notre attention. - *We acknowledge **receipt** of your letter . . .*

• Vous souhaitant **bonne réception** de ces pièces, . . . - *Wishing you **safe receipt** of these documents, . . .*

• **Dès réception de** vos doléances nous les avons transmises à nos

expéditeurs . . . - ***As soon as we received** your complaints we passed them on to our forwarding agents . . .*

recevoir *vt* receive, get; entertain, see; [take delivery of]

TENSES Pres *1 reçois 3 reçoit 4 recevons 6 reçoivent* Imp *recevais* Fut *recevrai* PP *reçu. -ue* Pres Part *recevant* Subj *1,3 reçoive 4 recevions 6 reçoivent*

• Je **reçois** à l'instant votre lettre du 7 octobre. - *I **have** just **received/got** your letter . . .*

• C'est avec le plus grand plaisir que je vous **recevrai** à cette heure ainsi que votre interprète. - *It is with the greatest pleasure that I will **see you** at that time together with your interpreter.*

• Je vous remercie infiniment de l'amabilité avec laquelle vous m'**avez reçu** à Londres. - *Thank you very much indeed for the kindness with which you **received/entertained** me in London.*

• Nous ne sommes pas équipés pour **recevoir** et manutentionner des caisses de 200 à 300kg. - *We are not equipped to **receive/take delivery of** and handle cases weighing 200 to 300kg.*

recherche *nf* investigation, lookout, research, search

• En conséquence, CIE est en ce moment **à la recherche d'**une organisation commerciale susceptible de distribuer ses produits en Allemagne. - . . ., *CIE is at present **looking for/on the look-out for** a commercial organization able to distribute its products in Germany.*

• Nous vous serions bien reconnaissants de bien vouloir **faire des recherches auprès du** service qui a été chargé de l'expédition de ce matériel. - . . . *to **make some inquiries of/to investigate this with** the department responsible for dispatching this material.*

rechercher *vt* look for, search for, seek out
• Ma cliente **recherche** des produits qui complètent les siens. - *My (lady) client is looking/searching/is on the look-out for products which complement her own.*
• ... afin que nous puissions, si nécessaire, **rechercher** des fabricants travaillant dans une gamme de produits différents. - *... so that we may, if necessary, look for/seek out manufacturers...*

réclamation *nf* claim, complaint
• Nous vous confirmons la **réclamation** formulée téléphoniquement à votre service commercial ... - *We confirm the complaint made by telephone to your sales department ...*

recommander *vt* recommend; register
• Nous signalerions d'abord les infractions par lettre **recommandée**. - *We should in the first instance report the infringements by registered letter.*

reconnaissant, -e (de) *adj* grateful
• Nous vous serions néanmoins **reconnaissants de** nous confirmer que notre interprétation est exacte.
• Nous vous serions **reconnaissants si** vous pouviez nous rendre ce service.

reconnaître *vt* acknowledge, admit, confess, recognize
TENSES See *connaître*
• Nous sommes persuadés que vous **reconnaîtrez** le bien-fondé de nos assertions. - *We feel sure you will acknowledge the soundness of our assertions.*
• Nous devons **reconnaître que** c'est habituellement dans ces délais que nous arrivent ces papiers. - *We*

have to **admit/confess that** *these papers do usually reach us within these times.*

recours *nm* recourse, resort; call upon
• Nous regrettons vivement que vous ayez dû **avoir recours à** un second rappel ... - *... that you have had to resort to/have recourse to a second reminder ...*
• Si l'occasion se présente à nouveau, nous ne manquerons pas d'**avoir recours à vous**. - *..., we shall not fail to call on you for assistance.*

rectificatif, -ive *adj* amended, corrected, rectified
• En nous excusant de cette erreur, nous vous adressons sous ce pli une facture **rectificative** annulant et remplaçant celle en votre possession. - *..., we enclose an amended invoice ...*

rectification *nf* amendment, correction, rectification
• ... malgré ces difficultés – frais de téléphone importants, **rectification** des documents, etc. - *... despite the difficulties – heavy telephone expenses, correction of the documents, etc.*

rectifier *vt* amend, correct, put right, put in order, rectify
• Nous vous serions reconnaissants de bien vouloir **rectifier** cette erreur. - *... kindly to correct this mistake.*

reçu *nm* receipt
• CIE devra vous donner décharge de ces paquets suivant le **reçu** ci-inclus, que vous voudrez bien mettre à notre disposition. - *CIE will take over these packets from you in accordance with the enclosed receipt, which you will kindly place at our disposal.*
• Au **reçu de** votre mémo du 29 novembre, nous avons demandé à CIE de nous envoyer un plan ... - *On receipt of your memo ...*

redevable à *adj* indebted to
• Nous sommes **redevables** de votre adresse à une revue française ... - *We are **indebted** for your address to a French journal* ...

rédiger *vt* draft, draw up, word
TENSES See *changer*
• Toutefois, la spécification exacte n'est pas encore **rédigée**. - *However, the exact specification has not yet been drawn up.*
• Nous vous confirmons les termes de notre câble de ce jour **rédigé** comme suit: ... - *We confirm the terms of our cable of today's date worded as follows:* ...

réduire *vt* reduce, lower, shorten; [minimize]
TENSES See *déduire*
• Nous vous demandons de bien vouloir **réduire** au maximum la livraison des MF. - *Kindly **minimize/ reduce as much as possible** delivery of the MF's.*

réduit, -e *adj* short
• Nous vous prions de bien vouloir nous faire connaître vos prix et délais de livraison **les plus réduits** pour ... - *... your prices and **shortest** delivery times for* ...

réel, réelle *adj* real
• CIE a exigé l'acceptation des clauses suivantes, confirmant l'importance **réelle** qu'elle attache à l'observance rigoureuse des délais avancés: ... - *..., confirming the **real** importance it attaches to the rigorous observance of the proposed deadlines:* ...

réexpédier *vt* return, send back; redirect
USAGE *The more usual word for 'send back' is 'retourner' vt.*
• L'appareil est réparé et prêt pour **être réexpédié** à l'adresse de votre

client M. X. - *The appliance is repaired and ready to **be returned/sent back** to your customer, Mr X.*

réexpédition *nf* return, sending back
• ... nous faire savoir si nous pouvons procéder à la **réexpédition** du fusil en cause. - *... let us know if we can go ahead with the **return** of the rifle in question.*

réexporter *vt* re-export
• ... un document complémentaire officiel certifiant que les marchandises ne **seront** pas **réexportées**. - *... certifying that the goods **will not be reexported**.*

référence *nf* reference; [above]
USAGE *In the second example, 'en référence' relates specifically to the heading or reference at the head of the present letter. Compare 'ci-dessus' and 'précité', which are more general words for Eng 'above'.*
• Nous avons bien reçu votre lettre **réf.** ABC du 30 novembre dernier ...
• Nous avons bien reçu votre lettre **citée en référence**. - *... **quoted above**.*
• Votre **réf.** ABC. Notre **réf.** DEF. (at the head of a letter)
• En effet, nos stocks sont pratiquement à zéro dans toutes les **références** commandées. - *In fact, our stocks are practically non-existant in all the **categories** ordered.*
• ... et, si vous le désirez, nous pouvons vous fournir des **références**. - *..., we can supply you with **references**.*

référencer *vt* reference, provide with a reference
• Nous sommes chargés par notre client, CIE, de l'expédition des marchandises **référencées**, ... - *We*

are instructed by our customer, CIE, to despatch the referenced/above goods, . . .

se **référer à** *vpro* refer to, [reference]
TENSES See *céder*
• **Nous référant à** votre bon de commande du 11 juillet, . . . - *Referring to/With reference to your order form of July 11, . . .*
• Nous **nous référons à** votre lettre du 9 courant et à vos télex du 11 courant.
• A ce sujet veuillez **vous référer à** notre bordereau modifié ci-annexé. - *In this connection please refer to our revised list herewith.*

refus *nm* refusal
• A chaque fois que nous avons désiré visiter . . ., on nous a opposé un **refus** catégorique. - *. . ., we have met with a categorical refusal.*

refuser (de) *vt* refuse, reject
• Notre client **a refusé de** régler le prix facturé de F123. - *Our customer has refused to settle the invoiced price of 123 francs.*
• Au cas où . . ., nous nous réserverions le droit de **refuser** tout le lot. - *In the event of . . ., we should reserve the right to reject the whole batch.*

région *nf* area, region
• . . . notre soumission pour la construction d'un hôpital important dans la **région** de Nantes.

régional, -e (*mpl* -aux) *adj* regional
• Nous avons immédiatement fait visiter cette entreprise par un de nos inspecteurs **régionaux**.

règle *nf* order; [straight; for the form, to keep things straight/above board]
• Enfin l'affaire est **en règle** de ce côté et nous pouvons marcher de

l'avant. - *At last the matter is in order/ straight in this regard and we can proceed.*
• Nous savons que vous vous êtes mis d'accord avec vos représentants: néanmoins, **pour la bonne règle**, nous aimerions avoir une confirmation de votre part. - *. . .: nevertheless, for the form/to keep things straight/above board, we should like to have your confirmation.*

règlement *nm* settlement, payment
• Ce **règlement** pourra s'effectuer soit par chèque bancaire au nom de CIE, soit par versement à notre CCP Paris 123. - *This settlement can be made either by cheque or . . .*
• Nous vous prions de bien vouloir indiquer votre mode de **règlement**. - *. . . your method of payment.*

régler *vt* pay, settle, straighten out
TENSES See *céder*
COLLOCATES *affaire, commande, compte, conflit, dette, dommages, facture, litige, montant, note, point, prix, problème, quelqu'un, question, solde, somme*
• Nous avons bien reçu, en son temps, votre versement postal de F330 **réglant** notre facture No 123 du 3 octobre 19--. - *. . ., your postal payment for 330 francs settling our invoice . . .*
• Nous espérons qu'il vous sera possible de **régler** prochainement le montant de cette fourniture. - *. . . to pay/settle in the near future the amount of this supply.*
• Notre lettre du 26 mars vous signalait que nous n'**étions** pas **réglés de** notre fourniture de calendriers . . . - *. . . that we had not been paid for our supply of calendars.*
• Nous espérions que ce litige **était réglé**, mais . . . - *We hoped that this dispute was settled/straightened out, but . . .*

regret *nm* regret, reluctance
• Nous sommes **au regret de** vous informer qu'il nous est impossible de vous faire offre dans ces articles. - *We regret to inform you that ...*
• Vous réitérant nos **regrets**, ... - *Repeating our regrets, ...*
• **A mon grand regret**, il me sera impossible de me rendre libre le 10 avril. - *To my great regret*, *it will be impossible for me to free myself ...*

regrettable *adj* regrettable
USAGE *'Il est regrettable que'* + Subjunctive.
• Il est évidemment **regrettable** que nous ayons omis de rectifier le cahier des charges. - *Clearly it is regrettable that we should have omitted to correct the specifications.*

regretter (de) *vt* regret, be sorry
USAGE *'Regretter que'* + Subjunctive.
• Croyez que je **regrette** cette occasion manquée d'une visite ... - *Believe me, I regret/am sorry about missing this opportunity for a visit.*
• Nous **regrettons** vivement **de** ne répondre qu'aujourd'hui à votre lettre. - *We deeply regret not replying to your letter until today.*
• Nous **regrettons que** M. X n'ait pas saisi cette occasion de faire une nouvelle affaire avec vous. - *We are sorry that Mr X has not taken this opportunity ...*

régulier, -ière *adj* regular
• Vous nous indiquez que vous n'avez pas de compagnie de navigation ayant un trafic **régulier** de Goole à Caen. - *... a shipping company with regular sailings from Goole to Caen.*
• ... laquelle vous marquait notre étonnement de n'avoir pas reçu votre commande **régulière**. - *... which (letter) expressed our surprise at not having received your regular order.*

régulièrement *adv* regularly; properly, [customary]
• Si nos produits vous intéressent, nous vous aviserons **régulièrement** de nos différents arrivages. - *..., we shall advise you regularly of our various arrivals.*
• Il était à ce moment trop tard pour enregistrer **régulièrement** votre commande. - *... to book your order properly/in the customary fashion.*

réimportable *adj* re-importable
• ... ces thermostats ne sont pas **réimportables**.

réitérer *vt* reiterate, repeat
TENSES See *céder*
• Dans cette attente et avec nos remerciements **réitérés**, ...

relatif, -ive **à** *adj* relating to, relative to
• Vous trouverez inclus une documentation **relative à** cet appareil. - *... literature relating to this appliance.*

relation *nf* relation, connection, dealings
• Je pense que nos conversations auront des répercussions très favorables dans l'avenir de nos **relations** commerciales. - *... very favourable repercussions on the future of our commercial relations.*
• A la suite de notre correspondance je **suis entré en relation avec** la maison CIE, parfumeur à Paris. - *I have opened a connection with CIE, ...*

relativement *adv* relatively, comparatively
• Le marché anglais est actuellement trés calme en ce qui concerne ce produit, ce qui motive naturellement un niveau de prix **relativement** bas. - *..., and this*

*naturally results in a **relatively** low price level.*

relevé *nm* statement (of account)
• ... soit 123 livres que nous déduisons sur notre **relevé** ci-joint. - *... namely £123 which we are deducting on our enclosed **statement**.*

relever *vt* discover, note, notice
TENSES See *acheter*
• Les différentes marques **relevées** sur le canon par M. X montrent que l'arme a été régulièrement éprouvée par CIE. - *The various marks on the barrel **discovered/noticed** by Mr X show that the weapon has been properly tested by CIE.*
• Nous **relevons que** la référence 123 n'a pas été repiquée sur la fiche technique. - *We **note that** the reference 123 has not been inserted on the technical sheet.*

reliquat *nm* remainder
• La livraison sera à faire à notre magasin en même temps que le **reliquat** de la commande en cours. - *... at the same time as the **remainder** of the current order.*

remarque *nf* comment, remark
• Toutes mes **remarques** n'ont qu'un seul but, ... - *All my **comments/remarks** have only one aim, ...*

remarquer *vt* note, notice, see; [point out, bring to one's attention/ notice]
• A notre retour en France, nous **avons remarqué que** nous n'avons pas reçu les 100 catalogues MF. - *We **have noted/noticed that** we have not received the 100 MF catalogues.*
• Comme vous pourrez le **remarquer**, nous avons pu maintenir l'ancien prix de F.280. - *As you can see, ...*
• Nous nous permettons de vous **faire remarquer que** tout ceci est

contraire à nos accords. - *May we **point out/bring to your notice that** all this is contrary to our agreements.*

remboursement *nm* refund, reimbursement, repayment
• ... et le **remboursement** des droits et des taxes va demander au minimum 6 mois. - *... and obtaining a **refund** of the duties and taxes will require a minimum of 6 months.*

rembourser *vt* refund, reimburse, repay
USAGE *Two constructions are possible, either 'rembourser quelque chose à quelqu'un' (as in these examples) or 'rembourser quelqu'un de quelque chose'.*
• Vous feriez bien de leur **rembourser** les 132 briques de la palette 47 et ... - *You would be well advised to **reimburse** them for the 132 bricks ...*
• Si vous n'êtes pas d'accord ..., votre argent vous **sera remboursé**. - *If you do not agree ..., your money **will be refunded**.*

remerciements *nm plur* thanks
• Avec nos **remerciements** anticipés, ... - *With our **thanks** in anticipation, ...*

remercier *vt* thank
USAGE *'Remercier' can take the* Preposition *'pour' as an alternative to 'de' before a* Noun Phrase, *as in the second example, but 'de' is more usual. However, only 'de' may be used before an* Infinitive, *as in the third example.*
• Vous en **remerciant** par avance, ... - ***Thanking** you in anticipation, ...*
• Nous avons bien reçu votre lettre réf. ABC et vous **remercions de** la demande qui en fait l'objet. - *... and **thank** you **for** your inquiry.*
• Nous vous **remercions** vivement **de** nous avoir contactés au sujet de

... - *We **thank** you very much **for** contacting us about* ...

remettre *vt* hand over, send; defer, postpone, put off
TENSES See *mettre*
USAGE *Usually 'remettre' is synonymous with 'envoyer', 'to send', but as in the first example it can mean 'to hand over', physically. When used in the general sense of 'to send', the 'things' sent are actually for the most part abstractions such as prices and specifications and occasionally small physical objects such as letters and other documents, rarely anything larger.* (Compare *'expédier'*)
• Comme convenu, nous **remettons** à votre porteur trois modèles de serrures ... - *As agreed, we **are handing over** to your messenger three types of lock* ...
• Nous avons le plaisir de vous **remettre** ci-inclus copie de la commande que nous passons ce jour à CIE ... - *We are pleased to **send** you herewith a copy of the order* ...
• Nous vous prions de nous **remettre** vos meilleurs prix et délai pour la fourniture éventuelle de ... - *Please **send** us your best prices and delivery* ...
• Avec votre accord, nous sommes disposés à **remettre** cette affaire à une date ultérieure. - *With your agreement, we are ready to **defer/postpone/put off** this matter **until** a later date.*

remise *nf* handing over, release; draft, remittance; discount, reduction; [overhaul, refurbishment, repair, restoration]
• CIE nous informe ce jour que votre maison se propose de régler contre **remise** des documents la marchandise destinée à leur adresse. - *... that your company proposes to pay*

against **handing over/release** of the documents for the goods ...
• ... une lettre nous informant que vous êtes porteurs d'une **remise documentaire à vue** de D.M. 20.860 tirée sur nous par notre fournisseur, CIE. - *... a letter informing us that you are holding a **sight draft** for 20,860 Deutschmarks drawn on us by our supplier, CIE.*
• Nous pourrions alors nous permettre de consentir des **remises** à des clients d'une telle importance. - *We could then see our way to granting **reductions/discounts** to such big customers.*
• Après avoir réexaminé cet appareil, nous vous confirmons que le montant de sa **remise en état/ remise à neuf** s'élèverait à F.B. 123. - *... the amount for its **overhaul/repair/ refurbishment** would come to 123 Belgian francs.*

remplacement *nm* replacement, [exchange]
• Nous avons pris à notre compte les frais occasionnés par le **remplacement** de ces deux pièces. - *We have taken responsibility for the costs involved in the **replacement** of these two parts.*
• Le pistolet **de remplacement** sera vraisemblablement expédié au début d'octobre. - *The **replacement** pistol will probably be dispatched* ...
• Nous avons fourni gratuitement à CIE 10 longueurs MF **en remplacement**. - *We have supplied free to CIE 10 lengths **as replacements/in exchange**.*

remplacer *vt* replace, substitute, supersede, take the place of
TENSES See *placer*
• Le client **a** immédiatement **remplacé** notre commande par la commande de 3 machines à CIE. -

The customer immediately **replaced** our order by the order for 3 machines given to CIE.

• Ce tarif **remplace** celui que nous vous avons fait parvenir en novembre 19--. - *This price list* **supersedes/takes the place of** *the one we sent you in November 19--.*

remplir *vt* fill, fill in; complete, go through

• Vous avez reçu une formule de bon de commande qui était à nous renvoyer, **remplie** et signée, pour le 20 juin. - *You have received an order form which should have been returned to us,* **filled in** *and signed, by 20 June.*

• Dans l'affirmative, nous vous ferons connaître les formalités **à remplir**. - *We will let you know the formalities* **to be completed/gone through**.

rémunération *nf* remuneration

• Il est important que le principe du montant de votre **rémunération** soit nettement indiqué dès la départ. - *It is important that the principle of the amount of your* **remuneration** *should be clearly indicated from the start.*

rémunérer *vt* remunerate

TENSES See *céder*

• Ces différents services pourront **être rémunérés**, soit sur la base d'un pourcentage du chiffre d'affaires, soit . . . - *These various services can* **be remunerated**, *either on the basis of a percentage of turnover, or . . .*

(se) rencontrer *vt & pro* meet; encounter, meet with

• J'espère, de toutes façons, avoir le plaisir de vous **rencontrer** au début de mai. - *. . ., to have the pleasure of* **meeting** *you . . .*

• Je vous confirme donc que nous **nous rencontrerons** le lundi 10 avril à déjeuner à la Chambre Syndicale. -

I confirm we **shall meet** *on Monday April 10 . . .*

• Notre transporteur habituel ne veut plus aller charger chez CIE par suite des difficultés , retards, etc qu'il **rencontre**. - *Our usual carriers are no longer willing to go and load at CIE's premises because of the difficulties, delays, etc which they* **encounter/meet with**.

rendez-vous *nm* appointment, rendez-vous

COLLOCATES *avoir, confirmer, convenir de, donner, fixer, obtenir, prendre*

USAGE *The* Indefinite Article *is often omitted after 'avoir', 'donner', 'fixer' and 'prendre', as in the first example.*

• Nous **avons rendez-vous** le vendredi 15 courant avec Monsieur X. - *We* **have an appointment/rendez-vous** *with/We* **have arranged to meet** *Mr X . . .*

• Je viens finalement d'obtenir un **rendez-vous** pour le mercredi 31 courant.

(se) rendre *vt & pro* make; deliver; go

TENSES Pres 1 *rends* 3 *rend* 4 *rendons* 6 *rendent* Imp *rendais* Fut *rendrai* PP *rendu, -ue* Pres Part *rendant* Subj 1,3 *rende* 4 *rendions* 6 *rendent*

• . . . et d'autre part, le Marché Commun . . . ne fait que **rendre** le problème plus vivant. - *. . . and furthermore, the Common Market . . . only* **makes** *the problem more pressing.*

• Ces prix s'entendent T.V.A. incluse, marchandises **rendues** à votre usine de Lunéville. - *. . ., goods* **delivered** *to your factory at Lunéville.*

• J'avais bien envisagé de **me rendre** à Zurich, au Salon de l'Hydraulique. - *I had hoped to* **go** *to Zurich, . . .*

renforcer *vt* reinforce, strengthen

TENSES See *placer*
* Nous vous demandons donc, à nouveau, de bien vouloir **renforcer** l'emballage. - . . ., *to be good enough to reinforce/strengthen the packing.*
* Ces dispositions permettent de **renforcer** le contrôle lors de la comptabilisation des opérations que vous nous confiez. - *These measures enable us to strengthen/tighten control when we record the transactions which you entrust to us.*

renommée *nf* fame, reputation
* Vous connaissez sans doute la **renommée** des cédrats de Corse. - *Doubtless you know of the fame/ reputation of Corsican citrons.*

renoncer à *vt indir* abandon, give up (the idea of), renounce, waive
TENSES See *placer*
* On nous a signalé que, dans ces conditions, CIE **renonçait** définitivement à tout nouvel essai. - *We were informed that, in the circumstances, CIE was definitely giving up the idea of any further trial.*

renouveler *vt* renew, repeat
TENSES See *appeler*
* Nos divers clients situés dans les régions sus-nommées, par les commandes **renouvelées** qu'ils nous ont passées, semblaient apprécier nos fabrications. - . . ., *to judge by the repeat orders which they gave us, (they) seemed to like our products.*
* Nous ne manquerons pas de vous tenir au courant des résultats et, en vous **renouvelant** nos remerciements, . . . - . . ., *and renewing our thanks./. . ., and with our thanks once again.*

renseignement *nm* (piece of) information
COLLOCATES *adresser, avoir, communiquer, demander, donner, faire*

parvenir, fournir, obtenir, prendre, transmettre; complémentaire, exact, indispensable, nécessaire, objectif, précis, utile
USAGE '*Renseignement*' is a Count Noun *as the examples show.* (See '*information*' *for the count/mass distinction.*)
* Nous nous tenons à votre disposition pour tous **renseignements** complémentaires. - *We are at your disposal for any further* **information**.
* Vous remerciant à l'avance de ce **renseignement**, . . . - *Thanking you in anticipation for this* **piece of** **information**, . . .

(se) renseigner *vt & pro* advise, brief, give information to; obtain information, find out, make inquiries
* Nous vous demandions de bien vouloir nous donner toutes précisions utiles pour que nous puissions **renseigner** cet acheteur éventuel. - . . . *so that we could* **advise** *this prospective purchaser./so that we could* **give** *this prospective purchaser* **the information he needs**.
* Mon adjoint essaiera de se **renseigner** concernant l'affaire en question. - *My assistant will try* **to find out/obtain information** *about the business in question.*

rentrée *nf* return
* Nous lui communiquerons votre réponse dès sa **rentrée** au bureau. - . . . *on his* **return** *to/as soon as he returns to the office.*

rentrer *vi* come back, go back, return
* J'ai trouvé votre lettre du 14 mars en **rentrant** de voyage. - *I found your letter on* **returning** *from a trip.*

renvoyer *vt* return, send back

TENSES See *payer*
• La meilleure solution serait que l'article nous **soit renvoyé** pour examen. - *The best solution would be for the article **to be returned**/**sent back** to us for examination.*

réouverture *nf* reopening
• Les deux commandes que vous nous avez fait parvenir seront expédiées dès la **réouverture** de notre usine début septembre. - *... on the **reopening** of our factory/as soon as our factory reopens at the beginning of September.*

réparation *nf* repair
• Nous avons décidé de prendre à notre compte les frais occasionnés par cette **réparation**. - *... the costs arising from this **repair**.*

réparer *vt* repair, make good
• L'appareil actuellement en notre possession est **réparé** ...

(se) répartir *vt & pro* allocate, allot, apportion, distribute, divide up, share out, split (up)
• ... concernant la livraison de 10.000 exemplaires de cet imprimé, **à répartir** suivant 21 bandes-adresses sur lesquelles est inscrit le nombre d'exemplaires à servir à chacun des 21 services. - *... concerning the delivery of 10,000 copies of this leaflet, **to be shared out**/**divided up** in accordance with 21 addressed wrappers on which there appears the number of copies to be supplied to each of the 21 departments.*
• Les qualités sont les suivantes: ..., dont les consommations **se répartissent** approximativement en 60% de pure pour 40% de brute. - *The qualities are as follows: ..., of which the amounts concerned **are distributed**/**split** approximately 60% pure, 40% crude.*

répartition *nf* allocation, allotment (etc *See* 'répartir' above)
• C'est ce dernier qui assurera la **répartition** des camions aux différents endroits de travail. - *It is the latter who will see to the **allocation** of the lorries to the various work places*

répéter *vt* repeat, reaffirm, reassert
TENSES See *céder*
• Je crois cependant utile de **répéter** qu'il ne s'agit pas d'une affaire comme les autres. - *However it seems to me worth **repeating** that this is not just a run-of-the-mill deal.*

repiquage *nm* insertion, insert
• Nous avons noté d'avoir à adresser à chacun 25 exemplaires de cette affiche complétés de 25 **repiquages** de leur nom et adresse. - *We have noted that we are to send to each 25 copies of this poster together with 25 **inserts**/**insertions** of their name and address.*

repiquer *vt* insert
• Nous relevons, pour ce qui concerne la fiche technique, que la référence 123 n'**a pas été repiquée** ... - *We note, as regards the technical information sheet, that the reference 123 **has** not **been inserted**.*

répondre (à) *vi & vt & vt indir* answer, reply; conform to, fit, match
TENSES See *rendre*
• Nous **répondons à** votre aimable lettre du 18 courant.
• Suite à notre rappel du 6 février 19--, vous nous **avez répondu que** vous seriez probablement en mesure de nous donner des nouvelles à ce sujet sous peu. - *..., you **replied that** you would probably be able to give us some news about this matter shortly.*
• Votre offre doit être ... et **répondra** en outre **aux** normes suivantes: ... - *your offer must be ...*

and will also conform to the following standards.

réponse *nf* answer, reply, response
COLLOCATES *affirmative, favorable, négative, positive, prompte, par retour du courrier (All after the* Noun *except 'prompte')*
• **En réponse à** votre lettre du 18 courant, . . .
• Une prompte **réponse** nous obligerait.
• Dans l'attente de votre **réponse**, . . .

reporter (à) *vt* defer, postpone, put off
• Pour cette raison nous préférons **reporter** ce genre d'offre à l'an prochain. - . . . *we prefer to* **put off/ defer** *this sort of offer* **until** *next year.*

se reporter à *v pro* refer back to
• Si vous voulez bien **vous reporter** à notre lettre du 28 novembre dernier, nous vous indiquions que . . . - *If you* **would refer back to** *our letter of Nov. 28 last, we pointed out to you that . . .*

reprendre *vt* refer to, revert to, take up; renew, resume; take back
TENSES See *prendre*
• Vous possédez les prix de la plupart des articles **repris** dans notre catalogue, . . . - *You have the prices of the majority of the articles* **referred to** *in our catalogue, . . .*
• Nous **reprenons** les différents points des entretiens téléphoniques que nous avons eus à propos de cette affaire. - *May we* **revert to/take up** *the various points from the telephone conversations we had about this matter.*
• Nous ne manquerons pas de **reprendre contact** avec vous à ce sujet. - *We shall not fail to* **renew contact/make contact again** *with you about this matter.*

• Il a dû **reprendre** tous les rails . . .
- *He had to* **take back** *all the rails . . .*

représentant, -e *nmf* representative
• Nous vous préviendrons lorsque nous serons en mesure de discuter de votre offre avec le **représentant** de votre Société. - *We will let you know when we are in a position to have discussions about your offer with your company's* **representative***.*

représentation *nf* agency, representation
COLLOCATES *avoir, confier, donner; exclusive*
• En effet, pour le moment nous ne vous avons en aucun cas confié la **représentation** de notre maison. - *For the moment we have certainly not entrusted you with our company's* **agency***.*

représenter *vt* represent
• Nous vous confirmons que nous **représentons** depuis plus d'un an la Société CIE en France.
• Nous vous ferons adresser un avoir de F.20,50 par kilo **représentant** la différence entre CIF et FOB. - *We shall send you a credit note for 20.50 francs per kg* **representing** *the difference between CIF and FOB.*
• Nous vous demandons de veiller à ce que le losange . . . figurant au recto soit bien celui **représenté** sur la maquette. - *Please take care that the diamond shape . . . appearing on the front (of a leaflet) is exactly like the one* **shown/represented** *in the artwork.*

reprise *nf* occasion, time, [repeatedly]; resumption; [take back]
• Après avoir essayé en vain, **à plusieurs reprises**, de rencontrer Monsieur X, . . . - *Having tried,* **on several occasions/repeatedly/several times** *to meet Mr X, . . .*

• Nous avons procédé à la **reprise** des 2 roues de notre fabrication, incriminées, pour examen. - *We have gone ahead with **taking back** the 2 offending wheels ...*

se reproduire *vpro* happen again, occur again, recur
TENSES See *déduire*
• ... car si les mêmes ennuis devaient **se reproduire**, le client retournerait l'ensemble. - *... for if the same problems were to **recur**, the customer would return the lot.*

réputation *nf* reputation, standing
• ... mais nous espérons que vous comprendrez que notre **réputation** est en jeu. - *... that our **reputation** is at stake.*

requis, -e *adj* required, requisite
• ... les chiffres ne correspondent pas aux conditions **requises**. - *... the figures do not tally with the **requisite** terms.*
• La qualité **requise** pour la susdite affaire est acier ... - *The quality **required** for the above transaction is steel ...*

requête *nf* request
• Avec l'espoir que cette **requête** sera accueillie favorablement ... - *Hoping that this **request** will be favourably received ...*

réseau *nm* network, organization
• Nous construisons un **réseau** de représentants sur l'ensemble de la France, ... - *We are building up a **network** of representatives/a sales force/ organization covering the whole of France.*

réservation *nf* booking, reservation
• Je pense qu'il serait utile de faire une **réservation** s'il est actuellement difficile de trouver une chambre à Londres.

réserve *nf* reserve, [spare]
• Une machine avait dû être remplacée par la dernière machine **en réserve**. - *A machine had to be replaced by the last machine **in reserve/ spare** machine.*
• Nous vous donnons notre accord **sous réserve d'**application des corrections signalées dans votre lettre. - *We give you our agreement **subject to** application of the corrections referred to in your letter.*

réserver *vt* book, reserve, put aside, put on one side
• Nous devons encore vous **réserver** 11% de commission sur ces prix. - *We still have to **reserve** 11% commission for you on these prices.*
• Nous vous prions de nous indiquer quelles quantités de MF nous devons vous **réserver** pour embarquement mars. - *... what quantities of MF we must **reserve/put aside** for you for shipment in March.*
• Nous **avons** pour le moment **réservé** notre réponse et étudions leurs propositions. - *For the moment we **have reserved** your response and are studying their proposals.*

se réserver (de) *vpro* intend, propose, reserve
• Nous **nous réservons** donc **de** revenir très prochainement sur cette question et ... - *We **intend/propose to** return to this matter shortly and ...*
• ... nous **nous réserverions** le droit de refuser tout le lot. - *... we **should reserve** the right to reject the whole batch.*

résilier *vt* cancel, terminate
USAGE *This word is restricted to legal matters. See 'annuler' for a more generally used synonym.*
• Nous nous réservons le droit de **résilier** le contrat dans le cas où il y

RÉSOUDRE

aurait insuffisance répétée de qualité ou de quantité. - *We reserve the right to* **cancel/terminate** *the contract in the event of repeated deficiencies of quality or quantity.*

résoudre *vt* resolve, settle, solve, sort out
TENSES Pres 1 *résous* 3 *résout* 4 *résolvons* 6 *résolvent* Imp *résolvais* Fut *résoudrai* PP *résolu, -ue* Pres Part *résolvant* Subj 1,3 *résolve* 4 *résolvions* 6 *résolvent*
• Nous prenons contact immédiatement avec Monsieur X pour voir quel est son problème et essayer de le **résoudre**. - *... to see what his problem is and to try to* **solve** *it.*

respecter *vt* abide by, keep to, observe, respect
COLLOCATES *caractéristiques, clause (d'un contrat), condition, délai, disposition, engagement, loi, règle, sentiments, stipulation, termes (d'un contrat)*
• Il ne nous a malheureusement pas été possible de **respecter** la seconde clause ci-avant pour des raisons indépendantes de notre volonté. - *Unfortunately it has not been possible for us to* **respect** *the second clause above ...*
• Il est indispensable que cette fois les délais **soient respectés**. - *It is essential that this time the delivery dates* **are kept to**.

respectif, *-ive adj* respective
• Un ou deux déplacements de M. X et de nous-mêmes seraient à nos charges **respectives**. - *One or two visits by Mr X and ourselves would be at our* **respective** *expenses.*

responsabilité *nf* liability, responsibility

RESTER

• Le fait de vous donner notre accord ne dégagera en rien votre **responsabilité** de fabricant, qui restera pleine et entière. - *Giving you our agreement will in no way release you from your* **liability/responsibility** *as manufacturer, ...*

responsable (de) *adj & nmf* responsible; authority, (person) in charge
• Nous ne saurions donc être tenus **responsables des** erreurs d'orthographe ... - *We would therefore not be held* **responsible for** *spelling mistakes ...*
• Ils pourront certainement vous mettre, dans chaque cas, en rapport avec les différents **responsables**. - *They will certainly be able, in each case, to put you in touch with the various* **authorities/persons in charge**.

restant, *-e adj* remaining
• Nous vous adressons un nouveau lot de 500 sacs pour le logement des 25 tonnes **restantes**. - *... for packing the* **remaining** *25 tons.*

reste *nm* rest, remainder; [moreover]
• ... votre lettre du 7 avril concernant nos prévisions approximatives pour le **reste** de l'année en cours. - *... our approximate forecasts for the* **rest** *of the current year.*
• Nous leur avons **du reste** téléphoné hier à ce sujet. - **Moreover**, *we phoned them yesterday about this.*

rester (à) *vi* remain, stay, [still]
• En conséquence notre tarif de vente **reste** inchangé. - *Consequently our price list* **remains/stays** *unchanged.*
• Les quatre carabines **restant à** fournir viennent précisément d'être terminées. - *The four rifles* **remaining/ still to** *be supplied have in fact just been finished.*

• Nous **restons** à votre disposition pour tous renseignements complémentaires. - *We remain at your disposal* . . .

restituer *vt* refund, return
• . . . ces taxes que nous vous **restituons** par un mandat-poste à votre ordre de F.123 que vous trouverez ci-inclus. - *. . . these taxes which we are refunding to you* . . .

résultat *nm* outcome, result
• Nous attendons de vos nouvelles concernant les **résultats** de ces essais le moment donné. - *. . . concerning the outcome/results of these trials when the time comes.*

résulter de *vt indir* follow from, result from, [mean]
• Il **résulte de tout ceci** que CIE ne peut prétendre plus longtemps à l'existence des contrats. - *It follows from all this/All this means that CIE can no longer maintain that the contracts exist.*

retard *nm* delay, [late, behind(hand)]
COLLOCATES *accumuler, aggraver, apporter, combler, occasionner, provoquer*
• Le **retard** à vous adresser les documents est dû à un oubli du transitaire. - *The delay in sending you the documents* . . .
• Nous souffrons en effet beaucoup des **retards** apportés à la dernière commande. - *We are indeed suffering a great deal from the delays which affected the last order.*
• Nous désirons que le contrat prévoie une amende en cas de **retard de livraison.** - *We wish the contract to provide for a penalty in the event of late delivery.*
• J'ai l'honneur d'accuser réception de votre lettre de décembre 19--, qui

nous est parvenue **avec beaucoup de retard. - . . .**, *which reached us after a long delay/very late.*
• Vous êtes **en retard** de livraison par rapport aux délais que nous vous avions demandés. - *You are behind with delivery in relation to the dates which we had requested.*

retarder *vt* delay, hold back/up
• Le mauvais temps **a retardé** le transport de nos marchandises. - *The bad weather has delayed/held up the transport of our goods.*

retenir *vt* book, reserve; detain, withold; consider
TENSES See *venir*
• Pouvez-vous me faire **retenir** une chambre à l'Hôtel X pour le mardi 28 et le mercredi 29 septembre. - *Can you book/reserve me a room* . . .
• Malheureusement, ma femme ne pourra être de ce voyage, **étant retenue** par la rentrée des classes. - *Unfortunately, my wife will not be able to make this trip, since she will be detained by the children's return to school.*
• Pour **être retenus**, vos prix devront être présentés suivant les indications du tableau ci-après. - *In order to be considered, your prices must be presented* . . .
• Nous avons bien reçu votre lettre du 30 juillet dernier, qui **a retenu** toute notre attention. - *. . ., which has had/received our closest attention.*

retour *nm* return, [back]
• Une réponse **par retour/par retour du courrier** est indispensable. - *A reply by return/by return of post is essential.*
• Nous ne trouvons pas trace d'une lettre concernant le **retour** de ces marchandises. - *We can find no trace of*

*a letter concerning the **return** of these goods.*

• Nous vous prions de trouver ci-joint **en retour** les contrats de CIE. - *... **in return** ...*

• **A notre retour** en France, nous avons remarqué ... - *On our return/ On returning to France, ...*

• **De retour de** voyage, je trouve votre lettre du 21 février ... - *Back from a trip, ...*

• J'espère que votre **voyage de retour** s'est bien effectué. - *I hope your **return journey** went well.*

retourner *vt & i* return; go back

• Ainsi que vous me le demandez, je vous **retourne** ces trois appareils afin qu'ils puissent nous être remplacés. - *..., I am returning these three appliances for replacement.*

• Nous sommes convenus que je **retournerai** le voir vendredi prochain, 17 avril, ... - *We are agreed that I will go back and see him ...*

retrouver *vt* locate

• Nous notons que vous **avez retrouvé** un certain nombre d'exemplaires de ce catalogue.

se retrouver *vpro* meet again

• J'espère que nous pourrons **nous retrouver** prochainement.

réunion *nf* meeting

• J'espère avoir le plaisir de vous rencontrer lors de la **réunion** annuelle de CIE, ...

réussir (à) *vi* succeed (in)

• J'espère que nous **réussirons à** enlever cette affaire contre les autres compétiteurs. - *I hope we shall **succeed** in bringing off this deal ...*

réussite *nf* success

• ... et nous formons des voeux pour la **réussite** de votre entreprise. -

*... and we send our good wishes for the **success** of your enterprise.*

revenir (sur) *vi* come back, return; reopen, revert to
TENSES See *venir*

• J'ai été heureux d'apprendre que vous envisagez de **revenir** à Paris au mois de mai prochain. - *... that you expect to **come back** to Paris next May.*

• Nous nous permettons de **revenir sur** votre correspondance du 15 octobre, ... - *If we may **revert to** your correspondence of 15 October, ...*

revêtir *vt* (*See* signature)

revient *nm* (*See* prix)

révisable *adj* revisable

• Vos prix seront fermes et non **révisables** pour une période de 12 mois à partir du 25 août 19--. - *Your prices will be firm and not **revisable** ...*

réviser *vt* revise

revoir *vt* see again; look at again, reconsider, re-examine, review; revise
TENSES See *voir*

• En attendant le plaisir de vous **revoir**, ... - *Looking forward to the pleasure of **seeing** you **again**, ...*

• J'insiste particulièrement pour que vous **revoyiez** les prix de ce matériel, qui me semblent prohibitifs. - *I insist in particular that you **reconsider/re-examine/review/ look again at** the prices of this material, ...*

• Les prix sont fermes pour toute l'année 19-- et **seront revus** le 1er janvier 19--. - *... and **will be reviewed** on 1 January, 19--.*

revue *nf* journal, magazine

• Suite à la publicité que nous faisons paraître dans diverses **revues** spécialisées, en France, nous recevons des demandes ... - *Following the advertisements which we are placing in various specialized journals, ...*

rigueur *nf* [hold it against someone]
• Nous nous excusons de l'erreur commise antérieurement et nous espérons que vous voudrez bien ne pas nous **en tenir rigueur**. - *We apologize for the mistake made previously and hope you will be kind enough not **to hold it against** us.*

risque *nm* risk
• Pour gouverne, les prix que nous avons faits comprennent l'assurance contre tous **risques**, sauf rouille. - *For your guidance, the prices we have quoted include insurance against all **risks**, except rust.*

risquer (de) *vt* risk
• ... et le client **risque** un arrêt de four. - *... and the customer **risks** a shutdown of the oven.*

• En revanche, nous ne voulons pas **risquer d'**investir des sommes considérables en désaccord avec les autorités. - *On the other hand, we do not wish to **risk** investing considerable sums contrary to the wishes of the authorities.*

rubrique *nf* heading; [above]
USAGE *In the second example, 'sous rubrique' relates specifically to the heading or reference at the head of the present letter. Compare 'ci-dessus' and 'précité', which are more general words for Eng 'above'.*
• J'ai pris note des différents changements qui sont intervenus dans plusieurs **rubriques** du contrat. - *I have noted the various changes which have been made under several **headings** in the contract.*
• A la réception de votre lettre nous avons pris contact avec la firme **sous rubrique**. - *... we contacted the **above** firm.*

S

saisir *vt* grasp, impound, seize, [refer, submit]
• Nous regrettons que M. X n'**ait** pas **saisi** cette occasion de faire une nouvelle affaire avec nous. - *We are sorry Mr X **did** not **grasp/seize** this opportunity to do business with us again.*
• M. X, le président de CIE, **est** actuellement **saisi de** trois propositions de fabrications nouvelles. - *Mr X, ..., has now had **referred/submitted to him** three proposals for new manufactures.*

salaire *nm* pay, salary, wage(s)

• A partir du 8 de ce mois une hausse de **salaires** a eu lieu. - *As of the 8th of this month a **wage** rise has taken place.*

salon *nm* exhibition, show
• Le prochain **salon** de l'équipement hôtelier, 'Équip'Hôtel', se tiendra du 8 au 19 octobre prochain. - *The next hotel equipment **exhibition**, 'Équip'Hôtel', will be held ...*

samedi *nm* Saturday (*See* lundi)

satisfaction *nf* satisfaction, [satisfy]

SATISFAIRE

- Nous espérons qu'il vous sera possible de **donner satisfaction à** notre client commun. - *We hope you will be able to **give satisfaction to**/ satisfy our mutual customer.*
- Le client serait prêt à payer un petit supplément pour obtenir **satisfaction**. - *The customer would be ready to pay a small supplement in order to obtain **satisfaction**.*

satisfaire (à) *vt & vt indir* satisfy, comply with, cater for
TENSES See *faire*
USAGE *When one satisfies a person, as in the first example, 'satisfaire' takes a Direct Object. With non-animates, such as 'demande', 'exigence' and 'loi', it is usual to employ 'à', as in the second example.*
- Afin de **satisfaire** vos agents, nous leur adresserons des formules de bon de commande, ... - *In order to **satisfy** your agents, we shall send them some order forms, ...*
- Je crois ainsi **avoir satisfait à** votre demande et ... - *I think in this way I **have satisfied**/complied with your request and ...*

satisfait, -e (de) *adj* satisfied (with)
- Ventes Belgique: j'**en** suis très **satisfait**. - *Belgian sales: I am very satisfied with them.*

sauf barring, except, save, [unless]
COLLOCATES *accord, avis contraire, cas de force majeure, contrordre, erreur (ou omission), imprévu, vente (entretemps)*
- Nous nous engageons par avance à ne pas les divulguer, **sauf** accord de votre part. - *We undertake in advance not to divulge them, **except**/ save with your agreement/**unless** you agree.*

savoir *vt* know, be aware, [let know, inform]

SEMBLER

TENSES Pres *1 sais 3 sait 4 savons 6 savent* Imp *savais* Fut *saurai* PP *su, sue* Pres Part *sachant* Subj *1,3 sache 4 sachions 6 sachent*
- Nous aimerions **savoir** quand vous comptez nous expédier ces marchandises.
- Comme vous le **savez**, nous devons procéder à la réorganisation de notre atelier tubes. - *As you **are** aware/**know**, we have to undertake the reorganization of our tube workshop.*
- Veuillez avoir l'obligeance de nous **faire savoir** si vous désirez remettre offre pour ce navire. - *Please be so kind as to **let** us **know**/**inform** us whether you wish to quote for this ship.*

à savoir namely
- Il conviendrait que la correspondance soit adressée directement au propriétaire de cette firme, **à savoir** le Dr X. - *... to the proprietor of that firm, **namely** Dr X.*

secrétaire *nmf* secretary

secteur *nm* sector, territory
- Ce représentant pourra organiser et travailler son **secteur** à partir du 13 février. - *This representative will be able to organize and work his **territory** from 13 February.*

selon according to, in accordance/ conformity with, as per
- Veuillez nous faire votre meilleure offre pour le matériel **selon** spécification ci-après. - *... for the material **in accordance with** the following specification.*

semaine *nf* week
- Nous lui communiquerons votre réponse au début de la **semaine** prochaine. - *... at the beginning of next week.*

sembler *vi & impers* appear, seem; [see fit]

USAGE *'Il semble que'* + Subjunctive.
• Cette notice nous **semble** très intéressante.
• Après remontage, cet outillage **semblait** fonctionner normalement. - *After reassembly, this equipment appeared/seemed to be working normally.*
• **Il semble que** ces briques fassent partie du troisième groupe de prix. - *It appears/seems that these bricks belong to the third group of prices.*
• Nous vous laissons donc toutes facultés pour marquer les paquets **comme bon vous semblera**. - *. . . to mark the bundles as you see fit.*

sens *nm* direction; lines, end, effect
• Soyez certain que nous ferons tous les efforts pour régler cette question dans le **sens** de nos intérêts communs. - *. . . to settle this question in the direction of our mutual interests.*
• J'espère que vous pourrez nous faire une proposition **dans ce sens**. - *I hope you will be able to make us a proposal along these lines.*
• Nous passons les instructions voulues **dans ce sens** à notre service facturation. - *We are giving the necessary instructions to this end/effect to our invoicing department.*

sensiblement *adv* appreciably, noticeably; approximately, more or less
• . . . votre prix de L.St.123 ne nous permet pas de faire affaire, ce prix étant **sensiblement** supérieur à celui des Autrichiens. - *. . ., this price being appreciably/noticeably higher than that of the Austrians.*
• M. X considérait que votre article et MF étaient de qualité **sensiblement** égale. - *. . . were of approximately/more or less the same quality.*

sentir *vi* feel
TENSES Pres 1 *sens* 3 *sent* 4 *sentons* 6 *sentent* Imp *sentais* Fut *sentirai* PP *senti, -ie* Pres Part *sentant* Subj 1,3 *sente* 4 *sentions* 6 *sentent*
• . . . mais il semble aujourd'hui que les effets de notre prospection se fassent **sentir**. - *. . . the effects of our canvassing are making themselves felt.*

séparé, -ée *adj* separate
COLLOCATES *colis, courrier, pli*
• Un modèle des échantillons envoyés à cette société vous est expédié par courrier **séparé** - *An example of the samples sent to this company is being sent to you by separate post.*

septembre *nm* September

série *nf* series
• Ce dernier tarif vient s'ajouter à la **série** de tarifs et barèmes déjà existante. - *The latter price list supplements the series of price lists and scales already in existence.*

sérieux, -ieuse *adj* serious; proper, reliable, strict, thorough
• . . . et il faut envisager maintenant de reprendre les questions **sérieuses**. - *. . . and we must now be thinking about taking up serious matters again.*
• Nous suggérons de plus qu'un contrôle **sérieux** soit organisé . . . pour faire respecter ces dispositions. - *We suggest moreover that a proper check should be carried out . . . to enforce these regulations.*

service *nm* department; facility, service; favour
• Effectivement, le chèque de règlement de vos calendriers a bien été reçu en son temps par notre **service** comptable. - *The cheque for your calendars was in fact duly received by our accounts department.*

• ... nous avons eu connaissance que CIE disposait d'un **service** de transport par chemin de fer directement de Birmingham sur Paris. - ... *we learnt that CIE had a transport service/facility by rail direct from Birmingham to Paris.*

• Veuillez nous indiquer des journaux professionnels dans lesquels nous pourrions faire des annonces pour proposer nos **services**. - ..., *in which we could place advertisements to offer our services.*

• Je vous serais très reconnaissant si vous pouviez me rendre ce **service**. - ... *if you could do me this favour.*

servir (à/de) *vi* serve, be used for
TENSES Pres 1 *sers* 3 *sert* 4 *servons* 6 *servent* Imp *servais* Fut *servirai* PP *servi, -ie* Pres Part *servant* Subj 1,3 *serve* 4 *servions* 6 *servent*

• Tous ces chiffres peuvent **servir de** base pour une discussion avec CIE. - *All these figures can serve as a basis for discussion with CIE.*

• Cet acier doit **servir à** la fabrication des pièces pliées à 18°. - *This steel is to be used for manufacturing parts bent through 18°.*

siège *nm* head office, registered office

• Nous avons l'honneur de vous faire connaître que les Actionnaires de notre Société sont convoqués par le Conseil d'Administration au **siège social** à Paris le 20 juin 19-- ... – ... *that the shareholders of our company are invited by the Board of Directors to the Head/Registered Office in Paris on 20 June, 19-- ...*

signaler *vt* bring to one's attention/ notice, point out, report
COLLOCATES *activité, cas, correction, création, ennui, erreur, incident, infraction, malfaçon*

• Nous vous **signalons** par cette lettre une erreur de date ... - *By this letter we wish to bring to your attention an error in the date ...*

• Ainsi que nous vous l'**avons** déjà **signalé**, nous devons décliner la fourniture ... - *As we have already pointed out, we must decline to supply ...*

• Nous vous donnons notre accord sous réserve d'application des corrections **signalées** dans votre lettre. - ... *subject to the corrections pointed out/reported in your letter.*

• Nous vous **signalons que** notre client a un besoin extrêmement urgent des aciers ... - *We would point out that our customer is in extremely urgent need of the steels ...*

signature *nf* signature, signing

• Je vous prie de trouver ci-joint le double du contrat de distributeur, **revêtu de ma signature**. - ... *the copy of the distributor's contract, with my signature appended/bearing my signature.*

• Veuillez nous faire signe quand vous serez en mesure de procéder à la **signature** de ce contrat. - ... *to go ahead with signing this contract.*

signer *vt* sign

• Pour la bonne règle, nous vous prions de nous retourner le double de la présente commande, dûment **signé** pour accord. - ... *the duplicate of the present order, duly signed to signify your agreement.*

similaire (à) *adj* similar

• ... une affaire située en Allemagne exerçant une activité **similaire à** la vôtre. - ... *a business in Germany engaged in activities similar to your own.*

simplement *adv* just, merely, simply

• Je n'ai pu obtenir les pourcentages d'alliages et l'on m'a **simplement** répondu qu'il s'agit d'acier à outils. - *I was not able to obtain the alloy percentages and they just/merely/ simply replied that it was tool steel.*

• ... avec, si vous le jugez néccéssaire, modification du message en question, ou même **tout simplement** suppression de ce message. - *... with, ..., modification of the message in question, or even quite simply deletion of this message.*

sincère(ment) *adj & adv* sincere(ly)

sinon *adv* if not, or else, otherwise

• Pouvez-vous joindre ces pieds réglables à la prochaine livraison et, **sinon**, me les envoyer par le train. - *Can you include these adjustable feet with the next delivery and, if not/or else/otherwise, send them by train.*

situation *nf* situation, state; job, post, vacancy

• Néanmoins, notre **situation** financière actuelle est fort instable. - *Nevertheless, our present financial situation/state is highly unstable.*

• Il est actuellement à la recherche d'une nouvelle **situation** en France. - *He is currently looking for a new job in France.*

(se) situer *vt & pro* be, be located, be situated; get an idea of

• Notre salle d'exposition, **située** au coeur de la ville, ... - *Our showroom, located/situated in the very centre of the city, ...*

• Nous vous adressons notre catalogue qui vous permettra de **mieux situer** les articles de notre fabrication. - *... which will enable you to get a better idea of the articles we manufacture.*

société *nf* company, firm

• Nous avons été contactés par les **sociétés** suivantes: ...

soi *pro* oneself; [it goes without saying (that)]

• Il **va de soi que** notre firme se porte garante pour tous les dégâts qu'elle pourrait occasionner à la voie publique. - *It goes without saying that our firm takes responsibility for any damage we might cause to the highway.*

soigné, -ée *adj* careful, meticulous
COLLOCATES *chargement, emballage, exécution, préparation, présentation, service, travail*
USAGE *'Soigné' is used to qualify things and actions but not persons, except in the sense of 'neat', 'well-groomed'.* Compare *'soin', 'veiller'.*

• Les emballages et le chargement seront particulièrement **soignés**. - *Packing and loading will be particularly careful.*

soigneusement *adv* carefully

• Ayant revu **soigneusement** nos calculs, ... - *Having carefully checked our calculations, ...*

soin *nm* care

• Nous tenons à vous remercier du **soin** que vous avez apporté dans la recherche des causes de ... - *Thank you for the care you have taken in seeking the causes of ...*

• J'ai examiné **avec soin** les termes de votre dernière lettre ... - *I have examined with care/carefully the terms of your latest letter ...*

• Nous vous **laissons le soin** d'adresser à Bulawayo une facture pour les besoins de la douane. - *We leave it to you to send an invoice to Bulawayo for customs' purposes.*

• Le dédouanement serait effectué **par nos soins**. - *Customs clearance would be done by us.*

soit namely, viz.; either . . . or

• Le montant de votre souscription, **soit** 400 Frs, n'était pas joint à votre envoi. - *The amount of your subscription, namely/viz. 400 francs, was not enclosed.*

• Ces calendriers vous sont cédés au prix unitaire de F.5,70, **soit** au total F.570. - *These calendars are supplied to you at 5.70 francs each, 570 francs in all.*

• Nous pensons que vous pourrez nous facturer **soit** directement **soit** par l'intermédiaire de CIE. - *We think you can invoice us **either** direct **or** through CIE.*

solde *nm* balance

• Paiement: 30% à la commande, le **solde** à 30 jours de facturation. - *Payment: 30% with order, the **balance** 30 days from invoicing.*

• . . . et prenons bonne note que le **solde** du matériel est souhaité le 25 courant. - *. . . and note that you desire the **balance** of the material on the 25th of this month.*

solliciter *vt* apply for, seek

• Par la présente nous avons l'avantage de **solliciter** de votre part l'autorisation d'imposer une interdiction de parquer . . . - *We hereby **apply** to you **for** authorization to impose a parking prohibition . . .*

solution *nf* solution, way out
COLLOCATES *accepter, apporter, arriver à, avancer, envisager, préconiser, trouver*

• Nous croyons que la meilleure **solution** serait de proposer à Monsieur X le nouveau matériel . . . - *. . . the best **solution**/way out would be to offer Mr X the new material . . .*

somme *nf* amount, sum
USAGE See '*montant*'.

• En ce qui concerne les frais de téléphone, nous avons laissé au budget une **somme** de F.90.000. - *As regards telephone expenses, we have left in the budget an **amount**/sum of 90,000 francs.*

sorte *nf* (*In* 'de sorte que' so that, in such a way that, so)
USAGE *When the following clause expresses **purpose** (first example), the verb is in the* Subjunctive. *When it expresses **consequence** (second example), the verb is in the* Indicative.

• Nous comptons sur vous pour que ce transfert soit effectué **de sorte que** cette somme soit certainement disponible ici le 31 août 19--. - *We are counting on you to have this transfer effected **so that**/in such a way that this sum is definitely available here on Aug. 31, 19--.*

• Nous sommes en situation de livrer ces marchandises avant la date que vos clients ont eux-mêmes fixée, **de sorte que** nous ne comprenons pas la raison qu'ils invoquent pour annuler la commande. - *We are in a position to deliver these goods before the date set by your customers themselves, **so** we do not understand the reason they give for cancelling the order.*

sortir *vi & t* come out, go out; bring out
TENSES See *partir*

• Nous nous permettons de vous envoyer la présente pour vous soumettre une nouveauté que nous venons de **sortir**. - *. . . in order to submit to you a new fashion which we have just **brought out**.*

en souffrance on demurrage, held up, awaiting delivery, pending

• La caisse est **en souffrance** à Mombasa depuis mai dernier. - *The crate has been **on demurrage**/held up at Mombasa since last May.*

souhait *nm* wish

• ... c'est un plaisir pour nous de vous présenter nos sincères **souhaits** de réussite et de prospérité. - ... *our sincere **wishes** for success and prosperity.*

souhaitable *adj* desirable, best, wise
USAGE *'Il est **souhaitable** que'* + Subjunctive.

• Nous pensons donc qu'il serait **souhaitable** que CIE intervienne auprès du transitaire à Mombasa ... - *We therefore think it would be **desirable** for CIE to approach the forwarding agent at Mombasa ...*

souhaiter *vt* wish, hope
USAGE *'Souhaiter'* is found most often in the expressions *'vous **souhaitant** bonne réception de'* and *'nous vous **souhaitons** bonne réception de'* (first example). Syntactically it behaves like *'désirer'* – *'souhaiter quelque chose'*, *'souhaiter faire'*, *'souhaiter que* + Subjunctive' – *except that , unlike 'désirer', it can take an* Indirect Object *(first example). However, the sense of 'souhaiter' is often close to that of 'espérer' (third example).*

• Vous **souhaitant** bonne réception de ces pièces, ... - ***Wishing** you safe receipt of these parts, ...*

• ..., mais il ne m'a pas caché qu'il **souhaite que** l'étude se fasse le plus tôt possible. - ..., *but he did not conceal from me that he **wishes** the study to be done as soon as possible.*

• Nous **souhaitons que** vous puissiez tenir compte de ces indications lors de la prochaine édition de votre tarif. - *We **hope that** you can take account of this information when your price list is next revised.*

soulever *vt* raise, bring up
TENSES See *acheter*

COLLOCATES *intérêt, point, problème, question*

• ..., et nous marquons notre accord sur les différents points **soulevés**. - ..., *and we confirm our agreement about the various points **raised**.*

souligner *vt* emphasize, underline

• Il est inutile de **souligner** auprès de vous l'importance de ... - *We hardly need to **emphasize** to you the importance of ...*

soumettre *vt* submit, put before
TENSES See *mettre*

• Il y aurait donc lieu de nous **soumettre** votre cotation par retour du courrier. - *It would therefore be well for you to **submit** your quotation to us by return.*

soumission *nf* tender

• Lorsque je recevrai d'autres **demandes de soumission**, je vous consulterai. - *When I receive other **invitations to tender**, I will contact you.*

soumissionner *vt* tender for

• A notre grand regret, il ne nous est pas possible de **soumissionner** les travaux ci-dessus. - ..., *it is not possible for us to **tender for** the above works.*

sous *prep* under; in, within

• Extras: 300 Frs la tonne pour emballage **sous** papier. - ... *for packing **in** paper.*

• Monsieur X nous avait dit que les MF pourraient être livrés **sous** 10 à 14 jours. - ... *the MF could be delivered **within** 10 to 14 days.*

se **souvenir de** *vpro* recall, remember
TENSES See *venir*

• Vous **vous souviendrez** en effet que les précédentes livraisons ne nous ont pas permis d'obtenir un rendement convenable. - *You will recall in fact that the previous deliveries did not enable us to obtain a satisfactory output.*

souvent *adv* often
• ... nous vous passons de plus en plus **souvent** des commandes pour des robinets. - ... *we are placing orders with you for taps more and more* **often.**

spécial, -e (*mpl* -iaux) *adj* special
• Au sujet du prix **spécial** que j'avais demandé, la remise est vraiment très faible. - *Regarding the* **special** *price I had asked for, the reduction is really very small.*

spécialement *adv* especially, particularly, specially
• Nous serions très intéressés par l'importation de ce matériel en France et plus **spécialement** par les modèles 301 et 302. - ... *and more* **especially** *by the 301 and 302 models.*

spécialisé, -ée (dans) *adj* specialized, specializing, [specialize]
• Suite à une publicité parue dans une revue **spécialisée** française, ... - *Following an advertisement which appeared in a* **specialized** *French journal, ...*
• Nous sommes devant un négociant **spécialisé dans** la vente des métaux non ferreux. - *We are faced with a merchant* **specializing in/ who specializes in** *the sale of non-ferrous metals.*

spécialiste (de) *nmf* specialist (in)
• Il est **spécialiste de** la mécanique. - *He is a* **specialist in** *mechanical engineering.*

spécialité *nf* speciality
• Voulez-vous avoir l'amabilité de nous dire si ces **spécialités** peuvent se vendre en Angleterre. - ... *if these* **specialities** *will sell in Britain.*

spécification *nf* specification
COLLOCATES *détaillée, exacte, précise, technique*
• Veuillez nous faire votre meilleure offre pour le matériel selon **spécification** ci-après. - ... *for the material conforming to the following* **specification.**

spécifier *vt* specify
• Veuillez bien **spécifier** les caractéristiques mécaniques. - *Please* **specify** *the mechanical characteristics.*

spécifique *adj* specific
• Je vous signale que ces demandes **spécifiques** doivent être traitées très rapidement. - ... *these* **specific** *inquiries must be dealt with very quickly.*

stage *nm* training course, work experience
• Monsieur X désirerait que son adjoint **fasse un stage de quelques semaines** dans vos bureaux. - *Mr X would like his assistant* **to have a few weeks work experience** *in your offices.*

stand *nm* stand
• Je vous joins croquis de notre **stand** à la Foire de Lille. - *I enclose a sketch of our* **stand** *at the Lille exhibition.*

standard (*Plural* invariable) *adj* standard
• Nous supposons qu'il vous serait difficile de changer la forme **standard.**

stipuler *vt* lay down, stipulate
• ... et nous établirons une facture pour les frais comme **stipulé** à votre lettre précitée. - ... *as* **stipulated** *in your aforementioned letter.*

stock *nm* stock

• En effet, nos **stocks** sont pratiquement à zéro dans toutes les références commandées. - *Our stocks are in fact practically exhausted . . .*
• A titre d'indication, j'ai actuellement **en stock** sauf vente: . . . - *By way of information, I have **in stock** at present, subject to prior sale: . . .*

subir *vt* suffer, be subjected to, undergo
COLLOCATES *accident, augmentation, avarie, conséquence, crise, dégâts, dommages, effet, hausse, influence, majoration, modification, perte, préjudice, traitement, transformation*
• Il se pourrait que 10 ou 20 barres puissent **avoir subi** un accident lors de l'extrusion. - *10 or 12 bars could **have suffered** an accident during extrusion.*
• A partir du 10 décembre les colis postaux **subiront une augmentation** de 10%. - *From 10 December parcel post **will be increased** by 10%.*

succès *nm* success
• En effet, l'essai de notre appareil n'a pas été un **succès**. - *It is indeed the case that the trial of our appliance has not been a **success**.*

succursale *nf* branch, branch office
• Ces conclusions ont été également transmises à notre **succursale** de Lyon.

suffire (de) *vi & impers* suffice, be sufficient
TENSES Pres 1 *suffis* 3 *suffit* 4 *suffisons* 6 *suffisent* Imp *suffisais* Fut *suffirai* PP *suffi* Pres Part *suffisant* Subj 1,3 *suffise* 4 *suffisions* 6 *suffisent*
• Les informations très générales que je leur ai données concernant l'affaire leur **suffisent** pour l'instant. - *The general information I gave them regarding the matter **is sufficient** for them for the moment.*

• Pour nous retourner les collections au bout d'un an, **il vous suffira de** conserver notre caisse emballage qui les contient. - *. . . **it will suffice for you/all you need do is** to keep the packing case they are in.*

suffisamment *adv* enough, sufficiently
• . . . afin que nous puissions nous approvisionner **suffisamment tôt** en jantes MF auprès de CIE. - *. . . so that we can stock up **soon enough/sufficiently early** with MF rims from CIE.*

suggérer (de) *vt* suggest
TENSES See *céder*
• Nous vous **suggérons** la livraison suivante: . . . - *We **suggest** the following delivery: . . .*
• Nous serons heureux de vous accueillir, **comme vous le suggérez**, le mardi 11 avril à Saint-Germain. - *We shall be glad to receive you, **as you suggest**, . . .*
• Je vous **suggère** donc **de** m'envoyer la bande en question. - *I **suggest** therefore that you send me the tape in question.*

suite *nf* continuation; [further to, pursuant to, re., reference; pursue, follow up; drop; accede to, agree to, comply with; following; due to, in consequence of, as a result of; afterwards, subsequently]
USAGE *An extremely frequent word in business letters, hence the large number of translation equivalents and examples which attempt to illustrate the more common uses.*
• **Suite** No 1 à notre offre du 28 février 19-- . . . - ***Continuation** No. 1 of our offer of 28 February, 19-- . . .*
• **Suite à/Comme suite à/Faisant suite à** votre demande, nous vous remettons sous ce pli notre facture

définitive relative à cette réparation. - *Further to/Re./Reference your request, . . .* (all interchangeable)

• Nous vous laissons le soin de **donner suite à** cette affaire et . . . - *We leave it to you to pursue/follow up/ proceed further with this matter and . . .*

• L'impossibilité d'obtenir une garantie du résultat a amené notre client à **ne pas donner suite à** cette affaire. - *The impossibility of getting a guarantee of the result has led our customer to **drop** this matter.*

• Nous regrettons de ne pouvoir **donner une suite favorable** à votre proposition . . . - *We regret we cannot accede/agree to/comply with your proposal . . .*

• **A la suite de** cette offre préliminaire, nous espérons être consultés de façon plus détaillée. - *Following this preliminary offer, we hope to be consulted in a more detailed way.*

• Notre transporteur habituel ne veut plus aller charger chez CIE **par suite des** difficultés qu'il rencontre. - *Our usual carrier is no longer willing to load at CIE's premises **due to/in consequence of/as a result of** the difficulties he meets with.*

• Les avaries ne surviennent pas sur le transport Londres-Paris, mais **par la suite** en cours d'expédition par chemin de fer chez nos clients. - *The damage does not occur between London and Paris, but **subsequently/ afterwards** during despatch by rail to our customers.*

suivant, -e *adj & nmf* following, next
USAGE See *'prochain'*.

• . . . un stock d'été qui perd toute sa valeur l'année **suivante**. - . . . *a summer stock which loses all its value the **following/next** year.*

• Je vous propose de prendre contact avec les personnes **suivantes**: . . . - *I suggest you contact the following people: . . .*

• Les caractéristiques de ces pneumatiques sont les **suivantes**: . . . - *The characteristics of these tyres are the following: . . .*

suivant *prep* according to, in accordance/conformity with, as per

• **Suivant** les calculs que nous avons faits, le surfret pour Glasgow ressortirait à . . . - *According to the calculations we have done, the freight surcharge for Glasgow would come to . . .*

• Les briques seraient exécutées **suivant** les formes et dimensions indiquées sur notre plan joint. - *The bricks would be executed **as per/in accordance with** the shapes and dimensions shown on the enclosed drawing.*

suivi, -ie *adj* regular, steady

• A vrai dire, nous n'avons travaillé d'une façon **suivie** qu'avec CIE. - *Truth to tell, it is only with CIE that we have worked on a **regular** basis.*

suivre *vt* follow, watch, keep an eye/tabs on; forward
TENSES Pres 1 *suis* 3 *suit* 4 *suivons* 6 *suivent* Imp *suivais* Fut *suivrai* PP *suivi, -ie* Pres Part *suivant* Subj 1,3 *suive* 4 *suivions* 6 *suivent*

• Nous vous confirmons les termes de notre câble de ce jour rédigé **comme suit**: . . . - . . . *our cable of today's date worded **as follows**: . . .*

• Nous **suivons** cette affaire **de près**. - *We **are following/watching/ keeping an eye/tabs on** this matter.*

• A vous à ce moment-là de les **faire suivre** à CIE. - *It will then be up to you to **forward** them (documents) to CIE.*

sujet *nm* subject, connection, matter, regard, [regarding]

• Nous aimerions vous lire **à ce sujet** dans un proche avenir et, ... - *We would like to hear from you **on this subject/matter/about this/in this connection/regard** in the near future and, ...*

• Nous nous référons à notre correspondance antérieure **au sujet des** olives farcies. - *We refer to our previous correspondence **on the subject of/regarding/with regard to** stuffed olives.*

sujet, -ette **à** *adj* subject to
• Cette affaire est **sujette à** l'acceptation définitive de la part des usines. - *This offer is **subject to** final acceptance by the factory.*

supérieur, -e (à) *adj* superior; higher, greater
• Nous pouvons vous offrir un article de remplacement nettement **supérieur** comme suit: ... – *We can offer you a replacement article which is distinctly **superior** as follows:...*
• ... les frais de transport par fer de Marseille jusqu'à Contes étaient **supérieurs au** fret direct de Dunkerque à Contes. - *... the transport costs by rail from Marseille to Contes were **higher/greater than** the freight direct from Dunkerque to Contes.*

supplément *nm* supplement, [extra]
• Le client serait prêt à payer un petit **supplément** pour obtenir satisfaction.
• Notre succursale de Paris nous demande 12 agendas **en supplément**. - *Our Paris branch is asking us for 12 **extra** diaries.*

supplémentaire *adj* additional, extra, supplementary
COLLOCATES *commande, crédit, délai, dépense, fret, paiement, prix, protection*
• ... et CIE demande si vous ne pourriez pas participer à une partie

de ces frais **supplémentaires**. - *... a part of these **additional/extra/supplementary** expenses.*

supporter *vt* bear
COLLOCATES *conséquences, démarque, frais, perte*
• Par ailleurs, si vous aviez à **supporter** une perte personnelle, nous serions heureux de vous assister. - *Furthermore, if you had to **bear** a personal loss, ...*

supposer *vt* assume, imagine, presume, suppose, take it that
• Nous n'avons pas reçu vos cotations pour les susdites demandes et nous **supposons** que le pli s'est égaré. - *... and we **assume** that the letter has gone astray.*

surcharge *nf* extra load, overload
• Ce retard est dû à la période des vacances et à la **surcharge** de travail qui en découle. - *... and to the **extra load/overload** of work resulting from it.*

surcharger *vt* overload, overwork
TENSES See *changer*
• Notre bureau technique est momontanément fort **surchargé** par d'importantes commandes. - *Our technical department is at the moment seriously **overloaded/overworked** by large orders.*

surprendre (de) *vt* surprise
TENSES See *prendre*
• Nous **étions** en effet **surpris de** ne pas encore avoir reçu de réponse de votre part. - *We **were** in fact **surprised** not yet **to** have received a reply from you.*

surtout *adv* above all, mainly, mostly, primarily
• ... et ce qui nous intéresse **surtout**, c'est d'en connaître la réputation technique. - *... and what*

interests us **above all** is to know their technical reputation.

surveiller *vt* supervise
• L'exécution du travail est sérieusement **surveillée**. - *Execution of the work is properly **supervised**.*

survenir *vi* arise, come about, happen, occur
TENSES See *venir*
COLLOCATES *amélioration, avarie, dévaluation, difficulté, incident, retard*
• Nous suivrons donc l'évolution de ce marché et, dès qu'une amélioration **surviendra**, nous ... - *We shall keep an eye on the way this market develops and, as soon as an improvement **comes about**, we ...*

en sus (de) in addition (to), over and above
• Dans ce cas le port et l'emballage seront facturés **en sus**. - *In this case carriage and packing will be invoiced **in addition**.*

susceptible de *adj* capable of, liable to
• Ces prix sont **susceptibles de** fluctuations ... - *These prices are **liable to** fluctuate ...*
• Nous avons remarqué votre appareil, qui est **susceptible d**'être adapté à nos produits. - *..., which is **capable of** being adapted to our products.*

susdit, -e *adj* above, above-mentioned
• Nous avons bien reçu votre **susdite** offre ... - *We have received your **above-mentioned** offer ...*

susmentionné, -ée *adj* above, above-mentioned
• Nous avons le plaisir de vous faire savoir que le fusil automatique MF, objet de votre ordre

susmentionné, pourra être expédié ... – ... *the MF automatic rifle, covered by your **above-mentioned** order, ...*

suspendre *vt* suspend
TENSES See *rendre*
• Nous vous confirmons notre communication téléphonique **suspendant** jusqu'à nouvel ordre de notre part les trois machines objet de notre commande en référence. - ... *suspending until further notice from us the three machines covered by our order referred to above.*

suspension *nf* suspension
• Le non-respect de cette clause entraînerait la **suspension** de tout paiement. - *Non-respect of this clause would entail **suspension** of all payments.*

système *nm* system
• Nous tenons à vous confirmer l'intérêt que nous portons au **système** d'assemblage MF. - ... *our interest in the MF assembly **system**.*

systématique *adj* systematic
• Ayant appris que vous seriez peut-être intéressés par une distribution **systématique** sur l'ensemble de la France de votre production, ... - *Having heard that you might be interested in the **systematic** distribution of your products throughout France, ...*

systématiquement *adv* systematically
• Nous envisageons d'améliorer encore nos ventes en engageant des représentants pour prospecter **systématiquement** et régulièrement toute la Belgique. - ... *by taking on representatives to canvass **systematically** and regularly the whole of Belgium.*

T

tableau (*mpl* -aux) *nm* table
• Afin de faire le point de nos commandes en cours nous avons établi le **tableau** ci-après: ... - *In order to take stock of our current orders we have drawn up the **table** below: ...*

tandis que whereas, while
• Nous vous prions de noter qu'un des fusils est actuellement disponible **tandis que** le second sera prêt vers la fin de cette semaine. - *... one of the rifles is now available **whereas/while** the second will be ready towards the end of this week.*

tant so long, so much; as long as, [until]; in one's capacity as; both ... and
• Je m'excuse d'avoir **tant** tardé à vous retourner ce document. - *I apologize for having delayed **so long** in returning this document to you.*
• Nous ne pourrons pas espérer de nouvelle commande à CIE **tant que nous n'aurons pas** de meilleure qualité de MF à proposer. - *... as long as we haven't/until we have a better quality MF to offer.*
• Nous tenons à vous préciser notre position **en tant qu'**agent import-export. - *We wish to make clear our position **in our capacity as** import-export agent.*
• Nous avons été amenés à faire une remise importante **tant** sur les appareils **que** sur la crème. - *We finished up giving a large discount **both** on the appliances **and** on the cream.*

tard *adv* late
• Il était à ce moment trop **tard** pour enregistrer régulièrement votre commande. - *It was by then too **late** to book your order properly.*

• Pour être prise en considération, votre offre devra nous parvenir **au plus tard** le 1er août 19--. - ..., *your offer should reach us **no later than/at the latest on** 1 August, 19--.*

tarder (à) *vi* delay (in), be/take a long time (to)
• ... et pour cette raison nous **avons tellement tardé à** vous fixer définitivement. - *... and for that reason we **have taken such a long time** to put you fully in the picture.*

tardif, -ive *adj* late, tardy
• ... cette demande, quoique bien **tardive**, pourrait être satisfaite ... - *... this request, although very **late/tardy**, could be satisfied ...*

tardivement *adv* belatedly
• Nous nous excusons de répondre **tardivement** à votre courrier du 10 mai.

tarif *nm* price list, tariff
• Veuillez trouver ci-joint notre **tarif** exportation 19--. - *... our 19-- export **price list**.*
• Vous trouverez sous ce pli notre **tarif** de publicité. - *... our advertising **tariff**.*

taux *nm* rate
USAGE Compare 'cadence'.
• Par la suite nous ne pourrons plus facturer de cette façon mais suivant le nouveau **taux** de change. - *... but in accordance with the new **rate** of exchange.*

taxe *nf* tax, duty
• Ces prix s'entendent nets unitaires, TVA incluse, pour marchandise rendue ... - *These prices*

*are net per unit, inclusive of **VAT**, delivered . . .*

• Nous avions remis à CIE le prix de F640, **toutes taxes comprises**, . . . - *. . ., inclusive of all taxes, . . .*

• Vos prix seront indiqués **hors taxes**, . . . - *Your prices will be shown exclusive of tax, . . .*

• Vos prix s'entendent pour tubes . . ., droits de douane et **taxe à l'importation** à notre charge. - *. . ., customs duties and **import duty** payable by us.*

technique *adj* technical

• Cette machine sera remise au début de la semaine prochaine à notre service **technique**, pour examen et . . . - *This machine will be passed at the start of next week to our **technical** department for examination and . . .*

tel, telle *adj* such

• Dans le cas d'une **telle** commande, quelques petites modifications seraient sans doute nécessaires. - *In the event of **such an** order, . . .*

• Il y a donc lieu de vous en séparer et de vous organiser **de telle façon/ sorte que** le travail n'en souffre pas. - *. . . organize yourselves **in such a way that** the work does not suffer as a result.*

• Enfin nous nous intéressons à tous vos autres appareils de bar **tels que**: MF, MF, . . . - *Finally, we are interested in all your other bar equipment **such as**: MF, MF, . . .*

• La quantité sera **telle qu'**on devrait facilement arriver à un tonnage de 350T. minimum. - *The quantity will be **such that** we should easily reach a tonnage of 350T. minimum.*

• **Tel** est donc le programme qu'aimerait suivre M. X. - *Such then is*

the programme that Mr X would like to follow.

tel quel, telle quelle *adj* as found, as it is

• Les marchandises, chargées par vos soins dans les remorques, arrivent **telles quelles** à destination. - *The goods, loaded by you in the trailers, arrive **as they are/undisturbed** at their destination.*

télégramme *nm* cable, telegram, wire

• Comme suite à votre **télégramme** et à votre lettre de confirmation du 8 octobre, . . . - *Reference your **cable/ telegram/wire** and your letter of confirmation . . .*

télégraphier *vt* cable, telegraph, wire

• . . . et nous avons à notre tour **télégraphié** comme suit: . . . - *. . . and we in turn **cabled/telegraphed/wired** as follows: . . .*

télégraphique *adj* cabled, telegraphic

• Votre réponse ou plutôt vos instructions **télégraphiques** nous obligeraient. - *Your reply or rather your **cabled/telegraphed** instructions would oblige us.*

téléphone *nm* telephone, phone

• Nous avons reçu ce matin, lundi 20, un **coup de téléphone** de Monsieur X de la S.N.C.F.. - *We received . . . a **telephone call** from Mr X of the SNCF.*

téléphoner *vt* telephone, phone

• **Téléphonez**-moi quand vous voudrez, pour que nous puissions prendre rendez-vous.

téléphonique *adj* telephone(d), phone(d)

COLLOCATES *appel, communication, conversation, demande, entretien*
• Faisant suite à notre entretien **téléphonique**, nous vous prions de ... - *Further to our **phone/telephone** conversation, ...*

téléphotocopie *nf* fax

télex *nm* telex
• Sans nouvelles de vous depuis notre échange de **télex** cité ci-dessus, nous vous prions de ... - *Being without news from you since our exchange of **telex** quoted above, ...*

télexer *vt* telex
• Nous comptons sur votre coopération pour que vous **télexiez** vos conditions de prix et délai dès réception de la présente. - *We are counting on you to **telex** your price and delivery terms as soon as you receive this letter.*

tellement *adv* so
• Pour vos machines à coudre une courroie étonnante – **tellement** étonnante que voici notre garantie: ... - *For your sewing machines an astonishing drive belt – **so** astonishing that here is our guarantee: ...*

temps *nm* weather; time; [punctually]
USAGE *The four expressions, 'en son/leur temps', 'en **temps** utile', 'en **temps** voulu' and 'en **temps** opportun' are used interchangeably. All four can be used both of past events (last but one example) and of future ones (last example).*
• Le mauvais **temps** a retardé le transport de nos marchandises ... - *The bad **weather** has delayed carriage of our goods ...*
• Comme suite à votre lettre du 15 ct., qui **a mis quelque temps à** nous parvenir, ... - *Further to your letter of*

*15th inst., which **took some time to** reach us, ...*
• En effet, nos services ministériels **ont pris un temps très considérable pour** nous accorder le remboursement des droits et taxes. - *In fact, our government departments **took a very considerable time to** grant us the reimbursement of the duties and taxes.*
• Nous avons appris qu'il s'agit d'une affaire qui est à l'étude **depuis un certain temps** déjà. - *... which has been under investigation **for some time** already.*
• Ce document, arrivé **peu de temps avant** les vacances de Pâques, s'est trouvé enfoui sous d'autres papiers. - *This document, having arrived **shortly before** the Easter holiday, got buried under other papers.*
• Comme demandé, nous vous enverrons la facture **en même temps** que l'avis d'expédition. - *As requested, we shall send you the invoice **at the same time** as the dispatch note.*
• Nous étions en droit de penser que la marchandise vous était parvenue **en son temps**. - *We were entitled to think that the goods had reached you **at the right/appropriate time/on time/punctually**.*
• ... et nous vous ferons parvenir **en temps utile/voulu/opportun** notre facture définitive concernant cette réparation. - *... and we shall send you **at the appropriate time/in due course** our final invoice for this repair.*

tenir *vt* keep to, honour
TENSES See *venir*
• ... mais nous insistons beaucoup pour que vous **teniez** rigoureusement les dates de livraison indiquées sur votre lettre. - *... but we emphasize strongly that you **should***

keep to/should honour the delivery dates . . .

tenir à *vt indir* be anxious to, be keen to, make a point of, wish to
TENSES See *venir*

• Nous **tenons à** vous préciser notre position en tant qu'agent import-export. - *We wish to/are anxious to make clear our position as import-export agents.*

• Lors d'un précédent numéro spécial vous **aviez tenu à** vous procurer cet important ouvrage. - *When a previous special issue came out you made a point of obtaining this important work.*

se tenir *vpro* be held, take place
TENSES See *venir*

• . . . le Congrès des Techniciens de la Santé, qui **s'est tenu** du 13 au 18 avril écoulé. - *. . . the Conference of Health Technicians, which was held/took place from 13 to 18 April last.*

terme *nm* term

• Les dénominations que vous suggérez nous semblent correctes en ce qui concerne les **termes** 'galvanisé' et 'alliage'. - *The designations you suggest seem to us correct as regards the terms 'galvanized' and 'alloy'.*

• J'ai examiné avec soin les **termes** de votre dernière lettre . . .

terminer *vt* close, end, finish

• En résumé, pour le 13 j'**aurai terminé** la mise en place des 6 représentants prévus pour notre première étape. - *To sum up, by the 13th I will have finished establishing the 6 representatives planned for our first stage . . .*

• Nous espérons votre accord pour considérer cette affaire comme **terminée**. - *We hope you will agree to consider this matter closed.*

texte *nm* text

• Toutes nos étiquettes comportent un **texte** anglais. - *All our labels include a text in English.*

tiers *nm* third party

• J'ai également noté vos scrupules à parler de ce problème à des **tiers** sans l'accord du propriétaire, M. X. - *I have also noted your scruples about speaking of this problem to third parties without the agreement of the owner, Mr X.*

tirer *vt* draw

• Nous pourrons **tirer** une traite à vue sur la Banque X, ainsi que vous nous le suggérez. - *We can draw a sight draft on the Bank X, as you suggest.*

(à) titre (de) *nm* basis; title; way, [as]; [deservedly, properly, rightly]
COLLOCATES *consultatif, confidentiel, exceptionnel, gracieux, gratuit, indicatif, informatif, permanent, personnel, privé, provisoire; d'accompte, de client fidèle, de compensation, d'essai, d'exception, d'exemple, d'indemnité, d'indication, d'information, de paiement, de prêt, de réciprocité*

• L'article que nous ferions paraître, **à titre absolument gratuit**, ne pourrait que vous être favorable. - *The article which we would publish, on an absolutely free-of-charge basis, could not fail to be favourable to you.*

• Nous avons conclu cette vente **à titre exceptionnel** sur juillet et . . . - *We made this sale on an exceptional basis/in this exceptional case for July and . . .*

• **A titre indicatif** et sans engagement de notre part, nous vous communiquons que les frais de transport sont . . . - *For information only and without obligation on our part,* *we advise you that transport costs are . . .*

• Mais nous sommes simplement en pourparlers **au même titre** qu'avec les maisons que vous nous avez indiquées. - *But we are simply negotiating **in the same way/on the same basis** as with the other firms which you have alluded to.*

• Tels sont les trois éléments qui, à **juste titre**, vous préoccupent peut-être. - *Such are the three factors which, **deservedly/rightly/with just cause/ quite properly**, are concerning you perhaps.*

• Nous vous confirmons qu'il vous sera réservé 10%, **à titre de** frais d'études, sur toute commande éventuelle . . . - *We confirm that 10% will be reserved for you, **as/by way of** research expenses, on any future order . . .*

tôt *adv* early, soon, [at your earliest convenience]
• Veuillez nous excuser de ne pas avoir répondu **plus tôt**. - *. . . for not having replied **earlier/sooner**.*
• . . . et vous serions très obligés de nous faire parvenir votre offre **au plus tôt**. - *. . . as soon as possible/at your earliest convenience*.
• Vous voudrez bien faire effectuer la livraison **le plus tôt possible** . . . - *Please have the delivery made **as soon as possible/at your earliest convenience** . . .*

total, -e (*mpl* -aux) *nm & adj* total, whole, [altogether, in all]
• Cette maison nous a acheté par très petites quantités 200 MF **au total** depuis le début de nos relations. - *This company has bought in very small quantities 200 MF **altogether/in all** since the start of our relationship.*
• . . . une quittance d'indemnité d'un montant de F68.900, plus

F.3.500 pour frais de transport, soit **au total** F.72.400. - *. . . a receipt in the amount of 68,900 francs, plus 3500 francs for transport charges, 72,400 francs **in all/in total**.*
• Crédit ouvert pour la durée **totale** de l'embarquement plus 15 jours . . . - *Credit open for the **whole** duration of loading plus 15 days . . .*

totalité *nf* whole, entirety, [all, entirely, wholly]
• **La totalité des** marchandises pourrait être mise à votre disposition dans un délai de trois mois. - *The **entirety/whole of/All** the merchandise could be placed at your disposal . . .*
• . . . car nous devrons éliminer certaines bottes, **en totalité** ou en partie. - *. . . for we shall have to discard certain bundles, **entirely/wholly/in whole** or in part.*

toujours *adv* always, at all times; still
• **Toujours** à votre disposition, . . .
• Cette affaire est **toujours** à l'étude. - *This matter is **still** under consideration.*

tour *nm* turn
• . . . et nous avons **à notre tour** *télégraphié comme suit: . . . - . . . and we **in turn** telegraphed as follows: . . .*

toutefois *adv* however
• **Toutefois**, le jeudi 13 avril ne me convient pas bien. - *However, Thursday 13 April does not suit me well.*
• Nous devons **toutefois** vous signaler que priorité doit être accordée à la nouvelle demande. - *We must, **however**, point out that priority must be given to the new inquiry.*

trace *nf* trace, record
• Malheureusement, nous **ne trouvons pas trace de** la copie qui

devait être jointe à votre lettre. - *Unfortunately, **we cannot trace/ cannot find any trace/record of** the copy which should have been enclosed with your letter.*

trafic *nm* traffic
• Concerne: **trafic** en provenance ou à destination d'Angleterre par remorques routières. - *Subject: **traffic** from or to England by road trailers.*

train *nm* train; [in the process of]
• Puisque vous arriverez le matin du 8 par le **train** de nuit, ...
• Nous **sommes en train d'examiner** ce problème et ... - *We **are in the process of examining**/We **are examining** this problem and ...*

traite *nf* bill, draft
• Nous vous prions de nous adresser une **traite à 60 jours.** - *... a **bill/draft at 60 days.***
• D'autre part, comme vous nous le suggérez, nous ferons présenter une **traite à vue** à votre banque, CIE, à Londres. - *Furthermore, as you suggest, we will arrange for a **sight draft** to be presented to your bank, CIE, in London.*

traiter *vt & i* handle, deal (with), do business, have dealings
• Nous avions remis à CIE le prix de F640 ... et nous pensions **traiter l'affaire** sur ces bases. - *We had quoted CIE a price of 640 francs ... and we thought we were **dealing with the business/handling the deal** on this basis.*
• ... et nous indiquer les prix auxquels vous pourriez **traiter.** - *... and indicate to us the prices at which you could **deal.***

traiter de *vt indir* be concerned with, deal with
• ... la disposition de votre règlement qui **traite de** cette

question. - *... the provision in your regulations which **is concerned with/ deals with** this question.*

tranche *nf* instalment
• Quantité: 31.000kg par an à livrer en 5 **tranches** de 5.630kg env.. - *Quantity: 31,000kg per annum to be delivered in 5 **instalments** of approximately 5,630kg.*

transaction *nf* transaction
• N'ayant encore effectué aucune **transaction** avec la Grande-Bretagne sur ce produit, ... - *Having as yet done no **transactions** with Great Britain in this product, ...*

transbordement *nm* transshipment
• Ce mode de transport vous permet d'éviter ... toutes les manutentions et tous les **transbordements.** - *This means of transport enables you to avoid ... all handling and **transshipments.***

transférer *vt* transfer
TENSES See *céder*
• ... votre accord pour **transférer** la distribution de vos fittings à CIE à Levallois. - *... your agreement to **transfer** the distribution of your fittings to CIE at Levallois.*

transfert *nm* transfer
• Nous notons que le règlement des marchandises fournies à Bamako sera subordonné à l'autorisation des **transferts** de fonds entre Mali et la France. - *We note that payment for the goods supplied to Bamako will be subject to **transfers** of funds being authorized between Mali and France.*

transformer *vt* convert, transform
• Je sais que les cotes de base de ces pièces en pouces ont été **transformées** en m/ms et ... - *I know the basic measurements of these parts in*

*inches have been **converted/
transformed** into millimetres and ...*

transit *nm* transit
• Voudriez-vous nous confirmer les
conditions de **transit** que vous
pouvez appliquer à notre trafic? -
*Would you confirm to us the **transit**
terms which you can apply to our traffic?*

transitaire *nm* forwarding agent
• Devons-nous procéder
directement à l'expédition de la
marchandise ou est-elle à remettre à
un **transitaire**? - *Are we to go ahead
and dispatch direct or are the goods to be
handed over to a **forwarding agent**?*

transmettre *vt* convey, forward,
pass on
TENSES See *mettre*
COLLOCATES *commande, conclusions,
confirmation, contenu, correspondance,
demande, documentation, doléances,
dossier, facture, instructions, lettre,
nom. paquet, photocopie, proposition,
remerciements, renseignements,
sentiments, voeux*
• Dès réception de vos doléances
nous les **avons transmises** à nos
expéditeurs, qui ... - *As soon as we
received your complaints, we **conveyed**
them to our forwarding agents, who ...*
• Nous vous remettons, en annexe,
un dépliant que nous vous prions de
vouloir bien **transmettre** à votre
client. - *... which we would ask you
kindly to **forward/pass on** to your
customer.*
• Nous vous prions de bien vouloir
**transmettre nos respectueux
sentiments** à Monsieur X ainsi que
notre bon souvenir à Monsieur Y. -
*Please **convey our respects** to Mr X
and **remember us** to Mr Y.*

transport *nm* transport, carriage,
conveyance, freight, movement,
transportation

• Ce mode de **transport** paraît avoir
un certain intérêt pour CIE. - *This
mode of **transport** appears to have a
certain attraction for CIE.*
• Le mauvais temps a retardé le
transport de nos marchandises. - *The
bad weather has delayed the **carriage/
transportation** of our goods.*
• Nous avons demandé les prix de
transport maritime à notre affréteur.
- *We have requested the prices for sea
freight from our charterers.*
• Les **transports** ont dû s'effectuer
partiellement de nuit pour atteindre
le départ. - *The **movements** (of goods)
had to take place partly at night in order
to catch the sailing.*

transporteur *nm* carrier, haulier,
shipper, transporter
• Notre **transporteur** habituel ne
veut plus aller charger chez CIE par
suite des difficultés qu'il rencontre. -
*Our usual **carrier** is no longer prepared
to load at CIE's premises ...*

travail (*Plural* -aux) *nm* work,
workmanship
COLLOCATES *se charger de, continuer,
effectuer, entreprendre, exécuter,
procéder à; accident du, endroit de, frais
de, méthodes de, organisation de,
surcharge de, vêtements de, volume de*
• Nous entreprenons
immédiatement le **travail** et ... - *We
are putting the **work** in hand straight
away and ...*
• Il y a lieu d'y joindre une liste de
références des **travaux** exécutés par
vous ... - *You should enclose a list of
references for the **work** you have carried
out ...*
• **Travail** soigné, transports et
placement compris, pour le prix de
... - *Careful **workmanship**, carriage
and installation included, ...*

travailler *vi & t* work

• D'autre part, si nous décidons de **travailler** ensemble, il vous faudra une collection complète. - *Moreover, if we decide to **work** together, ...*
• Ce représentant pourra organiser et **travailler** son secteur à partir du 13 février. - *This representative will be able to organize and **work** his territory from 13 February.*

trésorerie *nf* accounts, finances; cash flow, liquid assets
• ... ce qui vous permettra d'équilibrer votre **trésorerie** du mois de mai. - *... which will enable you to balance your **accounts** for May.*
• Vous voyez donc l'importance de l'effort que nous avons fait dans ce sens pour alléger vos problèmes de **trésorerie**. - *... to alleviate your **financial**/**cash flow** problems.*

triple *adj* triple, [triplicate]
• Vous trouverez, en annexe, notre facture commerciale **en triple exemplaire** pour ... - *... our commercial invoice **in triplicate** for ...*

(se) trouver *vt & pro* find; find oneself, be (located)

• Veuillez **trouver** ci-joint double de notre offre de ce jour à CIE.
• Elle **se trouve** dans l'impossibilité de nous donner le moindre renseignement. - *She **finds herself/is** unable to give us any information at all.*
• ... avant de partir pour le Portet, qui **se trouve** à une quinzaine de kilomètres de la ville. - *..., which **is located** about 15km from the town.*
• A l'heure actuelle les réfrigérateurs **se trouvent** concurrencés par les appareils français, qui sont mieux placés. - *At present the refrigerators **are in** competition with French appliances, which are better placed.*

type *nm* type, model
• Nous vous informons que nous avons reçu les deux MF, **type** 3600, objet de votre envoi No 123 ... - *... the two MFs, **type** 3600, of your dispatch No. 123 ...*
• Vous aurez à joindre à votre offre une nomenclature précisant les **types** et nombres de briques nécessaires ... - *... a list giving the **types** and numbers of bricks necessary ...*

U

ultérieur, -e *adj* further, future, later, subsequent
• Nous sommes disposés à remettre cette affaire à une date **ultérieure**. - *We are ready to defer this matter to a later date.*
• Nous aimerions également être tenus au courant des réactions **ultérieures** résultant de cette proposition. - *We should like to be kept informed of **future/subsequent** reactions to this proposal.*

ultérieurement *adv* later (on)
• ... un tarif plus complet vous sera expédié **ultérieurement**.

unique *adj* single, sole, unique, only
• Il ne s'agit pas, comme vous le pensez, d'un cas **unique** mais de plusieurs réclamations. - *This is not, as you imagine, a **single** case, but several complaints.*
• ... c'est pour l'**unique** raison que nous désirons faire l'effort nécessaire pour lancer votre article ici. - *... it is for the **sole** reason that we wish to make the effort necessary to launch your article here.*

uniquement *adv* exclusively, only, solely
• Nous offrons plusieurs possibilités: 1° – nous nous occupons **uniquement** de la vente sur Paris; ... - *...: 1) – we concern ourselves **exclusively/only/solely** with sales in Paris; ...*
• Nous pourrions livrer des MF, mais **uniquement** en modèle 123, ... - *We could deliver MFs, but **exclusively/only/solely** model 123, ...*

unitaire *adj* unit, individual

• Nous ajoutons que les prix nets **unitaires** ci-dessus ont été basés sur une production annuelle de 123 flasques. - *We should add that the above net **unit** prices have been based on ...*
• ... et l'emballage **unitaire** des paquets de MF est insuffisant pour ce mode de transport. - *... and the **individual** wrapping of the bundles of MF is inadequate for this means of transport.*

unité *nf* unit; boat, vessel
• Le délai, à la condition bien entendu qu'il ne s'agisse que de quelques **unités**, serait d'un mois environ. - *Delivery, provided of course that only a few **units** were involved, would be approximately one month.*
• Pourriez-vous nous indiquer si, avec cette nouvelle **unité**, vous obtiendrez des fréquences meilleures d'embarquement. - *Could you let us know whether, with this new **vessel**, you will obtain loadings at more frequent intervals.*

urgence *nf* urgency
• Nous attirons votre attention sur l'**urgence** de votre réponse et ... - *May we draw your attention to the **urgency** of your reply and ...*
• Si vous êtes d'accord, veuillez nous faire parvenir, **de toute urgence**, ces échantillons à l'adresse suivante: ... - *..., please forward us, **very urgently**, these samples to the following address: ...*

urgent, -e *adj* immediate, urgent
USAGE *This word is sometimes placed in isolation, at the beginning of a letter before the salutation ('Messieurs'), to emphasize its urgent nature.*

• Nous avons, en effet, un besoin **urgent** de cette matière première ... - *We do, in fact, have an **immediate/ urgent** need of this raw material ...*

usage *nm* use; action; [usual]
• Nous avons le plaisir de vous retourner inclus le mode d'emploi du MF à **usage** ménager. - *... the instructions for the MF for domestic **use**.*
• Une de ces pièces a été mise **hors d'usage** par un serrage excessif des écrous de fixation. - *One of these parts was put **out of action** by excessive tightening of the fixing nuts.*
• Conditionnement: en rouleaux, **comme d'usage** pour l'exportation. - *Packaging: in rolls, **as usual** for export.*

usine *nf* factory, works
• Nos prix s'entendent: **départ usine**, port et emballage en plus. - *Our prices are **ex-works**, carriage and packing extra.*

utile *adj* helpful, useful, of use
USAGE *'Il est utile que'* + Subjunctive.
• Nous espérons que ces renseignements vous seront **utiles** et ...
• Il serait peut-être **utile** que nous recevions couramment les doubles de toutes correspondances. - *It would*

*perhaps be **helpful/useful** for us to receive on a regular basis copies of all correspondence.*

utilisateur, -trice *nmf* user
• Nos appareils sont très appréciés des **utilisateurs**. - *Our appliances are very popular with **users**.*

utilisation *nf* use, utilisation
• ... mais l'**utilisation** de ces appareils nécessite des précautions toutes particulières. - *... but the **use/ utilisation** of these appliances requires very special precautions.*
• Ces robinets n'ont pas la même qualité que les vôtres, ni les mêmes **utilisations**. - *These taps are not of the same quality as yours, and do not have the same **uses**.*

utiliser *vt* use, make use of, employ
USAGE *To employ a **person** is 'employer', not 'utiliser'.*
• Combien de lames vos ouvriers **utilisent**-ils jusqu'à usure complète? - *How many blades do your workers **use** until they are completely worn out?*
• ... mais peut-être auriez-vous des placements en France ou dans d'autres pays **utilisant** le système métrique. - *... or in other countries **using/employing** the metric system.*

V

vacances *nf pl* holiday(s), break
• Nous nous excusons de ne pas y avoir répondu plus tôt, la période des **vacances** nous en ayant empêchés. - *We apologize for not replying to it sooner, the **holiday** period having prevented us from doing so.*
• Ce document est arrivé peu de temps avant les **vacances** de Pâques. - *... shortly before the Easter **holiday/ break**.*

valable *adj* valid; worthwhile
• Le présent offre est **valable** pour une durée d'un mois prenant cours aujourd'hui. - *The present offer is **valid** for one month with effect from today.*
• Nous pensons avoir, pour ce type de matériel, trouvé des débouchés qui peuvent être **valables**. - *... some outlets which may be **worthwhile**.*

valeur *nf* value
• ... nous ferons présenter à votre banque une traite à vue pour la **valeur** de notre fourniture. - *... we will arrange for a sight draft to be presented to your bank for the **value** of our shipment.*

validité *nf* validity
• Durée de **validité** de votre offre, au moins deux mois. - *Duration of **validity** of your offer, at least two months.*

valoir *vt* be worth; entitle, win
TENSES Pres 1 *vaux* 3 *vaut* 4 *valons* 6 *valent* Imp *valais* Fut *vaudrai* PP *valu, -ue* Pres Part *valant* Subj 1,3 *vaille* 4 *valions* 6 *vaillent*
• Nous nous permettons d'insister sur la précision et le fini de nos fabrications, qui nous **ont valu**, depuis de longues années, la confiance de nombreux fabricants de cycles de qualité. - *May we emphasize the precision and finish of our products, which for many years **have entitled us to/have won us** the confidence of many makers of quality cycles.*

à valoir sur to be deducted from
• Nous avons bien reçu votre dernier envoi de 252 appareils MF soldant la première tranche de 1000 appareils **à valoir sur** notre marché pour 19--. - *... completing the first instalment of 1000 appliances **to be deducted from** our contract for 19--.*

variante *nf* variant, variation
• ... la fourniture éventuelle de tubes droits en acier suivant les différentes **variantes** stipulées à la spécification ci-après. - *... straight steel tubes as per the several **variants** stipulated in the following specification.*

veille *nf* day before, eve
• Le début et les cadences à respecter vous seront communiqués au plus tard à 14 heures **la veille du** jour demandé. - *The start and the rates (of delivery) to be observed will be communicated to you at the latest by 2pm **on the day before** the requested day.*

veiller à *vt indir* attend to, ensure, make sure that, see to it that, take care that
USAGE *'Veiller à ce que'* + Subjunctive.
• Nous vous demandons de **veiller à ce que** le motif figurant au recto soit bien celui représenté sur la maquette. - *We ask you to **ensure/see to it/make sure/take care that** the motif on the recto side conforms to that shown in the paste-up.*

vendeur, -euse *nmf* seller, vendor

• Nous **sommes** actuellement **vendeurs de** cerneaux standard ... - *At present we **are sellers of/can sell** you standard half-shelled walnuts ...*

vendre *vt* sell
TENSES See *rendre*
• Cette puissante organisation commerciale a été constituée pour **vendre** des articles de consommation. - *... **to sell** consumer goods.*
• Nous devons toutefois attirer votre attention sur le fait que nous **avons vendu** à CIE sur la base d'un prix net. - *... that we **sold** to CIE on the basis of a net price.*

vendredi *nm* Friday (*See* lundi)

venir *vi* come; approach; [have just; coming]
TENSES Pres 1 *viens* 3 *vient* 4 *venons* 6 *viennent* Imp *venais* Fut *viendrai* PP *venu, -ue* Pres Part *venant* Subj *1,3 vienne* 4 *venions* 6 *viennent*
• J'ai bien retenu votre promesse de **venir** nous voir cette année et ... - *I have remembered your promise to **come** to see us this year and ...*
• ... nous **venons** vous demander si vous seriez intéressés par des cédrats de Corse ... - *... we **are approaching** you to inquire whether you would be interested in Corsican citrons ...*
• Nous **venons de** recevoir votre lettre du 29 janvier ... - *We **have just** received ...*
• Vous m'avez demandé récemment quelle pourrait être l'évaluation du tonnage pour l'année **à venir**. - *... the estimated tonnage for the **coming** year.*

vente *nf* sale(s); [if unsold]
• ... et même en triplant nos efforts nous n'augmenterons pas les **ventes**. - *... we shan't increase our **sales**.*

• Le dernier numéro, qui devait être mis **en vente** le 9 courant, est arrivé le 14 dans l'après-midi. - *The last issue, which should have been put **on sale** ...*
• ... les marchandises suivantes, que nous pouvons vous offrir, **sauf vente**, pour livraison avril. - *... the following goods, which we can offer you, **if unsold**, for delivery in April.*

verbal, -e (*mpl* -aux) *adj* verbal
• ... et notre client nous a donné un accord ferme mais **verbal** pour l'achat dans les conditions prévues ci-dessus. - *... and our customer has made a firm but **verbal** agreement with us to buy on the terms set out above.*

verbalement *adv* verbally
• Lors de notre visite à Dudley, nous vous avons passé **verbalement** une commande de machines que nous vous confirmons ci-dessous. - *..., we placed an order for machines with you **verbally** and we confirm it below.*

vérification *nf* audit, check, checking, verification
• Vos factures en titre nous sont parvenues et, **à la vérification**, nous remarquons que ... - *... and, on **checking/verifying (them)**, we note that ...*

vérifier *vt* audit, check, verify
• Nous **avons vérifié** les prix portés en compte par nos factures ... - *We **have checked/verified** the prices charged on our invoices ...*

vers *prep* about, around, towards
• Comme convenu, je partirai de Paris le samedi 6 août **vers** 5 ou 6 heures. - *... **about/around** 5 or 6 o'clock.*
• Nous espérons recevoir ceux-ci **vers** la fin de cette semaine. - *We hope*

*to receive the latter **towards** the end of this week.*

• CIE désirerait exporter ces matériels **vers** la Belgique. - *CIE apparently wishes to export these materials **to** Belgium.*

versement *nm* payment, remittance

• ... vous voudrez bien nous adresser un **versement** complémentaire de F.200. - *... will you kindly send us a further **remittance** of 200 francs.*

• Ce règlement pourra s'effectuer soit par chèque bancaire au nom de CIE, soit par **versement** à notre CCP Paris 123. - *This settlement may be made either by banker's cheque or by **payment** to our Giro account Paris 123.*

verser *vt* pay, remit

USAGE *This verb is used much less frequently than its synonym 'payer'. Its Direct Object is always inanimate ('de l'argent', 'une somme', etc); one cannot '*verser quelqu'un'.*

• Nous allons faire une démande pour le remboursement des droits de douane que nous **avons** déjà **versés**. - *... reimbursement of the customs duties which we **have** already **paid**.*

(au) **verso** *nm* back, reverse side, [overleaf]

• Nous attirons tout particulièrement votre attention sur nos conditions générales d'achat imprimées **au verso**. - *... our general conditions of purchase printed **overleaf**.*

vif, vive *adj* sincere, warm; [face to face, in person]

• Avec nos **vifs** remerciements, ... - *With our **sincere**/**warm** thanks, ...*

• ... et j'espère pouvoir vous en entretenir **de vive voix** prochainement. - *... and I hope to be able to speak to you about it **in person** soon.*

(en) **vigueur** in effect, in force, applicable, effective, operative; [enforce]

• Le salaire en question est celui d'un qualifié premier échelon, **en vigueur** au 24 novembre 19--. - *The salary in question is that of a skilled worker, grade 1, **in effect**/**in force**/ **applicable**/**effective** on 24 November, 19--.*

virement *nm* transfer

• Paîment: soit ...; soit sous dix jours de réception de facture par **virement** bancaire, sous déduction d'un escompte à débattre. - *Payment: either ...; or within ten days of receipt of invoice by bank **transfer**, subject to a discount to be negotiated.*

virer *vt* transfer

• Nous vous confirmons que nous faisons le nécessaire pour vous **virer** l'équivalent de 250.000 livres. - *We confirm we are arranging to **transfer** to you the equivalent of £250,000.*

vis-à-vis de vis-à-vis, concerning, regarding, with regard to

• Il a vivement insisté sur l'intérêt qu'il porterait à ce que la situation **vis-à-vis de** CIE soit éclaircie. - *He insisted strongly on the importance for him of having the situation **vis-à-vis**/ **concerning** CIE clarified.*

visite *nf* visit, call

COLLOCATES *au cours de, lors de, suite à, à la suite de; annoncer, avoir, recevoir; avoir lieu*

• Je n'ai pas oublié votre excellent accueil **lors de ma visite** en juin 19--. - *I haven't forgotten your excellent welcome **when I visited you** in June 19--.*

• Comme convenu, j'ai **rendu**/**fait visite** ce matin à M. X. - *As agreed, I **called on** Mr X this morning.*

visiter *vt* go round, inspect, look over/round, tour; call on

USAGE *'Rendre visite à' (more rarely 'faire visite à') is the general translation equivalent of Eng 'to visit' (a person). 'Visiter' implies either touring a place (a town, factory, etc) or, in the case of a person, company, etc, making a professional call on them.*

• ... votre lettre nous informant que Monsieur X désirerait **visiter** nos usines. - ... *your letter informing us that Mr X would like to* **go round/ inspect/tour** *our factories.*

• Étant donné que nous **visitons** déjà les hôtels et collectivités, il nous serait sans doute facile de vendre également vos machines à nettoyer et à cirer. - *Given that we already* **call on** *hotels and institutions,...*

vivement *adv* enormously, greatly, extremely, keenly, strongly, very much, warmly

COLLOCATES *apprécier, conseiller, désirer, s'excuser, féliciter, insister, intéresser, regretter, remercier, ressentir, souhaiter; reconnaissant, surpris*

• Nous vous remercions **vivement** de votre lettre du 15 courant. - *Thank you* **very much** *...*

• Nous regrettons **vivement** que vous ayez dû avoir recours à un second rappel. - *We are* **extremely** *sorry that you have had to resort to a second reminder.*

• Soyez certain que M. X vous en serait **vivement** reconnaissant. - *I assure you that Mr X would be* **extremely** *grateful to you.*

• Monsieur X a **vivement** apprécié vos scrupules. - *Mr X* **enormously/ keenly** *appreciated your scruples.*

voeu (*Plural* voeux) *nm* wish
• M. X m'a demandé de vous transmettre le **voeu** suivant: M. X

aimerait connaître le nom et l'adresse des sociétés américaines ... - *Mr X has asked me to convey the following* **wish** *to you: ...*

• Permettez-moi, à l'occasion de cette Nouvelle Année, de vous présenter mes **voeux** les meilleurs. - *Best* **wishes** *for the New Year.*

• Nous vous félicitons vivement de cette heureuse initiative et nous **formons des voeux** pour la réussite de votre entreprise. - *We congratulate you warmly on this happy initiative and we* **send you our good wishes** *for the success of your enterprise.*

voie *nf* way, process
• En raison des frais vraiment élevés de transport aérien, nous avons l'intention d'envoyer la collection **par voie maritime**. - *...., we intend to send the collection* **by sea.**

• Ces difficultés sont **en voie de** règlement. - *These difficulties are* **in the process of/on the way to** *being resolved.*

(se) voir *vt & pro* see, understand; find oneself

TENSES Pres *1 vois 3 voit 4 voyons 6 voient* Imp *voyais* Fut *verrai* PP *vu, vue* Pres Part *voyant* Subj *1,3 voie 4 voyions 6 voient*

• **Voir** nos lettres des 24 août et 16 octobre et votre lettre du 2 novembre. - *See our letters ...*

• ... mais je pourrai vous **voir** le mardi 11, si cela vous convient. - *... but I can* **see/meet** *you on Tuesday 11, ...*

• Il vous sera ainsi possible de **voir** exactement ce qu'une telle modification implique. - *... to* **see/ discover** *exactly what such a modification entails.*

• Puis-je vous demander de me préciser par avance les principaux points que vous aimeriez **voir** discuter? - ... *the main points you would like to* **see discussed**?

• ... et je ne **vois** pas en quoi un entretien en tête-à-tête pourrait changer un iota à ma position. - *... and I do not* **see/understand** *how a conversation face to face could alter my position one iota.*

• Nous **nous voyons** donc obligés de vous demander si vous optez pour l'envoi de 200 ou de 300 exemplaires. - *We* **find ourselves** *obliged therefore to ask you ...*

volonté *nf* will, [control]
• Sauf cas de force majeure indépendant de notre **volonté** (grève, inondation, incendie, ...), nous n'admettons ... - *Except in cases of* force majeure **beyond our control** *(strike, flood, fire, ...), we do not accept ...*

volontiers *adv* gladly, readily, willingly
• ... et j'aurais **volontiers** fait le détour par Dusseldorf ... - *... and I would* **gladly** *have made a detour via Dusseldorf ...*
• Aussi, nous convenons **bien volontiers** que ... - *So, we are* **quite willing to** *agree that ...*

volume *nm* amount, volume
• Le **volume** du travail de bétonnage à exécuter est approximatif ... - *The* **amount/volume** *of concreting work to be done is approximate ...*

vouloir *vt* want, wish; [kindly, please]
TENSES Pres 1 *veux* 3 *veut* 4 *voulons* 6 *veulent* Imp *voulais* Fut *voudrai* PP *voulu, -ue* Pres Part *voulant* Subj 1,3 *veuille* 4 *voulions* 6 *veuillent*
USAGE 1) *In business letters 'vouloir' is used only occasionally in the sense of 'want/wish':*

• Ces articles sont chers et peu de clients **veulent** payer un prix supérieur pour une marchandise similaire. - *... and few customers* **want/wish** *to pay a higher price for similar goods.* In this sense 'désirer' is usually preferred. See 'désirer'.
2) *Likewise, 'vouloir' is used only occasionally in the* Conditional – *'voudrais, voudrions, etc.'. Eng 'would like' usually corresponds to the* Conditional *of 'aimer' – 'aimerais, aimerions, etc.'* See 'aimer'.
3) *In business letters 'vouloir' is used overwhelmingly to make requests:*
• **Voulez-vous** tenir compte de ces indications. - *Will you take account of these instructions.* (This example is very abrupt, virtually amounting to a command. It would become more polite if 'bien' or 'avoir l'obligeance de' were inserted after 'voulez-vous' – *Will you kindly/please/be so good as to*.... But there are other, more common, ways of softening a request as shown in the following three examples, which are arranged in order of increasing politeness:
• **Vous voudrez bien** nous confirmer votre accord pour ce choix. - *Please/Kindly confirm that you agree with this choice.*
• **Veuillez** nous indiquer le délai approximatif de livraison. - *Please/Kindly let us know the approximate delivery.*
• **Nous vous prions de bien vouloir** nous excuser d'y répondre tardivement. - *We beg you kindly to excuse us for replying to it belatedly.*
4) *The expression 'bien vouloir' (less commonly 'vouloir bien') is highly characteristic of business letters. It is not confined to requests, as in the last example above, but adds a note of politeness in many contexts:*

• Nous souhaitons que les articles que vous **avez bien voulu** nous commander vous donnent entière satisfaction. - . . . *the articles which you kindly ordered/which you were kind enough to order from us* . . . Very many letters include 'bien vouloir' in their opening sentence:

• Nous vous demandons de **bien vouloir** nous adresser un chèque de 123 livres dès réception de ces documents. - *We ask you kindly to send us a cheque for £123 on receipt of these documents.* Similarly, 'Nous vous serions obligés de **b. v.** . . .' ; 'Nous vous serions reconnaissants de **b. v.** . . .' ; etc.

voyage *nm* journey, trip; [away]

• J'espère que votre **voyage** de retour s'est bien effectué. - *I hope your return journey went smoothly.*

• Je vous fixerai un peu plus tard la date exacte de ce **voyage**. - *I'll arrange with you a little later the exact date of this trip.*

• . . . et j'aurais volontiers fait le détour par Dusseldorf si votre secrétaire ne m'avait pas précisé que vous étiez **en voyage**. - . . . *if your secretary had not told me you were away.*

vrai, -e *adj* true, [truth; as a matter of fact, strictly speaking]

• Nous ne sommes **à vrai dire** pas complètement sûrs que la classe des produits de cette maison soit à un niveau conforme à celui que demande votre correspondant. - *To tell the truth/As a matter of fact, we are not completely sure* . . .

vraiment *adv* really

• Les tonnages disponibles dans les différents dépôts sont **vraiment** trop faibles pour justifier un déplacement. - *The tonnages available at the various depots are really too small to justify a journey.*

vraisemblablement *adv* in all likelihood

• J'ai surtout retenu que rien ne se passerait **vraisemblablement** avant le mois de septembre prochain. - *I remember above all that in all likelihood nothing would happen before next September.*

vu *prep* in view of

• En conclusion, nous pensons qu'il serait équitable, **vu** les circonstances énoncées, que nous puissions porter en compte les débours provenant de ce retard. - . . . *it would be fair, in view of these circumstances* . . .

vue *nf* sight, view

• Nous serions très intéressés par l'importation de ce matériel pour la France, et **à première vue**, plus spécialement les modèles 301 et 303. - *We should be very interested in importing this material to France, and at first sight, particularly models 301 and 303.*

• Nous nous réserverions la faculté de prélever des échantillons **en vue de** leur vérification. - *We should reserve the right to take samples with a view to checking them.*

• C'est un groupe très puissant **au point de vue** financier. - *It is a very powerful group from the financial point of view.*

W

wagon *nm* truck, wagon; truckload, wagonload

• Veuillez nous dire si vous pouvez indifféremment charger sur camion ou sur **wagon**. - *Please tell us whether you can load both on lorry and on* **railway wagon**.

• Rien n'est changé en ce qui concerne les commandes représentant un **wagon complet**. - *There is no change as regards orders representing a* **complete wagonload**.

A

abandon renoncer à *vt indir*
abide by respecter *vt*
be **able** pouvoir *vaux*
abnormal anormal, -e
about concernant, à **propos** de; environ, vers
about to en **instance** de, sur le **point** de
above ci-dessus; sous **rubrique**, en référence
above all surtout
above board en **règle**
above-mentioned précité, -ée; sous rubrique, en référence
abroad à l'étranger
absence absence *nf*
absolutely absolument
accede to [suite *nf*]
accelerate accélérer *vt*
accept accepter *vt*, admettre *vt*, agréer *vt*
acceptable convenable, [convenir à *vt indir*]
acceptance acceptation *nf*
accident accident *nm*, imprévu *nm*
accommodation chambre *nf*
accompany accompagner *vt*
accord accorder *vt*
in **accordance with** conformément à, [conforme *adj* à], selon, suivant
according to d'après, selon, suivant
accordingly en **conséquence**, par conséquent
account compte *nm*; exposé *nm*
account for expliquer *vt*
on **account of** à **cause** de, en **raison** de
on no **account** en aucun **cas**

accounts écritures *nf pl*, livres *nm pl*, trésorerie *nf*; [comptable *adj*]
accurate exact, -e
achieve atteindre *vt*, réaliser *vt*
achievement réalisation *nf*
acknowledge accuser *vt*; reconnaître *vt*
acknowledgement accusé *nm*
acquaint (with) informer *vt* (de)
acquaintance connaissance *nf*
acquire se **procurer** *vpro*
out of **action** hors d'**usage**
activity activité *nf*
in **actual fact** en **fait**
actually en **fait**
add ajouter *vt*
addition complément *nm*
in **addition** en **outre**, en **sus**
in **addition to** outre, en **sus** de
additional complémentaire, supplémentaire
address adresse *nf*
addressee destinataire *nmf*
adequate convenable
adjust modifier *vt*
administration administration *nf*
admit reconnaître *vt*, convenir de *vt indir*
adopt adopter *vt*
advance avance *nf*: [anticiper *vt*]; évoluer *vi*
advantage avantage *nm*, intérêt *nm*
take **advantage of** profiter de *vt indir*
advantageous avantageux, -euse
advertisement annonce *nf*, publicité *nf*
advertising publicité *nf*: publicitaire *adj*
advice avis *nm*, conseil *nm*
advisable convenable, opportun, -e

advise conseiller *vt*, renseigner *vt*
advise of annoncer *vt*, aviser *vt* de
affect affecter *vt*
affirmative affirmatif, -ive
be **afraid** craindre *vt*
after après (que)
after all malgré tout
afternoon après-midi *nm*
afterwards ensuite
again encore, à **nouveau**
against contre, en **exécution** de
agency agence *nf*, intermédiaire *nmf*,
　　représentation *nf*
agent agent *nm*
agree être d'**accord**
agree to accepter *vt* de, convenir de
　　vt indir, donner une **suite**
　　favorable à
agreement accord *nm*
aim but *nm*
air avion *nm*
aircraft avion *nm*
alert prévenir *vt*
all-in forfaitaire
all the more ... because d'autant
　　plus ... que
allocate affecter *vt*, répartir *vt*
allocation affectation *nf*, répartition
　　nf
allot répartir *vt*
allotment répartition *nf*
allow permettre *vt* (de), laisser *vt*;
　　accorder *vt*, consentir *vt*
allow for tenir **compte** de
allowance déduction *nf*
almost pratiquement, presque
also également, aussi
alter modifier *vt*
alteration modification *nf*
alternative possibilité *nf*: autre *adj*
alternatively à **défaut**
although bien que, quoique
altogether au **total**
always toujours
amend rectifier *vt*
amended rectificatif, -ive
amendment rectification *nf*

among parmi
amount montant *nm*, somme *nf*;
　　quantité *nf*, volume *nm*
amount to s'**élever** à *vpro*
annex annexe *nf*: annexer *vt*
annotation mention *nf*
announce annoncer *vt*
annoyed navré, -ée
annual annuel, -elle
another [encore]
answer réponse *nf*: répondre *vi & t*
　　(à)
anticipate compter *vt*, prévoir *vt*;
　　anticiper *vt*
anticipation avance *nf*, [anticiper *vt*]
anxious to désireux, -euse de
anyway de toute(s) **façon**(s)
apiece la **pièce**
apologies excuses *nf pl*
apologize (for) s'**excuser** *vpro* (de)
apparent évident, -e
appeal to faire **appel** à
appear paraître *vi*, sembler *vi*;
　　apparaître *vi*, figurer *vi*
appearance parution *nf*;
　　présentation *nf*
append annexer *vt*; revêtir *vt*
appendix annexe *nf*
appliance appareil *nm*
applicable en **vigueur**
be **applicable to** se rapporter à *vpro*
applicant candidat, -e *nmf*
application application *nf*; demande
　　nf
apply (to) (s')**appliquer** *vt & pro* (à)
apply for solliciter *vt*
apply to s'**adresser** à *vpro*
appoint désigner *vt*
appointment rendez-vous *nm*
apportion répartir *vt*
appreciably sensiblement
appreciate apprécier *vt*: [agréable
　　adj]; se rendre **compte** de *vpro*
approach contacter *vt*, [intervenir *vi*,
　　venir *vi*: rapport *nm*]; démarche
　　nf
approaching prochain, -e

appropriate opportun, -e, convenable: [convenir de *v impers*]
appropriate to propre à
approval accord *nm*
approve agréer *vt*
approximate approximatif, -ive
approximately approximativement, sensiblement; environ
April avril *nm*
area région *nf*
argument discussion *nf*
arise se **présenter** *vpro*, se **poser** *vpro*, survenir *vi*
arise from découler de *vt indir*, provenir de *vt indir*
around vers
arrange organiser *vt*; convenir de *vt indir*, faire le **nécessaire**
arrangement disposition *nf*, formule *nf*
(in) **arrears** arriéré, -ée *nm & adj*
arrival arrivée *nf*
arrive arriver *vi*
article article *nm*
as ainsi que, comme: en **qualité** de, à **titre** de
as ... as aussi ... que
as and when au **fur et à mesure** (que)
as for quant à
as found tel quel, telle quelle
as from à **compter** de, à **partir** de
as it is tel quel, telle quelle
as long as tant que
as per selon, suivant, conformément à
as to quant à
as well as ainsi que
as you say effectivement
ascertain se rendre **compte** de *vpro*
put **aside** réserver *vt*
ask demander *vt*, prier *vt*; poser *vt*

ask for demander *vt*
assemble monter *vt*
assembly montage *nm*
assent accord *nm*
assert prétendre *vt*
assess estimer *vt*
assign céder *vt*
assist aider *vt*
assistance aide *nf*
assume supposer *vt*
assurance garantie *nf*
assure assurer *vt*
assured certain, -e
assuredly certainement
astonish étonner *vt*
go **astray** s'**égarer** *vpro*
at au **prix** de
at once immédiatement
attach annexer *vt*
attempt (to) essayer *vt* (de)
attend assister à *vt indir*
attend to s'**occuper** de *vpro*, veiller à *vt indir*
attendance présence *nf*
attention attention *nf*, connaissance *nf*
attract attirer *vt*
attractive avantageux, -euse, intéressant, -e
audit vérification *nf*: vérifier *vt*
August août *nm*
authority autorisation *nf*: responsable *nmf*
authorization autorisation *nf*
authorize autoriser *vt*
avail oneself of profiter de *vt indir*
available disponible, en **main**
have **available** disposer de *vt indir*
average moyen, -enne *adj & nf*
avoid éviter *vt*
await attendre *vt*
awaiting delivery en souffrance
be **aware** savoir *vt*, ne pas **ignorer** *vt*
away absent, -e, en **voyage**

B

back (from) [retour *nm*]
on the **back** au **verso**
badly mal
bail out dépanner *vt*
balance solde *nm*
balance sheet bilan *nm*
bank banque *nf*: bancaire *adj*
banker banquier *nm*
banker's bancaire
bargain avantageux, -euse *adj*:
   occasion *nf*; marché *nf*
barring sauf
basic de base
basis base *nf*, titre *nm*
on the **basis of** en **partant** de
batch lot *nm*
bear porter *vt*, supporter *vt*, prendre
   vt à sa **charge**; revêtir *vt*
bear in mind tenir **compte** de *vt*
   indir
because car, parce que, puisque
because of à **cause** de, du **fait** de
become devenir *vi*
before avant (de/que)
beforehand au **préalable**
beg [honneur *nf*]
begin (to) commencer *vi* (à),
   entamer *vt*
beginning début *nm*, départ *nm*
on **behalf of** de la **part** de, pour le
   compte de
behind(hand) en retard
belatedly tardivement
believe penser *vt*, croire *vt*, entendre
   vt
belong to appartenir à *vt indir*, faire
   partie de
below ci-dessous: en dessous de
benefit avantage *nm*, intérêt *nm*,
   profit *nm*
benefit from bénéficier de *vt indir*
besides (en) outre; d'ailleurs

best meilleur, -e; préférable,
   souhaitable
the **best thing** mieux *nm*
better meilleur, -e
between entre
beyond [indépendant, -e: échapper
   vt]
big important, -e, gros, grosse, fort,
   -e, grand, -e
bill traite *nf*, facture *nf*: facturer *vt*
bill of lading connaissement *nm*
billing facturation *nf*
block cliché *nm*
blueprint plan *nm*
boat navire *nm*, bateau *nm*
body organisme *nm*
in **bond** sous **douane**
book livre *nm*: enregistrer *vt*;
   réserver *vt*, retenir *vt*
booking enregistrement *nm*;
   réservation *nf*
booklet brochure *nf*
books écritures *nf pl*, livres *nm pl*
boost développer *vt*
border frontière *nf*
borrow emprunter *vt*
both ... and aussi bien ... que, à la
   fois ... et, tant ... que
bother ennui *nm*: (se) **déranger** *vt &*
   pro
bottom bas *nm*
be **bound to** être **obligé**, -ée de
bound for à **destination** de
box boîte *nf*
branch agence *nf*, succursale *nf*
branch office succursale *nf*
brand marque *nf*
breadth largeur *nf*
break vacances *nf pl*
break down détailler *vt*,
   décomposer *vt*
breakdown décompte *nm*, détail *nm*

brief renseigner *vt*
briefly brièvement
bring apporter *vt*, porter *vt*
bring about entraîner *vt*
bring out sortir *vt*
bring to one's attention/notice
    signaler *vt*, faire **remarquer**
bring up soulever *vt*
broadly en gros
brochure brochure *nf*

building bâtiment *nm*, immeuble *nm*;
    construction *nf*
the **bulk (of)** la **plupart** (de)
bundle paquet *nm*
business activité *nf*, affaire *nf*
do **business** traiter *vi*
busy [occuper *vt*]
buy acheter *vt*
buyer acheteur, -euse *nmf*,
    placement *nm*

C

câble télégramme *nm*, câble *nm*:
    télégraphier *vt*
cabled télégraphique
calculate calculer *vt*
calculation calcul *nm*
call appel *nm*, communication *nf*,
    coup *nm*; visite *nf*: appeler *vt*
call for nécessiter *vt*
call on visiter *vt*
call upon faire **appel** à, avoir
    recours à
campaign campagne *nf*
can pouvoir *vaux*
cancel annuler *vt*
cancellation annulation *nf*
canvass prospecter *vt*
canvassing prospection *nf*
capable of susceptible de
capacity qualité *nf*, [tant]
card carte *nf*
cardboard carton *nm*
cardboard box carton *nm*
care soin *nm*
take **care of** prendre à sa **charge**
take **care that** veiller à *vt indir*
careful bon, bonne, soigné, -ée
carefully soigneusement, avec **soin**
carriage transport *nm*; port *nm*
carriage charge port *nm*

carrier transporteur *nm*
carry porter *vt*
carry on continuer *vt & i*, exercer *vt*
carry out effectuer *vt*, exécuter *vt*,
    procéder à *vt indir*, réaliser *vt*
carrying out exécution *nf*,
    réalisation *nf*
carton carton *nm*
case caisse *nf*; cas *nm*, façon *nf*
in that **case** alors, dans ce **cas**
cash comptant *nm*
cash flow trésorerie *nf*
catalogue catalogue *nm*
cater for satisfaire à *vt indir*
cause amener *vt*, occasionner *vt*
certain certain, -e
certainly certainement, bien
certificate attestation *nf*, certificat
    nm
certify certifier *vt*
chance chance *nf*, hasard *nm*,
    occasion *nf*
change changement *nm*: changer *vt*
    & i, échanger *vt*
channel canal *nm*
character caractère *nm*
characteristic caractéristique *nf &*
    adj
charge frais *nm pl*, prix *nm*; charge
    nf

charge for facturer *vt*, porter *vt* en compte

(person) in **charge** responsable *adj* & *nmf*

take **charge of** se charger de *vpro*

chargeable to à la charge de

cheap avantageux, -euse, bon marché

check contrôle *nm*, vérification *nf*: vérifier *vt*

checking contrôle *nm*, vérification *nf*: justificatif, -ive

cheque chèque *nm*

chiefly principalement

choice choix *nm*

CIF CIF, coût assurance et fret

circumstance circonstance *nf*, cas *nm*

cite citer *vt*

claim réclamation *nf*: prétendre *vt*

clarify éclaircir *vt*

clear évident, -e: écouler *vt*

clear (through customs) dédouaner *vt*

clear up éclaircir *vt*

make **clear** préciser *vt*

make it **clear** ne pas cacher *vt*

clearly évidemment; nettement

client client, -e *nmf*

clientele clientèle *nf*

clinch conclure *vt*

close (to) proche *adj*: près (de) *adv* & *prep*

close fermer *vt*, terminer *vt*

close-down fermeture *nf*

closely de près

closure fermeture *nf*

collaboration collaboration *nf*

colleague collaborateur, -trice *nmf*, collègue *nmf*, confrère *nm*

collect enlever *vt*, prendre *vt*

combine grouper *vt*

come venir *vi*, se présenter *vpro*

come about arriver *vi*, se produire *vpro*, survenir *vi*

come back rentrer *vi*, revenir *vi*

come from provenir de *vt indir*

come out sortir *vi*

come to s'élever à *vpro*

come to something se concrétiser *vpro*

come up se poser *vpro*

coming prochain, -e, à venir

commence commencer *vi*, entamer *vt*

comment commentaire *nm*, remarque *nf*

commerce commerce *nm*

commercial commercial, -e

commission commission *nf*

commit oneself to s'engager à *vpro*

commitment engagement *nm*

commodity marchandise *nf*

common commun, -e

commonly couramment

communicate communiquer *vt*, faire **part** de

communicate with se mettre en **rapport** avec

communication communication *nf*

company société *nf*, firme *nf*, compagnie *nf*, maison *nf*

comparative comparatif, -ive

comparatively relativement

compared with contre

compel to obliger *vt* à

be **compelled to** être obligé, -ée de

compete with concurrencer *vt*

competing concurrent, -e

competition concurrence *nf*

competitive compétitif, -ive

competitor concurrent, -e *nmf*

competitors concurrence *nf*

complain (about/of) se plaindre *vpro* (de)

complaint réclamation *nf*

complement complément *nm*

complementary complémentaire

complete complet, -ète: compléter *vt*

completely complètement

completion achèvement *nm*

in **compliance with** conformément à

complimentary gratuit, -e

comply with se **conformer à** *vpro*, satisfaire à *vt indir*, donner une **suite** favorable à
be **composed of** comporter *vt*
comprise comporter *vt*
compulsary obligatoire
conceal cacher *vt*
concede concéder *vt*
concern concerner *vt*; (s')**inquiéter** *vt & pro*: entreprise *nf*
concern oneself with s'occuper de *vpro*
concerned en **cause**
be **concerned with** traiter de *vt indir*
concerning concernant, à **propos** de
conclude conclure *vt*
conclusion conclusion *nf*, issue *nf*
concur [accord *nm*]
condition condition *nf*, état *nm*
conduct procéder à *vt indir*
confer accorder *vt*
confess reconnaître *vt*
confidence confidence *nf*
in **confidence** confidentiellement
confident [persuader *vt*]
confidential confidentiel, -ielle
confidentially confidentiellement
confine limiter *vt*
confirm confirmer *vt*
confirmation confirmation *nf*
conform to se **conformer à** *vpro*, répondre à *vt indir*
conforming to / in **conformity with** conformément à, selon, suivant: conforme *adj* à
congratulate féliciter *vt*
be **connected with** se **rapporter à** *vpro*
connection relation *nf*, rapport *nm*
in **connection with** au **sujet** de, à **propos** de
in this **connection** à ce **sujet**, à ce **propos**
consent accord *nm*
consequence conséquence *nf*
in **consequence** aussi, en **conséquence**, de ce **fait**

in **consequence of** du **fait** de, par **suite** de
consequently par **conséquent**, en **conséquence**, aussi
consider considérer *vt*; penser *vt*, juger *vt*; étudier *vt*
considerable considérable, important, -e
consideration considération *nf*; étude *nf*; obligeance *nf*
considering eu **égard** à
consign expédier *vt*
consignee destinataire *nmf*
consignment envoi *nm*, expédition *nf*, fourniture *nf*
consignor expéditeur, -trice *nmf*
consist in consister à *vt indir*
consist of comporter *vt*, consister en *vt indir*
be **consistent with** correspondre à *vt indir*
constitute constituer *vt*
construction construction *nf*
consult consulter *vt*, interroger *vt*
contact contact *nm*, rapport *nm*: contacter *vt*
contain contenir *vt*
contemplate envisager *vt* (de)
contend prétendre *vt*
contention litige *nm*
contents contenu *nm*
continuation suite *nf*
continue continuer *vt & i*
contract contrat *nm*, marché *nm*
contractual contractuel, -elle
contrary contraire *nm & adj*: contrairement à
contretemps contretemps *nm*
contrive to parvenir à *vt indir*
control contrôle *nm*, volonté *nf*
convenience convenance *nf*
be **convenient to** convenir à *vt indir*
conversation entretien *nm*, conversation *nf*
conversely inversement
convert transformer *vt*
convey transmettre *vt*

conveyance transport *nm*
convince (of) persuader *vt* (de)
cooperation coopération *nf*
copy copie *nf*, exemplaire *nm*
corporate name raison *nf* sociale
correct exact, -e: rectifier *vt*
corrected rectificatif, -ive
correction rectification *nf*
correspond to correspondre à *vt*
    indir
correspondence correspondance *nf*
correspondent correspondant, -e
    nmf
corresponding correspondant, -e
corroborate confirmer *vt*
cost coût *nm*, frais *nm pl*: coûter *vt*
costly cher, chère, onéreux, -euse
count compter *vt*
count on compter *vt*, compter sur *vt*
    indir
counting from à compter/dater de
country pays *nm*

course courant *nm*, cours *nm*
cover pli *nm*: couvrir *vt*
covered by objet de
crate caisse *nf*
create constituer *vt*
credit crédit *nm*, accréditif *nm*:
    créditer *vt*
credit note avoir *nm*
creep (into) se glisser *vpro* (dans)
crop up se **poser** *vpro*, se **présenter**
    vpro
cross se **croiser** *vpro*
currency monnaie *nf*
current actuel, -elle, courant, -e
currently actuellement
customary [régulièrement]
customer(s) client, -e *nmf*, clientèle
    nf
customs douane *nf*: douanier, -ière
    adj
customs clearance dédouanement
    nm

D

damage avarie *nf*, dommage *nm*:
    endommager *vt*
data données *nf pl*
date date *nf*: dater *vt & i*
date from dater *vi* de
to date à ce **jour**
dated en date du
day jour *nm*, journée *nf*
the day after lendemain *nm*
the day before veille *nf*
deal affaire *nf*: traiter *vi*
deal with s'occuper de *vpro*, traiter
    vt
dealer distributeur, -trice *nmf*
dealings rapports *nm pl*, relations *nf*
    pl
have dealings (with) traiter *vi* (avec)
dear cher, chère: cher *adv*

debit débit *nm*: débiter *vt*
December décembre *nm*
decide (to) décider *vt* (de)
decidedly nettement
decision décision *nf*
declare (oneself) (se) **déclarer** *vt &*
    pro
decline baisse *nf*: décliner *vt*
deduct déduire *vt*
be deducted from valoir *vi* sur
deduction déduction *nf*
defect défaut *nm*
defective défectueux, -euse
defer différer *vt*, remettre *vt*,
    reporter *vt*
definitely absolument, certainement
definitive définitif, -ive
definitively définitivement

delay retard *nm*: retarder *vt*, tarder *vi*
deliver livrer *vt*
deliverable livrable
delivery livraison *nf*; délai *nm*
awaiting **delivery** en **souffrance**
demand demande *nf*, impératif *nm*: exiger *vt*
in **demand** [demander vt]
demonstration démonstation *nf*
on **demurrage** en **souffrance**
depart partir *vi*
department bureau *nm*, direction *nf*, service *nm*
departure départ *nm*
depend on dépendre de *vt indir*; compter sur *vt indir*
in **depth** approfondi, -ie
describe décrire *vt*
deservedly à juste **titre**
design modèle *nm*
designate désigner *vt*
designed for/to [destiner *vt* à]
desirable souhaitable
desire désir *nm*: désirer *vt*
if so **desired** [désir *nm*]
desirous of désireux, -euse de
despatch *See* dispatch
despite malgré
destination destination *nf*
detail(s) détail *nm*, précisions *nf pl*: détailler *vt*
detailed account décompte *nm*, détail *nm*
detain retenir *vt*
determine déterminer *vt*
develop développer *vt*, évoluer *vi*
development développement *nm*, évolution *nf*
device appareil *nm*
devote consacrer *vt*
devoted dévoué, -ée
differ from différer de *vt indir*
difference différence *nf*, écart *nm*
different (from) différent, -e (de)
difficult difficile

difficulty difficulté *nf*
dimension cote *nf*, dimension *nf*
direct direct, -e: directement *adv*: diriger *vt*
direction indication *nf*; sens *nm*
directly immédiatement
disadvantage inconvénient *nm*
discharge décharger *vt*
discontinued [ne plus en fabrication]
discount escompte *nm*, rabais *nm*, remise *nf*
discover relever *vt*
discreetly discrètement
discretion discrétion *nf*
discuss discuter *vt & i*
discussion(s) discussion *nf*, entretien *nm*, pourparlers *nm pl*
have **discussions (about)** discuter *vi* (de)
dispatch envoi *nm*, expédition *nf*: expédier *vt*
display exposer *vt*; faire **preuve** de
displeased mécontent, -e
disposal disposition *nf*, [main *nf*]
dispose of disposer de *vt indir*; écouler *vt*
disposed to disposé, -ée à
dispute contestation *nf*, discussion *nf*, litige *nm*
disregard ne pas tenir **compte** de
dissatisfied mécontent, -e
distinctly nettement
distribute diffuser *vt*, distribuer *vt*, (se) répartir *vt & pro*
distribution diffusion *nf*, distribution *nf*
distributor distributeur, -trice *nmf*
disturb (se) **déranger** *vt & pro*, (s')**inquiéter** *vt & pro*
disturbance dérangement *nm*
ditto dito
diverse divers, -ses
divide up (se) **répartir** *vt & pro*
do faire *vt*, effectuer *vt*
do one's best/utmost mettre tout en oeuvre

DOCTOR

doctor docteur *nm*
document document *nm*, pièce *nf*
documentation documentation *nf*
domain domaine *nm*
dossier dossier *nm*
double double *adj*
doubt doute *nm*
doubtless sans **doute**
draft remise *nf*, traite *nf*: rédiger *vt*
draw attirer *vt*, tirer *vt*
draw up établir *vt*, rédiger *vt*
drawback inconvénient *nm*
drawing plan *nm*
drawing up établissement *nm*

ENTERPRISE

drop baisse *nf*: ne pas donner **suite** à
drop out se **désister** *vpro*
due date échéance *nf*
due to du **fait** de, par **suite** de
be **due to** devoir *vt & aux*; provenir
  de *vt indir*
be/fall **due** échoir *vi*
in **due course** en **temps** utile
duly dûment
duplicate double *nm*, duplicata *nm*
in **duplicate** en **double** exemplaire
duration durée *nf*
during pendant, durant
duty droits *nm pl*, taxe *nf*

E

each la **pièce**
earlier antérieur, -e, précédent, -e:
  antérieurement, précédemment
at your **earliest convenience** au plus
  tôt, le plus **tôt** possible
early tôt: court, -e, prochain, -e
economic économique
economic climate/conditions
  conjoncture *nf*
edition édition *nf*
effect incidence *nf*, effet *nm*:
  effectuer *vt*
in **effect** en **vigueur**
to this/that **effect** dans ce **sens**
effective efficace: en **vigueur**
efficient efficace
effort effort *nm*, démarche *nf*
either non plus
either ... or soit ...soit
eliminate éliminer *vt*
embark charger *vt*
embark upon entreprendre *vt*
emergency supply dépannage *nm*
emphasize insister sur *vt indir*,
  souligner *vt*
employ utiliser *vt*, employer *vt*

employment emploi *nm*
empower autoriser *vt*
enable to permettre *vt* de
enclose joindre *vt*, annexer *vt*
enclosed ci-joint, -e, **ci-inclus**, -e,
  sous ce **pli**
enclosure annexe *nf*
encounter rencontrer *vt*
end fin *nf*: (se) **terminer** *vt & pro*
in the **end** finalement
to this **end** à cet **effet**, dans ce **sens**
endeavour to essayer *vt* de
enforce appliquer *vt*, mettre *vt* en
  vigueur
engaged in [occuper *vt*]
enjoy bénéficier de *vt indir*
enlarge augmenter *vt*
enormously vivement
enquire (etc) *See* inquire (etc)
enough suffisamment
ensue from découler de *vt indir*
ensure faire le **nécessaire** pour,
  veiller à *vt indir*
entail entraîner *vt*, impliquer *vt*
enter into admettre *vt*, entamer *vt*
enterprise entreprise *nf*

entertain recevoir *vt*
entire entier, -ière
entirely entièrement, en **totalité**
entirety totalité *nf*
in its/their **entirety** entièrement
entitle valoir *vt*
be **entitled to** être en **droit** de
entrust to/with confier *vt* à; charger
    vt de
envelope pli *nm*
envisage envisager *vt* (de)
equally également
equip (with) équiper *vt* (de)
equipment matériel *nm*
equitable équitable
equivalent équivalent, -e *nm & adj*
erroneous erroné, -ée
error erreur *nf*
escape échapper *vi* (à)
especially particulièrement,
    spécialement
essential indispensable, essentiel,
    -elle
establish constituer *vt*, implanter *vt*,
    mettre *vt* en **place**
establish oneself s'implanter *vpro*,
    s'**installer** *vpro*
establishment établissement *nm*
esteem estimer *vt*
esteemed estimé, -ée, honorable
esteemed letter estimée *nf*
estimate devis *nm*: estimer *vt*
etc etc
eve veille *nf*
even encore, même
event cas *nm*
eventually finalement
everybody/-one tout le **monde**
ex works **départ** usine
exact exact, -e
exactly exactement
examination examen *nm*
examine examiner *vt*
example exemple *nm*
for **example** par **exemple**
exceed dépasser *vt*

excellent excellent, -e
except sauf
exceptional exceptionnel, -elle
exceptionally exceptionnellement
excessive exagéré, -ée
exchange échange *nm*: échanger *vt*
in **exchange** en remplacement
exclude exclure *vt*
excluding hors: [**non** compris, -e]
exclusive exclusif, -ive
exclusive of hors: [**non**-compris, -e]
exclusively exclusivement,
    uniquement
excuse excuser *vt*
execute effectuer *vt*, exécuter *vt*
exercise exercer *vt*, apporter *vt*
exert exercer *vt*
exhaust épuiser *vt*
exhibit exposer *vt*
exhibition exposition *nf*, salon *nm*
exist exister *vi*
existence existence *nf*
in **existence** existant, -e
existing existant, -e
exorbitant exorbitant, -e
expand (s')**étendre** *vt & pro*
expect attendre *vt*, prévoir *vt*
expectation attente *nf*
expedient opportun, -e
expedite accélérer *vt*
expeditious prompt, -e
expenditure dépense *nf*
expenses frais *nm pl*
expensive cher, chère, onéreux,
    -euse
experience expérience *nf*
experiment expérience *nf*
expire expirer *vi*, échoir *vi*
explain expliquer *vt*
export exportation *nf*: exportateur,
    -trice *adj*: exporter *vt*
exporter exportateur, -trice *nmf*
exporting exportation *nf*:
    exportateur, -trice *adj*
express exprès, -esse: exprimer *vt*
extend (s')**étendre** *vt & pro*
extent étendue *nf*, importance *nf*

extra en **supplément**, supplémentaire
extra load surcharge *nf*
extract extrait *nm*: extraire *vt*

extremely extrêmement, infiniment, vivement
ex-works **départ** usine
keep an **eye on** suivre *vt*

F

fabricate fabriquer *vt*
fabrication fabrication *nf*
face (up to) faire **face** à
face to face de **vive** voix
faced with devant
facility service *nm*
facing devant
fact fait *nm*, élément *nm*
in **fact** en **effet**, précisément
in actual **fact** en **fait**
factor élément *nm*
factory usine *nf*
fail to manquer de *vt indir*
failing défaut *nm*
fair foire *nf*: équitable *adj*
fairly assez
fall baisse *nf*: baisser *vi*
fall due échoir *vi*
fame renommée *nf*
be **familiar with** connaître *vt*
as **far as** [mesure *nf*]
fast rapide *adj*: rapidement *adv*
fault défaut *nm*
faulty défectueux, -euse
favour service *nm*: favoriser *vt*, honorer *vt*
in **favour of** en **faveur** de, au **profit** de
favourable favorable, intéressant, -e
favourably favorablement
fax téléphotocopie *nf*
fear craindre *vt*
feasibility possibilité *nf*
feasible faisable
feature caractéristique *nf*
February février *nm*

feel penser *vt*, sentir *vt*
make **felt** se faire **sentir**
few peu de, quelques
fewer moins
field domaine *nm*
(about) **fifteen** quinzaine *nf*
figure chiffre *nm*: figurer *vi*
file dossier *nm*: classer *vt*
fill (in) remplir *vt*
fill in documenter *vt*
final définitif, -ive, dernier, -ière, final, -e
final corrected proof bon *nm* à tirer
finalize mettre *vt* à **point**
finally définitivement, enfin, finalement
finances trésorerie *nf*
financial financier, -ière
find trouver *vt*
find a buyer/outlet for placer *vt*
find oneself se trouver *vpro*, se **voir** *vpro*
find out se **renseigner** *vpro*
fine amende *nf*
finish terminer *vt*
finishing achèvement *nm*
firm société *nf*, firme *nf*, maison *nf*, entreprise *nf*: ferme *adj*
first premier, -ière *adj & nm*: primo *adv*, au **préalable**
first and foremost avant toute chose
first-class/rate de **premier** ordre
at **first** d'abord
firstly primo
fit répondre à *vt indir*

fix fixer *vt*, établir *vt*
fixed fixe, forfaitaire
flaw défaut *nm*
fluently couramment
FOB FOB
folder dépliant *nm*
follow suivre *vt*
follow from résulter de *vt indir*
follow up donner **suite** à
following suivant, -e: à la **suite** de
for car: depuis; moyennant;
    pendant; pour
force to obliger *vt* à
in **force** en **vigueur**
be **forced to** être **obligé**, -ée de
forecast prévision *nf*
foregoing [précéder *vi*]
foreign étranger, -ère
foresee prévoir *vt*
forewarn prévenir *vt*
forget oublier *vt*
forget to manquer de *vt indir*,
    oublier *vt* (de)
forgive excuser *vt*
form bon *nm*, formule *nm*, imprimé
    nm; forme *nf*: constituer *vt*
for the **form** pour la bonne **règle**
formality formalité *nf*
format format *nm*
formation constitution *nf*
former ancien, -ienne
formulate formuler *vt*
forthcoming prochain, -e

forthwith dès **maintenant**
fortnight quinzaine *nf*
forward faire **suivre**, transmettre *vt*
forwarding expédition *nf*
forwarding agent transitaire *nm*
framework cadre *nm*
free franco *adv*: gratuit, -e *adj*; libre
    adj
free of charge gratuitement
freight transport *nm*
freight charge fret *nm*
frequent fréquent, -e
fresh nouveau, -elle
Friday vendredi *nm*
friendly amical, -e
friendship amitié *nf*
from de la **part** de
from ... onwards à **partir** de
frontier frontière *nf*
fulfil se **conformer à** *vpro*; réaliser *vt*
fulfilment exécution *nf*, réalisation
    nf
full complet, -ète
fully bien
furnish with approvisionner *vt* en;
    [fournir *vt*]
further complémentaire, nouveau,
    -elle, ultérieur, -e: encore, plus
    avant
further to suite à
furthermore d'autre **part**,
    d'**ailleurs**
future avenir *nm*: ultérieur, -e *adj*

G

gain gagner *vt*
gap écart *nm*
gather conclure *vt*
general général, -e
gentleman monsieur *nm* *(Plural messieurs)*
get obtenir *vt*, bénéficier de *vt indir*, recevoir *vt*
get an idea of situer *vt*
get hold of se **procurer** *vpro*
give donner *vt*, apporter *vt*, consentir *vt*, laisser *vt*, porter *vt*
give up (the idea of) renoncer à *vt indir*
given étant donné
glad heureux, -euse
gladly volontiers
global global, -e
go aller *vi*, se **rendre** *vpro*
go ahead with procéder à *vt indir*
go astray s'égarer *vpro*
go back rentrer *vi*, retourner *vi*
go by passer *vi*
go into examiner *vt*
go off se **passer** *vpro*
go out sortir *vi*
go round visiter *vt*
go through remplir *vt*
goal but *nm*

it **goes** without **saying** il va de **soi**
good bon, bonne, fort, -e
be **good** enough to avoir l'**amabilité** de, avoir l'**obligeance** de
make **good** réparer *vt*
goods marchandise *nf*
government department administration *nf*
grade choix *nm*, qualité *nf*
grant accorder *vt*, concéder *vt*, consentir *vt*
grasp saisir *vt*
grateful reconnaissant, -e: [obliger *vt*]
be **grateful** for/if savoir **gré** de
be **gratified** [agréable]
great gros, grosse
a **great** deal (of) beaucoup (de)
greater (than) supérieur, -e (à)
greatly beaucoup, vivement
gross brut, -e *adj & adv*
group groupe *nm*: grouper *vt*
grouping groupement *nm*
grow augmenter *vi*
growth augmentation *nf*, développement *nm*
guarantee garantie *nf*: garantir *vt*
for your **guidance** pour **gouverne**, à titre d'**indication**
guide diriger *vt*

H

habit habitude *nf*
half moitié *nf*
hand main *nf*
hand over remettre *vt*, céder *vt*
in **hand** en **cours**
on the one **hand** d'une **part**
on the other **hand** d'autre **part**; par **contre**
handing over remise *nf*
handle s'**occuper de** *vpro*, traiter *vt*; manutentionner *vt*
handling manutention *nf*
happen arriver *vi*, se **passer** *vpro*, se **produire** *vpro*, survenir *vi*
happen again se **reproduire** *vpro*
as it **happens** précisément
happy heureux, -euse
hardly [inutile *adj*]
hasten to s'**empresser de** *vpro*
haulier transporteur *nm*
have avoir *vt & aux*, posséder *vt*, entretenir *vt*
have to devoir *vaux*, avoir à *vaux*
head chef *nm*
head office siège *nm*
heading poste *nm*, rubrique *nf*
hear apprendre *vt*; entendre *vt*
hear from lire *vt*: [nouvelle *nf*]
height hauteur *nf*
held up en **souffrance**
be **held** se **tenir** *vpro*
help aide *nf*: aider *vt*

help out dépanner *vt*
helpful utile
henceforth désormais
here ici
hereunder ci-dessous
herewith sous ce **pli**
hesitate (to) hésiter *vi* (à), [manquer de *vt indir*]
hide cacher *vt*
high haut, -e, élevé, -ée, fort, -e
higher (than) supérieur, -e (à)
highly fort
hinder (from) empêcher *vt* (de)
hire location *nf*: louer *vt*
hire out louer *vt*
hiring out location *nf*
hitch contretemps *nm*
hitherto jusqu'à **présent**
hold contenir *vt*; disposer de *vt indir*; maintenir *vt*
hold back/up retarder *vt*
hold it against someone for tenir **rigueur** à quelqu'un de
holiday(s) congé *nm*, vacances *nf pl*
honour honorer *vt*, tenir *vt*
hope espoir *nm*: espérer *vt*, souhaiter *vt*
hotel hôtel *nm*
hour heure *nf*
however cependant, toutefois
however that may be quoi qu'il en soit
hundred cent *adj*: centaine *nf*

idea aperçu *nm*
identical (to) identique (à)
i.e. c'est à dire
if any [éventuel, -elle *adj*]
if not sinon
if so dans l'**affirmatif**, le cas **échéant**
ignore ne pas tenir **compte** de
imagine supposer *vt*
immediate urgent, -e
immediately immédiatement: **dès**
    que
imminent prochain, -e
impart communiquer *vt*
impending prochain, -e
implement réaliser *vt*
implementation réalisation *nf*
imply impliquer *vt*
import importation *nf*: importer *vt*
importance importance *nf*
important important, -e
importation importation *nf*
importer importateur, -trice *nmf*
importing importateur, -trice *adj*
impose imposer *vt*
impossibility impossibilité *nf*
impossible impossible:
    [impossibilité *nf*]
impound saisir *vt*
improve améliorer *vt & pro*
improvement amélioration *nf*
in all au **total**
in so far as dans la **mesure** où
inadequacy insuffisance *nf*
inadequate insuffisant, -e
incidence incidence *nf*
incident incident *nm*
include comprendre *vt*, inclure *vt*,
    comporter *vt*
inclusive forfaitaire
inclusive of [compris, -e, inclus, -e]
be **inconsistent with** ne pas
    correspondre à *vt indir*

inconvenience dérangement *nm*,
    inconvénient *nm*: déranger *vt*
increase augmentation *nf*, hausse *nf*:
    augmenter *vi & t*, majorer *vt*
increase to porter *vt* à
be **incumbent on** incomber à *vt indir*
incur encourir *vt*
indebted to redevable à
indeed bien, effectivement, en **effet**
indent commande *nf*: commander *vt*
independant indépendant, -e
indicate indiquer *vt*, manifester *vt*
indispensable indispensable
individual unitaire
induce (to) persuader *vt* (de)
indulgence compréhension *nf*
industrial industriel, -elle
industrialist industriel *nm*
industry industrie *nf*
infer conclure *vt*
infinitely infiniment
inform informer *vt*, indiquer *vt*, faire
    savoir
inform of indiquer *vt*, informer *vt*
    de, faire **savoir**
information renseignement *nm*,
    information *nf*, indication *nf*
information sheet notice *nf*
for **information only** à titre **indicatif**
for your **information** à toutes **fins**
    utiles, pour **mémoire**
give **information to** renseigner *vt*,
    documenter *vt*
obtain **information** se renseigner
    vpro
informed au **courant**
initial initial, -e: émarger *vt*
initially d'**abord**, initialement
initiative initiative *nf*
injury dommage *nm*
inquire demander *vt*
inquire (into) enquêter *vi* (sur)
make **inquiries** se **renseigner** *vpro*
inquiry demande *nf*; enquête *nf*

inscription inscription *nf*
insert insérer *vt*, repiquer *vt*
insertion insertion *nf*, repiquage *nm*
insist (on) insister *vi* (sur), exiger *vt*
in so far as / insomuch as dans la
    mesure où
inspect examiner *vt*, visiter *vt*
inspection contrôle *nm*, examen *nm*
inst. courant
install installer *vt*
installation installation *nf*,
    placement *nm*
instalment tranche *nf*
instance cas *nm*, exemple *nm*
in the first **instance** d'abord
instead au lieu de cela, plutôt
instead of au lieu de
instruct charger *vt*, inviter *vt*
instructions instructions *nf pl*
instructions sheet notice *nf*
insufficiency insuffisance *nf*
insufficient insuffisant, -e
insurance assurance *nf*
insure assurer *vt*
intend to avoir l'intention de
intend for destiner *vt* à
intention intention *nf*
intercession intervention *nf*
interest intérêt *nm*: (s')intéresser *vt*
    & *pro*

interested party intéressé, -ée *nmf*
interesting intéressant, -e
interlocutor interlocuteur, -trice
    nmf
intermediary intermédiaire *nmf*
international international, -e
interpretation interprétation *nf*
intervene intervenir *vi*
intervention intervention *nf*
introduce (oneself) (se) **présenter** *vt*
    & *pro*; lancer *vt*
introduction introduction *nf*
invaluable précieux, -ieuse
investigate enquêter *vi* sur; étudier
    vt, examiner *vt*
investigation enquête *nf*, recherche
    nf
invitation appel *nm*, invitation *nf*
invite inviter *vt*
invoice facture *nf*: facturer *vt*
invoicing facturation *nf*
involve s'**agir** de *vpro impers*,
    comporter *vt*, entraîner *vt*,
    impliquer *vt*
involve oneself intervenir *vi*
involvement intervention *nf*
irrevocable irrévocable
issue numéro *nm*; question *nf*
item poste *nm*; article *nm*
itemize détailler *vt*, décomposer *vt*

J

January janvier *nm*
job emploi *nm*, situation *nf*
joint commun, -e
journal revue *nf*
journey voyage *nm*
July juillet *nm*
June juin *nm*

just juste, simplement
just now à l'instant
just this instant/minute à l'instant
have **just** venir *vi* de
justice bien-fondé *nm*
justificatory justificatif, -ive
justify justifier *vt*

K

be **keen to** tenir à *vt indir*
keenly vivement
keep conserver *vt*
keep down limiter *vt*
keep to respecter *vt*, tenir *vt*
kind genre *nm*: aimable *adj*, bon, bonne *adj*

be so **kind as to** avoir l'**amabilité /** l'**obligeance** de
kindly [prier *vt*, vouloir *vt*]
kindness amabilité *nf*, bienveillance *nf*, obligeance *nf*
know connaître *vt*, savoir *vt*
not **know** ignorer *vt*
knowledge connaissance *nf*

L

label étiquette *nf*
labour (force) main-d'oeuvre *nf*
lack [manquer *vi & impers*]
large gros, grosse, important, -e, fort, -e
last dernier, -ière
last few days ces **jours**-ci
last month écoulé *nm*
at **last** enfin
lastly enfin
late tardif, ive *adj*: tard *adv*: [retard *nm*]
later ultérieur, -e
later on plus tard, ultérieurement
lately récemment
latest dernier, -ière
at the **latest** au plus tard, **dernier** délai
latter [-ci *suffix*], dernier, -ière
launch lancement *nm*: lancer *vt*
launching lancement *nm*
lay down imposer *vt*, stipuler *vt*
lead (to) amener *vt* (à), entraîner *vt*
leading principal, -e
leaf feuille *nf*
leaflet dépliant *nm*, imprimé *nm*
learn (of) apprendre *vt*, avoir **connaissance** de

least moindre *adj*
at **least** au **moins**
not in the **least** nullement
leave laisser *vt*; partir *vi*; quitter *vt*
length longueur *nf*
length (of time) durée *nf*
lengthy long, -ue
less moins, sous **déduction** de: inférieur, -e *adj*
lesser moindre *adj*
let laisser *vt*: location *nf*
let have céder *vt*; faire **parvenir**
let know faire **connaître**, faire **savoir**
letter lettre *nf*, courrier *nm*
letter of credit accréditif *nm*, crédit *nm*
level niveau *nm*; plan *nm*
liability responsabilité *nf*
liable to susceptible de
take the **liberty of** se **permettre** de *vpro*
licence licence *nf*
license autoriser *vt*
like aimer *vt*: comme
in all **likelihood** vraisemblablement
likely probable
likewise également, de **même**
limit limite *nf*: (se) **limiter** (à) *vt & pro*

LINE	MARKING
line ligne *nf*; article *nm*	**look after** s'occuper de *vpro*
along these **lines** dans ce **sens**	**look at** regarder *vt*
liquid assets trésorerie *nf*	**look at again** revoir *vt*
list liste *nf*, nomenclature *nm*, bordereau *nm*	**look for** chercher *vt*, rechercher *vt*
be **listed** figurer *vi*	**look forward to** attendre *vt* (avec plaisir)
literature documentation *nf*	**look into** étudier *vt*, examiner *vt*
little peu, **peu** de chose	**look over/round** visiter *vt*
load charge *nf*: charger *vt*, embarquer *vt*	**looking forward to** dans l'**attente** de
loading chargement *nm*, embarquement *nm*	on the **look-out for** à la **recherche** de
local local, -e	**lorry** camion *nm*
locate retrouver *vt*	**lose** perdre *vt*
be **located** se **situer** *vpro*, se **trouver** *vpro*	**loss** perte *nf*, préjudice *nm*
long long, -ue *adj*: longtemps *adv*	a **lot** beaucoup, cher *adv*, gros *adv*
a **long time** longtemps *adv*	a **lot of** beaucoup de
be/take a **long time (to)** tarder *vi* (à)	**low** bas, basse; faible, juste
at **long last** finalement	**lower** inférieur, -e
	lowering baisse *nf*
	lowest meilleur, -e, plus **bas**, **basse**
	lunch déjeuner *nm* & *vi*

M

magazine revue *nf*	**manager/-esse** chef *nm*, directeur, -trice *nmf*
mail courrier *nm*: adresser *vt*, envoyer *vt*	**manner** façon *nf*, manière *nf*
main principal, -e	**manning** permanence *nf*
the **main thing** essentiel *nm*	**manufacture** fabrication *nf*: fabriquer *vt*
mainly principalement, surtout	**manufactured goods** fabrication *nf*
maintain maintenir *vt*, entretenir *vt*	**manufacturer** fabricant *nm*, industriel *nm*
the **majority** la **plupart** *nf*	**many** beaucoup (de), de **nombreux**, -euses
make effectuer *vt*, faire *vt*, formuler *vt*, rendre *vt*	**margin** marge *nf*
make a point of tenir à *vt indir*	**marine** maritime
make out prétendre *vt*; établir *vt*: [au **nom** de]	**mark** marque *nf*, mention *nf*: marquer *vt*
make the most of profiter de *vt indir*	**markedly** nettement
make up of composer *vt*	**market** marché *nm*, débouché *nm*: diffuser *vt*
maker fabricant *nm*	**marketing** diffusion *nf*
manage diriger *vt*	**marking** marquage *nm*
manage to parvenir à *vt indir*	
management direction *nf*	

March mars *nm*
match correspondre à *vt indir*
matching conforme à
material matériau *nm*, matière *nf*
materialize se **concrétiser** *vpro*, se réaliser *vpro*
matter question *nf*, sujet *nm*: être important, -e
as a **matter of fact** à **vrai** dire
as **matters stand** dans l'**état** actuel des choses
maximum maximum *nm & adj*
May mai *nm*
mean for destiner *vt* à
mean to avoir l'**intention** de
means moyen *nm*
by no **means** nullement
(in the) **meantime / meanwhile** entre-temps, en **attendant**
measure mesure *nf*, cote *nf*
medium intermédiaire *nmf*: moyen, -enne *adj*
meet rencontrer *vt*; faire la **connaissance** de; correspondre à *vt indir*
meet again (se) **retrouver** *vt & pro*
meet with rencontrer *vt*
meeting entretien *nm*, réunion *nf*
member membre *nm*
memory mémoire *nf*
mention mention *nf*: mentionner *vt*
merchandise marchandise *nf*
merely simplement
method mode *nm*, méthode *nf*, formule *nf*
meticulous soigné, -ée
message communication *nf*

to my/our **mind** à mon/notre **avis**
minimize réduire *vt* au maximum
minimum minimum *nm & adj*
ministry administration *nf*
minor petit, -e
be **mislaid** s'**égarer** *vpro*
miss manquer *vt*
be **missing** manquer *vi & impers*
mistake erreur *nf*
misunderstand mal comprendre *vt*
misunderstanding malentendu *nm*
mode mode *nm*
model modèle *nm*
modest avantageux, -euse
modification modification *nf*
modify modifier *vt*
modus operandi processus *nm*
moment moment *nm*
at any **moment** incessament
at the **moment** actuellement, en ce moment
for the **moment** pour le **moment**, pour l'**instant**
Monday lundi *nm*
money order mandat-poste *nm*
month mois *nm*: [courant]
more or less sensiblement
moreover d'autre part, d'**ailleurs**
morning matin *nm*, matinée *nf*
most la **plupart** *nf*
mostly principalement, surtout
move écouler *vt*
movement transport *nm*
much beaucoup (de)
multiple multiple
must devoir *vaux*, falloir *vimpers*
mutual commun, -e, mutuel, -elle

N

name nom *nm*
namely à savoir
naturally bien entendu, naturellement
nature nature *nf*, caractère *nm*, ordre *nm*
near près (de) *adv & prep*: proche *adj*
in the near future prochainement
nearly presque
necessary nécessaire
be necessary to falloir *vimpers*, avoir lieu de
if necessary éventuellement, s'il y a lieu
necessitate nécessiter *vt*
necessity nécessité *nf*
need besoin *nm*: avoir besoin de, [falloir *vimpers*]
if need be éventuellement, s'il y a lieu
be in need of [manquer *vimpers*]
need to avoir à *vaux*, falloir *vimpers*
needed nécessaire
negative cliché *nm*: négatif, -ive *adj*
neglect to manquer de *vt indir*, omettre *vt* de
negotiate négocier *vi*, être en pourparlers
negotiation(s) négociation *nf*, pourparlers *nm pl*
neither non plus
net/nett net, nette *adj & adv*

network réseau *nm*
nevertheless néanmoins
new neuf, -ve, nouveau, -elle
next prochain, -e, suivant, -e
next few days ces jours-ci
no aucun, -e
nomenclature nomenclature *nf*
nonetheless néanmoins
normal normal, -e
normally normalement
not non
not very peu
notably notamment
note note *nf*, bordereau *nm*: noter *vt*, constater *vt*
take note of noter *vt*
notice remarquer *vt*, relever *vt*
notice to quit congé *nm*
give notice to prévenir *vt*
until further notice jusqu'à nouvel ordre
noticeably sensiblement
notify aviser *vt*
notwithstanding malgré
November novembre *nm*
now actuellement, maintenant, ici, à présent
from now on désormais
null nul, nulle
number nombre *nm*; numéro *nm*: numéroter *vt*
numerous nombreux, -euses

O

object objet *nm*
objection contestation *nf*
objective but *nm*
obligation obligation *nf*,
  engagement *nm*
obligatory obligatoire
oblige obliger *vt*, avoir l'**obligeance**
  de
observation observation *nf*
observe constater *vt*; respecter *vt*
obstacle difficulté *nf*
obtain obtenir *vt*
obtain supplies (of)
  s'**approvisionner** *vpro* (en)
obvious évident, -e
obviously évidemment
occasion occasion *nf*
have **occasion to** être **amené**, -ée à
on several **occasions** à plusieurs
  reprises
on the **occasion of** lors de
should the **occasion arise**
  éventuellement
occupy occuper *vt*
occur arriver *vi*, se **produire** *vpro*,
  survenir *vi*
occur again se reproduire *vpro*
October octobre *nm*
of course bien entendu,
  évidemment
offer offre *nf*: offrir *vt*, proposer *vt*
office bureau *nm*, direction *nf*
through the **offices of** par
  l'**intermédiaire** de
official officiel, -elle
old ancien, -enne: [dater *vi* (de)]
omission omission *nf*
omit (to) omettre *vt* (de)
on and after à partir de
on it/them dessus
once and for all définitivement
only seulement, uniquement:
  unique *adj*

the **onus** [incomber à *vt indir*]
onwards [à partir de]
open ouvrir *vt*
opening ouverture *nf*
operation opération *nf*
operative en **vigueur**
opinion avis *nm*, opinion *nf*
opportune opportun, -e
opportunely opportunément
opportunity occasion *nf*
option option *nf*, faculté *nf*
or else sinon
order commande *nf*, ordre *nf*:
  commander *vt*
in **order** en **règle**
in **order to/that** afin de/que, de
  façon à/que
ordinary ordinaire
organism organisme *nm*
organization organisation *nf*, réseau
  nm
organize organiser *vt*
origin origine *nf*, provenance *nf*
original original, -e *adj & nm*, initial,
  -e *adj*
originally à l'origine
originate from provenir de *vt indir*
other autre
on the **other hand** d'**autre** part, par
  contre
otherwise sinon, dans le cas
  contraire
ought to devoir *vaux*
out of stock (of) démuni, -ie (de).
  dépourvu, -ue (de)
outcome résultat *nm*, issue *nf*
outgoings dépenses *nf pl*
outlet débouché *nm*, placement *nm*
outline exposé *nm*
outlook perspective *nf*
output production *nf*
from the **outset** dès le **départ**

outside en dehors (de)
outstanding impayé, -ée;
   exceptionnel, -elle
over and above en sus de
overdue arriéré, -ée *adj*
overheads frais *nm pl* généraux
overleaf au verso
overload surcharge *nf:* surcharger *vt*

overlook oublier *vt*
overseas outremer
oversight oubli *nm*, omission *nf*
overwork surcharge *nf* (de travail):
   surcharger *vt*
owe devoir *vt*
owing to à cause de, en raison de
own propre *adj:* posséder *vt*

P

pack emballer *vt*
package paquet *nm:* conditionner *vt*
packaging conditionnement *nm*
packet paquet *nm*
packing emballage *nm*
packing note bordereau *nm* de
   colisage
page page *nf*
on **pain of** sous **peine** de
pair paire *nf*
pallet palette *nf*
pamphlet brochure *nf*
parcel colis *nm*
part part *nf;* partie *nf;* pièce *nf:*
   partiel, -ielle *adj*
partial partiel, -ielle
partially partiellement
participate in participer à *vt indir*
participation participation *nf*
particular particulier, -ière
in **particular** notamment
in this **particular instance**
   exceptionnellement
particularly particulièrement
particulars données *nf pl*, précisions
   nf pl
partly en **partie**, partiellement
party partie *nf*
pass passer *vi & t*, porter *vt*
pass for press donner le **bon à tirer**
pass on transmettre *vt*

past passé *nm*
pattern modèle *nm*
pay salaire *nm:* payer *vt*, régler *vt*
pay for régler *vt*
payable (to) payable, établi, -ie à
   l'**ordre** de
payable by à la **charge** de
payment paiement *nm*, règlement
   nm
penalty amende *nf*
pending en **souffrance**
percentage pourcentage *nm*
perfect parfait, -e
perfectly parfaitement
perform effectuer *vt*
performance exécution *nf*
period période *nf*
periodically périodiquement
permanently définitivement
permission autorisation *nf*
permit (to) permettre *vt* (de)
person personne *nf*
in **person** de **vive** voix
person spoken to interlocuteur,
   -trice *nmf*
personal personnel, -elle
personally personnellement
personnel personnel *nm*
persuade (to) persuader *vt* (de)
phone téléphone *nm:* téléphoner *vt*
phoned téléphonique
photocopy photocopie *nf*

photograph photographie *nf*, photo *nf*

pick up prendre *vt*

in the **picture** au **courant**

in the **pipeline** en **cours**

it is a **pity (that)** c'est **dommage** (que)

place lieu *nm*; place *nf*: mettre *vt*, passer *vt*, placer *vt*; faire **paraître**

plan projet *nm*; plan *nm*: compter *vt*, prévoir *vt*

on the ... **plane** sur le **plan** ...

planning stage étude *nf*

plant matériel *nm*

pleasant agréable

please [prier *vt*, vouloir *vaux*]

pleased heureux, -euse

be **pleased to** avoir l'**avantage** de

pleasure plaisir *nm*

have **pleasure in** avoir l'**avantage** de

point point *nm*

on the **point of** en **instance** de, sur le **point** de

point out signaler *vt*, faire **remarquer**

pointless (to) inutile (de)

policy police *nf*

popular [apprécier *vt*]

port port *nm*

pose poser *vt*

position position *nf*

in a **position to** en **mesure** de, à **même** de

positive positif, -ive

possess posséder *vt*

possession possession *nf*

be in **possession of** posséder *vt*

possibility possibilité *nf*: [éventuel, -elle *adj*]

possible possible, éventuel, -elle

possibly éventuellement

post situation *nf*; courrier *nm*, poste *nf*: postal, -e *adj*

postage port *nm*

postal postal, -e: [poste *nf*]

postal order mandat-poste *nm*

postpone différer *vt*, remettre *vt*, reporter *vt*

potential éventuel, -elle: possibilité *nf*

pound livre *nf*

practically pratiquement

in **practice** en **fait**

precaution précaution *nf*

precede précéder *vt*

preceding précédent, -e

precise précis, -e

prefer préférer *vt*

preferable préférable

preferably de **préférence**

preference préférence *nf*

to be **preferred** être **préférable**

prejudge préjuger de *vt indir*

prejudice préjugé *nm*: [préjuger de *vt indir*]

premises local *nm*

preparation préparation *nf*, établissement *nm*

prepare préparer *vt*, établir *vt*

prepared (to) prêt, -e (à), disposé, -ée à

presence présence *nf*

present actuel, -elle, présent, -e

at **present** actuellement, en ce **moment**

be **present at** assister à *vt indir*

present itself/oneself se présenter *vpro*

presentation présentation *nf*

pressure impératif *nm*

presume supposer *vt*

prevent (from) empêcher *vt* de; éviter *vt*

previous antérieur, -e, précédent, -e

previously précédemment, antérieurement

price prix *nm*

price list tarif *nm*

principal principal, -e

principally principalement

principle principe *nm*

print imprimer *vt*

printed matter imprimé *nm*

prior antérieur, -e, préalable
prior to avant
priority priorité *nf*
prize apprécier *vt*
probable probable
problem inconvénient *nm*,
    problème *nm*
procedure processus *nm*
proceed opérer *vi*, procéder *vi*
process procédé *nm*: exécuter *vt*
in the **process of** en **train** de, en **voie**
    de
procure se procurer *vpro*
produce fabriquer *vt*; éditer *vt*
producer producteur, -trice *nmf &*
    adj
product(s) produit *nm*, production
    nf, fabrications *nf pl*
production fabrication *nf*,
    production *nf*
professional professionnel, -elle
profit bénéfice *nm*, profit *nm*
pro-forma pro-forma *adj invar*
programme programme *nm*
progress évolution *nf*: évoluer *vi*
in **progress** en **cours**
project projet *nm*
promise (to) promesse *nf*:
    promettre *vt* (de)
promising intéressant, -e
prompt prompt, -e
promptly rapidement
proof preuve *nf*, justificatif *nm*;
    épreuve *nf*
proper sérieux, -ieuse: [convenir de
    vimpers]
properly régulièrement; bien, à juste
    titre

proportion partie *nf*
proportionately d'autant
proposal proposition *nf*, projet *nm*
propose proposer *vt*, se **réserver** de
    vpro
proposition proposition *nf*
proprietor propriétaire *nmf*
prospect perspective *nf*; client(e)
    éventuel(le) *nmf*
prospective éventuel, -elle
prove s'avérer *vpro*
prove itself faire ses **preuves**
provenance provenance *nf*
provide fournir *vt*, assurer *vt*
provide for prévoir *vt*
provided that à **condition** que
provisional provisoire
provisionally provisoirement
proviso condition *nf*
P.S. P.S.
publication parution *nf*
publish éditer *vt*, faire **paraître**
punctual exact, -e
punctually en son/leur **temps**
purchase achat *nm*: acheter *vt*
purchaser acheteur, -euse *nmf*
purchasing achat *nm*
purpose but *nm*, intention *nf*, objet
    nm, effet *nm*
pursuant to suite à, conformément
    à
pursue donner **suite** à
put mettre *vt*, poser *vt*; lancer *vt*
put aside réserver *vt*
put before soumettre *vt*
put off différer *vt*, remettre *vt*,
    reporter *vt*
put together monter *vt*
put up majorer *vt*

Q

qualify for bénéficier de *vt indir*
quality qualité *nf*, choix *nm*
quantity nombre *nm*, quantité *nf*
quay quai *nm*
question question *nf*: interroger *vt*
be a question of s'agir de *vpro impers*
in question en cause, en question

quick rapide
quickly rapidement
quite assez; bien
quota quota *nm*
quotation offre *nf*, prix *nm*
quote offre *nf*: indiquer *vt*, proposer
    vt; citer *vt*, rappeler *vt*

R

rail/railway/railroad chemin *nm* de
    fer
raise majorer *vt*, porter *vt*; poser *vt*,
    soulever *vt*
at random au hasard
range gamme *nf*, ensemble *nm*
range between [aller *vi*]
rapid rapide
rapidly rapidement
rate cadence *nf*; taux *nm*
rather plutôt
re. concerne, objet, faisant suite à
reach parvenir à *vt indir*, arriver *vi* à;
    atteindre *vt*
reaction réaction *nf*
read lire *vt*; [libeller *vt*]
ready (to) prêt, -e (à), disposé, -ée à
reaffirm répéter *vt*
real réel, réelle
reality réalité *nf*
realize se rendre compte (de)
really bien, vraiment
realm domaine *nm*
reason raison *nf*
reasonable abordable, raisonnable
reassert répéter *vt*
rebate rabais *nm*
recall se souvenir de *vpro*
receipt réception *nf*, reçu *nm*

receive recevoir *vt*; accueillir *vt*
recent récent, -e
recently récemment
reception accueil *nm*
reckon on compter *vt*
recognize reconnaître *vt*
recommend conseiller *vt*
recondition(-ing) [neuf, -ve]
reconsider revoir *vt*
record document *nm*; trace *nf*:
    enregistrer *vt*, marquer *vt*
recording enregistrement *nm*
recourse recours *nm*
rectification rectification *nf*
rectified rectificatif, -ive
rectify rectifier *vt*
recur se reproduire *vpro*
redirect réexpédier *vt*
reduce réduire *vt*, ramener *vt*
reduction diminution *nf*, remise *nf*
reexamine réexaminer *vt*
reexport réexporter *vt*
refer back to se reporter à *vpro*
refer to se référer à *vpro*, reprendre
    vt; [saisir *vt*]
reference référence *nf*: référencer *vt*
for reference (purposes)
    [documentation *nf*]
with reference to (faisant) suite à,
    nous référant à

refund remboursement *nm*:
  rembourser *vt*, restituer *vt*
refurbish(-ment) [neuf, -ve]
refusal refus *nm*
refuse (to) refuser *vt* (de)
regard sujet *nm*: concerner *vt*
having **regard to** eu **égard** à
with **regard to** en ce qui **concerne**, à
  l'**égard** de, vis-à-vis de
regarding concernant, à **propos** de,
  au **sujet** de
as **regards** en ce qui **concerne**, sur le
  plan
region région *nf*; ordre *nm*
regional régional, -e
register enregistrer *vt*, marquer *vt*,
  recommender *vt*
registered office siège *nm* social
registration enregistrement *nm*
regret (to) regret *nm*: regretter *vt*
  (de)
regrettable regrettable
regular régulier, -ière, suivi, -ie
regularly couramment,
  régulièrement
reimburse rembourser *vt*
reimbursement remboursement *nm*
reimportable réimportable
reinforce renforcer *vt*
reiterate réitérer *vt*
reject refuser *vt*
relate to se **rapporter** à *vpro*
relation relation *nf*, rapport *nm*
relative to relatif, -ive à
relatively relativement
release remise *nf*
relevant (to) [s'**appliquer** *vpro* (à)]
reliable sérieux, -ieuse
reluctance regret *nm*
be **reluctant (to)** hésiter *vt* (à)
rely on compter sur *vt indir*
remain rester *vi*
remainder reliquat *nm*, reste *nm*
remaining restant, -e
remark observation *nf*, remarque *nf*
remarkable exceptionnel, -elle

remember se **souvenir** de *vpro*;
  [transmettre *vt*]
remember to penser à *vt indir*
remind rappeler *vt*
reminder rappel *nm*
remit verser *vt*
remittance versement *nm*
remove enlever *vt*
remunerate rémunérer *vt*
remuneration rémunération *nf*
rendez-vous rendez-vous *nm*
renew renouveler *vt*
renounce renoncer à *vt indir*
rent location *nf*: louer *vt*
reopen revenir *vi* sur
reopening réouverture *nf*
reorder [nouveau, -elle]
repair réparation *nf*, **remise** *nf* à
  neuf: réparer *vt*
repay rembourser *vt*
repayment remboursement *nm*
repeat répéter *vt*, réitérer *vt*:
  [nouveau, -elle]
repeatedly à plusieurs **reprises**
repercussions conséquences *nf pl*
replace remplacer *vt*
replacement remplacement *nm*
reply réponse *nf*: répondre *vt*
report rapport *nm*: signaler *vt*
represent représenter *vt*
representation représentation *nf*
representative représentant, -e *nmf*
reputation réputation *nf*, renommée
  nf
request (to) demande *nf*, requête *nf*:
  demander *vt* (de), inviter *vt* (à),
  prier *vt* de
require avoir **besoin** de, nécessiter
  vt, exiger *vt*
required requis, -e
requirement(s) besoin *nm*,
  exigences *nf pl*
requisite requis, -e
research étude *nf*, recherche *nf*
reservation réservation *nf*
reserve réserve *nf*: (se) **réserver** *vt &*
  pro, retenir *vt*

resolve résoudre *vt*; décider *vt* (de)
resort to avoir **recours** à
as a last **resort** en dernier **lieu**
respect égard *nm*: respecter *vt*
in **respect of** quant à
with **respect to** à l'**égard** de
respective respectif, -ive
response réaction *nf*, réponse *nf*
responsibility responsabilité *nf*
be the **responsibility of (to)**
    appartenir à *vimpers* (de)
responsible responsable
rest reste *nm*
rest with (to) appartenir à *vimpers*
    (de)
restoration remise *nf* à neuf
restrain from empêcher *vt* de
restrict (to) (se) **limiter** *vt & pro* (à)
result résultat *nm*
result from résulter de *vt indir*
as a **result of** par **suite** de
resume reprendre *vt*
resumption reprise *nf*
retail détail *nm*: détailler *vt*
retailer détaillant, -e *nmf*
retain conserver *vt*
return retour *nm*, rentrée *nf*;
    réexpédition *nf*: retourner *vt & i*;
    rentrer *vi*, revenir *vi*; renvoyer *vt*,
    restituer *vt*
in **return** de ma (etc) **part**
in **return for** moyennent

reveal faire **apparaître**
on the **reverse side** au **verso**
revert to reprendre *vt*, revenir *vi* sur
review revoir *vt*
revisable révisable
revise réviser *vt*, revoir *vt*
revoke annuler *vt*
get **rid of** écouler *vt*
right droit *nm*, faculté *nf*: exact, -e,
    opportun, -e: [convenir de
    vimpers]
right from dès
rightly à juste **titre**
sole **rights** exclusivité *nf*
ring coup *nm* de fil/téléphone
ripe opportun, -e
rise hausse *nf*, majoration *nf*
give **rise to** occasionner *vt*, donner
    lieu à
risk risque *nm*, inconvénient *nm*:
    risquer *vt* (de)
room chambre *nf*
rough brutal, -e; approximatif, -ive
as a **rough guide** à **titre** indicatif
roughly approximativement, en
    gros
route route *nf*: acheminer *vt*
routinely habituellement
rule out exclure *vt*
as a **rule** en **général**
ruling décision *nf*
run diriger *vt*; libeller *vt*

S

safe receipt bonne réception
safely bien
sailing départ *nm*
salary salaire *nm*
sale vente *nf*
put on sale lancer *vt* sur le marché
sales force réseau *nm* de
    représentants
same même *pro & adj*
sample échantillon *nm*
satisfaction satifaction *nf*
satisfied (with) satisfait, -e (de)
satisfy satisfaire *vt*, donner
    satisfaction à
Saturday samedi *nm*
save éviter *vt*; gagner *vt*: sauf *prep*
saving gain *nm*
say dire *vt*
scale of charges barême *nm*
scarcely [inutile *adj*]
schedule emploi *nm* du temps; liste
    nf
schedule of conditions cahier *nm*
    des charges
scheme projet *nm*
scope cadre *nm*
scrap mettre *vt* au rebut
scrutinize examiner *vt*
scrutiny examen *nm*
sea mer *nf*
search for rechercher *vt*
second deuxième
secondhand d'occasion
secretary secrétaire *nmf*
sector secteur *nm*
secure obtenir *vt*
see voir *vt*, remarquer *vt*; recevoir *vt*
see again revoir *vt*
see for oneself se rendre compte
    (de)
see to s'occuper de *vpro*
see to it that veiller à *vt indir*

as you see fit comme bon vous
    semblera
seek (to) chercher *vt* (à)
seek out rechercher *vt*
seem sembler *vi & impers*
seize saisir *vt*
selection choix *nm*
sell vendre *vt*, placer *vt*
seller vendeur, -euse *nmf*
send envoyer *vt*, adresser *vt*,
    remettre *vt*, faire parvenir
send back retourner *vt*, renvoyer *vt*
sender expéditeur, -trice *nmf*
sending back retour *nm*,
    réexpédition *nf*
sensible raisonnable
separate séparé, -ée
September septembre *nm*
series série *nf*
serious grave, sérieux, -ieuse
serve servir *vi*
service disposition *nf*, service *nm*
set jeu *nm*: constituer *vt*
set off partir *vi*
set out détailler *vt*, exposer *vt*
set up constituer *vt*, (s')installer *vt &*
    pro, mettre sur pied
setting up constitution *nf*
settle régler *vt*, mettre au point
settlement règlement *nm*
settlement date échéance *nf*
several plusieurs
shape forme *nf*
share participation *nf*
share in participer à *vt indir*
share out (se) répartir *vt & pro*
shared commun, -e
sheet feuille *nf*, feuillet *nm*
ship navire *nm*: expédier *vt*
shipment expédition *nf*, fourniture
    nf
shipper transporteur *nm*
shipping expédition *nf*: maritime *adj*

shop magasin *nm*

short court, -e

be **short of** manquer *vi & impers*

shortage insuffisance *nf*

shorten réduire *vt*

shortfall insuffisance *nf*

shortly prochainement, sous **peu**

shortly after/before peu de **temps**
    après/avant

show salon *nm*; indiquer *vt*;
    présenter *vt*; manifester *vt*, faire
    preuve de

showing avec l'**indication** de

showroom salle *nf* d'**exposition**

side côté *nm*

put on one **side** réserver *vt*

sight vue *nf*

sight draft traite *nf* à vue

sign signer *vt*

signature signature *nf*

significant important, -e

signify marquer *vt*

signing signature *nf*

similar similaire, pareil, -eille

similarly de **même**; de la même
    manière

simply simplement

since puisque, comme; depuis

sincere sincère, vif, vive

sincerely sincèrement

single unique

be **situated** se **situer** *vpro*

situation situation *nf*, [où en est]

size dimension *nf*, format *nm*;
    importance *nf*, grandeur *nf*

slight faible

slightest moindre

slightly un **peu**

slip bordereau *nm*

slip (into) se glisser *vpro* (dans)

small petit, -e, faible

so tellement; donc, aussi, de **sorte**
    que

so as to de façon à

so long tant

so many/much autant (de)

so that afin que, de **façon** que

sole exclusif, -ive, unique

solely exclusivement, uniquement

solution solution *nf*

solve résoudre *vt*

somewhat plutôt

soon prochainement, sous **peu**, tôt

as **soon as** dès que

as **soon as possible** au plus **tôt**, le
    plus **tôt** possible

be **sorry** regretter *vt*

very **sorry** désolé, -ée

sort genre *nm*

sort out résoudre *vt*

soundness bien-fondé *nm*

source provenance *nf*

space out (s')**échelonner** *vt & pro*

spare en **réserve**: éviter *vt*; disposer
    de *vt indir*

speak parler *vi*

special spécial, -e

specialist spécialiste *nmf*

speciality spécialité *nf*

specialized/-izing spécialisé, -ée

specially particulièrement,
    spécialement

specific spécifique

specification spécification *nf*

specify spécifier *vt*, préciser *vt*

speed up accélérer *vt*

speedy prompt, -e, rapide

spell out préciser *vt*

spend passer *vt*

sphere domaine *nm*

in **spite of** malgré

split (up) répartir *vt*

on the **spot** sur **place**

spread (out) (s')**échelonner** *vt & pro*

staff personnel *nm*

staffing permanence *nf*

stagger échelonner *vt*

at **stake** en **jeu**

stand stand *nm*

standard qualité *nf*; norme *nf*:
    standard *adj*

standing réputation *nf*

start début *nm*, départ *nm*:
    commencer *vi* (à); entamer *vt*

starting up démarrage *nm*
state état *nm*, condition *nf*: dire *vt*
state of the market conjoncture *nf*
statement exposé *nm*; relevé *nm*
station gare *nf*
stay rester *vi*
in my (etc) stead à ma (etc) place
steady suivi, -ie
step(s) démarche *nf*, dispositions *nf*
   pl
stick coller *vt*
stick to maintenir *vt*
still encore: [rester *vi*]
stipulate stipuler *vt*
stock stock *nm*
stock up (with) s'approvisionner
   vpro (en)
in stock en stock, disponible
out of stock (of) démuni, -ie (de),
   dépourvu, -ue (de)
straight directement; en règle
straight away immédiatement, dès
   maintenant
straighten out régler *vt*
strengthen renforcer *vt*
strict sérieux, -ieuse
strictly speaking à vrai dire
strike grève *nf*
strong fort, -e
strongly vivement
study étude *nf*: étudier *vt*
subject sujet *nm*, objet *nm*: concerne
subject to sujet, -ette à
be subjected to subir *vt*
submit soumettre *vt*
subsequent ultérieur, -e
subsequently ultérieurement, par la
   suite
subsidiary (company) filiale *nf*
substantial important, -e

substitute remplacer *vt*
succeed (in) réussir *vi* (à)
success succès *nm*
such tel, telle, pareil, -eille
such as to de nature à
in such a way that de sorte que
suffer subir *vt*
suffice (to) suffire *vi & impers* (de)
be sufficient suffire *vi*
sufficiently suffisamment
suggest (to) proposer *vt* (de),
   suggérer *vt* (de)
suit convenir à *vt indir*
suitable convenable
be suitable for convenir à *vt indir*
sum somme *nf*
sum up faire le point (de)
superb excellent, -e
superior (to) supérieur, -e (à)
supersede remplacer *vt*
supervise surveiller *vt*
supplement supplément *nm*:
   compléter *vt*
supplementary supplémentaire
supplier fournisseur, -euse *nmf*
supply (to) fournir *vt* (à)
supply with approvisionner *vt* en
suppose supposer *vt*
sure certain, -e
be sure to ne pas manquer de *vt*
   indir
make sure that veiller à *vt indir*
surprise surprendre *vt*
suspend suspendre *vt*
suspension suspension *nf*
swift rapide
sympathetically avec bienveillance
system système *nm*
systematic systématique
systematically systématiquement

T

table tableau *nm*
keep **tabs on suivre** *vt* de près
take prendre *vt*, extraire *vt*, prélever *vt*, [mettre *vt*]
take account of tenir **compte** de
take away enlever *vt*
take back reprendre *vt*: [reprise *nf*]
take care of s'**occuper de** *vpro*
take delivery of recevoir *vt*
take it that supposer *vt*
take off déduire *vt*
take on entreprendre *vt*, s'**occuper** de *vpro*
take part in participer à *vt indir*
take place se **tenir** *vpro*, intervenir *vi*
take shape se **concrétiser** *vpro*
take stock (of) faire le **point** (de)
take the place of remplacer *vt*
take up reprendre *vt*
talk discussion *nf*, entretien *nm*: parler *vi*
talk to (about) entretenir *vt* (de)
talks pourparlers *nm pl*
tally with correspondre à *vt indir*
tardy tardif, -ive
target but *nm*
tariff tarif *nm*
tax taxe *nf*
technical technique
telegram télégramme *nm*
telegraph télégraphier *vt*
telegraphic télégraphique
telephone téléphone *nm*: téléphonique *adj*: téléphoner *vt*
telephoned téléphonique
telex télex *nm*: télexer *vt*
tell dire *vt*, indiquer *vt*
temporarily momentanément, provisoirement
temporary provisoire
(about) **ten** dizaine *nf*
tender soumission *nf*

tender for soumissionner *vt*
term(s) terme *nm*; conditions *nf pl*
terminate résilier *vt*
territory secteur *nm*
test épreuve *nf*: essayer *vt*
text texte *nm*
thank remercier *vt*
thanks remerciements *nm pl*: merci *inter*
thanks to grâce à
thank you merci *inter*
that is c'est-à-dire
then alors, ensuite
therefore donc, aussi, par **conséquent**, en **conséquence**
thickness épaisseur *nf*
as **things are** dans l'**état** actuel des choses
think penser *vt*, juger *vt*, croire *vt*
think about penser à *vt indir*; penser de *vt indir*
think of penser *vt*, envisager *vt* de; penser de *vt indir*
think to penser à *vt indir*
third party tiers *nm*
thorough approfondi, -ie, sérieux, -ieuse
thoroughly en **détail**
though bien que, quoique
through direct, -e: par l'**intermédiaire** de
Thursday jeudi *nm*
thus ainsi
till jusqu'à
time fois *nf*; heure *nf*, moment *nm*, temps *nm*
time allowed délai *nm*
at the **time of** lors de
for the **time being** provisoirement, pour l'**instant**
on **time** en son/leur **temps**
timely opportun, -e
at all **times** toujours

timetable emploi *nm* du temps; horaire *nm*
title titre *nm*
today ce **jour**, aujourd'hui
of **today's date** de ce **jour**
together ensemble
together with accompagné, -ée de, en **compagnie** de
top haut *nm*: premier, -ière *adj*
top management direction *nf* générale
total total, -e *adj* & *nm*, global, -e *adj*
touch contact *nm*, rapport *nm*
tour visiter *vt*
towards vers
trace trace *nf*
trade commerce *nm*: commercial, -e *adj*, professionnel, -elle *adj*
trade fair foire *nf*
trademark marque *nf* de fabrique
trading commerce *nm*: commercial, -e *adj*
traffic trafic *nm*
train train *nm*
training course stage *nm*
transaction transaction *nf*, affaire *nf*
transfer transfert *nm*; virement *nm*: transférer *vt*; virer *vt*

transform transformer *vt*
transit transit *nm*
transport transport *nm*: transporter *vt*
transportation transport *nm*
transporter transporteur *nm*
transshipment transbordement *nm*
travel/travelling déplacement *nm*, voyage *nm*
treat considérer *vt*
trial essai *nm*
tried and tested [preuve *nf*]
trip déplacement *nm*, voyage *nm*
triple triple
in **triplicate** en **triple** exemplaire
trouble dérangement *nm*, ennui *nm*: déranger *vt*
truck camion *nm*, wagon *nm*
true vrai, -e
trust confiance *nf*: espérer *vt*
truth [vrai, -e]
try (to) essayer *vt* (de)
Tuesday mardi *nm*
turn tour *nm*
turn out s'avérer *vpro*
turnover chiffre *nm* d'affaires
twice deux **fois**
type type *nm*, modèle *nm*, genre *nm*

U

ultimate final, -e
ultimately finalement
ultimo écoulé, -ée *adj* & *nm*
be **unable** ne pas **pouvoir** *vaux*
unaltered inchangé, -ée
be **unaware of** ignorer *vt*
unchanged inchangé, -ée
under sous
undergo subir *vt*
underline souligner *vt*
understand comprendre *vt*, entendre *vt*

understanding compréhension *nf*; interprétation *nf*
undertake se **charger de** *vpro*, entreprendre *vt*
undertake to s'engager à *vpro*
undertaking entreprise *nf*; engagement *nm*
unexpected imprévu, -e
unforeseen imprévu, -e
unfortunate [dommage *nm*]
unfortunately malheureusement
unique unique

unit unité *nf*: unitaire *adj*
unless [sauf]
unload décharger *vt*
unloading déchargement *nm*
unnecessary inutile
unpaid impayé, -ée
unreasonable exagéré, -ée
unsettled impayé, -ée
if **unsold** sauf **vente**
until jusqu'à (ce que), [tant]
unusual anormal, -e
up to jusqu'à
up to date au **courant**
be **up to (to)** appartenir à *vimpers*
    (de), incomber à *vt indir* (de)
update mettre *vt* à **jour**
uphold maintenir *vt*
up-to-date récent, -e

urge (to) conseiller *vt* (de)
urgency urgence *nf*
urgent urgent, -e
use utilisation *nf*, emploi *nm*, usage
    nm: utiliser *vt*
use up épuiser *vt*
make **use of** utiliser *vt*
of **use** utile
used d'**occasion**
be **used (for)** servir *vi* (à)
useful utile, intéressant, -e
useless inutile
user utilisateur, -trice *nmf*
usual habituel, -elle, normal, -e
as **usual** comme d'**habitude**
usually habituellement,
    normalement
utilisation utilisation *nf*
utmost maximum *nm*

V

vacancy situation *nf*
vacate quitter *vt*
valid valable
validity validité *nf*
valuable intéressant, -e
value valeur *nf*; montant *nm*
variant variante *nf*
variation variante *nf*
varied divers, -ses *adj pl*
a **variety of** divers, -ses *adj pl*
various différents, -es *adj pl*, divers,
    -ses *adj pl*
vary changer *vt & i*
vary from différer de *vt indir*
vendor vendeur, -euse *nmf*
verbal verbal. -e
verbally verbalement
verification vérification *nf*

verify vérifier *vt*
version édition *nf*, version *nf*
very très, fort, bien: même *adj*
very much vivement
very much indeed infiniment
vessel navire *nm*
vice versa inversement
view avis *nm*, opinion *nf*, vue *nf*
in **view of** vu
in **view of this** en **conséquence**
in my (etc) **view** à mon (etc) **avis**
with a **view to** dans le **but** de
virtually pratiquement
vis-à-vis vis-à-vis de
visit visite *nf*, passage *nm*
vital indispensable
viz soit
volume volume *nm*
vouch for garantir *vt*

W

wages salaire *nm*
wagon wagon *nm*
wait for attendre *vt & i*
waiting to en **instance** de
waive renoncer à *vt indir*
want désirer *vt*
for **want of** à **défaut** de
warehouse entrepôt *nm*, magasin
   nm
warm vif, vive
warmly vivement
warn (of) prévenir *vt* (de)
warranty garantie *nf*
waste perdre *vt*
wasted inutile
watch suivre *vt*
way façon *nf*, manière *nf*, titre *nm*;
   voie *nf*
way out solution *nf*
in this **way** ainsi
in no **way** nullement
the **way things are** dans l'**état** actuel
   des choses
weather temps *nm*
Wednesday mercredi *nm*
week semaine *nf*
weigh peser *vt & i*
weight poids *nm*
welcome accueil *nm*; bienvenu, -e
   nmf: accueillir *vt*; apprécier *vt*
well bien
be as **well to** y avoir **lieu** de
well-known connu, -e
what quoi *pro*: quel, quelle *adj*
whatever quoi *pro* que: nullement
whatsoever nullement
when lorsque, quand
where où
whereas alors que: or
while **pendant** que
whole ensemble *nm*, totalité *nf*:
   entier, -ière *adj*, total, -e *adj*

wholly en **totalité**
wholesale gros *nm*
wholesaler grossiste *nmf*
width largeur *nf*
will volonté *nf*
willing to disposé, -ée à, prêt, -e à
willingly volontiers
win gagner *vt*: [valoir *vt*]
wire télégramme *nm*: télégraphier *vt*
wise souhaitable
wish (to) désir *nm*, souhait *nm*, voeu
   nm: désirer *vt*, souhaiter *vt*; se
   permettre de *vpro*, tenir à *vt indir*
withdraw prélever *vt*; se **désister**
   vpro
withhold retenir *vt*
within d'ici
without fail sans **faute**
witness assister à *vt indir*
word mot *nm*: rédiger *vt*, libeller *vt*
wording libellé *nm*
work travail *nm*: travailler *vi & t*
work experience stage *nm*
work out calculer *vt*, déterminer *vt*,
   établir *vt*
workforce main-d'oeuvre *nf*
working ouvrable
working day journée *nf* (de travail)
working from en **partant** de
workmanship travail *nm*
works usine *nf*
world monde *nm*
worldwide mondial, -e
worry ennui *nm*: s'**inquiéter** *vt & pro*
be **worth** valoir *vt*
be **worth it** [intéressant, -e]
worthwhile intéressant, -e, valable
would [se **permettre** de *vpro*]
wrap emballer *vt*
wrapping emballage *nm*
write écrire *vt*
writing écrit *nm*
wrong erroné, -ée

Y

year an *nm*, année *nf*: [courant, -e]
yearly annuel, -elle

yesterday hier
yet encore: néanmoins

APPENDIX

The Salutation

Most business letters are directed to organizations rather than to individuals and the standard salutation to begin the letter is 'Messieurs'. For an individual it will normally be 'Monsieur' or 'Madame', though a more specific one may be used as appropriate, for example 'Monsieur le Président', 'Madame la Directrice'. The abbreviations 'M.' and 'Mme' are not used in these.

When the correspondents know each other, 'Cher Monsieur', 'Chère Madame' are preferred. Notice, however, that 'Cher Monsieur X', 'Chère Madame X' tend to be patronizing. If a stronger personal rapport develops, more familiar salutations are in order, but it is best to take your cue from the native speaker with whom you are corresponding.

The Complimentary Close

The standard 'formules de politesse' to close the letter are:

Nous vous prions d'agréer, . . ., nos salutations distinguées
Veuillez agréer, . . ., mes/nos salutations distinguées

Slightly more deferential alternatives are:

Nous vous prions d'agréer, . . ., l'expression de nos sentiments distingués
Veuillez agréer, . . . , l'expression de mes/nos sentiments distingués

In all cases the exact title used for the salutation is inserted into the complimentary close at the position indicated by the dots in the above examples.

These four closes may safely be employed in letters both to organizations and to named individuals within organizations. A wealth of alternatives is possible but, as with the salutation, it is best to let yourself be guided by your French-speaking correspondent.